Coleridge

POET AND REVOLUTIONARY

1772-1804

A CRITICAL BIOGRAPHY

John Cornwell

16069

√6

ALLEN LANE

First published in 1973

ALLEN LANE
Penguin Books Ltd
21 John Street, London, WC1

ISBN 0 7139 0461 5

Printed in Great Britain
by Ebenezer Baylis and Son Limited
The Trinity Press, Worcester, and London
Set in Monotype Caslon

TO
J.W. & A.W.

Contents

1 Childhood and Youth   1
2 Pantisocracy   33
3 The Ebullience of *Schematism*   66
4 Bristol   86
5 Marriage   101
6 The Watchman   117
7 In Search of a Role   134
8 Alfoxden   157
9 *The Ancient Mariner*   223
10 Germany   247
11 Greta Hall   282
12 '. . . a little theological'   345
13 'A Comet tied to a Comet's Tail'   364
14 Going Away   379
Postscript   397
Abbreviations   401
References   403
Index   417

Those pilgrimings to Coleridge ... indicate deeper wants beginning to be felt, and important ulterior resolutions becoming inevitable ...

Carlyle

Acknowledgements

I AM indebted to the courtesy of Professor E. L. Griggs and the Clarendon Press for permission to quote from the *Collected Letters of S. T. Coleridge*, and to Professor Kathleen Coburn and Princeton University Press for permission to quote from Coleridge's *Notebooks*.

My debt to the above editors for information and enlightenment, and to many other Coleridgeian scholars, will be apparent throughout the book and in my source references.

I also wish to thank the librarian of Victoria College Library, Toronto, for assistance by correspondence and for permission to quote from a MS in the library's keeping.

J. C.

Childhood and Youth

To many of his contemporaries Coleridge manifested a striking affectation of rootlessness. It was said of him that he seemed to have fallen out of the sky. In fact, he often spoke of himself as if he were an orphan, and many noted his tendency to self-abasement – the hat in hand, the 'undulant' step, the habit of 'assentation'. But Coleridge's roots were sturdy and respectable, if somewhat impoverished. His father was a pious, absent-minded clergyman and schoolmaster of Ottery Saint Mary in Devon, who interspersed his sermons with Hebrew, which his parishioners thought was 'the immediate language of the Holy Ghost'. Samuel was born on 21 October 1772, the youngest of ten children by his father's second marriage, a child of his father's old age, and intended for the Church. It seems that the other eight boys (there was only one girl, Anne) might be apprenticed to tradesmen for all the Reverend John Coleridge cared; it was left to 'maternal ambition' to set them on the right path for careers in the Church, the Indian Army and Medicine. The father was the son of a woollen-draper who had gone bankrupt, and this man of 'primitive manners' acquired an education, Coleridge tells us, 'in consequence of his own exertions, not of his superior advantages'. His father's origins, Coleridge insisted, were humble, his veins 'uncontaminated with one drop of gentility'.

Ingenuous and absent-minded though the father was (he once stuffed a considerable portion of a lady's dress down his trousers, thinking it to be his own shirt tail), he was a scholarly man with literary leanings, contributing to the *Gentleman's Magazine*, and writing sundry schoolbooks and commentaries on the Old Testament. The young Samuel was his father's favourite; indeed, it was said that he strongly resembled his father in person and mind. Yet Coleridge seems to have spent a lonely and miserable childhood, and later traced the 'untoward circumstances' which led to his defects in character to this period of his life. He was 'hardly used from infancy to boyhood', he lamented, 'and from boyhood to youth most, MOST, cruelly'. The family was large, and the numbers were swelled by boarders from his father's school; Coleridge became the butt of bullying from his elder brother Frank, and a nurse, Molly, who felt that he was overindulged by his parents. So he became 'fretful, and timorous, and tell-tale', tormented by the schoolboys and driven from their games. He became a solitary child, playing alone and burying himself in nursery books : *Tom Hickathrift, Jack the Giant-Killer, Robinson Crusoe, Seven Champions of Christen-dom*, and *The Arabian Nights*. Yet even in these solitary pleasures he was not to remain undisturbed. There was a tale in the Arabian Nights – 'the tale of a man who was com-pelled to seek for a pure virgin' – which made such a deep impression on him that he was haunted by spectres whenever he was in the dark: 'I distinctly remember the anxious and fearful eagerness, with which I used to watch the window, in which the books lay – and whenever the sun lay upon them, I would seize it, carry it by the wall, and bask, and read.' His father eventually discovered the effect of such books and burnt them; consequently, Coleridge tells us, he developed an 'indisposition to all bodily activity'. He became a 'dreamer', 'inordinately passionate', and 'slothful'. By his own admission he had a memory and understanding 'forced into almost an unnatural ripeness', and he very soon took refuge in 'vanity', despising with a 'deep and bitter contempt . . . all who traversed the orbit of my understanding'.

Of Coleridge's mother we know very little. He says briefly of her, 'My Mother was an admirable Economist, and managed exclusively', and that she had a 'pride and spirit of aggrandizing her family'. Throughout his life he rarely speaks of her, and on the few occasions that he wrote letters home, he sent his 'duty' rather than his 'love'. That a deep tension existed in his relationship towards her at an early stage is revealed by a curious incident that occurred when he was about seven years of age. One evening, after a squabble, Coleridge flew at his brother Frank, who threw himself on the ground pretending to have been seriously hurt. 'I hung over him', says Coleridge, 'moaning & in a great fright – he leaped up, & with a horse-laugh gave me a severe blow in the face.' Seizing a knife, Coleridge ran at him, but at that moment his mother entered the room and took him by the arm. 'I expected a flogging,' remembered Coleridge, ' – & struggling from her I ran away . . .' Hiding at the bottom of a hill close to the river Otter, he whiled away the time reading a little shilling book of prayers. 'I very devoutly repeated them – thinking *at the same time* with inward & gloomy satisfaction, how miserable my Mother must be.'

Eventually he fell asleep, darkness came and it began to rain. 'I felt the cold in my sleep, and dreamt that I was pulling the blanket over me, & actually pulled over me a dry thorn bush, which lay on the hill – in my sleep I had rolled from the top of the hill to within three yards of the River, which flowed by the unfenced edge of the bottom.' In the meantime his mother had sent out several men and boys to search for him. 'My Mother was almost distracted – and at ten o'clock at night I was *cry'd* by the crier in Ottery, and in two villages near it – with a reward offered for me.' He goes on to describe how half the town were up all night, how he lay paralysed at dawn, incapable of moving, his cries

too weak to attract the labourers on their way to work :
' – and there I might have lain & died.' Eventually, however,
he was found by the local squire and carried back to the
vicarage, where his father wept and his mother was 'outrageous with joy'. Relating this story to an intimate friend
in his twenty-fifth year, he adds an intriguing sequel : after
the rapturous home-coming : 'in rushed a *young lady*, crying
out – "I hope, you'll whip him, Mrs Coleridge !" This
woman still lives at Ottery, & neither Philosophy or Religion
have been able to conquer the antipathy which I feel
towards her, whenever I see her.' As it was, he was put to
bed, and recovered in a day or so : but from that time
onwards he claims to have been 'weakly' and 'subject to the
ague for many years after'.

The incident clearly had a deep effect on him ; in fact, it is
the only substantial story that survives from his early
childhood. Coleridge's first publisher, Joseph Cottle,
records another version of the tale in his *Early Recollections*.
Cottle was notoriously unreliable in his biographical
sketches, but one fails to see how he could have been wrong
about almost every detail. He says that Coleridge's sister
Anne had given him a hook and line to catch a fish in the
gutter that flows through Ottery. 'Sammy' decided, however,
to go after a whale, and went down to the river Otter where
he wandered a great distance and fell asleep. During the
night he caught hold of a willow branch, and was on the
point of pulling himself into the water when he was found
by a waggoner who heard his cries.[1]

The intended knife attack on the brother, the fear of
punishment, the aggressive feelings towards his mother,
have been entirely suppressed. All that remains of the
'drama' of the story is the cry for help : 'A waggoner proceeding along, at four in the morning, thought he heard a
child's voice ! He stopped and listened. He now heard the
voice cry out.' It is interesting, too, that the mother should
be replaced by his sister, another shadowy figure, who died

when he was at Cambridge, and yet a person on who
seems to have placed much dependence.

The central importance of both versions is clearly contained in the plea for help. However much he may have been
his parent's darling, he was lonely, bullied and obviously
unhappy. Understandably he had staged a confrontation.
The question was, had it worked? One psychoanalyst,
Professor Eli Marcovitz, who thinks that it had not, comments that Coleridge's attempt on his brother's life required
punishment – the fact that he was not punished probably
produced a reaction; the chronic muscular and arthritic
pains of later life which Coleridge attributed to his exposure
during that night were in all probability a mode of self-
punishment. He would also have us trace Coleridge's later
obsession with the Cain and Abel theme back to this un-
resolved occasion of brotherly guilt.[2] The view is intriguing ;
but then, we shall never know. What does seem certain is
that Coleridge developed an early antipathy for his mother,
while closely identifying with his father. In contrast to the
mother's 'aggrandizing' spirit, his father was 'indifferent to
the good & evil of this world'. His father would take him
on his knee, and hold long conversations with him. And
Coleridge remembers that when he was eight years of age,
his father walked with him one winter evening and told him
the names of the stars ' – and how Jupiter was a thousand
times larger than our world – and that the other twinkling
stars were Suns that had worlds rolling round them – &
when I came home, he shewed me how they rolled round'.
The young Coleridge listened to him with 'a profound
delight & admiration'.

It was in Coleridge's ninth year that his secure, if not
entirely happy, world was totally destroyed. Uncharacteris-
tically, his father had taken Frank to Plymouth to secure
him a midshipman's berth under Admiral Graves : we may
take it that he was implementing one of his wife's 'ambitious'
plans. Before returning home he had a dream in which

'Death had appeared to him, as he is commonly painted, & touched him with his Dart'. He came home, took to his bed and accordingly died. That Coleridge later associated his father's death with his mother's ambition is by no means certain ; yet the errand to Plymouth is given much prominence in his account. He also remarks that he did not know of his father's return. 'Her *shriek* awaked me,' he wrote, ' – & I said, "Papa is dead." . . . How I came to think of his Death, I cannot tell ; but so it was – Dead he was . . . '

The home was uprooted, and for the next few months Coleridge's mother negotiated for a suitable boarding school for her youngest son. At length, in April 1782, 'Judge Buller, who had been educated by my Father, sent for me, having procured a Christ's Hospital Presentation'. He went up to London, stayed briefly with relatives, spent six weeks at the preparatory school in Hertford, and at last, in September, 'was drafted up to the great school at London'. At one blow Coleridge lost his father, his mother and his home, and it is difficult not to believe that the scars would remain for a lifetime.

Christ's Hospital in those days was spartan. The boys were 'under excessive subordination to each other, according to rank in school', the food was poor and scarce as befitted 'orphans' ('Our appetites were damped, never satisfied'), and they froze in their dormitories in winter. Once again Coleridge became a 'playless dreamer', and sought consolation in books and insulated fantasies.

Conceive what I must have been at fourteen ; I was in a continual low fever. My whole being was, with eyes closed to every object of present sense, to crumple myself up in a sunny corner and read, read read – fancy myself on Robinson Crusoe's Island, finding a mountain of plum-cake and eating a room for myself, and then eating it into the shapes of tables and chairs – hunger and fancy![3]

It seems that he was regarded a dull boy until he was discovered reading Virgil 'for pleasure' out of school hours.

After this he was taken up into the Grammar School, where he came under the severe regime of James Boyer, who impressed on his pupils the rigorous logic of the best classical authors : 'In the truly great poets, he would say, there is a reason assignable, not only for every word, but for the position of every word.' Coleridge never forgot the advice, although it took him some years to emulate it.

He rarely went home to Devon ; and he was clearly lonely in his first years, particularly on whole-day holidays when the boys were locked out of the school. In 1785, however, his kind and generous brother George, who became something of a substitute father, came to teach close by at a school in Hackney, and his brother Luke was training to be a surgeon at the London Hospital. In his sixteenth year he also became the object of much warmth and affection in the home of a friend, Tom Evans : there were three sisters and Coleridge soon developed an attachment for Mary, the eldest. Letters passed between them, and Coleridge sent love-rhymes wrapped round nosegays. He later claimed that Mary had given him his first experience of love, and home life. For Mary Evans's mother, he felt a 'tenderness scarcely inferior to the solicitude of maternal affection', and later in life went so far as to say, she 'taught me what it was to have a mother ! I loved her as such'.[4] The breach with Ottery seemed final, and somewhat self-imposed.

At school Coleridge showed signs of developing those propensities towards 'myriad-mindedness' that he exhibited in later life. Looking back on his childhood in his twenty-fifth year, he chose to think of himself as a kind of pre-cocious Berkeleian idealist (understandably, he had been soaking himself in Berkeley during that year). He says that from his early reading of fairy tales his mind 'had been habituated *to the Vast* – & I never regarded *my senses* in any way as the criteria of my belief'. Yet this was clearly a retrospective exaggeration of only one of a variety of mental experiences, and does little to explain his periodic preoccupation with empirical and necessitarian thought, his remarkable sense of the tangible in poetry, his aptitude for metaphysical systems which cannot be easily reconciled with Berkeley's form of idealism.

Solitude had turned him into a *helluo librorum*, and he gained access to a circulating library by the kindness of a stranger with whom he had collided in the Strand. The man had taken the young Coleridge for a pickpocket; but as Coleridge winningly explained, he had been imagining himself swimming the Hellespont in the character of Leander. Much speculation surrounds the 'catalogue' of this 'circulating library' – which clearly formed the extra-curricular source of Coleridge's reading at this time. If we are to take Coleridge at his word, and Lamb (who seemed to find little difficulty in doing so), his reading at school was impressive in its range and depth. Lamb talks of him un-folding the 'mysteries of Jamblichus and Plotinus', which he may have read in the form of Thomas Taylor's translation of the sixth Book of the First Ennead, on the Beautiful, published in 1787.[5] From this relatively small work he may have acquired his lifelong absorption with the notion of the reconciliation of the many and the one. Closely related to this transcendental material were his forays into Boehme's *Aurora*, a mind-spinning work of theosophy – which reaches out into the realms of metaphysics, seventeenth-century science, angels and mysticism – over which Coleridge says he 'conjured' at school. On the other hand there was the cynical rationalism of Voltaire's *Philosophical Dictionary* – a work specially written for the entertainment and con-firmation of atheists. Presumably he had this work in mind when he claimed that he had read all the arguments for atheism by the age of fifteen. He even professed his atheism to Boyer on one occasion – an admission that resulted in a sound flogging. He also had ambitions to be a surgeon, reading a great many medical and scientific works, and spending Saturdays with Luke at the London Hospital.

It was at school, too, that he first demonstrated his extraordinary eloquence. Charles Lamb records how he had seen him surrounded by an audience of amazed schoolboy listeners in the school cloisters, and Coleridge himself recalls in his *Biographia* how his loneliness drove him to seek out an accommodating clerical ear on which to vent his inner preoccupations : 'In my friendless wanderings on our leave-days (for I was an orphan, and had scarce any connections in London), highly was I delighted if any passenger, especially if he were dressed in black, would enter into conversation with me.'

The subject of these conversations and their effect on the young Coleridge are of great interest. They were, he tells us, quoting *Paradise Lost* –

> Of providence, fore-knowledge, will, and fate,
> Fixed fate, free will, fore-knowledge absolute,
> And found no end in wandring mazes lost.

This 'preposterous pursuit', Coleridge tells us, was injurious both to his natural powers and to the progress of his education. But he was fortunately extricated from these 'quicksilver mines of metaphysic depths' by his relationship with the Evans family and his timely discovery of the poet William Lisle Bowles. These 'abstruse researches' were marked in his mind as exercising 'the strength and subtlety of the understanding without awakening the feelings of the heart'. It was Bowles's twenty-one sonnets, published in 1789, which provided an antidote – 'so tender and yet so manly, so natural and real, and yet so dignified and harmonious'. To Bowles he directly attributed the beginning of a 'long and blessed interval, during which my natural faculties were allowed to expand and my original tendencies to develop themselves'.

The actual influence of Bowles on Coleridge's own poetry is very slight indeed :[6] he seems to have absorbed little of his style and practically nothing of his thinking. On the other

hand it is easy to see how Bowles's 'friend of the friendless'
regard for Nature consoled a lonely boy, how his ingenuous
emotion and sense of pity led the young Coleridge away
from the 'writings of Mr Pope and his followers'. Even at
that early stage he claims to have seen that the excellence
of these 'modern' writers 'consisted in just and acute
observations on men and manners in an artificial state of
society as its matter and substance'. The more obvious
influence on Coleridge's early productions are to be found in
Milton, who together with Shakespeare was set as a lesson :
'And they were the lessons, too, which required most time
and trouble to *bring up*, so as to escape his [Boyer's] censure.'
In avoiding the trap of the Augustans, Coleridge seems to
have taken an independent course at school ; talking of his
schoolfellows in the *Biographia*, he says, 'Among those
with whom I conversed there were, of course, very many
who had formed their taste and their notions of poetry from
the writings of Mr Pope . . . ' In rebelling against the
Augustans he was perhaps more a child of his age than he
knew. But the rejection of 'Ignoramuses & Pope-admirers',
and 'the usual trash of Johnsons', was not merely a preference
for the 'simple, sensuous, passionate' Milton ; as Coleridge
approached the end of his schooldays he was to come in
contact with upheavals which were something more than a
revolution in aesthetics, or a mere generation gap.

The *Destruction of the Bastile*, which Coleridge wrote at
school in 1789 is interesting more for its earnestness and
optimism, than its political awareness or literary promise :

> I see, I see ! glad Liberty succeed
>   With every patriot virtue in her train !
>   And mark yon peasant's raptur'd eyes ;
>   Secure he views his harvests rise ;
>   No fetter vile the mind shall know,
>   And Eloquence shall fearless glow,
> Yes ! Liberty the soul of Life shall reign,
> Shall throb in every pulse, shall flow thro' every vein !

Enthusiasm glows through the juvenile rhetoric: yet when he turns his attention to England there is not a glimmer of precocious revolutionary insight: 'Freedom' is described as a conquering hero spreading throughout the globe from its true centre — Britain :

> And wider yet thy influence spread,
> Nor e'er recline thy weary head,
> Till every land from pole to pole
> Shall boast one independent soul!
> And still, as erst, let favour'd Britain be
> First ever of the first and freest of the free!

Here the young Coleridge was acknowledging the prevalent Whig attitude that the French Revolution was bringing France in line with an enlightened constitution that had existed in England since 1688. Yet it was precisely his expression of ingenuousness, optimism and seriousness that separated him from the attitude that presumed such a contention. If it was smugness that led George III to declare that the British constitution was 'the most beautiful combination that was ever framed', it was earnestness which would shortly lead many of Coleridge's generation to disagree with him. By the same token they would find the world of Pope, Johnson and Gibbon, with all its polish, wit and confident generalization, trivial. It was not merely a question of 'style', it ran to a basic difference in attitudes and feelings. 'Gibbon's style is detestable,' said Coleridge a good many years later, 'but his style is not the worst thing about him.'8

No doubt his very presence at Christ's Hospital, where he suffered a sense of exile, and the 'orphan's' precariousness, did much to preclude any feelings of smugness about his role or position in life. Outwardly Coleridge may have exhibited signs of 'charity boy' deference to his 'superiors', yet he would also be capable of pride, self-righteousness and moral outrage. One can never overestimate the effect of an adolescent's heroes. Coleridge's father, 'an Israelite without guile' as Coleridge liked to call him, was clearly his first and most abiding object of worship. Coleridge evidently inherited much of his piety, simplicity and dreaminess, but in large measure, too, his sense of indifference to worldly considerations. In his younger days, one of the worst insults Coleridge could hurl at anybody (as will be seen) was the accusation 'WORLDLY PRUDENCE'.

Apart from Bowles, the other strong hero figure of his late schooldays was Thomas Chatterton, the orphan poet of Bristol. Like Coleridge, Chatterton had been educated at a charity school, although he soon learnt to despise the city merchants who had provided him with an education. Sitting in the Muniment Room over the north entrance to St Mary Redcliffe's Church in Bristol he composed 'medieval' poems and wrote them down on scraps of parchment he had found in a chest there. But the 'Rowley forgeries', as they came to be known, were not just a whimsical mode of self-expression : the young Chatterton was deriving considerable pleasure from debunking the 'privileged' arbitrators of taste and excellence. Eventually he unsuccessfully approached a representative of this 'literary class' when he applied to Horace Walpole for patronage. His subsequent flight to London, where he committed suicide in poverty and depression, captured the imagination of the latter half of the eighteenth century ; but more importantly he became something of a cult hero for a great many young 'geniuses' who suspected that the world of literature had comfortably organized itself into an exclusive club. And what realms of privilege might lie beyond that ?

In his last year at school Coleridge wrote his *Monody on the Death of Chatterton*, which reveals a definite progression from the chauvinistic self-congratulation of *The Destruction of the Bastile*. It is a much more personal poem; his identification with Chatterton is complete, and he has evidently been thinking. In fact he had had plenty of time to think, for he spent half of his final school year in the sick ward recovering from rheumatic fever.

> Now prompts the Muse poetic lays,
> And high my bosom beats with love of Praise!
> But, Chatterton! methinks I hear thy name,
> For cold my Fancy grows, and dead each Hope of Fame.

It is 1790 and he is on the point of leaving school. But what sort of world was he entering? And how would he be received into it? There were many questions to be asked, but already some of the most vexing ones were purely rhetorical:

> Is this the land of liberal Hearts!
> Is this the land, where Genius ne'er in vain
> Pour'd forth her soul-enchanting strain?

Although Coleridge later bewailed his schooldays 'pent mid cloisters dim', he often looked back on Christ's Hospital with a certain nostalgia: the school became, perforce, an 'Alma Mater' in a literal sense; and on leaving it he wrote a sonnet which paralleled his loss of this parental substitute with the loss of his home at Ottery:

> Farewell parental scenes! a sad farewell!
> To you my grateful heart still fondly clings ...
> Lingering I quit you, with as great a pang,
> As when erewhile, my weeping childhood, torn
> By early sorrow from my native seat,
> Mingled its tears with hers – my widow'd Parent lorn.

He brought away from Christ's Hospital a fine training in classical scholarship, and a deep sense of confidence in his own powers: as he noted, 'Advantage of public schools – content with school praise where others publish'.[9] Yet there was to be another, not so happy legacy. In 1802 he wrote: 'N.B. The great importance of breeding up children *happy* to at least 15 or 16 illustrated in my always dreaming of Christ Hospital and when not quite well having all those uneasy feelings which I had at School/feelings of Easter Monday &c.'[10] The unhappiness of Coleridge's childhood emerges repeatedly in his later writings. We have seen already that he suffered loneliness and persecution. But there had been other miseries, less clearly defined. In a piece of interesting self-analysis Coleridge later wrote : 'It is a most instructive part of my Life the fact, that I have always been preyed on by some Dread, and perhaps all my faulty actions have been the consequence of some Dread or other on my mind/from fear of Pain, or Shame, not from prospect of Pleasure / – So in my childhood & Boyhood the horror of being detected with a sore head ; afterwards imaginary fears having the Itch in my Blood – / then a short-lived Fit of Fears from sex.'[11] Certainly he suffered much pain at school ; when he tried to describe the acuteness of his suffering in subsequent illnesses, he frequently compared it with his illness at Christ's Hospital, and his poem *Pain*, written when he was eighteen, is a moving testimony of his sufferings at that time :

> Now that my sleepless eyes are sunk and dim,
> And seas of Pain seem waving through each limb –

Yet the fear of 'Shame', the 'horror of being detected with a sore head', the 'imaginary fears', indicate sufferings of a more subconscious nature. One naturally turns to Coleridge's dreams with curiosity, particularly the 'Christ's Hospitalized dreams', as he once called them. To interpret a man's dreams without the advantage of the subject's living presence and cooperation would, of course, be hazardous : on the other hand, Coleridge's dreams are interesting for their own sake, and in many instances gratify the biographer's thirst for 'inner' revelation. In the first place it may be said that the recurrent 'school-dream' is fairly common with Englishmen. Cyril Connolly has remarked in his *Enemies of Promise* how he often dreamt that he was back at Eton searching for his place and finding it filled.

He tells us that a number of his contemporaries had the same dream. And so it was with Coleridge:

I dreamt that I was asleep in the Cloyster at Christ's Hospital & ⟨had⟩ awoken with a pain in my hand from some corrosion/boys & nurses daughters peeping at me/On their implying that I was not in the School, I answered yes I am/I am only twenty – I then recollected that I was thirty, & of course could not be in the School – & was perplexed – but not the least surprize that I could fall into such an error/...[12]

The suggestion of insecurity arising from the rejection of the parent-substitute figure needs no further comment. But a more fundamental sense of deprivation is recurrent in other dreams. In November of 1803, for example, when Coleridge was thirty-one, he says that he awoke from the following 'persecuting' dream:

The Tale of the Dream began in two *Images* – in two Sons of a Nobleman, desperately fond of shooting – brought out by the Footman to resign their Property, & to be made believe that they had none/ they were far too cunning for that/as they struggled & resisted their cruel Wrongers, & my Interest for them, I suppose increased, I became they – the duality vanished – Boyer & Christ's Hospital became concerned – yet still the former Story was kept up – & I was conjuring him, as he met me in the Street, to have pity on a Nobleman's Orphan.[13]

The disinherited 'Orphan', surrounded by 'cruel Wrongers' and pleading for pity, naturally points back to Coleridge's 'expulsion' from Ottery, an event that surely had a profound and lasting effect upon him. Psychoanalysts have suggested that the loss of the father before puberty may result in severe inner conflict leading to depressive, or manic-depressive reactions in later life; yet one is protected from a simple, all-embracing interpretation of the effect of Coleridge's loss by the sheer proliferation of speculation. Would he internalize his anger against the absent father, who was such a valued love object, and with whom he identified so closely? Or would he see the father's death as his own handiwork – a consequence of the childhood competition with the father for his mother's affection? Would he, as Charles Baudouin has suggested, suffer from a marked degree of conflict between the practical tendencies of the mother and the visionary nature of the father, which had ended in the father's death? And might this not produce a lifelong internal struggle between objective and subjective reality, the progressive tendency and regression, the 'reality' and the 'pleasure principle'? Or were there, as Professor M. Schulz suggests, deep feelings of guilt and insecurity arising from the lack of conflict with a father in puberty and the consequent development of a weak 'super ego'?[14] Perhaps the most intriguing psychoanalytic question in this last regard might relate to the history of Coleridge's youthful revolutionary tendencies and their eventual outcome. Marxist and Freudian writers have recently engaged in much polemic over the importance of the 'autonomous ego' as developed through 'constructive conflict with parents' in any sustained political struggle.[15] The contour of Coleridge's political allegiances might furnish an interesting illustration for the exponents of such hypotheses.

The debate is naturally open-ended, yet there is one common and inescapable conclusion amongst the psychoanalysts, that Coleridge, in view of his deprived childhood, would enter adulthood with abnormal dependency needs, that he would be subject to the depressive defences common in such cases. Coleridge's dreams are certainly fraught with depressive content, and there are recurrent features of sexual guilt, castration, persecution, harassment by debtors and duns, the experience of skin disease and deformity, a sense of being lost, and, frequently, of his own death.[16] Against these may be set the typically manic images of grandiosity and triumph : taking possession of the hall of an emperor, wandering amongst magnificent groves and noble buildings, an arrogant sense of superiority in 'quizzing' his old school fellows, Allen and Legrice, and of delivering the profound lecture.[17]

It is not difficult to read all manner of neurotic symptoms into Coleridge's waking life ; in fact, the quest for symptoms has developed into something of a sport in recent years : the tendentious diagnoses range from the suggestion that his later opium addiction was a deprived child's reversion to the 'oral stage', to the assertion that his fascination with the reconciliation of opposites arose from a 'primary process' love-hate conflict with his mother. There have been suggestions that the rise and fall of his friendships resulted from his frustrated search for father figures (or mother figures), and that his extraordinary verbal flights, his frequent attempts to escape reality, his dreams of the great epic, or the vast unifying philosophy were manic-defence mechanisms. So far his minor foibles have mercifully escaped unscathed – his inability at one stage to open letters, his craving for clotted cream, or his stern contention that all musicians are 'almost uniformly Debauchees'. But then, any tendency away from the habitual moral finger-wagging in Coleridge biography is probably a good one, and nobody more than Coleridge would have been delighted with the idea that there were any number of complicated psychological explanations for his failings, not to mention his aches and pains. As he once wrote to Robert Southey : 'God have mercy on us ! – We are all sick, all mad, all slaves !' As for the relationship between genius and neurosis, of this he had no doubt, although his mischievous speculation would possibly be found wanting in orthodoxy by our contemporaries :

It is a theory of mine that Virtue & Genius are Diseases of the Hypochondriacal & Scrofulous Genus – & exist in a peculiar state of the Nerves, & diseased Digestion – analogous to the beautiful Diseases, that colour & variegate certain Trees. – However, I add by way of comfort, that it is my Faith that the Virtue & Genius produce the Disease, not the Disease the Virtue &c tho' when present, it fosters them. Heaven knows! there are fellows who have more vices than scabs, & scabs countless – with fewer Ideas than Plaisters.[18]

Coleridge was awarded a modest exhibition by his school which was intended to maintain him at Jesus College, Cambridge, for seven years. He had been marked out for favour, and it was expected that he would proceed to Holy Orders and possibly a fellowship. Although Cobbett was to denounce both universities as 'dens of dunces' it seems that Coleridge found sufficient intellectual challenge to keep him at full stretch. Shortly after going up, in November 1791, he wrote to George : 'I read Mathematics three hours a day – by which means I am always considerably before the Lectures, which are very good ones ... After Tea ... I read Classics till I go to bed – viz – eleven o'clock.' He was convinced that if he continued to work at his present rate he would be a 'Classical Medallist' and a very 'high Wrangler', that is, a 'champion' mathematician. But he adds the sceptical comment : *'Freshmen always begin very furiously.'*

Coleridge had been fortunate in being sent to the university where mathematics and the natural sciences flourished, yet he soon neglected these studies and found ample reason to repent it in later years. In 1818 he wrote a note to his sons in the flyleaf of a book : 'O with what bitter regret, and in the conscience of such glorious opportunities ... at Jesus College, Cambridge, under an excellent Mathematical Tutor, Newton, all neglected.'[19]

He was equally fortunate in being sent to the university where family background counted for little. It was mainly prejudice that prompted Coleridge's Unitarian friend, John Prior Estlin, to assert that at the 'Established & Idolatrous Universities' only one thing would be learnt – 'Indifference to all Religions but the Religion of the *Gentleman*'. The accusation was more true of Oxford, perhaps. As Thomas

Carlyon, who wrote from experience, noted : '. . . at Oxford, the candidate for a fellowship must be well dressed, of gentle lineage, and moderately learned, the humble sizar, at Cambridge, was invited to enter the lists for academic honours and emoluments, without there being any question asked as to the tailor who made his coat, or the situation of his parents.[20]

The more liberal outlook at Cambridge, probably due to its long tradition in the empirical sciences, revealed itself in a strong Whig allegiance. And as far as the university was concerned the burning political issue of the times was the debate over the Test Act, which deprived the Dissenters of university places. It was this long-standing dispute which brought Coleridge in contact with reforming groups, and their initial appeal was more likely to be religious and emotional.

The champion of Church Establishment in Cambridge was Isaac Milner, Vice-Chancellor and staunch Tory, later to be immortalized for his opium habit in De Quincey's *Confessions*. Since his youth he had consistently and fanatically fought the Dissenters, and even as an undergraduate had distinguished himself by being the only man in his year to refuse to sign a 'round-robin' against compulsory subscription to the Thirty-nine Articles. At the opposite extreme there was William Frend, a fellow of Coleridge's college, who had not only conducted an arduous campaign against Milner but had actually resigned his Church ministry, gone over to the Unitarians, and braved the common room in a blue coat with brass buttons. The influence of Frend, right down to the sartorial bravado, was clearly decisive in Coleridge's early development, and the reason for this influence is not far to seek. Here was a university teacher in whom a high degree of religious sincerity merged with a deep social concern, a man who was prepared to throw caution and 'WORLDLY PRUDENCE' to the winds and court professional disaster in the interests of a just

2

cause – a cause so closely associated with the support of a persecuted and deprived minority.

Frend's main activity was confined to the writing of pamphlets. In 1788, after his 'conversion', he had published *Thoughts on Subscription to Religious Tests*, shortly followed by *An Address to the Inhabitants of Cambridge and its Neighbourhood, exhorting them to turn from the false worship of Three Persons to the Worship of the One True God*. The Unitarians are chiefly known, as their title implies, for their rejection of the Trinity, but of equal importance was their repudiation of the central 'Establishment' doctrines of Original Sin and Atonement. If anything their creed was distinguished by an absence of doctrine, rather than any set of positive tenets, and their faith held strong attractions for the scientific mind which sought to reconcile Christianity and empirical method. Yet if there was a single and fundamental doctrine in Unitarianism it was the primacy of reason.

Joseph Priestley, the Birmingham scientist and chief exponent of the sect, had preached this message far and wide in books and pamphlets during the 1780s – and it was due to Priestley that Frend had joined the Unitarian ranks in 1788. Nor would Coleridge have come under Priestley's influence merely through the medium of Frend. Even from Birmingham Priestley had spread his nets in the universities by the publication of his *Letters to the young men, who are in a course of education for the Christian Ministry at the university of Oxford and Cambridge*. His message was clear : 'If you would not set your hand to a common bond, without previously reading it, and approving of it, surely your minds ought to revolt at the idea of subscribing to articles of faith which you have not examined.'[21] Early in Coleridge's time at Cambridge, he published his *Appeal to the serious and candid Professors of Christianity*, where the encouragement to 'examine' is developed a stage further : his readers were asked to be on guard for the sinister manipulations and impositions of the guardians of faith : 'Distrust, therefore, all those who deny human reason, and who require you to abandon it, wherever religion is concerned. When once they have gained the point with you, they can lead you whither they please, and impose upon you every absurdity which their sinister views make it expedient for them that you should embrace.'[22] The tone of this, in spite of the qualification, 'Wherever religion is concerned', extends far beyond religious controversy; indeed there are strong echoes from France, and of Thomas Paine's *Rights of Man* which in that same year sold 200,000 copies.[23]

Extending a new religious hope with one hand Priestley was offering social and political optimism with the other. A notable example of this was his view of Original Sin, which led men to accept not only a depressing religious *status quo*, but a social one too. Original Sin he wrote, was 'the cause of fatal despair in some, and as fatal security in others. If the opinion were true, and men were really aware of their situation, I should think it impossible to prevent their falling into absolute distraction, through terror and anxiety.'[24] And in support of his social and religious optimism Priestley could bring to bear the emerging contemporary theories of determinism and necessity as expounded by the psychologist Hartley. Hartley will appear later in this narrative, but the importance of his connection with Priestley and his consequent influence on Coleridge at this stage is paramount.

If the world of Pope, Johnson and Gibbon represented a philosophy about which one could generalize, it was the vision of a secure and tidy universe. The prevailing intellectual climate of certainty and contentment in the eighteenth century was largely induced by the satisfaction derived from gazing out on a codified and mathematical universe, a view that was no doubt reinforced by a sense of political confidence inspired by the acquisition of a vast empire and the conviction that the British constitution was more or less divinely inspired. But tendencies from the opposite direction had been gathering momentum, albeit in confused eddies and cross-currents. There came an emphasis on feeling and instinct, the sensible apprehension of the particular as opposed to the bland generalizations of armchair philosophers. As Locke, the father of the movement had proclaimed, 'In truth the immediate object of all our reasoning and knowledge is nothing but particulars'. Knowledge was seen to be the result of sensation, and reflections on sensation. Locke had allowed judgment as the principle which studies the agreement or disagreement of ideas ; but Hume was far more sweeping : for him, the whole of mental life – knowledge of matter and mind, phenomena of emotions and wills – was explicable in terms of the association of ideas, an all-embracing law in the mental world as Newton's was in the physical. Hartley took this as a principle and developed it into a psychological-mechanical hypothesis. In its simplest terms they argued that ideas which are similar, or which have repeatedly occurred simultaneously or in succession, tend automatically to evoke one another. Thus it was only by repeated experience that perception of a cause led one to look for an effect. For those who were convinced by such arguments, a great many certainties suddenly disappeared. The implications of such theories in the realms of politics, religion and aesthetics were, to say the least, revolutionary.

At the same time the age of science and industry had been gradually getting under way ; by the 1770s an iron bridge had been thrown over the Severn, Richard Arkwright's spinning mills were humming day and night, and James Brindley's galleries and aqueducts were carrying coals from Worsley to the Mersey. The days of political economy, trade wars, income tax, industrial disputes and the workhouse, were fast approaching, and suitable men were at hand to fulfil the new roles. In 1783 the younger Pitt came to power – as Coleridge so aptly put it in the jargon of the times, 'he was cast rather than grew' ; and already Adam Smith was sneering at the 'myth' of the British Empire.

'The rulers of Great Britain,' he wrote in *Wealth of Nations*, 'have, for more than a century past, armed the people with the imagination that they possessed a great empire on the west side of the Atlantic. This empire, however, has hitherto existed in the imagination only.' By the 1770s the popular eighteenth-century Whig party ballad, 'Rule Britannia', seemed as inappropriate to some as it does in the 1970s.

Equally inappropriate was the notion that Englishmen, any more than other men, lived in the best of all possible worlds. 'I have frequently endeavoured to image the possibility of a perfect government,' says the prince in Johnson's *Rasselas*, 'by which all wrong should be restrained, all vice reformed, and all the subjects preserved in tranquility and innocence.' Experience had taught Dr Johnson, and the prince, that this was a dangerous indulgence. But it was precisely the knowing acceptance of the human condition that was about to be called in question, and a new spirit of dissatisfaction, curiosity and enquiry would range across the whole of human affairs, not to speak of 'creation's ample range'.

In his *Essay on Man* Pope had rejoiced in the rigid, unerring universal laws, which separated rather than correlated. Thus a question could resolve itself in a smooth tautology:

> Why has not man a microscopic eye?
> For this plain reason, man is not a fly.

With Coleridge there would be no such easy answers, for the least of his questions found him at the threshold of undiscovered worlds of intellectual adventure. On gazing at a waterfall in his early manhood he remarked: 'Hung over the bridge, and musing, considering how much of this scene of endless variety in Identity was Nature's – How much the living organism's! what would it be if I had the eyes of a fly! – what if the blunt eye of a Brobdignag.'

Yet if Pope's neat questioning led paradoxically to a compartmentalized attitude of mind, Coleridge's wide-ranging enquiries tended towards an all embracing unity. The inescapable materialist substratum of Priestley's and Hartley's world descended on him like a revelation : for by employing a simple and incontrovertible physical analogy, the myriad disparate elements of the universe could be brought together. As Priestley explained in his *Matter and Spirit* :

> Suppose then that the Divine Being, when he created *matter*, only fixed certain *centres of various attractions and repulsions*, extending indefinitely in all directions, the whole effect of them to be upon each other ... It cannot be denied that these spheres may be diversified infinitely, so as to correspond to all kinds of bodies that we are acquainted with, or that are possible. For all effects in which bodies are concerned, and of which we can be sensible by our eyes, touch &c. may be resolved into attraction or repulsion.[25]

Positing the 'Divine Being' as the principle of energy, the Pantheistic picture was complete. The view might involve a great many later difficulties, but the vision of a universe soaked in 'divinity' in which each belonged to each was surely a thrilling and consoling one to a young man emerging from a lonely and dislocated youth. As Priestley put it : 'the Divine Being, and his energy are absolutely necessary to that of every other being. His power is the very *life* and *soul* of everything that exists ; and strictly speaking, *without him, we* ARE, as well as, *can* DO *nothing*.'[26]

It was out of the excitement of such ideas as these that religious and philosophical movements merged with agitation for political reform and a total reconstruction of society amongst the young intellectuals of Coleridge's day. It was, as Hazlitt later remarked, an 'unconstrained period', a time when 'nothing was not given for nothing', a time when, as Coleridge exultantly proclaimed in *Reflections on Entering into Active Life*, 'it was a luxury – to be !' In the year of the

French Revolution Frend had tramped through Europe on foot and returned to Cambridge via France – he was in no doubt as to the enormous importance of what was happening, and was fired with hope that the revolutionary precedents could be extended to the situation in his own country. The Unitarian organization would be mobilized, like the Corresponding Societies amongst the artisans, and the message of hope spread throughout the land; as Hazlitt commented, describing the exchange of visitors amongst Unitarian ministers: 'A line of communication is thus established, by which the flame of civil and religious liberty is kept alive.' The way had already been paved, in fact, by the Society for Commemorating the Revolution in Great Britain, established among a dissenting congregation in London. In 1789 this Society turned its energies to the encouragement of the Revolution in France. And in November of that year Richard Price, author of *Observations of the Nature of Civil Liberty*, preached to them on the subject of a possible British Revolution : 'Tremble all ye oppressors of the world !' he cried. 'You cannot now hold the world in darkness. Struggle no longer against increasing light and liberality. Restore to mankind their rights ; and consent to the corrections of abuses, before they and you are destroyed together.'

Yet the new reforming zeal of the Dissenters, whether they shared Price's radicalism or not, was to lay them open to the same accusations of Jacobinism, atheism, republicanism and levelling that would be aimed at the non-religious Corresponding societies. The euphoria of danger was to merge with the excitement of religious and social righteousness. Persecution, perhaps martyrdom, was in the air. In 1791 a Church-and-King mob destroyed Priestley's house and laboratory in Birmingham. Meanwhile back in Cambridge Frend was writing and preaching himself out of a job. All that Coleridge could do at the moment was emulate his new hero as best he could in an orgy of undergraduate discussion. His rooms in Jesus, 'on the right hand ground floor of the staircase facing the gate, were a centre of conversation, largely on politics'. At these parties, says Charles Legrice, 'Aeschylus and Plato and Thucydides were pushed aside with a pile of lexicons to discuss the pamphlets of the day. Ever and anon a pamphlet issued from the pen of Burke. There was no need of having the book before us. Coleridge had read it in the morning, and in the evening he would repeat whole pages verbatim.'

A young, politically active, and largely deplored group was rallying round Frend. In fact, there was a reactionary slogan at the time – 'FREND of Jesus, Friend of the Devil'.[27] Even among the liberal minded there had been a stern reaction, an example of which was Burke's *Reflections on the Revolution*, published in 1790, which was intended to curb the excesses of Richard Price and put a case for the moderating virtues of tradition. The young reformers demonstrated their repudiation of the standards of the Establishment by their clothes and hair-styles, adopting the striped pantaloons of the French revolutionaries, growing their hair long and wearing it loose. The ingenuity of their graffiti remains unparalleled to this day. Not satisfied with merely chalking 'Frend for ever ! ! !' on college walls throughout the city, the slogan 'LIBERTY and EQUALITY' was burnt into the smooth lawns of Trinity with gunpowder.

Meanwhile Coleridge was emulating the example of the Unitarian 'visits' by making trips to Manchester. Robert Owen, who profoundly believed in the shaping influence of the social environment, remembers how Coleridge occasionally made the journey to Manchester College to join his own group of reformers, and he records an interesting portrait of the eloquent young undergraduate :

At this period Coleridge was studying at one of the universities, and was then considered a genius and eloquent. He solicited permission to join our party, that he might meet me in discussion, as I was the one who opposed the religious prejudices of all sects, though always in a friendly and kind manner, having now imbibed the spirit of charity and kindness for my opponents, which was forced upon me by my knowledge of the true formation of character by nature and society. Mr Coleridge had a great fluency of words, and he could well put them together in high sounding sentences; but my few words, directly to the point, generally told well; and although the eloquence and learning were with him, the strength of the argument was generally admitted to be on my side.'28

Early in 1793 matters came to a head for Frend. At the very time when the tensions between France and Britain were escalating into war, Frend published his *Peace and Union*, which he outlined in a later publication in this way:

The reforms recommended were classed under three heads, representation, law and religion. Under the first, the shortening of the duration of parliaments, increase of votes in boroughs, extension of the rights of suffrage to copy holders as well as freeholders, and the antient system of government introduced . . . by the king, were recommended. Under the second head, some evils in the modern system of law were enumerated . . . Under the third head, some changes in the religious establishment were desired.29

As Frend completed the pamphlet King Louis XVI was executed and war finally broke out between France and England. This led him to write a vitriolic appendix on the injustice of the war, not only for its principles, but because of the direct effect it would have on the manufacturing classes. The pamphlet immediately brought the rage and vengeance of patriotism and orthodoxy in Cambridge down on his head. He was expelled from his college and later brought to trial before the Vice-Chancellor's court for offending the University statutes. After sustaining a long and arduous defence, Frend was eventually expelled from the University. Coleridge was at the trial, and himself narrowly missed being disciplined for his noisy demonstrations:

[The undergraduates] were unanimous in favour of Mr Frend and every satirical remark reflecting on the conduct and motives of his persecutors was vociferously applauded. At length the Court desired

2*

the Proctors to interfere. Mr Farrish, the Senior Proctor, having marked one man who had particularly distinguished himself by applauding, and noted his position in the gallery, and having previously ascertained the exact situation of the culprit, he touched a person, whom he supposed to be the same, on the shoulder, and asked him his name and college. The person thus addressed assured him that he had been perfectly quiet. Farrish replied, 'I have been watching you for a long time, and have seen you repeatedly clapping your hands'. 'I wish this was possible', said the man, and turning round exhibited an arm so deformed that his hands could not by any possibility be brought together; this exculpation was received with repeated round of applause, which continued for some minutes. The name of the young man was Charnock, and his college Clare Hall; the real culprit was S. T. Coleridge, of Jesus College, who having observed that the Proctor had noticed him, and made an offer of changing places, which was gladly accepted by the unsuspecting man. Coleridge immediately retreated, and mixing with the crowd, entirely escaped suspicion.[30]

But in this same year Coleridge was overtaken by a plague of personal troubles which had been accumulating since he first arrived in Cambridge. In the first place he had been falling heavily into debt. It seems that he had naïvely allowed a crafty Cambridge tradesman to furnish his rooms in college, expense no object, then rapidly acquired further debts in every direction, but notably to the college itself. 'To real happiness I bad adieu from the moment, I received my first Tutor's Bill.' Also in his first year his sister Anne died, and we must judge the profound effect of this loss from two poems he wrote at that time. The first, *On Receiving an Account that his only Sister's Death was inevitable*, returns to the former deaths in his family, and laments the death of Anne not only as the loss of one whom he had only recently come to love, but more particularly as the loss of somebody who might have loved *him*.

> Scarce had I lov'd you ere I mourn'd you lost;
> Say, is this hollow eye, this heartless pain,
> Fated to rove thro' Life's wide cheerless plain –

Nor father, brother, sister meet its ken –
My woes, my joys unshared! Ah! long ere then
On me thy icy dart, stern Death, be prov'd; –
Better to die, than live and not be lov'd!

The other, *On Seeing a Youth Affectionately Welcomed by a Sister*, similarly dwells on the theme of the loss of her love to him :

Cease, busy Memory! cease to urge the dart;
Nor on my soul her love to me impress!

Coleridge had lost his only sister, yet there were still the Evans girls who continued to be a source of solace and affection, and to whom he addressed himself as 'brother Coly'. By 1792, however, he had probably fallen deeply in love with the eldest, Mary, and undoubtedly had her in mind in his poem *Lines – On an Autumnal Evening*, of the following year, where an uncomfortable – though heartfelt – blending of Milton and Priestley finds expression :

With faery wand O bid the Maid arise,
Chaste Joyance dancing in her bright-blue eyes;
As erst when from the Muses' calm abode
I came with Learning's meed not unbestowed;
When as she twin'd a laurel round my brow,
And met my kiss, and half return'd my vow,
O'er all my frame shot rapid my thrill'd heart,
And every nerve confess'd the electric dart.

Although the details are vague, 1793 was a year of crisis for Coleridge. While he had done well enough to win the Browne Medal for a Greek Sapphic ode on the slave trade in the previous year, he was bitterly disappointed at narrowly failing to win the much coveted Craven Scholarship early in 1793. Then followed illness, further depression over his debts, and news of the death of his brother Frank – who had been killed the year before at the fall of Seringapatam. But while this latest bereavement filled him with melancholy, he

confessed to his brother George that he felt no 'Anguish'.
He explains his state of mind :

> I quitted Ottery, when I was so young, that most of those en-
> dearing circumstances, that are wont to render the scenes of our
> childhood delightful in the recollection, I have associated with the
> place of my education – and when at last I revisited Devon, the
> manners of the Inhabitants annihilated whatever tender ideas of
> pleasure my Fancy rather than my Memory had pictured to my
> Expectation. I found them (almost universally) to be gross without
> openness, and cunning without refinement.[31]

Even at this stage, George seems to have helped him
financially,[32] but things were going from bad to worse. It is
probably to this period, early in 1793, that he referred in a
later confession of his failings to George.

> I became a proverb to the University for Idleness – the time,
> which I should have bestowed on the academic studies, I employed
> in dreaming out wild Schemes of impossible extrication. It had been
> better for me, if my Imagination had been less vivid – I could not
> with such facility have shoved aside Reflection! How many and how
> many hours have I stolen from the bitterness of Truth in these soul-
> enervating Reveries – in building magnificent Edifices of Happiness
> on some fleeting Shadow of Reality! My Affairs became more and
> more involved – I fled to Debauchery – fled from silent and solitary
> Anguish to all the uproar of senseless Mirth! Having, or imagining
> that I had, no *stock* of Happiness, to which I could look forwards,
> I seized the empty gratifications of the moment, and snatched at the
> foam, as the wave passed by me.[33]

In the summer of 1773 Coleridge returned to Ottery, and
an attempt was made to straighten out his debts. The
brothers clubbed together, and a 'fair Road seemed open to
extrication'. But it was all to no purpose. On his way back
to college, via London, he went on a spending spree, and
returned to Cambridge and a 'multitude of petty Embarrassments which buzzed round me, like a Nest of Hornets –
Embarrassments, which in my wild carelessness I had

forgotten, and many of which I had contracted almost without knowing it'. At the same time he was suffering from a 'love-fit' as he called it, on discovering that there was a rival for Mary Evans's hand, and on realizing that he would not be in a position to compete for her. 'I never durst even in a whisper avow my passion, though I knew she loved me.' It was the final blow, the loss of love, security and 'home' all over again.

My agitations were delirium – I formed a Party, dashed to London at eleven o'clock at night, and for three days lived in all the tempest of Pleasure – resolved on my return – but I will not shock your religious feelings – I again returned to Cambridge – staid a week – such a week! Where Vice has not annihilated Sensibility, there is little need of a Hell! On Sunday night I packed up a few things, – went off in the mail – staid about a week in a strange way, still looking forwards with a kind of recklessness to the dernier resort of misery –

The identification with Chatterton had become very strong indeed. But instead of committing suicide, he put an end to it all in a less drastic fashion. At the beginning of December he enlisted as a trooper in the 15th Light Dragoons under the pseudonym Silas Titus Comberbache. And as much as the night by the river Otter in his childhood, one supposes that it was a way of punishing his family, and calling for help. It was very clear from the start that Coleridge would not make a good soldier.

'Whose is this rusty carbine?' an officer once demanded.

'Is it very rusty?' came Coleridge's voice from the troop.

'Very rusty!' replied the officer.

'Then, Sir, it must be mine.'

Not for long did Trooper Coleridge remain undetected. Who was this preposterous Comberbache who chalked up Latin tags, spouted Euripides, crammed a Greek text in his saddle holsters, and could not stay in the saddle?

Once again his brothers bailed him out. He was discharged as insane and in April of 1794 returned to

Cambridge, where he was gated and given the task of translating Demetrius Phalereus. His debts were fully paid and he addressed himself to a life of self-discipline. 'Every enjoyment, except of necessary comforts, I look upon as criminal', he solemnly wrote.

But the hectic experiences of the past year had unsettled him for the life of an undergraduate : and perhaps, in any case, he had already taken the best that Cambridge could offer him. He was now looking further afield.

Pantisocracy

EARLY in June 1794, in his twenty-second year, Coleridge set out from Cambridge on a tour with a college friend, Joseph Hucks. They had planned to do most of the walking in Wales, but first there was to be a brief diversion to Oxford to look up a school acquaintance. As they walked beneath the blazing sun of that summer which was to be remembered for many years for its drought, Coleridge carried in his hand a 'curious' walking stick, five feet in length, which he later described in detail:

On one side it displays the head of an Eagle, the Eyes of which represent rising Suns, and the Ears Turkish Crescents. On the other side is the portrait of the Owner in Wood-work. Beneath the head of the Eagle is a Welch Wig – and around the neck of the Stick is a Queen Elizabeth's Ruff in Tin. All adown it waves the line of Beauty in very ugly Carving.[1]

In those days, even without his 'curious' stick, Coleridge would have cut an extraordinary figure. Perhaps the best surviving description of him in his early twenties was this which he wrote himself:

As to me, my face, unless when animated by immediate eloquence, expresses great Sloth, & great, indeed almost ideotic, good nature. 'Tis a mere carcase of a face: fat, flabby, & expressive chiefly of inexpression. – Yet I am told, that my eyes, eyebrows, & forehead are physiognomically good – ; but of this the Deponent knoweth not. As to my shape, 'tis a good shape enough, if measured – but my gait is awkward, & the walk, & the *Whole man* indicates indolence *capable of energies.* . . . I cannot breathe thro' my nose – so my mouth, with sensual thick lips, is almost always open.

Like the other young university radicals of the time he wore his hair loose and unpowdered in the manner of the French revolutionaries, and as a demonstration against Pitt's powder tax ; moreover, he was careless in dress by nature, and notoriously unfastidious about soiled linen.

The ninety miles walk to Oxford was not likely to enhance his appearance. As his walking companion, Hucks, re-marked : 'We are so completely metamorphosed, that I much doubt whether you would recognize us through our disguise ; we carry our clothes, etc. in a wallet or knapsack, from which we have not hitherto experienced the slightest inconvenience : as for all ideas of appearance and gentility, they are entirely out of the question – our object is to see not be seen.' Vain hope no doubt, with Coleridge's walking stick. But there was a seriousness of intent about this tour, a consciousness of doing something unusual and urgent. It was an exercise altogether different from the spanking 'routs' of young gentlemen, or even the leisurely, philosophical, 'pedestrian tours' of the previous generation. Like Frend's march through Europe in 1789, or that of another young man, William Wordsworth, in the same year, it marked the new generation's distaste for the Grand Tour mentality. Notwithstanding the purported disguise, they were setting out in a blaze of declared earnestness to discover the truth about their country – especially in its remote regions. And the most important truths to both Coleridge and Hucks were, of course, political. Their enthusiasm and energetic awareness was strengthened further by an almost apocalyptic urgency. As Hucks put it, they were setting out 'at a time so peculiarly alarming to the affairs of this country, that every hour comes attended with some fresh calamity'.[2]

Britain had been at war with France for over a year. A French invasion was rumoured, and war fever was rife with all the flurry of military parades, volunteer corps and public subscriptions. The zeal of the reform movement in England, now closely identified with the Revolution in France, had been followed by a fierce Church-and-King reaction from all levels of society. Anything could happen on a six hundred mile walk. Spies abounded ; and in the previous month the Habeas Corpus Act had been suspended to allow political suspects to be held without trial. In some parts of the country the 'Democrats' and 'Jacobins' were being hounded by patriotic mobs, and effigies of Tom Paine had been burnt on bonfires – giving him the notorious distinction of a Guy Fawkes, or a Pope. For Coleridge and Hucks, with their fierce republican sympathies, there were obvious dangers, which they seemed to relish unabashed. Yet their motives for making such a tour were not entirely single-minded. To the gentle and serious young Hucks it almost amounted to a desire to see the country while the going was good : 'to explore the hidden beauties of nature unmechanized by the ingenuity of man'. And for his part, Coleridge purchased a little notebook and portable inkhorn to record 'the wild Flowers of Poesy'.[3]

The Oxford Coleridge entered that June was far from his liking. Whereas the student radicals at Cambridge had clashed violently with the university authorities throughout the past year, Oxford, with its preponderance of theologians and 'Aristocrats', had slumbered peacefully on, 'plus royaliste que le roi', as if unaware of the tumultuous times. Oxford, as far as he was concerned, was 'a blighted Corn-field, where the sleepy Poppy nods its red-cowled head, and the weak-eyed Mole plies his dark work'. But in the midst of these dullards he found at least one under-graduate whose political views were sympathetic to his own when he was introduced to Robert Southey at Balliol College.

Southey, 'tall, dignified,' and 'possessing great suavity of manners',[4] was the son of a bankrupt tradesman who had been imprisoned the year before and had died of a broken heart. 'At the age of nineteen', wrote Southey, who had actually visited his father in the prison, 'I have known more calamity than many who deserve it more, meet with in long lives.'[5] Rising at five every morning to study Homer, he strove to adopt the highest standards of self-discipline and morality, and avoided all but his most sober friends. Yet, he had himself only recently undergone a conversion.

His career at Westminster School had been marked by wild pranks and hooliganism, involving such diversions as defacing monuments in Westminster Abbey and leading gangs in raids on a private school close to St Margaret's Churchyard. The *Public Advertiser* of 1791 records a 'terrible fracas' in which all the boys at Westminster School rushed out to 'Green' in Dean's Yard to witness a fight between two boys over a piece of ribbon. All attempts by the headmaster to gain control were repulsed, and when he announced that he was going to flog the head boy the whole school staged a walk-out. It took 'the persuasion of Lord Stormont and some distinguished characters' to restore the head boy and the school to order. Ten years later Southey could boast that he still possessed the piece of ribbon![6] Meanwhile back in Bristol, where his hair – 'all ringlets' – and his complexion – 'beautifully fair' – were the envy of a Miss Sara Fricker, he was known to parade in the streets dressed as a girl. Miss Fricker, who will shortly return to our narrative, actually walked some way with him one evening before recognizing his true identity and gender.[7]

His outstanding achievement at Westminster, however, was his collaboration in a satirical school magazine, the *Flagellant*. Some biographers have called attention to Southey's early radicalism in this escapade. But, as the title of the periodical suggests, a more amusing although hardly less knowing propensity was the case. Magazines featuring flagellation – 'The English Vice' – were something

of a rage in the late eighteenth century. To mention just a
few, there were available in London the *Bon Ton Magazine*,
English Woman's Domestic Magazine, *The Annals of Gallantry*,
and *Glee and Pleasure*; descriptions of flagellation orgies,
erotic gossip and advertisements for willing flagellants were
the main topic. Southey's famous article, couched in its
callow attempt at a medieval friar's anathemata, was a clear
suggestion that his schoolmasters were guilty of sado-
masochism in their practice of corporal punishment. Such
behaviour, he wrote, was 'utterly inconsistent with the
character of a schoolmaster, particularly with ministers of
the Church of England as most schoolmasters are, thus by
making use of so beastly, so idolatrous a custom of the
children of morals, of the Hittites and the Shittites and the
Gergusites and other idolators'. Naturally, the masters
expelled him.

But by 1794 all this was in the past. The young Southey
was determined to 'despise folly and execrate vice' and felt
'compelled to seek internal resources'.[8] Lean, ascetic-
looking, with angular features, he was a plodder. In his
youth he might be capable of rashness, but he was blessed
with a sensible attitude towards self-survival, and what he
lacked in the higher flights of imagination and emotion he
compensated with industry, perseverance and self-discipline.

Quite what it was that attracted Coleridge to this clever
and pretty young man with such spontaneous and lasting
ardour is difficult to say. Certainly Southey exhibited all the
necessary reforming tendencies and breadth of mind that
would be essential to earn his respect : not only was Southey
a fine classical scholar, and a promising poet, he had also
shocked the Balliol refectory with his loose unpowdered
ringlets. Perhaps in this first absence from Cambridge
after being gated, Coleridge's defences were down and he
felt for the first time the need to replace the loss of Mary
Evans. And it would be preferably somebody far distant
from Cambridge where his youthful excesses had been

proverbial; somebody who, like himself, had suffered and been deprived, who had adopted a life of austerity and high seriousness, who could keep him to the straight and narrow. Whatever the case, the relationship was deep, generous and enthusiastic from the very beginning, and it seemed to be sublimated out of the ordinary run of such youthful English intimacies with all the epithets of 'civic' greetings and 'fraternal' well-wishing that were current at that time. And if Southey was to hesitate in the face of a total personal commitment, the eloquent Coleridge could offer overwhelming political arguments.

Warmth of particular Friendship [he told Southey] does not imply absorption. The nearer you approach the Sun, the more intense are his Rays – yet what distant corner of the system do they not cheer and vivify? The Ardour of private Attachments makes Philanthropy a necessary *habit* of the Soul. I love my *Friend* – such as *he* is, all mankind are or *might be*! The deduction is evident – Philanthropy (and indeed every other Virtue) is a thing of *Concretion* – Some home-born Feeling is the *center* of the Ball, that, rolling on thro' Life collects and assimilates every congenial Affection.[9]

From the outset he lavished Southey with the highest praise. Although he could not resist a playful jibe at his regular habits: 'I would say, thou art a Nightingale amongst Owls – but thou art so songless and heavy towards night, that I will rather liken thee to the Martin Lark.' Southey had creative powers of 'Genius', declared Coleridge; but, even more, he could make 'the adamantine gate of Democracy turn on its hinges to the most sweet music'.

There were excited discussions in Southey's rooms in Balliol, which were situated close to a gate which led into St Giles's and had a view over the newly planted Fellows' grove. And their friendship, which found its origin in political fervour, was further cemented by collaboration in a scheme for putting their political theories into practice. They would be the architects of a new society, founders of a commune in which personal property would be abolished.

The commune would be based on twelve men and their wives, although they would hold an open mind about the dissolubility of marriage. They would emigrate to America, buy land and live in a Utopia – free of personal possessions, sharing an equal burden of manual labour (which, pinning their confidence on an assertion of Adam Smith's, they were convinced would absorb no more than two hours of the day). With each member pulling his or her weight, they would be equally privileged in their freedom to pursue the things of the mind. 'When Coleridge and I are sawing down a tree we shall discuss metaphysics', enthused Southey, 'criticise poetry when hunting buffalo, and write sonnets whilst following the plough.'[10] Isolated from the depravities of 'civilized' society they would shape their children's minds and hearts according to a master plan that would ensure predictable results. They would be the elect; a unique society who by the second generation would combine 'the innocence of the patriarchal age with the knowledge and general refinements of European culture'.[11] At the same time it would become increasingly clear, particularly on Southey's part, that this self-exiled commune was to flee from the wrath to come; for the mighty upheavals in France – anticipating revolution in England – heralded who knew what? War, famine, persecution, the demise of civil liberty were already in evidence. Who could say what devastation, conflagration, apocalypse even, might not come to pass before the glorious millennium of a recon- structed Society?

The phenomenon of Pantisocracy, as the ideology of this band of revolutionary 'saints' was to be called, united many echoes from the past with the beckoning voice of the future. On the one hand, its Garden of Eden simplicity, its sense of righteousness and freedom of spirit, puts one in mind of the millennial sects of the Middle Ages. The pantheism of Priestley here blends with the Neoplatonism of so many of those former adepts of the 'Free Spirit': not only was God

'All that is', but the perfect man is 'both God and man', for 'You shall order all created beings to serve you according to your will, for the glory of God. . . . You shall bear all things up to God. If you want to use all created beings, you have the right to do so ; for every creature that you use you drive up into its Origin.'[12] Yet while the repudiation of ownership harked back to early Christianity and the sects of the 'Blessed', it looked forward to the communist ideology of a later age. And if the commune smacked of religious exclusiveness and initiation, it also anticipated the necessity for shedding the taboos and unquestioned prejudices of society as they knew it. At the same time it was very much of its own age. As the commune gradually took shape in the form of a heated correspondence between Coleridge and Southey – it became apparent that its basic theory was associated with necessitarianism. As Priestley had pointed out, 'the doctrine of necessity supplies the only theoretical foundation of moral governments, and . . . the opposite affords no foundation for it at all'.[13]

On many points, too, it coincided with views of William Godwin, whose *Political Justice* had appeared the year before. Godwin would have entirely agreed that the characters of men originate in their external circumstance. There were no innate principles, no instincts. 'What is born into the world is an unfinished sketch, without character or decisive feature.'[14] In his view children were no more than a 'sort of raw material . . . a ductile and yielding substance', and if we failed to mould them exactly to our wishes it was because we 'throw away the power commuted to us, by the folly with which we are accustomed to exert it'.[15] Man and society, then, were perfectible not through the 'mysterious philosophy' of Free Will but under 'necessity in a mature volitional act'. A trifle puzzling perhaps, but then Godwin never did succeed, any more than his contemporaries, in explaining the paradox satisfactorily, although it was not difficult to improve on his unhappy recourse to imagery : 'The case . . . is similar to that of the pair of bagpipes', he hazarded, 'which being pressed in a certain manner, utters a groan, without anything more being necessary to account for this phenomenon, than the known laws of matter and motion.'[16] Like the Pantisocrats he too had notions of the elimination of arduous labour : yet his principle of equalization of work and property would involve himself and Coleridge in an interesting divergence of opinion at a later stage.

But the thesis in *Political Justice* which provoked most interest, and consternation, during his day, and seemed to be endorsed in the early blueprint of Pantisocracy, was the 'evil of marriage as it is practised in European Countries'. 'Marriage', he asserted, 'is a system of fraud', and he would replace it with a custom whereby, 'each man will select for himself a partner, to whom he will adhere, as long as that adherence shall continue to be the choice of both parties'. On yet another fundamental point, however, they would totally disagree. While Godwin had not by this stage professed atheism, he was clearly tending in that direction. Institutional religion had elevated virtue into 'something impossible and unmeaning : and those who, spurning the narrow limits of science and human understanding, have turned system-builders and fabricated a universe after their own peculiar fancy'.[17] While Coleridge intended to spurn the 'mongrel-whelp' of Christianity as it was commonly accepted by members of the Established Church, his simplified version of Christianity had, and would remain for him, an absolute condition in the reconstruction of society. It was only later, in fact, in the autumn, that Coleridge learnt of Godwin's 'infidel' inclinations. 'I set him at Defiance', Coleridge wrote to Southey ' – tho' if he convinces me, I will acknowledge it in a letter in the Newspapers.'[18] The letter, of course, was never to appear.

Yet in spite of its discrepancies with Godwin's proposals, Pantisocracy shared the same rarefied and intellectual appeal.

It was this more than anything else that separated them from the working-class movements in the cities as represented by the London Corresponding Society. The founder of the L.C.S., Thomas Hardy, was a shoemaker, not a scholar, and while his movement owed something to Locke and Rousseau their proposals were derived from the actual conditions of life as it was lived by the masses in London, Manchester, Stockport and Sheffield. And their manifesto was composed of immediate and tangible demands : manhood suffrage, annual parliaments, cheaper government, the end of unjust land enclosure, and a more feasible legal system. Where Hardy's agitation arose from an aspiring, collective unrest, Godwinism and Pantisocracy descended from an almost paternalist dogmatism from above. Godwin and Southey were convinced that their rulers were depraved and in darkness – but they were in no doubt as to their own irreproachable rightness and enlightenment. Yet at least Coleridge and Southey had enthusiasm and willingness on their side, and their determination to realize the scheme would soon call them down from the ivory tower.

In the meantime, however, they could enjoy their exaltation. There might be one or two practical snags – which, as they occurred, tell us much about the Pantisocrats' preoccupations and priorities : for one thing they would have to get wives ; for another, Coleridge knew as little about forestry and carpentry as Southey did about farming. More ominous still was the question of money : neither of them had any. But all that could wait. Now that Coleridge was on point of continuing his tour, now, while they could postpone the vexing details, their enthusiasm soared, and it cost little to celebrate it with optimistic discussion.

Coleridge and Hucks had intended leaving Oxford after three days. Three weeks had passed when they continued their journey on 5 July, Coleridge's head 'full of confluent

ideas' and a determination that Southey should keep him
posted about Pantisocratic developments. They marched in
the intolerable heat through the Cotswolds to Gloucester,
Coleridge grumbling about the whiteness of the roads and
the dreariness of the stone walls. And with his newly discovered friend behind him, he found Hucks wanting in
orthodoxy. Hucks had objected to a beggar woman with
baby in arms putting her head in at the window of their
dining room and asking for a piece of bread and meat ; he had
proclaimed her action 'impertinent and obtrusive'. Coleridge
was outraged. As he confided to Southey : 'My companion
is a Man of cultivated, tho' not vigorous, understanding –
his feelings are all on the side of humanity – yet such are the
unfeeling Remarks, which the lingering Remains of
Aristocracy occasionally prompt.' In the Pantisocratic
commune, he assured Southey, 'these things will not be
so – !' Ill-tempered with Hucks, the scorching weather,
and the carriages of the over-privileged, he struck off some
verses which were to be his first mature political effusion,
and his most promising piece so far :

> The Dust flies smothering, as on clatt'ring Wheels
> Loath'd Aristocracy careers along.
> The distant Track quick vibrates to the Eye,
> And white and dazzling undulates with heat.
> Where scorching to th'unwary Traveller's touch
> The stone-fence flings it's narrow Slip of Shade,
> Or where the worn sides of the chalky Road
> Yield their scant excavations (sultry Grots!)
> Emblem of languid Patience, we behold
> The fleecy Files faint-ruminating lie. –

The 'fleecy Files' and 'sultry Grots' are an unfortunate
lapse, but otherwise it has tactile immediacy and great
energy, the senses fully engaged. 'Emblem of languid
patience' is a characteristically Coleridgean mannerism
which he was liable to employ in his didactic mood at this
time.

Asking Southey to forward the post to Wrexham, they left Gloucester behind them, a town in which Coleridge had found little to interest him – except the sight of a girl in a boat on the Severn bandying words with thirty naked men bathing. And so they proceeded to Ross on Wye where they stayed at the King's Arms, and Coleridge scribbled an effusion on the window shutter in memory of the so called 'Man of Ross', famous for his humanitarian deeds :

> Richer than Misers o'er their countless hoards
> Nobler than Kings or king-polluted Lords,
> Here dwelt the Man of Ross! O Stranger, hear!
> Departed Merit claims the glistening tear . . .
> Beneath this roof if thy cheer'd moments pass,
> Fill to the good man's name one grateful glass :
> To higher zest shall Memory wake thy soul,
> And Virtue mingle in the ennobled bowl.

Significantly there is an atmosphere of swashbuckling heartiness and bar-politics about it which would be the keynote of the two political 'confrontations' he was to have in Wales. Not that tavern polemic was less dangerous politically : in 1793, John Frost, a member of the Corresponding Society of London, had been imprisoned for being found in 'seditious' conversation in a coffee house. Coleridge's first public 'appearance' was at an inn in Llanvillin where he 'preached Pantisocracy and Aspheterisin' (a word doubtless coined by Coleridge from the Greek – against private property), 'with so much success that two great huge Fellows, of Butcher like appearance, danced about the room in enthusiastic agitation – And one of them of his own accord called for a large Glass of Brandy, and drank it off to this, his own Toast – God save the King. And may he be the Last – '. The gloating reference to the jibe at monarchy was characteristic too ; as he records in another didactic emblem written about that time : 'The Cockatrice is emblematic of Monarchy – a *monster* generated by *Ingratitude* on *Absurdity*. When Serpents *sting*, the only

Remedy is – to *kill* the *Serpent*, and *besmear* the *Wound* with the *Fat*.' A seditious enough statement by any reckoning during these times.

The second 'confrontation' was in the inn at Bala a few days later, where he was greeted by a 'Welch Democrat' who grasped him so enthusiastically by the hand that it sustained bruises. Shortly afterwards, five men joined them. They got to drinking and Coleridge was asked to propose a toast. He says that he chose Joseph Priestley who had now emigrated to America. The town's apothecary was next, and he countered with, 'I gives a sentiment, Gemmen ! May all Republicans be *gulloteened* !' The Welsh Democrat hand-bruiser immediately jumped up and declared 'May all *Fools* be gulloteen'd – and then you will be the first.' In the row that followed, Coleridge tried to soothe them with the ironic observation, 'however different our Political Opinions might be, the appearance of a Clergyman in the Company assured me, that we were all *Christians* – though I found it difficult to reconcile the last sentiment with the spirit of *Christianity*'.

'Pho,' retorted the clergyman, 'Christianity ! why an't at *church* now – are we ?'

The party dispersed in friendly mood, all the men, except the clergyman, shaking hands with Coleridge and commending his open-speaking, honest fashion – notwithstanding his politics.

They continued on to Llangollin, meeting two fellow students of Jesus College on the way, and to Coleridge's great glee he could record that like the 'loath'd Aristocracy' of his verses they were 'Vigorously pursuing their tour – in a *post chaise* !' Not only this, the reason they gave for such style was that one of them was suffering from the clap.

Whatever political ideologies Coleridge may have been ruminating during the tour, it is clear that the 'manners' of revolution were uppermost in his mind. In this sense he was probably unfair on Hucks, who seems to have recorded the more serious observations, in spite of his fastidiousness.

Hucks noted, for example : 'The [Welsh] children are remarkably beautiful, and usually well made, but this only continues during their infancy ; for, from the age of ten and upwards, they begin to bear marks of hard labour, and still more precarious substance. – A haggard countenance ; a reduced appearance, and, in short, all the traces of a premature old age.'[19] Again, on the road from Llangollin to Wrexham, his attention was seized by an industrial scene :

Upon the hill above us were seen the dark figures of the miners; the confused noise of the men, who were preparing to descend these gloomy caverns, and of the busy team, returning with its busy load; while the thick volumes of black smoke, that continued to ascend into a clear and beautiful atmosphere, formed an uncommon and striking contrast.[20]

At the same time, Hucks was not entirely blind to the humour of some of the situations which offended his own 'respectable' sensibilities. One night, for example, he had thrown aside the sheets thinking them to be damp. When the maid came to take away the candle she remonstrated : 'Lard Sir, it be impossible, for they have been slept in four or five times within this last week.' Poor Hucks was clearly used to better things.

The fact was that Coleridge had been in a rumbustious, agitated mood, snatching at a variety of impressions and recording few of them in any depth. The anticipation of the Pantisocratic scheme, no doubt, largely accounted for this effervescence. But something else occurred at Wrexham which was to unsettle him in other ways. At Wrexham lived the sister of his beloved Mary Evans, Eliza. In spite of the fact that Eliza had corresponded with him, Coleridge seems to have forgotten where she lived. Consequently it was with profound shock that he recognized her while attending service at the parish church. Eliza turned pale, Coleridge hastened away to his inn. A little later, as he stood at his window, Eliza passed by, this time accompanied by Mary herself – the girl he had loved 'desperately and to distraction'

(*Quam efflictim et perdite amabam*), 'yea, even to anguish –'.
The two sisters gave a short scream on seeing him, but
Coleridge hid from them, terrified to acknowledge that he
had recognized them: 'My fortitude would not have
supported me.'[21] The sisters continued to pass to and fro
in front of the window four of five times, but Coleridge
would not present himself, hoping they might think
themselves mistaken.

This act of concealment seems to have had the significance
of providing a definite break for him. Incapable of eating that
day, or sleeping that night, he wrote a Latin verse to mark
the event:

> Vivit sed mihi non vivit – nova forte marita
> Ah dolor! alterius carâ a cervice pependit
> Vos, malefida valete accensae Insomnia mentis
> Littora amata, valete! Vale ah! formosa Maria![22]

*She lives, but lives not for me: as a loving bride perhaps – ah
sadness! – she has thrown her arms around another man's neck.
Farewell, ye deceitful dreams of a love-lorn mind; ye beloved
shores, farewell; farewell, ah, beautiful Mary!*[23]

The next day he hastened the sixteen miles to Ruthin
where he sat down to confide the experience in a letter to
Southey: 'Southey! There are few men of whose delicacy
I think so highly as to have written all this – I am glad, I have
so deemed of you – We are soothed by communication.'
Little did Coleridge know, Southey was the last person from
whom he might expect a sympathetic, or even compre-
hending ear in matters of the heart, either then, when
Southey was still only twenty, or later in their lives.

While claiming to have survived the worst of the experience – 'Love is a local Anguish – I am 16 miles distant
and am not half so miserable', he nevertheless makes an
assertion that belies his apparent resilience: 'Her Image is
in the sanctuary of my Heart, and never can it be torn
away but with the strings that grapple it to Life.'

It is likely that he composed *The Sigh* at this time, and once again – while yielding 'to the stern decree' of unrequited love, the final stanza expresses a determined devotion.

> And though in distant climes to roam,
> A wanderer from my native home,
> I fain would soothe the sense of Care,
> And lull to sleep the Joys that were!
> Thy Image may not banish'd be –
> Still, Mary! still I sigh for thee.

They walked towards Anglesey which was 'repaid by scarcely one object worth seeing'; visited Snowdon, and scaled 'at the imminent hazard of our Lives the very Summit of Penmaenmawr – it was a most dreadful expidition!' So the strenuous tour continued – 'now philosophising with Hucks,' records Coleridge, 'now melancholizing by myself, or else indulging those day-dreams of Fancy, that make realities more gloomy'. The only outstanding event on this leg of the trek was the theft of Coleridge's 'curious' walking stick at Abergely, which was retrieved after the town crier had announced a full description of it along the beach. A lame old man had 'borrowed' it, and they marched him back to Coleridge's inn, 'the solemn Cryer before him and a various Cavalcade behind him'.

They were supposed to await Southey in Wales, but – without warning – Coleridge pressed on to Bristol where Southey was living during the vacation with his formidable aunt, Miss Tyler. But during Coleridge's absence, Southey had been assailed by certain scruples about the Pantisocratic venture. For one thing, he was anxious about the finances; for another, he was contemplating the immediate repercussions that would follow on his decision not to enter the Church – a choice of career that had long been expected of him. When he had communicated these misgivings to Coleridge by letter they had been peremptorily dismissed from the Welsh mountains : 'For God's sake, Southey! enter

not into the church.' For his immediate needs, Coleridge
advised, he could procure 'the office of Clerk in a Compting
House'. But at all costs he must steer clear of employment
under the Government. 'A Friend of Hucks,' he sternly
related '. . . accepted a place under Government – he took
the Oaths – shuddered – went home and threw himself in
an Agony out of a two pair stairs Window !'

Southey, however, continued anxious. 'I am doomed to
take orders,' he wrote to his close friend Grosvenor Bedford,
'and little less than a miracle can rescue me.'[24] But if
Southey had not envisaged the actual realization of the
Pantisocratic plan with as much seriousness as Coleridge,
it seemed likely that he would contemplate it with increasing
resignation for reasons less than worthy. Pantisocracy
might, after all, be the miracle he so much desired. For in
spite of the elevated discussions in college rooms, the
idealism and euphoric altruism, when it came down to it
Southey had been approaching the demanding call to found
a new society as if it were no more than a desperate
alternative to finding a suitable career in England. 'Either in
six months I fix myself in some honest means of living or
I quit my country – my friends – and every fondest hope I
indulge for ever. I may be wretched but never will I be a
villain.'[25] Thus had the political reformer spoken just a week
before Coleridge's visit to Oxford. Yet even after meeting
Coleridge his tone had hardly changed : '. . . whether I
linger out existence in England in America or among the
convicts of New Holland is a matter of indifference',[26] he
wrote to Grosvenor Bedford.

In any case, by the time Coleridge marched into Bristol –
having walked six hundred and twenty nine miles, as
Hucks scrupulously noted, things had taken a temporary
turn for the better. Southey would not have to depart for
America without his friends after all. Robert Lovell, an
old family friend in Bristol, noted chiefly for his attachment
to boxing and tennis,[27] had been finally persuaded to come

along ; and Southey's brother Tom — who was at sea, and
had recently been ill-treated by his captain — expressed an
interest. Finally, his own mother not only approved of the
scheme but declared herself one of the party. Southey's
spirits revived : 'My mother is fully convinced of the
propriety of our resolution. She admires the plan, she goes
with us. Never did so delightful a prospect of happiness
open upon my view before.' This was well and good, but
with the inclusion of the mother, a pugilist, and a disaffected
sailor, the scheme was already becoming somewhat untidy.
Moreover, by augmenting the numbers with members of
his own family, who were in no position to lend financial
support, Southey was exacerbating the most vexing problem
of all : money.

So far, Southey had pinned his main hopes on literary
earnings. There was his *Joan of Arc*, a lengthy poem of
radical sentiments which he had started a year before and
was completing with Coleridge's assistance. He hoped to
publish it by subscription and evidently thought for a time
that it would buy his own place in the commune. 'Should the
publication be any ways successful it will carry me over and
get me some few acres a spade and a plough.'[28] The money
would continue to be a source of anxiety. There was also the
question of female companions. For Robert Lovell, the
problem was already solved — he had recently married a
Mary Fricker, daughter of the widow of a manufacturer of
chimney pots whose business had toppled. The widow
and her five daughters, Mary, Edith, Sara, Martha and
Eliza, lived in reduced circumstance in Bristol, making
a precarious living with their needles. The Southeys were
customers of the Frickers, and the two families were fairly
intimate. Coleridge, quite naturally, was introduced to the
family circle.

With Mary Fricker (now Mrs Lovell) destined for
America, it is not surprising that further alliances were
precipitated in the heady atmosphere of the moment

between the eligible sisters and Southey and Coleridge.
Whatever speculations one might make about misguided
emotions and concealed motives, the plain fact is that
Southey became engaged to Edith Fricker, and Coleridge
(the image of Mary Evans still 'in the sactuary' of his heart)
to Sara Fricker. George Burnett – another friend of
Southey's, also in the scheme, proposed to the fourth
sister, Martha, who promptly turned him down, declaring
that he was more interested in getting 'a wife in a hurry
than her individually of all the world'.[29] Martha's sentiment
on this occasion is revealing. For the Fricker family, as for
Southey and Coleridge, the future was unpromising.
Without even meagre fortunes the girls' marriage prospects
were dismal; the most they could hope for were poor, if
respectable, young men with sufficient education to make
their way in the world. Duty, initiative and industry, allied
to strict morality, were virtues that must have flourished
strongly in the Fricker family – virtues which might spell
success in the new world of North America where social
background and carefully graded fortunes counted for little.
Southey, who matched their sensible ideals, was already
popular amongst the sisters, and they were no doubt
inspired by the irrepressible and eloquent optimism of the
strange unkempt Coleridge. It would not have taken much to
induce them to join forces. If George Burnett was simply
after a wife in a hurry, it is not unlikely that the remaining
sisters were after a husband.

There is a curious problem, however, as to which sister
was intended for Southey. It has always been presumed
by past biographers that the second daughter, Edith, who
did in fact become Mrs Southey, had always been Southey's
girl. Sara Fricker, the third daughter, later to become
Mrs Coleridge, saw it otherwise. For whatever reasons, she
claimed in later life that he had been *her* man.[30] Apparently
Southey's own mother was much surprised at his eventual
choice of Edith, a fine, but 'inanimate' girl. But of all the

3

sisters, Coleridge's new fiancée, Sara, was the prettiest and probably the best educated. The surviving portrait of her reveals a slender but full bosomed woman of pale complexion. Her chin is small and delicate, almost too delicate for her full throat and long neck. Her large eyes are dark and lustrous, her lips full and well shaped, but her mouth a trifle too large for that frail chin. It is a portrait in which the features too readily reveal the personality behind them — a petulance about the mouth, a sidelong glance from those slightly protruding dark eyes — of self-consciousness and pride on the defensive. There is no doubt that Coleridge found her attractive physically as some of his later letters will testify. Doubtless, too, the warmth of a family of ready listeners must have appealed to this young man who had spent an emotionally lonely youth, who, as will be seen, had a fatal weakness for any sympathetic circle of females he could adopt as sisters. But, above all, he was still smarting from the recent encounter with Mary Evans, and it is not unlikely that his hasty proposal was an engagement 'on the rebound'. Nevertheless, it is still extraordinary that Coleridge should have failed to study his own interests, at least to the extent of waiting several weeks. Perhaps Southey forced his hand ; for if he spoke of marriage to Coleridge as he did when extending a Pantisocratic invitation to Grosvenor Bedford's brother, Horace, he would have talked of it as a prime condition of membership : 'Would you could come with us – do Horace consider well,' he wrote. 'What prospects have you in England? Were it not better to marry now than linger out years in solitary wretchedness?'[31] In any case, where compelling motives were lacking the very headiness of the times would have encouraged precipitance. 'The mind opened,' wrote Hazlitt, 'and a softness might be perceived coming over the heart of individuals, beneath "the scales that fence" our self-interest.'

When Sara Fricker first saw Coleridge arriving from his long walk, bedraggled and 'brown as a berry', she thought him 'plain but eloquent and clever'. His clothes, she reminisced many years later, 'were worn out – his hair wanted cutting. He was a dreadful figure.' She said as much to Southey, which prompted the somewhat ponderous remark: 'Yes! he is a diamond set in lead.'[32]

During Coleridge's stay in Bristol, he would walk in the evening in Crescent Fields with Southey, Mrs Fricker and Sara. 'There was a great deal of conversation about the Pantisocratic scheme,' remembered Sara in her matter-of-fact way. Before Coleridge was due to return to Cambridge, he asked her if she would write to him, and it was this request that brought on a proposal of marriage. Coleridge asked her if she could accompany him to America, and the match was agreed upon.[33]

But another meeting took place during the stay in Bristol – which was to have important implications for the engaged couple. In the middle of August Coleridge and Southey took time off from courting and Pantisocratic discussions to visit Nether Stowey, where Thomas Poole lived, a wealthy tanner with republican sympathies. Southey amusingly records the first night of their journey:

We reached Cheddar about ten, anticipating the delights of a good supper and comfortable inn. We inquired the best inn, and arrived at a poor pot-house in a little village. 'Can you give us a bed?' He snorted 'No' and turned round again. We agreed to go back to the other inn, get some supper and sleep in the stable. Down we sat, demolished the bread and cheese and cold *à la mode* beef, and petitioned for straw in the stable. They said they would make us up a bed. It was in a garret, the only piece of furniture except another bedstead, on which lay a bed and quilt. . . . Coleridge is a vile bed-fellow and I slept but ill. In the morning rose – and lo! We were fastened in! They certainly took us for footpads and had bolted the door on the outside for fear we should rob the house.[34]

Coleridge was already slightly acquainted with Poole, but the visit marks the beginning of an intimacy that was to continue for many years. Seventeen years older than

Coleridge, Poole was a confirmed bachelor, dedicated to his trade and his large collection of books. He had started a Sunday school in Stowey and ran a book society from his house. It was said that he was as much at home with Virgil as he was with the 'new anti-friction steam roller', recently invented by an American friend, which stood in his tanyard.[35] But for all his learning and humanitarian interests, his radical tendencies were viewed with dark dismay by his family. He had been chosen to represent the tanners of the West of England in their efforts to appeal against anomalies in the trade; but more sinister yet, he was known to be influenced by Tom Paine's *Rights of Man*, and actually walked about with his hair loose and unpowdered. 'I am sure from his conversation and conduct,' wrote his cousin Charlotte, 'he would be glad to see all law and order subverted in this country. What can be the cause of such conduct? Certainly pride and the love of power : for though the democrats so eloquently talk of the wickedness of the world, and declaim against tyranny, I do not find that their lives are more spotless, and I am sure in their own little concerns they display a great deal of tyranny. In short, his mind is poisoned – I fear irrecoverably poisoned.'[36] Certainly the visit of Coleridge and Southey to Stowey did little to allay the family fears. Both Charlotte and a cousin John have left on record their sentiments about the two young revolutionaries. 'Tom Poole', wrote Charlotte of a later visit, 'has a friend with him of the name of Coleridge [*sic*] : a young man of brilliant understanding, great eloquence, desperate fortune, democratic principles, and entirely led away by the feelings of the moment.'[37] Cousin John's verdict was a good deal less delicate : 'Each of them was shamefully hot with Democratic rage as regards politics, and both Infidel as to religion.' Southey, he found particularly obnoxious : for on delivering the ominous news that Robespierre had died, Southey had exclaimed, 'I had rather have heard of the death of my own father.'[38]

Yet for all his cousins' anxieties Poole was no hothead, and his initial verdict on the two young men shows great insight:

> Coleridge, whom I consider the Principal in the undertaking . . . possesses splendid abilities – he is, I understand, a shining scholar . . . He speaks with much elegance and energy, and with uncommon facility, but he, as it generally happens to men of his class, feels the justice of Providence in the want of those inferior abilities which are necessary to the rational discharge of the common duties of life. His aberrations from prudence, to use his own expression, have been great; but he now promises to be as sober and rational as his most sober friends could wish. In religion he is a Unitarian, if not a Deist; in politics a Democrat, to the utmost extent of the word.
>
> Southey, who was with him, is of the University of Oxford, a younger man, without the splendid abilities of Coleridge, though possessing much information, particularly metaphysical, and is more violent in his principles than even Coleridge himself. In Religion, shocking to say in a mere boy as he is, I fear he wavers between Deism and Atheism.

His response to the Pantisocratic plans is sadly ironic: 'Could they realize them they would indeed, realize the age of reason; but, however perfectible human nature may be, I fear it is not perfect enough to exist long under the regulations of such a system, particularly when the Executors of the plan are taken from a society in a high degree civilized and corrupted.'[39]

And in the weeks which followed, Coleridge and Southey had ample opportunity to reflect upon the question of human perfectibility. One evening at the end of August when the Pantisocrats were walking in Crescent Fields, a gentleman with a shovel hat stopped and said to Coleridge: 'Sir, when are we to expect you back in Cambridge?'

'I am coming back in a few days, Sir', replied Coleridge.

As the gentleman, a Tutor of Jesus College, passed on, Coleridge remarked to the rest of his group: 'I would not have met him on any account.'[40]

The fact was that while Southey had decided to leave Oxford without a degree, Coleridge had not committed himself to follow suit. He set off from Bristol a few days later, taking with him the manuscript of a play, *The Fall of Robespierre*, which he and Southey had completed in two days. He hoped to sell it in London where he was to stop briefly on his way to Cambridge, with the double object of spreading political enlightenment and defraying the expenses of Pantisocracy. Although the work was highly topical (Robespierre had been executed on 27 July), the haste with which it had been completed and put together ensured its lack of merit and subsequent failure. Coleridge had written the first Act, and Southey the second and third. Apparently Robert Lovell had been commissioned to do the third, but his production was considered unsuitable. In the letter of dedication, Coleridge wrote on Southey's behalf, 'it has been my sole aim to imitate the empassioned and highly figurative language of the French Orators, and to develope the characters of the chief actors on a vast stage of horrors'. As it is, only the final speech of Barère is passable rhetoric, and Coleridge's contribution is employed as an opportunity to indulge in Pantisocratic propaganda :

> Tell, me, on what holy ground
> May Domestic Peace be found?
> Halcyon daughter of the skies,
> Far on fearful wings she flies,
> From the pomp of Sceptered wings she flies,
>
> From the Rebel's noisy hate.
> In a cottag'd vale She dwells,
> Listening to the Sabbath bells!
> Still around her steps are seen
> Spotless Honour's meeker mein,
> Love, the sire of pleasing fears,
> Sorrow smiling through her tears,
> And conscious of the past employ
> Memory, bosom-spring of joy.

As far as one contemporary reader, Thomas Seward, was concerned the composition soared on 'wax plumes', but although he doubted whether many would read it twice, he granted that it was not 'without some emanations of the Aonian light from whence it sprung'.[41] Coleridge failed to place the manuscript with a London publisher, and it later appeared in Cambridge under his own name.

In London he stayed at the 'Angel' in Newgate Street, and spent his evenings at the 'Salutation and Cat' close by. Among new acquaintances he met George Dyer, another Christ's Hospital and Cambridge man who had written a work entitled *Complaints of the Poor People of England*. Dyer, who was a Unitarian and an old comrade of Frend's, was immediately captivated with the idea of Pantisocracy – Joseph Priestley, he told Coleridge, would assuredly join them when they landed in America. It would have surprised the aspiring Pantisocrats to learn that Priestley, far from seeking an ideal republic across the seas, was busily engaged in land speculation.[42] One evening, however, Coleridge actually met a land agent, a 'most intelligent' fellow, at the 'Salutation and Cat', and could now advise Southey about regions and estimates of the cost. The agent recommended Susquehannah, 'from it's excessive Beauty, & it's security from hostile Indians'. The party would need no more than £2000, the passage would only cost £400, and 'for 600 hundred Dollars a Thousand Acres may be cleared, and houses built upon them'.

Since the agent knew his job he would hardly have failed to dwell on the paradisal beauty and fertility of his recommended region. As one contemporary travel writer described that area :

The strength and rapidity of vegetation in that country are incredible, the size of the trees enormous, and their variety infinite . . . The crops of Indian corn are prodigious, the cattle acquire an extraordinary size, and keep the whole year in the open fields . . . A man in that country works scarcely two hours in a day for the support of himself and family; he passes most of his time in idleness hunting or drinking.[43]

A promised land, indeed. Coleridge also learnt that 'literary Characters make *money* there', but in this instance he would have been sadly disabused by the travel books. In that same year Thomas Cooper had recorded in his *Some Information Respecting America* that 'Literature in America is an amusement only – collateral to the occupation of the person who attends (and but occasionally attends) to it'.[44] It is more than likely that Coleridge would have eventually come across this, for a friend of Cooper's, James Watt, the button-making magnate's son, was to have joined the commune.

Stimulated to greater enthusiasm by the encouraging information Coleridge returned to Cambridge by 17 September 1794 and wrote to Southey: 'My God! How tumultuous are the movements of my Heart... America! Southey! Miss Fricker!' The allurements of Pantisocracy and Miss Fricker seemed to run confusingly, dangerously together. Yet far from reflecting on emotional realities back in the sceptical atmosphere of the university, criticism of his plans only served to engage him more stubbornly in the defence of his theory. His Tutor Dr Pearce tried to reclaim him, to no avail. After a long discussion on the 'visionary and ruinous tendency of his conduct and schemes', Coleridge cut short the argument by bluntly assuring his friend and master that 'he mistook the matter altogether. He was neither Jacobin ... nor Democrat, but a Pantisocrat'.[45] But there was no lack of other more youthful, more contentious critics. Undaunted, Coleridge took them on with glee: 'I have drawn up my arguments in battle array – they shall have the *Tactician* Excellence of the Mathematician with the Enthusiasm of the Poet.' A few years later he would describe his own vehement eloquence: 'In conversation I am impassioned, and oppose what I deem (error) with an eagerness, which is often mistaken for personal asperity – but I am ever so swallowed up in the *thing* that I forget my *opponent.*'[46]

We have glimpses of him in Cambridge rooms surrounded by friends posing objections – Coleridge arising 'terrible in reasoning' to refute them. Indeed, he could report back to Southey that Pantisocracy was 'the universal Topic at this University'. But the euphoria was shortlived. One night returning from a discussion lasting six hours, Coleridge perceived the first break in the embattled ranks, the first hint of unorthodox politics – and from no less a person than Southey himself. 'I came home at one o'clock this morning exulting in the honest consciousness of having exhibited closer argument in more eloquent and appropriate Language than I had ever conceived myself capable of. Then my heart smote me – for I saw your Letter on the propriety of taking Servants with us.'[47]

The servant in question was Shadrack Weekes, or 'Shad' as they called him, who worked for Southey's aunt. Shad had a family and there had been some doubt as to whether they would be taken out to America : doubts that Coleridge thought he had conclusively dismissed on 18 September, when he emphasized in a letter : 'SHAD GOES WITH US. HE IS MY BROTHER.' Practical considerations apart, it was for Coleridge an important gesture of equality. But Southey, it seemed, was now incapable of entertaining the fundamental equalities that Coleridge envisaged. Yes, he could agree to the 'servants' accompanying the party to America ; he could agree to Shad's children being educated, but it would be an education such 'as to render them incapable of blushing at the want of it in their Parents'. Furthermore, they might 'dine with us and be treated with as much equality as they would wish – but perform that part of Labor for which their Education has fitted them'. Coleridge was aghast.

Southey should not have written this Sentence – my Friend, my noble and high-souled Friend should have said – to his Dependents – Be my Slaves – and ye shall be my Equals – to his Wife & Sisters –
3*

Resign the *Name* of Ladyship and ye shall retain the *thing*. – Again –
Is every Family to possess one of these Unequal Equals – these Helot
Egalité-s? Or are the few, you have mentioned – 'with more toil than
the Peasantry of England undergo' – to do for all of us 'that part of
Labor which their Education has fitted them for?'

Talk of servitude, moreover, prompted Coleridge to
deliver himself of his views on the place of women in their
new society: 'Let the married Women do only what is
absolutely convenient and customary for pregnant Women
or nurses – Let the Husbands do *all* the Rest – and what
will that all be – ? Washing with a Machine and cleaning
the House. One Hour's addition to our daily Labor – and
Pantisocracy is practicable.'[48] Progressive sentiments indeed :
but dubiously practicable.

Two days later, in a list of queries he wishes Southey to
ponder, he returns to the same theme :

Quere. Whether our Women have not been taught by us habitually
to contemplate the littleness of individual Comforts, and a passion for
the *Novelty* of the Scheme, rather than the generous enthusiasm of
Benevolence? Are they saturated with the Divinity of Truth sufficiently to be always wakeful? In the present state of their minds
whether it is not probable that the *Mothers* will tinge the Mind of the
Infants with prejudications? *These* Questions are meant *merely* as
motives to you, Southey! to be strengthening the minds of the Women
and stimulating them to literary Acquirements.

If one detects a jarring note of paternalism, that the men
must watch out for the innate self-indulgence and weak-
mindedness of their females, it is also the first note of
scepticism with regard to human perfectibility. It is also a
prelude to some searching questions about the commune's
children.

But, Southey! – there are *Children* going with us. Why did I never
dare in my disputations with the Unconvinced to *hint* at this circumstance? Was it not, because I knew even to certainty of conviction,
that it is subversive of *rational* Hopes of a permanent System? These

children – the little Fricker for instance and *your* Brothers – Are they not already *deeply* tinged with the prejudices and errors of Society? Have they not learnt from their Schoolfellows *Fear* and *Selfishness* – of which the necessary offspring are Deceit, and desultory Hatred? *How* are we to prevent them from infecting the minds of *our* Children?'

Locke and Hartley, Priestley and Godwin, were all very well : but how did one start with a barrel of sound apples? Was he at last beginning to realize just how difficult a task they had undertaken? As yet, there was no hint of compromise : he infers that he would rather rewrite the list of members than submit to an alteration in the ideal. But by November the bickerings between Coleridge and Southey over the servants, the women and the children, threatened to open a gulf of enmity as the contentious letters winged their way back and forth from Cambridge to Bristol. The impassioned enthusiasm of Coleridge's prose begins to slump in weary sullenness. On 3 November, Coleridge wrote, 'My feeble and exhausted Heart regards with a criminal indifference the Introduction of Servitude into our Society.' Again it was the question of shared labour; Coleridge was determined that no member of the commune would be more privileged than another, even if, as Southey had pointed out, certain members would prefer to be so. 'To be employed in the Toil of the Field while *We* are pursuing philosophical Studies – ' retorted Coleridge, 'can Earldoms or Emperorships boast so huge an Inequality? Is there a human Being of so torpid a Nature, as that placed in our Society he would not feel it? – A *willing* Slave is the worst of Slaves – his *Soul* is a Slave.' He added a final plea with regard to the mothers and children : 'I wish, Southey! in the stern severity of Judgment, that the two Mothers were *not* to go and that the children stayed with them.'

And yet for Southey's part, the disagreement must have had little more significance than an academic quibble. For all this time he had continued to worry about the financial difficulties and the reception these ideas would have with Miss Tyler, the aunt who provided for him, and his uncle in Portugal. In the middle of October his worst fears were realized. Miss Tyler heard of the plan, and her reaction was sudden and tempestuous. Southey reported to his brother Tom : 'Here's a kick up. Here's a pretty commence. We have had a revolution at College Green, and I have been turned out of doors in a wet night . . . I was penniless : it was late in the evening ; the wind blew and the rain fell, and I had walked from Bath in the morning.' The 'open war — declared hostilities' were not merely Miss Tyler's response to the eccentric Pantisocratic plans, which were far from finalized, but more particularly her nephew's engagement to Edith Fricker. Miss Tyler swore that she would never even open a letter from him again, a vow which she kept. What little prospects Southey could entertain in the event of the commune failing now seemed forever lost. We must conclude that the effects were sobering, to say the least. Hardly a situation that Coleridge could be expected to appreciate fully, for he had no such discreet alternative hopes, no such patronage.

But following closely on Southey's setback, Coleridge became involved in his own family disputes, less stormy perhaps, but equally conducive to serious self-searching. His schoolmaster brother, George, had written to him, a letter of 'remonstrance, and anguish and suggestions, that I am deranged ! !' It was a verdict that George was to pronounce with increasing conviction as the years passed. But this first letter was followed by another of 'inexpressible consolation', in which George evidently spoke of brotherly love and Christian duty, themes which never failed to evoke a spirit of self-examination and remorse in Coleridge. Taking stock of his position, he wrote to George on 6 November, 'The appeal of Duty to my Judgement, and the pleadings of affection at my Heart — have been heard indeed

– and heard with deep regard.' Was he, in truth, quite so radical as he appeared to be? 'How often and how unkindly,' observed Coleridge solemnly, 'are the ebullitions of youthful disputatiousness mistaken for the result of fixed Principles!' It had come to George's ears that his youngest brother had taken the extreme position of Democrat, with all its over-tones of atheism and reform by violence that the label then implied. 'Solemnly, my Brother! I tell you – I am *not* a Democrat.' Had he not revealed his position in this regard in his recent play – *The Fall of Robespierre*?

> And Herbert's atheist Crew, whose maddening herd
> Hurl'd down the altars of the living God
> With all the Infidel's Intolerence.[49]

Whatever the case, he had certainly fooled the mature judgment of Thomas Poole who had declared him 'a Democrat, to the utmost extent of the word'. Possibly, he had overstated his case at that meeting; possibly, he had been infected by the vehemence of Southey's violent principles. Perhaps he was simply beginning to change his mind.

However, he now wished to state his position – to set his brother's mind at rest.

> I see evidently, that the present is *not* the *highest* state of Society, of which we are *capable* – And after a diligent, I *may* say, an intense study of Locke, Hartley and others who have written most wisely on the Nature of Man – I appear to myself to see the point of *possible* perfection at which the World may perhaps be destined to arrive – But how to lead Mankind from one point to the other is a process of infinite Complexity, that in deep-felt humility I resign it to that Being – 'Who shaketh the Earth of her place and the pillars thereof tremble.'

The statement, brutally simplistic as it stands, was obviously intended to pacify brother George. But the Priestleian conviction, that materialist and necessitarian

ideas could be entertained alongside the notion of a transcendental reality giving purpose to the 'infinite complexity'
of human existence, is clear. As yet the duality of vision
remained arbitrary; but before long he would be enticed by
the inconsistencies and ever proliferating implications and
qualifications on a path of his own. At the same time,
Southey's reforming zeal, initially more radical than
Coleridge's, was beginning to collapse with embarrassing
suddenness. As the weeks wore on, he seemed to descend
by rapid stages through a series of ever increasing com-
promises to the values of the 'civilized and currupted'
society to which he belonged – as Thomas Poole had so
accurately predicted. With Southey, it was not simply a
question of theory – such as the dispute about servants; his
basic attitude seemed at fault. Not only had he originally
rejoiced in the plan as an escape from a dismal future in
England, but he had consistently boasted to his friends that
his emigration would ensure his safety when the great
bloodbath of revolution came to England. He could not
resist gloating at the idea of himself and his family and
closest friends living in a haven of peace and plenty when
England would be engulfed in a savage civil war or a French
invasion.

But what if, after all, the apocalypse should not come?
What if his prospects for a successful career in England
could be resurrected? By the end of November Southey
seemed to have undergone a change of heart, and certain
practical considerations forced him to present Coleridge
with yet another major compromise. How would they cope
with the farming, he asked, never having had experience?
Surely it would be better to give the commune a trial run
nearer home, where failure would not spell utter disaster.
Why not make the first experiment in Wales, for example?

Coleridge answered him coldly and bluntly: 'As to the
Welsh scheme – pardon me – it is nonsense – We must go
to America, if we can get Money enough.' But Coleridge's

own interest in America at this point was no more than an empty gesture : he could continue to suggest it, one feels, because he knew that it would never materialize. His disillusionment with Southey was deep and bitter. His doubts about the feasibility of Pantisocracy with the present group of people were serious. But his reluctance was not basically due to a disillusionment with the idea itself. There were other reasons for his fading interest at this stage, which belong to the strange story of Coleridge's emotional life since he left Bristol at the end of the summer.

3

The Ebullience of *Schematism*

IN his *Biographia* Coleridge claims to have led a life of gross
sexual irregularity in Cambridge prior to meeting Southey.
Recollecting the period of his 'Unchastisies' from his nineteenth to his twenty-second year, he later spoke as if his
lusts had been so gross and so brutish that he had no
memory of the objects of them : 'I could here recollect no
name at all – no, nor even a face or feature. I remembered
my vices, & the times thereof, but not their objects.'[1]
Apart from the inconclusive testimony of harlot and homo-
sexual dreams, most of them in a Cambridge setting, there
is no factual evidence available to ascertain the extent to
which he may have over-dramatized his behaviour, apart
from a notebook reference to his 'short-lived fit of fears from
sex'. But then, the 'fit of fears' and its implication of depressive sexual guilt are probably more significant than any
actual deed or event.

Whatever Coleridge's fears and anxieties of the previous
year at Cambridge, Southey, with his 'strict purity of
disposition and conduct', had dispelled them. In grappling
Southey to his soul, he felt perhaps that he had found a
secure retreat from the turmoil of impulse and remorse. In
any event Coleridge was convinced that Southey had
wrought a swift reformation in his character. In the *Biographia* he could 'dwell with unabated pleasure on the strong
and sudden, yet I trust not fleeting influence, which my
moral being underwent on my acquaintance with him at
Oxford'. His irregularities he learnt 'to feel as degrading,

learnt to know that an opposite conduct, which was at that time considered by us as the easy virtue of cold and selfish prudence, might originate in the noblest emotions, in views the most disinterested and imaginative'.

As their friendship ebbed and flowed over the years, one of the constant features of Coleridge's regard for Southey was this acknowledgement of his dependable qualities. Later when they were married and their families shared the same house the practical value of Southey's reliability would emerge very strongly. But at this early stage one is more inclined to remember that Southey was two years Coleridge's junior; that when they met in Balliol in the summer, he had still two months to go to his twentieth birthday. In attaching himself to Southey, as to a safe anchor, there were obvious dangers: Southey was, after all, rather tender in years to assume the role of dependable authority figure in matters of morals. Furthermore the trouble with Southey's views about morality was that they were combined with a marked disinclination for spontaneous feeling. He was not a man of romantic disposition, whereas however much Coleridge assented to Southey's pure ideals he would remain deeply emotional and subject to passionate attachments. 'A man ought to be able to live with any woman,' Southey told Shelley many years later, 'You see that I can, and so ought you. It comes to pretty much the same thing I apprehend. There is no great choice or difference.'² It is not unlikely that Southey felt this conviction as strongly in his early years as he did in middle age. We cannot be certain to what extent he persuaded Coleridge that Sara Fricker would make an ideal wife, even in the absence of romantic feelings; Southey says that he received the news of Coleridge's engagement 'not a little to my astonishment, for he had talked of being deeply in love with a certain Mary Evans'. But he was liable to make such utterances as, 'It is better to sacrifice happiness than integrity'.³ And Coleridge was deeply impressed by a remark of Southey's to the effect that one could grow to love a person if there was sufficient reason to do so.[4] His idolization of Southey, then, was likely to entice him into a way of thinking and feeling which was not true to himself, although the blame can by no means be placed entirely on Southey's shoulders.

At the same time one cannot ignore the strong over-tones of asceticism which often overtake the revolutionary spirit, not unlike sexual guilt recoiling on the uncertain child who has challenged his father in abnormal circum-stances. The moral outrage that urged the revolutionaries in Paris to disinter Madame de Pompadour's bones and scatter them in the streets was perhaps not so different from the developing strain of puritanism which led Coleridge to assert that 'a fellow that puts his arm inside the Girls & so walks cuddling to her, is in lust with her'.[5] For the rest of his life Coleridge would betray signs of prejudice and prudishness in sexual matters. Yet it was hardly the sum of his most permanent and characteristic propensities which led him to be attracted to a marriage in which the major allurement was the 'virtuous' network of relationships which existed in the arrangement of three friends marrying three sisters (however much he may have been habitually drawn to becoming an adopted member of other people's families). For it was this prospect that seems to have initially pre-occupied him at the end of August when he departed for Cambridge. 'Remember me to your Mother – to our Mother – am I not affiliated? . . . To Lovell and Mrs Lovell my *fraternal* Love – to Miss F. *more*. To all remember me – tell Edith and Martha and Eliza that I even *now* see all their faces and that they are my very dear Sisters.' His fiancée, the Miss F, seems to be rather buried amongst these brotherly greetings; and while he seemed to find it difficult to write to her, he can write to her sister Edith in a tone of intimacy that no doubt gave rise to some embarrassment :

I *had* a sister – an only Sister. Most tenderly did I love her! Yea, I have woke at midnight, and wept – because *she was not*.

There is no attachment under heaven so pure, so endearing. The Brother, who is blest with it I have envied him! Let whatever discompose him, he has still a gentle Friend, in whose soft Bosom he may repose his Sorrows, and receive for every wound or affliction, the Balm of a Sigh.

My Sister, like you, was beautiful and accomplished – like you, she was lowly of Heart. Her Eye beamed with meekest Sensibility. I know, and *feel*, that I am *your Brother* – I would, that you would say to me – 'I *will* be your Sister – your *favorite* Sister in the Family of the Soul.'[6]

There are ominous implications even in his first letter to Southey and the Fricker family, in which Coleridge expresses his most open enthusiasm about Sara. 'Yes – Southey – you are right – Even Love is the creature of strong Motive – I certainly love her. I think of her incessantly & with unspeakable tenderness – with that inward melting away of Soul that symptomizes it.' Indeed preoccupation with the motives and his own symptoms seems to be excluding the very object of his love. And two paragraphs later he returns to Edith: 'Make Edith my sister – surely, Southey! we shall be *frendotatoi meta frendous*. Most friendly where all are friends. She must therefore be more emphatically my Sister.' He finishes with a sonnet, celebrating his new resolutions and dedication to a life of virtue:

No more my Visionary Soul shall dwell
On Joys that were! No more endure to weigh
The shame and Anguish of the evil Day,
Wisely forgetful! O'er the Ocean swell
Sublime of Hope I seek the cottag'd Dell,
Where Virtue calm with careless step may stray,
And dancing to the moonlight Roundelay
The Wizard Passions weave an holy Spell.

Strange that he should reject his visionary soul only to

anticipate virtue in the form of moonlight roundelays and wizard passions.

And two days later his shaky conviction took a serious blow : 'Southey – ! Precipitance is wrong. There may be too high a state of *Health* – perhaps even *Virtue* is liable to a *Plethora* !' Southey had written to Coleridge demanding an explanation for his not having written to himself or Sara on his return to Cambridge ; and now Coleridge was deeply wounded by the suggestion that he had failed in friendship. He gave reasons for his silence. He had lingered in London and suffered illness and sickness of heart over shortage of money – the tone is plaintive. But finally he cannot resist repaying Southey in kind, calling him to task over his priggishness : 'Your undeviating Simplicity of Rectitude has made you too rapid in decision – having never erred, you feel more *indignation* at Error, than *Pity* for it. There is *Phlogiston* in your heart.'[7]

But the matter did not end there. A week after sending this letter of rebuke, a mutual friend, Samuel Favell, received a letter from Southey reporting Coleridge's strange silence, and asking that he should seek Coleridge out and demand an explanation. Coleridge was at once irritated and anguished ; explaining again that he had already sent a whole parcel of letters which 'should have arrived on Sunday morning', he suddenly explodes : 'Perhaps you have not heard from Bath – perhaps – damn perhapses – My God ! my God ! what a deal of pain you must have suffered – before you wrote that Letter to Favell.' There are none of the usual epithets of fraternal love in *this* letter, and in the place of a greeting to Miss F at the end, he writes : 'I am in the queerest humour in the world – and am out of love with every body.'[8]

The fact of the matter was that in a waking 'Night-mair of Spirits', no doubt induced by Southey's previous letter, and growing doubts about Sara, he had embarked on yet another romantic adventure. Making the acquaintance of an acting family from Norwich, the Bruntons, he was already being treated as one of the family, and had formed an attachment for the youngest daughter, Ann. The pattern was becoming familiar : 'Much against my Will,' he reports coyly to Southey, 'I am engaged to drink Tea and go to the Play with Miss Brunton (Mrs Merry's Sister). The young Lady and indeed the whole Family have taken it into their heads to be very much attached to me – tho' I have known them only 6 days . . . The young Lady is said to be the most literary of the beautiful, and the most beautiful of the literate.' But he adds a disclaimer barely concealing the undercurrent of brazenness : 'It may be so – my faculties & discernments are so completely jaundiced by vexation, that the Virgin Mary & May Flanders – alias Moll, would appear in the same hues.' So too would Sara Fricker, he might have mentioned.

Jaundiced by vexation though he was, he diverted himself with the translation of Latin love verses addressed to the eldest sister, Elizabeth Brunton (the Mrs Merry mentioned in the letter), and composed verses of his own for Ann, 'I have *my* Brunton too', which he himself describes as 'very pretty, but rather silly or so.'

This new dalliance was taking place in the last week of September, and by the beginning of October he had arranged to spend part of the Christmas vacation with the Brunton family – 'an invitation too pressing to be refused'. Sara Fricker was well out of his thoughts. But it was also during the first week of October that he received a letter which completely somersaulted him : it was unsigned, but unmistakably in Mary Evans's handwriting. She had heard of his Pantisocratic scheme, which she took for a crazy, desperate aberration, and his strange new views, verging on atheism. It was a plea, possibly prompted by Coleridge's brother George, calling him to reason : 'I conjure you, Coleridge ! earnestly and solemnly conjure you, to consider long and deeply, before you enter into any rash Schemes.

There is an Eagerness in your Nature, which is ever hurrying you into the sad Extreme.' But worse yet, there was an ambiguous passage which seemed to open up hopes for their old relationships : 'We thought in all things alike. I often reflect on the happy hours we spent together, and regret the Loss of your Society. I cannot easily forget those whom I once loved – nor can I easily form new Friendships.' With a sad irony she signs herself – 'Farewell – Coleridge – ! I shall always feel that I have been your *Sister*.'⁹

It was enough to awaken all his vain hopes, utterly destroying the uneasy composure he had found in the summer. In a frenzy of emotion he renewed his overtures towards Ann Brunton, hoping 'that her Exquisite Beauty and uncommon Accomplishments might have cured one Passion by another'. And after her return to Norwich, at the end of the first week in October, he reluctantly reconsidered Sara Fricker : 'Her, whom I do not love – but whom by every tie of Reason and Honor I ought to love.'

Eventually he wrote to Southey enclosing the Mary Evans letter and pouring forth his heart : 'I loved her, Southey! almost to madness. Her Image was never absent from me for three Years – for *more* than three Years – My Resolution has not faltered – but I want a Comforter.' He states emphatically that he does not love Sara Fricker, but just stops short of renouncing the engagement. 'I am resolved,' he says plaintively 'but wretched.' It would have been a clear plea to be let off the hook – to any man but Southey. Neither would the moving sonnet which he enclosed in this letter, saying in poetry what he could not say in prose, fare any better.

> Thou bleedest, my poor Heart! & thy Distress
> Doth Reason ponder with an anguish'd smile
> Probing thy sore wound sternly, tho' the while
> Her Eye be swoln and dim with heaviness.
> Why didst thou *listen* to Hope's whisper bland?
> Or, listening, why *forget* its healing Tale,

Why Jealousy with feverish Fancies pale
Jarr'd thy fine fibres with a Maniac's hand?
Faint was that Hope and rayless: yet 'twas fair
And sooth'd with many a dream the Hour of rest!
Thou should'st have lov'd it most when most opprest,
And nurs'd it with an Agony of Care,
Ev'n as a Mother her sweet infant heir
That pale and sickly droops upon her Breast.

'When a Man is unhappy, he writes damn'd bad Poetry,' reflected Coleridge in a footnote. But he had managed to express the confused agony of mind of a man who has discovered, only too late, that he has failed, not in entertaining vain hopes, but rather in the quality and perseverance of his original hope. For had not Mary Evans, after all, opened up the way to re-establishing their relationship? He later entitled the sonnet *On a Discovery Made Too Late*.

With his thoughts 'floating about in a most Chaotic State', Coleridge vacillated for more than a week between going to Bath to talk with Southey, and communicating with Mary Evans. In the meantime Southey had replied to his letter; he offered sympathy, and evidently tried to console his friend with the thought that all passions could be conquered by an effort of will. 'Whatever of mind we *will* to do, we *can* do!' retorted Coleridge, as if throwing the words back in his face. 'What then palsies the Will? The Joy of Grief! A mysterious Pleasure broods with dusky Wing over the tumultuous Mind — "and the Spirit of God moveth on the darkness of the Waters"! She WAS VERY lovely, Southey! We formed each others' minds — our ideas were blended — Heaven bless her! I cannot forget her — every day her Memory sinks deeper into my heart. — ' But it was falling on deaf ears, and Coleridge at last departed for London to write to Mary Evans.

It is an extremely poignant letter hovering on the brink of self-pity — but in the final analysis courageous, for he knew that it would provoke the truth for once and for all:

Too long has my Heart been the torture house of Suspense. After
infinite struggles of Irresolution I will at last dare to request of you,
Mary! that you will communicate to me whether of no you are
engaged to Mr — . [the rival was a Mr Fryer Todd, a man of 'good
fortune', whom Mary Evans eventually married the following year.]
I conjure you not to consider this request as presumptuous Indelicacy.
Upon mine Honor, I have made it with no other Design or Expectation than that of arming my fortitude by total hopelessness . . .

For four years I have *endeavoured* to smother a very ardent attach-
ment — in what degree I have succeeded, you must know better than
I can . . . you regarded me merely with the kindness of a Sister —
What expectations *could* I form? I formed no expectations — I was
ever resolving to subdue the disquieting Passion : still some inexplicable
Suggestion palsied my Efforts, and I clung with desperate fondness to
this Phantom of Love, its mysterious Attractions and hopeless
Prospects . . .

Indulge, Mary! this my first, my last request — and restore me to
Reality, however gloomy. Sad and full of heaviness will the Intelligence
be — my heart will die within me — I shall receive it however with
steadier resignation from yourself, than were it announced to me
(haply on your marriage Day!) by a Stranger! Indulge my request —
I will not disturb your Peace by even a *Look* of Discontent — still
less will I offend your Ear by the Whine of selfish Sensibility. In a
few months I shall enter at the Temple — and there seek forgetful
Calmness — where only it can be found — in incessant and useful
Activity . . .[10]

In less than a year Coleridge would be taking Southey to
task for making a similar suggestion about entering the
Law, a course of action 'more opposite to your avowed
principles, if possible, than even the Church'. But as this is
the only reference Coleridge makes to such a career for
himself, we can take it that it was merely a romantic tactic.

Meanwhile the agony of waiting for a reply began. He
seems to have gone back to Cambridge where he remained
silent, until yet again returning to London, where he
eventually replied to the letter from Southey suggesting
that they try the Pantisocratic scheme in Wales and in

which Southey had also remonstrated with Coleridge once again for not writing to Sara Fricker. Coleridge's reply, abrupt and hostile with regard to the Welsh innovation, was even more harsh on the hapless Miss Fricker:

I am not conscious of having injured her otherwise, than by having mistaken the ebullience of *schematism* for affection, which a moment's reflection might have told me, is not a plant of so mushroom a growth — had it ever not been counteracted by a prior attachment/but my whole Life has been a series of Blunders! God have mercy upon me — for I am a most miserable Dog — The most criminal action of my Life was the 'first letter I wrote to — [Sara]' I had worked myself to such a pitch, that I scarcely knew I was writing like an hypocrite.[11]

It was an open invitation to sever all ties, for to continue any further correspondence with Sara on the basis of their engagement would be no less hypocritical. But still Southey could not, or would not, take the hint; and Coleridge continued to commit himself to Sara out of duty: 'it still remains for me to be externally Just though my Heart is withered within me'. One wonders how he would have reacted had Mary Evans given him fresh hopes when replying to his last letter. Coleridge clearly spoke hysterically and unjustly a year later when he accused Southey of losing for him 'the Woman whom I loved to an excess which you in your warmest dream of fancy could never shadow out'.[12] For in spite of his professed commitment to Sara, he had done all in his power to regain Mary's affection; and it was she herself who rejected him firmly and finally in a letter he received on Christmas Eve.

Thus Coleridge sat down to write to her for the last time. 'To love you Habit has made unalterable. This passion, however, divested, as it now is, of all Shadow of Hope, will lose its disquieting power. Far distant from you I shall journey thro' the vale of Men in calmness. He cannot long be wretched, who dares be actively virtuous.'[13]

The worst of the agony was over. He would pine for her

and recriminate Southey for losing her. But she now lay
beyond hope. Only once would he see her again, when she
came briefly into his life of her own accord fourteen years
later. In 1808, seeing Coleridge listed for a lecture at the
Royal Institution, she was prompted by curiosity to waylay
him after he had spoken. They were both astonished at the
changes wrought in the other by age and suffering. Coleridge visited her for tea and saw in her life 'a counterpart of
the very worst parts of my own fate in exaggerated form'.
Her marriage with the 'man of fortune' had been even less
successful than his own. His rival, Fryer Todd, eventually
went bankrupt and their only child was taken into care. But
still, through the ravages of time 'the Mary Evans of 14
years ago, flashed across my eyes', mused Coleridge sadly,
'with a truth and vividness as great as its rapidity'.[14]

By Christmas, then, Coleridge was resigned forever to
losing the girl 'who was my first attachment, and who with
her family gave me the first idea of an *home*, and inspired
my best and permanent feelings'. But the sense of exile
would linger with him throughout a lifetime.

It is frequently suggested that Coleridge's loss of Mary
Evans became the source of an inner tension out of which he
wrote some of his finest poetry. The thought had not escaped
Coleridge himself. 'But all Thing work together for Good,'
he observed calmly at the end of December. 'Had I been
united to her, the Excess of my Affection would have
effeminated my Intellect. I should have fed on her Looks
as she entered into the Room – I should have gazed on her
Footsteps when she went out from me.'[15] And during this
agonizing period of emotional conflict he does not seem to
have been idle, nor downhearted, in his literary activity.
Having now left Cambridge for good, he seemed to be
settling down in London ; his sonnets on Eminent Characters were appearing in the *Morning Chronicle*, a Miltonic
paean of praise for his current heroes, among them, Burke,
Priestley and Godwin. He was meeting editors for dinner,

and spending his evenings with Charles Lamb in the smoky atmosphere of the 'Salutation and Cat' with 'all its associated train of pipes, tobacco, Egghots, Welch Rabbits, metaphysics and poetry'.[16] The friendship with Lamb, who was now employed in the counting house of the East India Company, had been renewed from Christ's Hospital where Coleridge had been three years his senior. At this time there was a close emotional bond between the two men, for Lamb's sister was seriously ill. It evoked Coleridge's deepest sympathies, and he incorporated some of the main themes of his 'brotherly' letter to Edith Fricker into a poem of consolation for him.

On the same day that Coleridge wrote his farewell to Mary Evans he was also working on the first draft of *Religious Musings* his most ambitious poem so far. It was not to be published until 1796, and certainly went through a number of drafts after Christmas 1794, but some of his main political, philosophical and religious preoccupations at this time travel through the later revisions. Lamb, who was the first to read it, referred to it as 'a gigantic hyperbole by which you describe the Evils of existing society'.[17] Early in the poem there is a description of Christ as the simple Galilean of the Unitarians and archetype of the reformer, whom he contrasts with the traditional heavenly 'Angelblaze' of pomp :

> Thou Man of Woes!
> Despiséd Galilean! For the Great
> Invisible (by symbols only seen)
> With a peculiar and surpassing light
> Shines from the visage of the oppressed good man,
> When heedless of himself the scourgéd saint
> Mourns for the oppressor.

He goes on to talk of 'the elect' — the small band of men, who in religious terms are like the Old Testament remnant preserving the true faith, but foreshadowing the highly individualistic élite, independent of mass movements. It was an idea he would develop further in his political lectures early in 1795.

> Their's too celestial courage, inly armed –
> Dwarfing Earth's giant brood, what time they muse
> On their great Father, great beyond compare!
> And marching onwards view high o'er their heads
> His waving banners of Omnipotence.

And the existence of the elect would be further justified by the ignorance and desperation of the masses, a view which would be increasingly substantiated in Coleridge's mind by the excesses of the French Revolution. He, like many others, considered the anarchy and bloodshed in France due to lack of education as much as oppression. The people must be educated for revolution by the elect.

> O ye numberless,
> Whom foul oppression's ruffian gluttony
> Drives from Life's plenteous feast! O thou poor Wretch
> Who nurs'd in darkness and made wild by want,
> Roamest for prey, yea thy unnatural hand
> Dost lift to deeds of blood.

There were millennial expectations, too, in which the apocalypse of revolution, associated with the Book of Revelations, would reach even greater excesses before the glorious millennium began, and all government would disappear save the self-government of each human heart ; and

> the vast family of Love
> Raised from the common earth by common toil
> Enjoy the equal produce.

The tone of the work is positively Miltonic : yet the influence of Priestley, and once again Hartley, emerges in the underlying theories. In fact, Hartley – 'he first who marked the ideal tribes/Up the fine fibres through the sentient brain', and Priestley – 'patriot, and saint, and sage', are addressed as foremost amongst the elect, along with Milton and Newton.

There is every indication that Coleridge had read one or the other of Priestley's two recent publications *The Present State of Europe Compared with Ancient Prophecies*, or his *Conclusion to Hartley's Observations*, both published in 1794. Both these works give Priestley's reasons for escaping to America. According to him, on the opening of the fifth Seal the Revolution had begun, and it would reach its climax at the establishment of the Millennium. In support of his theory he could cite Newton and Hartley in their interpretation of prophecy: thus they both naturally find a place amongst Coleridge's heroes. Moreover both in *Religious Musings* and *Destiny of Nations* (a revised portion of his contribution to Southey's epic, *Joan of Arc*) Coleridge expounds an interesting Priestleian quasi-scientific theory which also finds its parallels in Erasmus Darwin and French writers such as Diderot. The whole of Nature consists of teleological atoms of energy called 'monads' which constitute the total organism of the Infinite Mind, which have propensities towards an orchestrated act of total purpose. The French Revolution was seen as a first stage in an inexorable revolutionary development through struggle and turmoil towards harmony and perfection, soon to be followed by earthquakes and volcanoes, before the Millennium and the Resurrection of the dead.[18]

> Contemplant Spirits! ye that hover o'er
> With untired gaze the immeasurable fount
> Ebullient with creative Deity!
> And ye of plastic power, that interfused
> Roll through the grosser and material mass
> In organizing surge! Holies of God!
> (And what if Monads of the Infinite mind?)
> I haply journeying my immortal course
> Shall sometime join your mystic choir!

Or as he puts in *Destiny of Nations*:

> Glory to Thee, Father of Earth and Heaven!
> All-conscious Presence of the Universe!
> Nature's vast ever-acting Energy!
> In will, in deed, Impulse of All to All.

Here quite clearly was Coleridge's intoxication 'with the vernal fragrance & effluvia from the first fruits of Pantheism'. Commenting on this period in later life he claims that he was 'unaware of its bitter root', that he pacified his religious feelings with the dim distinction 'that tho' God was = the World, the World was not = God, as if God were a whole composed of Parts, of which the World was one !'[19]

His reading of Hartley, whose *Observations on Man* was reprinted in 1791, only served to reinforce the above notions. Although Hartley maintained a distinction between mind and matter, Coleridge had clearly accommodated his theories to Priestley's all-embracing materialist exposition. He had mentioned Hartley, it will be remembered, when writing to his brother George on 6 November, 1798. 'And after a diligent, I *may* say, an intense study of Locke, Hartley and others who have written most wisely on the Nature of Man – I appear to myself to see the point of *possible* perfection at which the World may perhaps be destined to arrive.'[20] Yet in December, he wrote to Southey : 'I am a compleat Necessitarian – and understand the subject as well almost as Hartley himself – but I go farther than Hartley and believe the corporeality of *thought* – namely, that it is motion.'[21] Hartley's *Observations* is a two-volume work, the first part attempting to explain all human activity in terms of matter. The human mind is seen as a kind of mechanism which receives vibrations due to palpable extramental stimulus of the organs of sense, the process of thought depending on the association of these sensations in spatiotemporal contexts. A parodied interpretation of Hartley's theory is to be found in a note Coleridge sent to a friend who had been beaten by James Boyer, the

Master of the Upper School at Christ's Hospital. It elucidates Hartley's general drift more instructively and amusingly perhaps than many a commentary :

I condole with you the unpleasant motions, to which a certain Uncouth Automaton has been mechanized; and am anxious to know the motives, that impinged on it's optic or auditory nerves, so as to be communicated in such rude vibrations through the medullary substance of It's Brain, thence rolling their stormy surges into the capillaments of it's Tongue, and the muscles of it's arm. The diseased Violence of It's thinking corporealities will, depend upon it, cure itself by exhaustion – In the mean time, I trust, that you have not been assimilated in degredation by losing the ataraxy of your Temper, and that the Necessity which dignified you by a Sentience of the Pain, has not lowered you by the accession of Anger or Resentment.'[22]

Even in 1794 Coleridge found the idea eccentric enough to be amused by it ; later in the *Biographia* he would reject Hartley's cumbersome 'solid fibres', 'hollow tubes' and 'oscillating ether'. But taken with the second part of the *Observations*, which expounds on the direction and regulation of this quasi-mechanical human behaviour through the teachings of Christianity, it answered the need for a system which united the empirical convictions of the late eighteenth century with a reaffirmation of Christian belief.

The extent of Coleridge's Christian belief within the framework of his political thinking found contentious expression during his stay in London when he came in contact with such notable and atheistic reformers as Thomas Holcroft, of whom Coleridge dryly remarked, 'He absolutely infests you with Atheism'. Thomas Holcroft, a leading radical and author of *Road to Ruin*, had been indicted for high treason and imprisoned in October. He had recently been released without trial when Coleridge met him in December at a dinner given by the proprietors of the *Morning Chronicle*. But Coleridge was not impressed, particularly with such remarks of Holcroft's as : 'Every Man not an atheist is only not a fool.'[23] They seemed to

have clashed violently at this first meeting: 'I had the
honor of *working* H[olcroft] a little – and by my great
coolness and command of impressive Language, certainly
did him over.'

'There is a fierceness and *dogmatism* of conversation in
Holcroft,' Coleridge observed scornfully, 'for which you
receive little compensation either from the variety of his
information, the closeness of his Reasoning, or the splendour
of his Language. He talks incessantly of Metaphysics, of
which he appears to me to *know nothing* – to have *read
nothing.*'[24] Coleridge clearly intended to dissociate himself
from those reformers who did not measure up to his own
standards of intellectual excellence, and more especially
those who were tainted with atheism.

He had clearly made an impression in political and
journalistic circles in London during December, and with
the support of Lamb's friendship it seems likely that he
would have stayed on there indefinitely. It seems too that
emotional considerations might have kept him there. For at
the end of the month, several days after communicating
with Mary Evans for the last time – he writes to Southey.

To lose her! – I can rise above that selfish Pang. But to marry
another – O Southey! bear with my weakness. Love makes all things
pure and heavenly like itself: – but to marry a woman whom I do *not*
love – to degrade her, whom I call my Wife, by making her the
Instrument of low Desire – and on removal of a desultory Appetite, to
be perhaps not displeased with her Absence! – Enough! – These
Refinements are the wildering Fires, that lead me into Vice.

But even yet he drew back from the obvious decision:
'Mark you, Southey – *I will do my Duty.*' And still Southey
kept him inexorably to his word, insisting that he should
come down to Somerset to fulfil that duty. Through the
first half of January Coleridge was expected daily in Bath;
he wrote frequently to say that he was on his way; each
letter from London was about to be his last, only to be

followed by another of vague excuse: 'Think you, I wish to stay in Town?' he wrote on Monday, 29 December. 'I am all eagerness to leave it – and am resolved, whatever be the consequence, to be at Bath by Saturday – I thought of walking down. I have written to Bristol – and said, I could not assign a particular Time for my leaving Town – I spoke indefinitely that I might not disappoint.'[25] But on Friday, 2 January, Coleridge was still in London, writing, 'The roads are dangerous – the horses soon knock'd up – The outside to a Man who like me has no great Coat, is cold and rheumatismferous – . . . Shall I walk? I have a sore throat – and am not well. – . . . The Waggon does not set off before Sunday Night – I shall be with you by Wednesday, I suppose.'[26] On receiving this Southey set out with Lovell and walked to Marlborough to meet the wagon halfway, 'but *no S. T. Coleridge was therein*!'[27] Southey was beside himself with anger. And so it continued into the second week of January when Southey wrote to Sara Fricker:

'Friday night – no Coleridge! . . . This state of expectation totally unfits me for anything. When I attempt to employ myself the first knock at the door wakes all my hopes again and again disappoints them . . . I am kept in exercise by walking to meet the coaches – Did he say Wednesday (January 7th) positively to you? I told you about the middle of the week. Why will he ever fix a day if he cannot abide by it?

Finally, Southey bluntly announced that he was coming to London to fetch him, undoubtedly one of the most outrageous acts of assurance he was to commit in his life. When he arrived in London a despondent note from Coleridge awaited him off the coach: 'Come to me at the Angel . . . I am not glad that you are come to town – and yet I am glad. – It was total want of cash that prevented my Expedition.'

The proprietor of the 'Salutation and Cat' demanded that Coleridge leave his clothes behind until his bill should be paid, while the inn-keeper of the 'Angel' wept at his departure and offered him free lodgings if he would stay.[28]

4

But Southey meant business and insisted on transporting his hapless friend back to Bristol, Miss Fricker and the fulfilment of his duty; '*nor would he, I believe, have come back at all*, if I had not gone to London to look for him,' wrote Southey later.[29] Lamb, for one, who considered 'London . . . the only fostering soil for Genius,' viewed Southey's highhandedness with dismay. As he wrote to Coleridge shortly afterwards, 'I must say I have borne him [Southey] no good will since he spirited you away from among us.'

So at last, Coleridge returned to Bristol by way of Bath, to face his long neglected fiancée. And on arriving in Bristol he discovered to his astonishment that Sara had received two other proposals in his absence, one of them from a man of large fortune, whom she had rejected because of her 'perseverant attachment' to him. 'These peculiar circumstances', wrote Coleridge, 'she had with her usual Delicacy concealed from me until my arrival at Bristol.' It seemed that he had been put on the spot : the 'rivals' continued to propose ; a Fricker uncle persistently admonished her for refusing ; Sara wrung her hands and made no secret of how heavy her heart was with anxiety, 'how disquieted by Suspense'. As a perplexed Coleridge explained to a friend : 'So commanding are the requests of her Relations, that a short Time must decide whether she marries me whom she loves with an affection to the ardour of which my Deserts bear no proportion – or a man whom she strongly dislikes, in spite of his solicitous attentions to her.' Coleridge was being given a chance, then, to turn down his Miss Fricker – but the scales of guilt, such was Sara's 'perseverant attachment', were being heavily weighed against him. Staying in Bristol he could not long hold out.

Meanwhile the Pantisocracy squabbles were being resurrected. Southey was still keen on rehearsing the scheme in Wales : Coleridge was equally reluctant to take the commune to any place but America. But finally, in a letter to Southey in mid-January, he capitulated, at the same time taking the opportunity to castigate Southey for his 'self-centering Resolve'. The 'frail & unpiloted Bark' of Pantisocracy was once again afloat; and by the end of January 1795, Coleridge, Southey and George Burnett were sharing a house in College Street, Bristol, with a tantalizing view from the dormer window of the masts and rigging of the ships in the port, a constant reminder of that voyage to the American Utopia which Coleridge had longed for with such ardour. But at last, in spite of so many setbacks, Southey and Coleridge were writing at the same table. 'Our names are written in the book of destiny, on the same page,' declared Southey. Their friendship seemed to have regained some of its former momentum.

4
Bristol

IN the late eighteenth century Bristol was one of the most dynamic and wealthy cities in England; a port and trading centre whose interests extended to the Mediterranean, Scandinavia, West Africa, North America and the West Indies. Iron ore, tobacco, wine, sugar and cocoa were deposited on its wharves; iron and brass were turned into bangles and trinkets beneath the smoking chimneys of its factories. As Southey once remarked, 'This city is peopled with rich fools.'[1] Yet if Bristol enticed men who were bent on making their fortunes, especially out of the unpleasant ramifications of the slave trade, it also attracted people of an opposite tenor, such as Thomas Clarkson, the 'moral steam-engine' of anti-slavery, as Coleridge called him, or Hannah More who set herself the task of educating the poor through her Mendip schools. For young reformers like Coleridge and Southey there was much to engage and enliven their interest: there would be objects in plenty for their criticism and outrage, and attentive sympathizers to applaud their principles.

Here Coleridge and Southey determined to establish writing careers that would bring sufficient income to marry and launch the Welsh commune, estimating £150 a year each the minimum sum.[2] They both tried to obtain posts on *The Telegraph* and *The Citizen* during the following two months, but nothing came of it. Meanwhile they determined to embark on a series of lectures on political and religious topics which would partially keep them in funds and give expression to their theories and creative energies. At the same time they began to ransack the Bristol library for works of history, philosophy and theology.

'I am, & ever have been', [wrote Coleridge in the following year], 'a great reader – & have read almost everything – a library-cormorant – I am *deep* in all out of the way books, whether of the monkish times, or of the puritanical æra – I have read & digested most of the Historical Writers – ; but I do not *like* History. Metaphysics, & Poetry, & 'Facts of mind' – (i.e. Accounts of all the strange phantasms that ever possessed your philosophy – dreamers from Thoth, the Egyptian to Taylor, the English Pagan,) are my darling Studies – In short, I seldom read except to amuse myself – & I am almost always reading.'[3]

And while their methods of reading, and the mode of employment of their reading matter, was entirely different, it is likely that they shared each other's books and acquired new interests through collaboration. Southey for example, had long been interested in reviving epic poetry by the employment of mythologies and exotic materials, and undoubtedly introduced Coleridge to some of the 'out of the way books' which he devoured with such relish.[4]

And in all their affairs at this time, they were to find a useful and generous friend in Joseph Cottle, an affluent young Bristol bookseller and publisher, with literary aspirations and a soft spot for poets. Against all rules of good business he extended large advances, and constantly made himself available for odd jobs and small loans. A vain, slightly preposterous but well-meaning figure, his protégés frequently scoffed at him behind his back.[5] The two poets, however, were prompt to invite him to join the Pantisocratic scheme, but he held back from what he termed 'this epidemic delusion'. 'Young as I was,' he wrote in his *Recollections*, 'I suspected there was an old and intractable leven in human nature, that would effectually frustrate the airy schemes of happiness which had been projected in every age, and always with the same result.'[6] Cottle, in fact, hoped for a different kind of association with Coleridge and Southey: he aspired to become their first publisher; and he records with pride the following conversation with Coleridge, assigning it the importance of the beginning of Coleridge's career. Cottle had been persuading him to publish a volume of his poetry as Coleridge had been downcast about money:

'Oh,' he replied, 'that is a useless expedient.' He continued: 'I offered a volume of my poems to different booksellers in London, who would not even look at them! The reply being, "Sir, the article will not do." At length, one, more accommodating than the rest, condescended to receive my M.S. poems, and, after a deliberate inspection, offered me for the copy-right, six guineas, which sum, poor as I was, I refused to accept.'

'Well,' said I, 'to encourage you, I will give you twenty guineas.' It was very pleasant to observe the joy that instantly diffused itself over his countenance. 'Nay,' I continued, 'others publish for themselves, I will chiefly remember you. Instead of giving you twenty guineas, I will extend it to thirty, and without waiting for the completion of the work, to make you easy, you may have the money, as your occasions require.' The silence and the grasped hand, showed, that, at that moment, one person was happy.[7]

Coleridge seems to have given his first lecture, which was subsequently published as *A Moral and Political Lecture*, by early February 1795. And in assuming this new role he shocked the sensibilities of at least one member of his predominantly radical audience: 'his person is slovenly. . . . Mr. C[oleridge] would . . . do well to appear with cleaner stockings in public, and if his hair were combed out every time he appeared in public it would not depreciate him in the esteem of his friends.'[8] But as an orator, he appeared, 'like a comet or meteor' on the Bristol horizon.[9] 'Undaunted by the storms of popular prejudice,' reported the Bristol *Observer*, 'unswayed by the magisterial influence, he spoke in public what none had the courage in this city to do before, – he told Men that they have Rights.'[10] The comment suggests a close identification with Tom Paine; and it seems, indeed, that faced with an audience, Coleridge was easily carried away towards the radical extremes on the current of excited rhetoric. Once more his reputation as a Democrat and a Jacobin was gathering stature. Later he claimed that it was no more than the spirit of the moment: nobody more than Coleridge could appreciate the temptations that lie in wait for a brilliant speaker.

'And tho' I detested Revolutions in my calmer moments, as attempts, that were necessarilly baffled and made blood horrible by the very causes, which could alone justify Revolutions (I mean, the ignorance, superstition, profligacy, & vindictive passions, which are the natural effects of Despotism & false Religion)... yet with an ebullient Fancy, a flowing Utterance, a light & dancing heart, & a disposition to catch fire by the very rapidity of my own motion, & to speak vehemently from mere verbal associations. ... I aided the Jacobins, by witty sarcasms & subtle reasoning & declamations full of genuine feeling agains all Rulers & against all established Forms![11]

We know from Cottle that Coleridge's political lectures were witty, amusingly arch and enthusiastically applauded. He seems to have been particularly gifted, moreover, with the political speaker's most devastating weapon – repartee. At one meeting a group of 'Aristocrats' began to demonstrate by hissing. The rest of the audience were seized with alarm, wondering how Coleridge would deal with the intrusion. But their fears were soon assuaged when Coleridge remarked with great coolness, 'I am not at all surprised, when the red hot prejudices of Aristocrats are suddenly plunged into the cool water of reason, that they should go off with a hiss!' Cottle remembers that 'the words were electric. The assailants felt, as well as testified, their confusion, and the whole company confirmed it by immense applause! There was no more hissing.'[12]

On another occasion, 'A fellow came and hissed him for professing public principle,' reminisced Crabb Robinson from a conversation with Coleridge, 'and said: "Why, if

you are so public-spirited, do you take money at the door ?"
"For a reason," said Coleridge, "which I am sorry in the
present instance has not been quite successful – to keep out
blackguards." '13

These political lectures, given in February, were delivered
against a background of renewed unrest and political
agitation on the part of the reformers. The war with France
was in its second year, and the radicals accused the government of delaying peace negotiations in order to achieve
reactionary political objectives at home and abroad. Moreover, it was considered that the war had caused a loss of
national integrity ; that it was to blame for a plague of
hardships that afflicted the whole country. And the hardships, coupled with natural disasters, were severe indeed.
The summer drought of 1794 had been followed by a winter
of intense cold ; the death rate doubled ; many who escaped
death by famine were killed by exposure. At the same time
the impact of the disruption of trade was being felt in the
manufacturing areas ; there was widespread unemployment
and the crime-rate soared in spite of severe penalties. These
were times when a pickpocket might be sentenced to death
or deportation. Yet, as the radicals were quick to point out,
many preferred to run the risk of hanging, or Botany Bay,
rather than enter the army where a savage death on the Continent seemed equally certain ; to be sent home mutilated to
join the hundreds of thousands of vagrants on England's
roads was the best that could be hoped for. Even the great
sides of beef hung outside the recruiting stations, or the
promise of exhorbitant bounties, did little to persuade the
people that volunteering was the answer to starvation. As it
was, the military resorted to press-gangs and 'crimping'.
But more than this, the reformers raged with indignation at
the system of spies who mingled with the people : who were
said to sit in coffee houses and inns, and insinuate themselves
into people's homes. An unguarded outburst against the
government might be interpreted as sedition, a clandestine

meeting as a plot against the Constitution. To facilitate the
arrest of suspects, the Habeas Corpus Suspension Act was
again voted through Parliament on 5 February. Yet while
there were many amongst the moderates who would have
agreed with the anti-war sentiments of the radicals – few
would have accepted that Pitt's measures against treason
were vicious. As Southey's friend Seward said: 'Truly,
the acquittal of Hardy and Tooke affords fresh and irre-
fragable proof how totally unfounded their and their
fellow wretches ungrateful clamours against the powers of
the English constitution to protect the liberties and safety of
Englishmen.'[14] Coleridge, who outlines the discontent of
the radicals in a powerful and moving flow of rhetoric in his
third lecture (*On the Present War*), summed up the situation
thus: 'Our national faith has been impaired; our social
confidence hath been weakened, or made unsafe; our
liberties have suffered a perilous breach, and even now are
being (still more perilously) undermined.'[15] It was an
opportune time for preaching the reconstruction of society;
he might have plunged into the sort of rhetoric that was
designed to exacerbate the spirit of unrest, and by his
own admission seems to have done so. Yet in his speeches in
published form, he shrinks from the excesses of violence.
If there was to be a revolution, Coleridge preferred it to be
benevolent and bloodless.

We know for certain that the text of Coleridge's first
address, *A Moral and Political Lecture*, was a good deal more
restrained than his actual words in the lecture hall. In fact,
Coleridge claims that he was obliged to publish it, 'it
having been confidently asserted that there was Treason in
it'.[16] Reminiscent of *Religious Musings*, it is a passionate
plea for universal education – the prerequisite for any
revolutionary movement that is not to degenerate into
bloodshed: 'The annals of the French revolution have
recorded in letters of blood, that the knowledge of the
few cannot be counteracted by the ignorance of the many;

that the light of philosophy, when it is confined to a small
minority, points out the possessors as the victims, rather
than the illuminators, of the multitude.' Coleridge was
concerned with analysing what had gone wrong with the
revolution in France, and by the same token what was
likely to go wrong with a revolution in England. He
enumerates the classes of imperfect revolutionaries –
pointing out, in each case, a want of education and fixed
principles. There are those 'unaccustomed to the labour of
thorough investigation', whose political opinions depend
'with weather-cock uncertainty on the winds of rumour . . .
on the report of French victories they blaze into Republicanism, at a taste of French excesses they darken into Aristocrats'. Another class are those who understand the issues,
but are influenced only by the 'mad-headed enthusiast'.
'Unillumined by philosophy and stimulated to a lust of
revenge by aggravated wrongs . . . these men are rude
materials from which a detestable minister manufactures
conspiracies.' Amongst this class, too, potentially the most
powerful, are those with the 'ignorance of brutes'. 'This
class, at present, is comparatively small – yet soon to form
an overwhelming majority, unless great and immediate
efforts are used to lessen the intolerable grievances of our
poorer brethren, and infuse into their sorely wounded
hearts the healing qualities of knowledge.' Finally, there
were those who pursued revolution with 'self-centering
views'. They are prepared to join in 'digging up the rubbish
of mouldering establishment and stripping off the tawdry
pageantry of governments.' But they do not go far enough.
'Whatever tends to improve and elevate the ranks of our
poorer brethren, they regard with suspicious jealousy, as
the dreams of a visionary ; as if there were anything in the
superiority of Lord to Gentleman, so mortifying in the
barrier, so fatal to happiness in the consequences, as the more
real distinction of master and servant, of rich man and poor.'

Against these classes of dangerous revolutionaries he sets the 'small but glorious band, whom we may truly distinguish by the name of thinking and disinterested Patriots'.

... Calmness and energy mark all their actions, benevolence is the silken thread that runs through the pearl chain of all their virtues. Believing that vice originates not in man, but in the surrounding circumstances; not in the heart, but in the understanding; he is hopeless concerning no one – to correct a vice or generate a virtuous conduct he pollutes not his hands with the scourge of coercion; but by endeavouring to alter the circumstances removes, or by strengthening the intellect disarms, the temptation.[17]

Here, in a more extended form, are the familiar themes : fixed principles, the elect, universal education, abolition of servitude; and now, additionally, the doctrine of a benevolent reconstruction of society which would act upon deterministic human nature precluding any need for coercion. Such were Coleridge's basic political views early in 1795, and they were elaborated in the following two lectures he gave in February. But an interesting development in the second, which, in its published form, was entitled *Conciones ad Populum or Addresses to the People*, is his further dissociation from Godwin who had recommended that knowledge should be diffused from the top to the bottom of society through the various classes. Coleridge thought the idea plausible rather than just or practicable.

Society as at present constituted does not resemble a chain that ascends in a continuity of links. – There are three ranks possessing intercourse with each other: these are well comprized in the superscription of a Perfumer's advertisement, which I lately saw – 'The Nobility, Gentry, and the People of Dress.' But alas! Between the Parlour and the Kitchen, the Tap and the Coffee-Room – there is a gulph that may not be passed. He would appear to me to have adopted the best as well as the most benevolent mode of diffusing Truth, who uniting the zeal of the Methodist with the views of the Philosopher, should be *personally* amongst the Poor, and teach them their *Duties* in order that he may render them susceptible of their *Rights*.[18]

No doubt Coleridge had in mind the Unitarian preacher travelling amongst the labouring class — a role that he himself would assume briefly the following year. Significantly, he would later refer to these first political lectures as lay sermons.

Meanwhile, the reconciliation with Southey proved to be only temporary. Southey had started a series of historical lectures in March, but he seems to have made less impact than Coleridge. One critic commented, 'his gesticulation and attitude when he is speaking is not the most pleasing, his body is always too stiff, his features are apt to be distorted'.[19] In spite of the fact that the two poets were living in the same house and writing at the same table there was an undercurrent of tension which was liable to erupt at any moment. Both had been equally guilty of upbraiding the other in tones of high moral indignation : we may take it that they were both equally wounded, and anxious not to be caught out again. At the same time, while Southey was contemplating withdrawing from the Pantisocracy scheme altogether, Coleridge continued to be galled by the fact that it was to be in Wales rather than America. The first harsh words were spoken in early March, precipitated by a typical instance of Coleridge's unreliability. Southey was scheduled to deliver a lecture on 'The Rise, Progress and Decline of the Roman Empire', but Coleridge requested that he should give the lecture himself as it was a subject he had studied closely. The request was readily granted, and the lecture and speaker announced the previous week. Cottle records the outcome :

At the usual hour, the room was thronged. The moment of commencement arrived. No lecturer appeared! Patience was preserved for a quarter, extending to half an hour! — but still no lecturer! At length it was communicated to the impatient assemblage, 'that a circumstance, exceedingly to be regretted! would prevent Mr Coleridge from giving his lecture, that evening, as intended.' Some few present learned the truth, but the major part of the company retired, not very well pleased, and under the impression that Mr C had either broken his leg, or that some severe family affliction had occurred.[20]

It happened that the next day, Coleridge, Southey, Edith, Sara and Cottle set off on an excursion to Chepstow and Tintern. They crossed on the Severn ferry, visited the castle at Chepstow and went on to dine at the Beaufort Arms. After dinner Southey proceeded to upbraid Coleridge for his failure to appear the evening before. A fierce quarrel arose, each girl taking the side of her man. It was left to Cottle to patch up the tempers. And when, eventually, they set off for Tintern, they had wasted so much time that it was already getting dark. Cottle amusingly records the wanderings of the extraordinary party as they lost their way in a wood:

On emerging into the wood, for such it was, extending the whole way down to Tintern, we all suddenly found ourselves deprived of sight; obscurity aggravated almost into pitchy darkness! We could directly see nothing, whilst we floundered over stones, embedded, as they appeared, in their everlasting sockets, from the days of Noah. The gurgling of the unseen stream, down in the adjacent gully, (which we, perchance, might soon be found, reluctantly, to visit!) never sounded so discordant before. Having some respect for my limbs (with no bone-setter near) I dismounted, resolving to lead my steed, who trembled, as though conscious of the perilous expedition in which he had entered. Mr Coleridge, who had been more accustomed to rough riding than myself, upon understanding that I through cowardice, had forsaken the saddle, without speaking a word, put his foot in the stirrup, and mounting, determined to brave, at all hazards, the dangers of the campagne.[21]

Coleridge cantered to and fro searching for the road, while 'Mr Southey marched on like a pillar of strength, with a lady pressing on each arm, while the relator [Cottle] lagged in the rear, without even a pilgrim's staff to sustain his tottering steps'. At last, they emerged from the wood, regained the road, and passed on to Tintern where they

spent the night. The quarrel had shaken Coleridge badly,
he was 'agitated, even to many tears', but Southey assured
him afterwards that he was certainly coming to the commune
in Wales.

Later, on another occasion, Southey told Coleridge that
he liked him better than ever – to which Sara Fricker,
nothing if not honest, retorted: 'What a story!' But the
antipathy between the two poets ran deep. It was not long
before Southey began to accuse Coleridge of not pulling his
weight in literary output, of sponging on Cottle and himself.
A glance at Coleridge's private and public productions, not
to speak of his omnivorous reading, refutes the accusation of
idleness. Unfortunately it was a reputation that would
dog him for a life time, an opinion that his memory would
inherit long after his death. Coleridge himself, even, tended
to lend credence to the legend by regular self-castigation on
this score. But he did more justice to himself when he
answered Southey's accusation by saying: 'The Truth is –
You sate down and wrote – I used to saunter about and
think what I should write. And we ought to appreciate our
comparative Industry by the quantum of mental exertion,
not the particular mode of it: By the number of Thoughts
collected, not by the number of lines; thro' which these
Thoughts are diffused.'[22] Still smarting from this accusation
of 'INDOLENCE' eight months later, Coleridge would carry
his rebuff even further:

But neither is the charge a true one. My own lectures I wrote
for myself – eleven in number – excepting a very few pages, which
most reluctantly you eked out for me – And such pages! I would
not have suffered them to have stood in a Lecture of your's. To
your Lectures I dedicated my whole mind & heart – and wrote one
half in *Quantity* – ; but in Quality, you must be conscious, that all
the *Tug* of Brain was mine: and that your Share was little more than
Transcription.'[23]

Fundamentally, however, it was a difference of temperament that separated the two men, a difference that Southey

would only recognize more clearly as the years passed :
'Coleridge goes to work like a hound,' he would write in
1810, 'nosing his way, turning, and twisting, and winding
and doubling, till you get weary with following the mazy
movements. My way is, when I see my object, to dart at it
like a greyhound.' But the view would still lack a full
appreciation of Coleridge's worth. His final verdict on their
Bristol collaboration, '[Coleridge] did me much good – I
him more', never altered basically from his first. Perhaps the
final word, however, should be Wordsworth's who, comparing their poetry and methods of work fifty years later,
wrote : 'Observe the difference of execution in the poems of
Coleridge and Southey, how masterly is the workmanship of
the former, compared with the latter ; the one persevered
in labour unremittingly, the other could lay down his work
at pleasure and turn to anything else.'[24] Yet it was precisely
in their poetical collaboration that their friendship suffered
least : in fact, even during Coleridge's worst period of
stress, before Christmas, he could write a long and detailed
letter of advice and encouragement about Southey's latest
verse.

Undoubtedly the immediate cause of the rift between
them was occasioned by the degeneration of the Pantisocracy
scheme. Yet the issue was not so simple. Each of them had
been receding from its realization for their own separate
reasons ; yet for either of them to compromise it, or radically
alter its shape, would be an admission of moral weakness.
There was an air of unreality, of hypocrisy, even, about the
squabbles, which does little credit to either of them. Then,
in June, Coleridge learnt of Southey's retreat from yet
another of the basic principles of their much compromised
scheme. Apparently Southey proposed to George Burnett at
a 'strawberry party' at Long Ashton, that the idea of a
commune without personal ownership should be abandoned
for a jointly owned farm. 'It scorched in my throat,' wrote
Coleridge later. 'Your private resources were to remain your

individual property, and every thing to be separate except on five or six acres. In short, we were to commence Partners in a petty Farming Trade. This was the Mouse of which the Mountain Pantisocracy was at last safely delivered.'[25] Southey also proposed that they should think in terms of delaying the establishment of the commune for about fourteen years, by which time they should have sufficient money.

But there were other developments in Southey's private affairs which would shortly spell the end of the Pantiso-cratic dream, mountain or mouse. In the spring of 1795 Southey had received a letter from his uncle, Herbert Hill, in Lisbon, suggesting that he should come out to Portugal until a reconciliation could be effected with Miss Tyler. Then in August Herbert Hill turned up in England in person, and wrote to Southey offering financial assistance and urging him to take Holy Orders. He also renewed the invitation to stay in Lisbon. Meanwhile Charles Wynn, a family friend, offered an annuity of £160 to start in October after Southey's twenty-first birthday. Southey showed the letter from Herbert Hill to Coleridge as if genuinely undecided, and Coleridge put his response in writing, in a controlled and lofty letter with little indication of explicit reproof. He does not seem concerned that the Pantisocracy scheme now seems forever doomed : 'Southey ! Pantiso-cracy is not the Question – it's realization is distant – perhaps a miraculous Millennium – What you have seen, or think that you have seen of the human heart, may render the formation even of a pantisocracy *seminary* improbable to you but this is not the question.' The only question, as far as Coleridge was concerned, was that of Holy Orders ; all other considerations paled, even Pantisocracy, by the side of the glaring wickedness of such a decision. The real point, wrote Coleridge, was 'whether or no you can *perjure* your-self ... you disapprove of an Establishment altogether – you believe it iniquitous – a mother of Crimes ! – It is impossible that *you* could uphold it by assuming the badge of Affiliation.'[26] But then, very indiscreetly, Coleridge proceeded to spread the news abroad that Southey might defect to the Established Church – giving Southey fresh occasion to remonstrate with him for his treachery. Although Southey had plainly given Coleridge the impression that he was hovering on the brink of such a decision, it seems from the testimony of letters to friends that it was out of the question for him to take Orders, and that he himself considered such a course 'the gate to Perjury'.

But the break up was now inevitable. Southey finally decided on the Law as a career, which seemed to Coleridge as much a betrayal of their radical principles as taking Orders. From this point onwards Coleridge regarded Southey 'as one who had *fallen back into the Ranks* ; as a man admirable for his abilities only, strict indeed in the lesser Honesties, but like the majority of men unable to resist a Temptation – You were become an Acquaintance.' Southey was quick to notice Coleridge's coldness, and wrote asking why he was only showing the 'face of friendship' and withholding his former intimacy. Coleridge responded by avoiding Southey even more. Only on literary topics did he open up : 'I spoke to you as I should have done to any other Man of Genius who happened to be my Acquaintance . . . Our Muses had not quarrelled.'

George Burnett, it should be mentioned, also played a minor role in these quarrels and the final break up. It was Burnett who had carried back the tale about Southey's proposal to retain his own possessions. We hear from Coleridge that after Southey had produced his uncle's letter, Burnett 'sat half-petrified – gaping at the pigmy Virtue of his supposed Giant'. Burnett also put it about that Southey's defection was due to an unwillingness to share his money ; that he had become selfish and mercenary. It was a sorry and sordid end for a plan that had been conceived out of the ingenuous and optimistic ebullience of youth. At last,

towards the end of August, Coleridge moved out of the
house in College Street to a cottage in Clevedon overlooking
the Bristol Channel in preparation for his forthcoming
marriage with Sara Fricker. Southey moved back to Bath.
And although they continued to come into Bristol, they ran
into each other but rarely – and were barely civil to each
other beyond shaking hands.

5

Marriage

IN gradually working himself free of the strong influence of Southey, and in realizing that the Pantisocratic commune was increasingly unlikely, Coleridge had become more settled; he began to deal with the world as it was rather than look forward to an improbable Utopia. In May and June he delivered six lectures on Revealed Religion which show further evidence of his coming to grips with a personal political philosophy. The religious lectures clarify and supplement many of the issues raised in the political lectures of February, and reaffirm the importance he laid on Christian belief in the formation of a healthy society. Yet while he showed signs of a developing social conscience, he was giving fuller rein to his prejudiced attitude towards atheism. The theological lectures are prefaced by an allegory in which Sensuality and the Monster Blasphemy are discovered together in a 'Vast and dusky Cave'. So profound, indeed, was his disgust for the atheist, that he does not even accord him aesthetic experience.[1] In his third lecture he says:

... to a Sensualist and to the Atheist that alone can be beautiful which promises a gratification to the appetite – for of wisdom and benevolence the Atheist denies the very existence. The wine is beautiful to him when it sparkles in the Cup – and the Woman when she moves lasciviously in the Dance but the Rose that bends on its stalk, the Clouds the imbibe the setting sun – these are not beautiful.

Coleridge's attitude towards atheism naturally put him at

variance with the likes of Holcroft and John Thewall. But as much as their tendency to atheism, he objected to the official organizations appealing *to* the people, not for them.[2] Throughout the early months of 1795 he became increasingly convinced that the education of the masses was impossible in their present state of 'demoralization' and 'depravity'. He felt that the corresponding societies were operating unrealistically, that the only effective path to reform and enlightenment was a general conversion of the people to the spirit of Christian morality. It was an attitude that arose from distrust of mass movements, mobs and rioting, of which there had been no lack in the past two years. Each individual must undergo a personal, spiritual reform, before any general amelioration could take place : 'Let us exert over our own hearts a virtuous despotism, and lead our passions in triumph, and then we shall want neither Monarch nor general. If we would have no Nero without, we must place a Caesar within us, and that Caesar must be religion !'[3]

Meanwhile his loathing for the Church of England had intensified, and he denounces them as no better than the Church of Rome : 'Do they not both SELL the Gospel – Nay, nay, they neither sell, nor is it the Gospel – they forcibly exchange Blasphemy for the first fruits, and snatching the scanty Bread from the poor Man's Mouth they cram their lying Legends down his throat.' His central view of the function Christianity in Society was that Christ's precept that all personal property should be rejected was to be taken literally. Even the notion of equalization of property, Coleridge considered unacceptable.

Our Saviour by no means authorizes an Equalization of Property, which in the first place is impracticable for how are we to equalize ? Measuring will not do it – one soil is better than another – and where is the scale to adjust the differences, and balance Quality with Quantity ? and secondly, if it were practicable, it would answer no end, for this Equalization could not continue for a year, and while it continued,

it would only narrow the theatre, and exclude the actors. . . . That
we use money is a proof that we possess individual property, and
Commerce and Manufactures, and while these evils continue, your
own vices will make a government necessary, and it is fit that you
maintain Government and King which are but the Lord lieutenants
of conquered souls.[4]

In this we see a clear dissociation not only from Godwinism but the Priestleian notion that 'all trade and commerce,
all buying and selling, is wrong unless it be to the advantage
of both parties'.[5] In Coleridge's estimation, Priestley's
view was both impracticable and reactionary. At the same
time he found the Unitarian preoccupation with the wrongs
committed against the Dissenters equally untenable, for it
tended to eclipse the general wrongs against the poor as a
whole.

With such independent views it is perhaps a little
surprising that Coleridge should have contemplated
becoming a dissenting minister. Yet it appears that he at
least gave it a trial. Naturally, the only denomination that
suited was the Unitarians, and an experiment was made
at the chapel of the Reverend David Jardine in Bath early in
Coleridge's time at Bristol. Cottle, who is vague about the
date, went along with another friend to give support.

Coleridge, wearing a blue coat and white waistcoat, had
refused to wear the 'hide-all sable gown'. There was a
meagre congregation, and after an 'undevotional prayer' and
some 'somniferously languid' singing, the moment for
announcing the text arrived. Curiosity was excited, Cottle
relates :

With little less than famine in the land our hearts were appalled at
hearing the words, 'When they shall be hungry, they shall fret themselves, and curse their king, and their God, and look upward.' But to
the immense relief of the congregation Coleridge delivered a lecture on
the Corn Laws which he laboured to show were a cruelty to the poor
and the main cause of the prevailing sufferings and popular discontent

Later, at dinner in the local tavern, Coleridge decided that he would like to take the afternoon service as well, and Jardine agreed. This time Coleridge lectured on the Hair Powder Tax, a lecture Cottle had heard before back in Bristol: 'the twice-told tale, even to the ear of friendship, in truth, sounded rather dull !' Neither did the congregation take very kindly to Coleridge's harangue :

Two or three times Mr C looked significantly toward our seat, when, fearful of being thrown off my guard into a smile, I held down my head, from which position I was aroused, when the sermon was about half over, by some gentleman throwing back the door of his pew, and walking out of the Chapel. In a few minutes after, a third door flew open, and the listener escaped !'

Fortunately, at least David Jardine the minister stayed on until the end of the 'sermon'. So ended Coleridge's inaugural chapel service, and the three friends returned to Bristol with a feeling of disappointment: 'Mr C. from the little personal attention paid to him by Mr Jardine; and we, from a dissatisfying sense of a Sunday desecrated.' For the time being Coleridge laid aside his aspiration to become a minister.

Meanwhile, he was becoming more settled in his private life. He had come to terms with his loss of Mary Evans, and he was beginning to find a rewarding relationship with Sara Fricker. Soon after he came to Bristol, probably in March, he bought a new common-place book which came to be known as the *Gutch Notebook*, and this was an early entry :

I mix in life & labour to seem free,
With common persons pleas'd & common things –
While every thought & action tends to thee
And every impulse from thy influence springs.

It has been suggested that this was Coleridge's farewell to Mary Evans. It is equally likely that it aptly expressed the sense of stability he was discovering in spiritual renewal, and it certainly echoes many passages in the lectures expressing the dependence of man on the person of Christ. In any case, two entries later he writes : 'The flames of two candles joined give much stronger light than both of them separate – evid. by a person holding two Candles near his Face, but separate, and then joined in one. Picture of Hymen.' While this might also be a religious reflection suggested by a similar image in Jeremy Taylor's sermons,[6] the reference to Hymen indicates the anticipation of the new strength he would find in his marriage with Sara.

The notebook was to become an essential part of Coleridge's literary work, a kind of workshop in which he freely experimented in verse, gathered ideas, recorded observations, transcribed from his reading, and confided the shaping of his inmost thoughts, alongside jokes, recipes and haphazard financial accounts. It was as if his wide ranging reflections had found an anchor in the pages of a commonplace book, that between its covers he could harness the mercurial activity of his mind.

And as the spring of 1795 slipped into summer his poetry began to express an unfamiliar quality of simplicity, dreaminess and lyricism. Sara figures in most of them. She is 'the chaste-eyed Maiden mild'; 'the dear-loved maid'; 'My pensive Sara !', 'meek daughter in the family of Christ'. His admiration for her is almost entirely associated with Christian purity. And even when he does allow himself a sensual reflection – it is only in a dream closely modelled on Milton's sonnet, 'Methought I saw my late espousèd Saint' – and hastily to be qualified with the purest sentiments :

> My Sara came, with gentlest look divine ;
> Bright shone her eye, yet tender was its beam :
> I felt the pressure of her lip to mine !
> Whispering we went, and Love was all our theme –
> Love pure and spotless, as at first, I deem,
> He sprang from Heaven ! Such joys with Sleep did 'bide,

> That I the living Image of my Dream
> Fondly forgot. Too late I woke, and sigh'd –
> 'O! how shall I behold my Love at eventide!'

These summer poems, many of them relaxed, meditational and in loose blank verse, have a constant theme of music: the flute, with its 'magic spell'; the Eolian harp, with its 'sweet upbraiding'; the 'soft impassion'd' singing voice. And the human voice and musical instruments find their pastoral counterpart in the nightingale's 'soft diversities of tone'; the sky-lark's 'gladdest song'; the moaning of 'sea-breeze, the mimic thunders of the onward surging tides'. There is a preoccupation with sound and motion, in wind, water, sighs, kisses, the beating of the heart, singing and music. Nor is this preoccupation merely a newly discovered harmony: in the 'mountain surges bellowing deep', the 'stormy Midnight howling round', 'diversities of tone', the 'impassion'd voice, correctly wild', we find a Miltonic attempt to encompass many contrarieties of mood. In the finest of these poems, *The Eolian Harp*, this pervasive sense of music and motion reaches an ecstasy of delight:

> And that simplest Lute,
> Placed length-ways in the clasping casement, hark!
> How by the desultory breeze caress'd,
> Like some coy maid half yielding to her lover,
> It pours such sweet upbraiding, as must needs
> Tempt to repeat the wrong! And now, its strings
> Boldlier swept, the long sequacious notes
> Over delicious surges sink and rise,
> Such soft floating witchery of sound
> As twilight Elfins make, when they at eve
> Voyage on gentle gales from Fairy-Land,
> Where Melodies round honey-dropping flowers,
> Footless and wild, like birds of Paradise,
> Nor pause, nor perch, hovering on untam'd wing!

Here he acknowledges the transcendental implications in music – binding the universal and the particular. The possibilities were surely infinite. Through all the differences, inconsistencies, contrasts and contradictions of life and the universe he had experienced a binding principle – through all shades of diversity, from sound to silence, movement to stillness, radiance to darkness. And this discovered unity in diversity had brought a new peace, and a new excitement. Just as his soul, listening to the nightingale in an earlier poem –

> Waked by those strains to thousand phantasies,
> Absorb'd hath ceas'd to listen!

so too as he lies on the midway slope of a hill at noon, in *The Eolian Harp*,

> And tranquil muse upon tranquility;
> Full many a thought uncall'd and undetain'd,
> And many idle flitting phantasies,
> Traverse my indolent and passive brain,
> As wild and various as the random gales
> That swell and flutter on this subject Lute.

If the random diversity could give rise to the tranquillity of unity, so too could the tranquillity of unity give rise to random diversity. Yet the philosopher in him could not resist probing further; the felt experience was not enough. In a manuscript version of *The Eolian Harp* we find this reflection :

> And what if All of animated Life
> Be but as Instruments diversely fram'd
> That tremble into thought, while thro' them breathes
> One infinite and intellectual Breeze?
> And all in different Height so aptly hung,
> That Murmurs indistinct and Bursts sublime,
> Shrill Discords and most soothing Melodies,
> Harmonious from Creation's vast consent –
> Thus *God* would be the universal Soul
> Mechaniz'd matter as th' organic harps
> And each one's Tunes be that, which each calls I.

In the published version the image is severely reduced to this :

> And what if all of animated nature
> Be but organic Harps diversely fram'd,
> That tremble into thought, as o'er them sweeps
> Plastic and vast, one intellectual breeze,
> At once the Soul of each, and God of all?

But perhaps the longer version more clearly demonstrates Coleridge's attempt to reconcile the interpenetration of finite and infinite, the sense in which all natures share in the infinite breeze only differing according to their varying material limitations; the sense in which the animated, the infinite, the 'I', combines with the mechaniz'd matter and the organic – the 'shrill Discords' with 'soothing Melodies'. This fascination is, of course, nothing new in the history of ideas, nor is the explanation in terms of music; but it marks the beginning of one of Coleridge's most passionate quests, the driving force behind his finest poetry, the constant theme of his philosophical speculations. Although he had been strongly influenced by Locke and Hartley over the past year, he was now embarking on the strange adventure of reconciling their restricting materialist philosophy with the realms of the transcendental, in Poetry. What had led him in this new direction is intriguing. We have seen that as a schoolboy he had come under the influence of Plotinus, and it seems extremely likely that his source for Plotinus at that time had been Thomas Taylor. From Taylor's translation he may have acquired his life long absorption with the notion of organic unity in aesthetics; the theme is constant, but perhaps the best definitive formulation was written in 1814 : 'The safest definition, then, of Beauty, as well as the oldest, is that of Pythagoras :

THE REDUCTION OF THE MANY TO ONE – or, as finely expressed by the sublime disciple of Ammonius . . . of which the following may be considered both a paraphrase and a corollary. *The sense of beauty subsists, in the simultaneous intuition of the relation of parts, each to each, and of all to a whole: exciting an immediate and absolute complacency, without inconvenience, therefore, of any interest, sensual or intellectual.*[7]

But undoubtedly the stimulus for Coleridge's enlivened interest in the transcendental during the summer of 1795 was provided by Ralph Cudworth's *True Intellectual System of the Universe* (1678), which he borrowed from the Bristol Library from 15 May to 1 June. Cudworth, a Cambridge Platonist, held the notion of 'one original mind' in which each individual participated – so that 'truths are not multiplied by the diversity of minds which apprehend them; because they are all but ectypal participations of the one, and the same original or archetypal mind and truth'.[8] The importance of Cudworth is that he proceeded from strong *a priori* standpoint, and upheld the theory of universals, but probably the most effective antidote to Hartley was an emphasis on the 'self-active' character of the human mind, which, as Professor Kathleen Coburn has suggested, 'helped to release Coleridge from associationism and necessitarianism'.[9]

But there were other new influences at work, too. Late in August Coleridge had taken the Clevedon cottage. It was a place of retirement in surroundings of great beauty – 'The prospect around us is perhaps more *various* than any in the kingdom,' Coleridge wrote to Poole. ' – Mine Eye gluttonizes. – The Sea – the distant Islands ! – the opposite Coasts ! – I shall assuredly write Rhymes – let the nine Muses prevent it, if they can – .'[10] Earlier, in March, he had written to George Dyer :

It is melancholy to think, that the best of us are liable to be shaped & coloured by surrounding Objects – and a demonstrative proof, that Man was not made to live in Great Cities ! Almost all the physical Evil in the World depends on the existence of moral Evil – and the long-continued contemplation of the latter does not tend to meliorate the human heart. – The pleasures, which we receive from rural beauties, are of little Consequence compared with the Moral Effect of these pleasures – beholding constantly the Best possible we at last become ourselves the best possible. In the country, all around us smile Good and Beauty – and the Images of this divine καλοκάγαθόν are miniatured on the mind of the beholder, as a Landscape on a Convex Mirror.[11]

The Hartleian determinism is familiar enough, but the beneficence of 'rural beauties' is a new departure. Absorbing the principles of Christianity, then, was not the only path to amelioration. Already there is the attitude of mind and feeling that would find its counterpart in Wordsworth. Coleridge had read Wordsworth's *An Evening Walk* and *Descriptive Sketches* in the summer of 1793. 'Seldom, if ever,' wrote Coleridge some years later, 'was the emergence of an original poetic genius above the literary horizon so evidently announced.' And in *Lines written at Shurton Bars*, during this summer of 1795, he had paid tribute to Wordsworth in the lines :

> I mark the glow-worm, as I pass,
> Move with 'green radiance' through the grass,
> An emerald of light.

In a footnote to the poem he writes : 'The expression "green radiance" is borrowed from Mr Wordsworth, a Poet whose versification is occasionally harsh and his diction too frequently obscure ; but whom I deem unrivalled among the writers of the present day in manly sentiment, novel imagery, and vivid colouring.'[12] And it was now, in the summer of 1795, that Coleridge met Wordsworth for the first time. Wordsworth had turned up in Bristol in August to stay with his friends the Pinneys. It is not certain whether the two poets met in Coleridge's house on College Street, or whether it was at one of Coleridge's lectures ; but later, in October, Wordsworth wrote, 'Coleridge was at Bristol part of the time I was there, I saw but little of him. I wished indeed to have seen more – his talent appears to me very great.'[13] Wordsworth was also impressed with Southey's 'power of mind', a verdict he was later to retract on reading the preface to his *Joan of Arc*, which he pronounced 'a very conceited performance' proving its author 'certainly a coxcomb'. Wordsworth also met at this time the serviceable Cottle who would prove to be as helpful to Wordsworth as he had been to Southey and Coleridge.

At the end of this summer of new insights and lyrical poetry came Coleridge's marriage with Sara Fricker. They were married on 4 October in the church of St Mary's Red Cliff – which put Coleridge in mind of Chatterton, the hero of his youth – and they retired to the cottage at Clevedon. It was situated at the extremity of the village, one storey high with a small garden and a tall rose tree that peeped in at the bedroom window. The marriage seems to have brought Coleridge much happiness initially. She was the woman, he told Thomas Poole, whom he loved best of all created beings. To Southey he wrote, 'I love and I am beloved, and I am happy!' And the cottage at Clevedon was no less a part of that happiness. *The Eolian Harp* gives us a glimpse of the young couple in their idyllic pastoral setting:

> My pensive Sara! thy soft cheek reclined
> Thus on mine arm, most soothing sweet it is
> To sit beside our Cot, our Cot o'ergrown
> With white-flower'd Jasmin, and the broad-leav'd Myrtle,
> (Meet emblems they of Innocence and Love!)
> And watch the clouds, that late were rich with light,
> Slow saddening round, and mark the star of eve
> Serenely brilliant (such should Wisdom be)
> Shine opposite! How exquisite the scents
> Snatch'd from yon bean-field! and the world *so* hush'd!
> The stilly murmur of the distant Sea
> Tells us of silence.

It was a strangely felicitous outcome after Coleridge's former rejection of Sara; but was the prospect so serene?

Even at this time there are ominous hints that it might not
be so. Following on the philosophical passage in *The
Eolian Harp*, 'And what if all of animated nature ...'
there is this reflection :

> But thy more serious eye a mild reproof
> Darts, O belovéd Woman! nor such thoughts
> Dim and unhallow'd dost thou not reject,
> And biddest me walk humbly with my God.
> Meek Daughter in the family of Christ!
> Well hast thou said and holily disprais'd
> These shapings of the unregenerate mind;
> Bubbles that glitter as they rise and break
> On vain Philosophy's aye-babbling spring.

Coleridge's sentiment here is generous indeed, but
hopelessly out of character : how long could he sustain a
subordinate attitude in the face of Sara's 'mild reproof' of
his 'vain Philosophy'? Sober too, is his comment in August
1795 '(this last) twelvemonth ... has improved my head
and heart whatever effect it may have had on my happiness'.
Moreover, Mrs Sandford, in her *Thomas Poole and His
Friends*, talks of rumours doing the rounds by the 'un-
conventional manner' in which Coleridge and Southey were
constantly seen walking about Bristol with the Fricker girls
– and the impression that Pantisocracy meant a system of
things which dispensed with the marriage tie.[14] She suggests
that Coleridge contracted his marriage when he did to
dispose of such imputations against Sara's character.

But these are no more than hints, and it seems that they
settled down quickly to a happy life together, although they
had to send to Cottle for some last minute household things :
kitchen utensils, one pair of candlesticks, two mats, assorted
spices, a Bible, and, of course, a pair of slippers. 'It happened
in this case,' observed the useful Cottle, '... where a duty
devolves equally on two ; both neglect it'.[15] Cottle came
down the day after the marriage and found to his astonishment that he was greeted 'with hearty congratulations'

instead of wine and cake. Noticing with some disgust that the parlour was only whitewashed he sent a man down on returning to Bristol, 'with a few pieces of sprightly paper, to tarnish the half immaculate sittingroom walls'.

We hear of Coleridge and Sara writing verses together, although Mrs Coleridge later claimed that she wrote little of the 'beautiful little poetic epistle' ascribed to her – *The Silver Thimble*, published in 1796. George Burnett now lived with them and Coleridge recorded the division of household duties in his notebook. The Pantisocratic dream might remain unfulfilled – but he intended putting some of its principles to the test.

Meanwhile the break with Southey became final. In November Southey prepared to depart for Lisbon to stay with his uncle, but before leaving he contracted a secret marriage with Edith Fricker, and his estrangement with Coleridge was now complicated by the fact that he had become Sara's brother-in-law. The marriage was an act of duty and principle consonant with Southey's strict standards. 'Why did I marry, do you ask?' he wrote to Grosvenor Bedford. 'It is Grosvenor a satisfaction to myself. If the tongue of malice should whisper that I have forsaken her (and calumny has been busy with me) there is now an answer that will make it dumb. And what is more of consequence – if I should not return alive – she has a claim upon the protection of those I am now satisfying – for "the bitter little that would then be left of life". '[16] After the ceremony the couple parted, Edith tying the wedding ring about her neck to be hidden out of sight until Southey should return from Portugal. Coleridge was not present at the wedding; in fact the day before, he had passed Southey in the street 'and, unsaluted and unsaluting, passed by the man to whom for almost a year I had told my last thoughts when I closed my eyes, and the first when I awoke'. That very day Coleridge had, in fact, been composing a letter of 'farewell' to Southey: a 5,000 word

stream of hysterical indignation and poisoned eloquence –
it was probably the closest Coleridge would ever come to an
expression of hatred. The letter – when it reached Southey –
and one hopes he did not read it on his wedding day – could
not have failed to wound deeply, for its intention was to
destroy any self-respect he might have thought he enjoyed in
Coleridge's eyes. Coleridge knew exactly where Southey
was most vulnerable, and he plunged in the knife and twisted
it again and again. Recounting the history of their relationship, Coleridge enlists a series of indictments, punctuated by
moral exhortations :

> You are *lost* to *me*, because you are lost to Virtue. . . . My hand
> trembles when I think what a series of falsehood and duplicity I am
> about to bring before the Conscience of a Man, who has dared to
> write me, that 'his conduct has been uniformly open' . . . O Selfish,
> money-loving Man! what Principle have you not given up? . . . O
> God! that *such a mind* should fall in love with that low dirty, gutter-
> grubbing Trull, WORLDLY PRUDENCE !! . . . If there be in nature a
> Situation perilous to Honesty, it is this – when a man has not heart to
> *be*, yet lusts to *seem*, virtuous.

Thus raged Coleridge at the back of his departing erst-
while friend ; but his final words were surely the cruellest
revenge possible for the sanctimonious sermons he had
stomached from Southey about duty and virtue over the
past year :

> May God Almighty bless & preserve you! And may you live to
> know, and feel, and acknowlege that unless we accustom ourselves to
> meditate adoringly on him, the Source of all Virtue, no virtue can be
> permanent.[17]

Southey, for one, now knew to his cost how thoroughly
unpleasant it was to get on the wrong side of Coleridge.

It is easy to interpret the end of the Southey relationship
as an instance of Coleridge's inability to maintain a close
relationship. Coleridge was sincere, generous and deeply

affectionate in his friendships, and if he erred it was possibly because he hoped for too much : he was certainly not the man to measure friendship by its palpable returns, by constant proofs of gratitude and loyalty, and he hoped that others would love him in the same way. As he once wrote to a friend, '... believe me to be what you believe me'. And again, 'there is that within me which passeth all verbal professions'.[18] But if in this first important friendship of his manhood he was continually weighed in the balance, badgered and bullied into keeping within the strict and narrow code Southey reserved for his intimates, it was the price Coleridge had to pay for his dependence on Southey. Yet it was a severe blow for Coleridge at the end of the summer of 1794 when he realized that Southey did not love him sufficiently to trust that he would write when he could. 'Surely had I written to *you* the *first* Letter you directed to me at Cambridge, I *would* not have believed that you *could* have received it without immediately answering.' As it was, he admitted his failings and pleaded for pity rather than indignation. The friendship was probably damaged from that first rebuke, and it is unlikely that Coleridge ever forgave Southey for his attitude towards the engagement with Sara Fricker. As he wrote to Charles Morgan in 1808 : 'O had I health and youth and were what I once was – but I played the fool and cut the throat of my own happiness ; of my own genius, of my utility, in compliment to the merest phantom of over-strained honour – O, Southey, what an unthinking man were you, and an unjust.'

It was a harsh verdict, and the spontaneity and generosity of Coleridge's nature as contrasted with Southey's coldness and inflexibility makes it tempting to endorse it. Yet Southey was the younger man, and if he erred in high-handedness it only reflected the extent to which Coleridge was unwisely subservient to him. Perhaps more than most Coleridge was conscious of his own helpless and fatal penchant for transforming a friend into more than he

5

could ever be. As he admitted to Southey some years later :
'I said to myself — O when wilt thou be cured of the idle
trick of letting thy Wishes make Romances out of men's
characters?'[19]

6

The Watchman

WITH marital responsibilities facing him, the matter of finding a suitable career now became urgent. Joseph Cottle was offering a guinea for every hundred lines of poetry he could write, which was helpful; but he needed something more substantial. An earlier idea of starting a provincial magazine he now rejected – largely because Southey had been connected with the scheme : he also felt that a magazine would be a hazardous financial enterprise. For the immediate future he planned to complete *Imitations* of the Latin poets – a work which he hoped would give him a sound reputation ; and to do this he thought he might return to Cambridge and take lodgings in the town with Sara. But in the long term view he was nourishing a new idea. Several days after his marriage he wrote to Thomas Poole about 'my school plan', and the desire to 'publish proposals for a school etc.' The career of schoolmastering ran strongly in the Coleridge family ; his father had run a school in Ottery, and George had now followed in his footsteps. Earlier in the year Coleridge had thought of becoming a tutor in the family of the Earl of Buchan in Edinburgh – a plan he had been forced to reject after the confirmation of his engagement to Sara, and the lingering possibility of the Pantisocracy scheme.

Born into an educated but impoverished family, Coleridge was in a difficult position. The careers open to him were restricted to the Church, the university, schoolmastering, and the law : yet even the last of these might have proved too much of a financial burden. With his political convictions, Coleridge felt alienated from the very institutions which made any of these careers possible, although as a private tutor, or as proprietor of his own school, he might have felt sufficiently free to maintain a sense of integrity and self-respect. Unlike Lamb he seemed unable to write in his spare time and take a humble clerical position which would afford financial security. Coleridge wanted more than this : he was seeking a role beyond that of writer ; a role which would actively involve him in the amelioration of society ; yet that very society exerted pressures which restricted his prospects. Moreover, his deep religious convictions, and, possibly the restraints of his down-at-heel but 'respectable' family, who always induced feelings of guilt in him, prevented him from breaking out altogether and taking his chances with the mainstream of the reformers who might have been glad of his talents. To play a role in education then, might be the answer, provided he was sufficiently independent. But history intervened to send him, perhaps somewhat recklessly, in a new direction.

On 26 October 1795 there was a mass meeting in the field behind Copenhagen House, Islington, to protest against the war with France. Three days later George III was hissed and booed on his way to open Parliament, and the window where he was seated was shattered by a stone or bullet. On the way back from Parliament the royal carriage once again ran the gauntlet of an angry mob, which according to Parson Woodforde was 'composed of the most violent & lowest Democrats' crying 'Bread ! Peace ! No Pitt !' Later, when the king alighted, his carriage was almost destroyed. If the government had been acting nervously over the past year, they were now frantic. Seizing on the Islington meeting as the probable cause for the attack on the King's person, a proclamation was issued on 5 November to urge the peace officers to exercise vigilance in guarding against seditious and treasonable persons and meetings. The day after,

Grenville introduced into the Lords an Act for the Safety
and Preservation of His Majesty's person and Government
against Treasonable and Seditious Practices and Attempts,
which came to be known as the Treasonable Practices Act.
Even more severe measures were tabled when Pitt introduced into the Commons an Act for the More Effectually
Preventing Seditious Meetings and Assemblies, or the Con-
vention Bill. In the prevailing atmosphere of suspicion
and repression the reform movement stood in peril of being
entirely suppressed.

Coleridge's way was now clear. The battle for civil
liberties, for freedom of speech and freedom of the press,
was on, and he took the platform with courage and
impetuous confidence. On 17 November there was a meeting
of the citizens of Bristol at the Guildhall, ostensibly to
congratulate the king on his escape ; but a large group at the
meeting wished to register their protest over the war against
France. The London *Star* reported : 'After a considerable
time spent in fruitlessly calling *"Mr Mayor! Mr Mayor!"* in
a tone of voice, and with that sweetness of emphasis which
would have fascinated the attention even of a Robespierre ;
Mr Coleridge began the most elegant, the most pathetic,
and the most sublime Address that was ever heard, perhaps,
within the walls of that building.' After saying ' "Though
the war . . . may take much from the property of the rich,
it left them much ; but a PENNY taken from the pocket of a
poor man might deprive him of a dinner" ', Coleridge was
authoritatively stopped 'by the countenance of some person
on the bench'.[1] Three days later the anti-war group who had
asserted themselves at the meeting convened again, this
time to send a petition to Parliament against the Two Bills.
They agreed unanimously and signed a petition to be for-
warded to London. Coleridge meanwhile addressed a
meeting with a lecture entitled *Against the Two Bills*, and
the text was later incorporated in a pamphlet entitled *The
Plot Discovered*. 'All political controversy is at an end,' he

proclaimed. 'Those sudden breezes and noisy gusts, which purified the atmosphere they disturbed, are hushed to death like silence. The cadaverous tranquility of despotism will succeed the generous order and graceful indiscretions of freedom – the black moveless pestilential vapour of slavery will be inhaled at every pore.' He proceeded to sum up the situation :

> There are four things, which being combined constitute despotism.
> 1. The confusion of the executive with the legislative branches.
> 2. The direct or indirect exclusion of all popular interference.
> 3. A large military force kept separate from the people.
> 4. When the punishments of state offenders are determined and heavy, but what constitutes state-offences left indefinite, that is, dependent on the will of the minister, or the interpretation of the judge. Let the present Bills pass, and these four things will be *all* found in the British Government.

If Coleridge had hesitated about the course his life should take earlier in October, he now had no doubts. His mission was obvious, he must assume the mantle of the champion of liberty ; and like so many youthful reformers, before and since, as the editor of his own magazine. The driving force to teach and to write would come together in the production of a periodical that would provide a commentary on the current political situation, and ensure the voice of freedom. And consonant with the 'small band' of philosophers, supervising and guiding the affairs of men – he would call his magazine *Watchman*.

But it was no easy matter to run a magazine in these times. The very Acts against which he sought to stir up public opinion would put him in constant danger of prosecution ; if he wished the publication to have anything more than a parochial distribution he must travel far and wide for subscribers ; he would be obliged, moreover, to set off on that financial tightrope that is the lot off small periodical proprietors. Most ominous of all he would be forced to remove

himself from the tranquillity he had found in retirement at
Clevedon. The work on the *Imitations* would be put aside,
and also his *Poems* which Cottle had hoped to publish at an
early date and for which he had already received payment.
The longsuffering Cottle claims not to have been daunted
by the further delays – 'but they were not so acceptable to
the printer who grievously complained that his "types, and
his leads ; and his formes, were locked up", week after week,
to his great detriment'.[2] But duty called, and Coleridge's
Reflections On Having Left a Place of Retirement expresses
how seriously he viewed his new task :

> Ah! quiet Dell! dear Cot, and Mount sublime!
> I was constrained to quit you. Was it right,
> While my unnumber'd bretheren toil'd and bled,
> That I should dream away the entrusted hours
> On rose-leaf beds, pampering the coward heart
> With feelings all to delicate for use? . . .
> I therefore go and join head, heart and hand,
> Active and firm, to fight the bloodless fight
> Of Science, Freedom and the Truth in Christ.

The *Watchman* was born late in December in the Rummer
Tavern in Bristol, where Coleridge gathered together in
'dextrous secrecy' a founding group of subscribers, 'sundry
Philanthropists and Anti-polemists', 'to determine on the
size, price and time of publishing with all other pre-
liminaries'.[3] Cottle, who was to become the mainstay of the
business side of the periodical – generous in gifts of paper,
financial support and time – was not invited to the first
meeting, and Coleridge was obliged to write him a letter of
apology and explanation :

My dear friend,
    I am fearful that you felt hurt at my not mentioning to you the
proposed 'Watchman', and from my not requesting you to attend the
meeting. My dear friend, my reasons were these. All who met were
expected to become subscribers to a fund; I know there would be

enough without you, and I knew, and felt, how much money had
been drawn away from you lately.

God Almighty love you!

S.T.C.[4]

Chief amongst these subscribers was Josiah Wade ; and it
was to Wade that Coleridge frequently wrote when he embarked on a tour of the Midlands to collect subscriptions.
But first, more subscriptions were sought in Bristol – Cottle,
energetic as ever in Coleridge's interests, collecting 250,
and another bookseller, Reed, 120.[5] A 'Flaming prospectus'
was published for the Midlands tour in which the people
were offered a 'Miscellany by S.T.Coleridge, author of
Addresses to the People and *A Plot Discovered'*. It would
contain domestic and foreign news, parliamentary reports,
essays and poetry of political interest. It would be published
every eighth day to exempt it from the stamp-tax and avoid
contributing to the war. There would be no advertisements,
and its thirty-two pages would cost only fourpence. Its chief
objectives, Coleridge proclaimed, would be cooperation
with the Whig Club in their efforts to repeal the Two Bills,
and with 'the PATRIOTIC SOCIETIES, for obtaining a Right
of Suffrage general and frequent'. Above all the Prospectus
claimed that the periodical would be 'a faithful WATCHMAN,
to proclaim the State of the Political Atmosphere, and
preserve Freedom and her Friends from the attacks of
Robbers and Assassins ! !'[6]

Coleridge set off from Bristol on 9 January with letters of
introduction and a heap of prospectuses. His first letter to
Josiah Wade was humorous and energetic : He was evidently
enjoying his new extrovert role. Climbing into the Worcester coach, he encountered his first amusing episode :

We were five in number, and twenty five in quantity – The
moment I entered the Coach I stumbled on a huge projection which
might be called a Belly with the same propriety that you might name
Mount Atlas a Molehill – Heavens ! that a man should be un-
conscionable enough to enter a stage-coach, who would want elbow-

room if he were walking on Salisbury Plain!!! This said Citizen Squelch-gut was a most violent Aristocrat.[7]

Worcester he found a beautiful city, but the Aristocrats were so numerous and the influence of the clergy so extensive that he doubted whether he could persuade any bookseller to publish the work. He proceeded to Birmingham where he was more successful, and here he preached at the invitation of John Edwards the Unitarian minister of the New Meeting. Editor, and now travelling preacher, Coleridge was indeed living out the ideals of the 'elect', although, as Cottle observed, the idea to preach was shrewd, for it was the nearest way to collect subscribers. But the service at Birmingham gave rise to a fit of scruples, for before entering the pulpit Coleridge suffered himself to be 'overpersuaded' to wear a gown, symbol of the whore of Babylon. He was grievously conscience-stricken, but rationalized that since his sermon had such a political tendency, and since the congregation was of all sorts – 'Arians, Trinitarians etc' – he might have shocked a 'multitude of prejudices'. He would not, he assured Wade, do it in a place where he intended to preach often. 'I have that within me,' confessed Coleridge, 'which makes it difficult for me to say, No! repeatedly to a number of persons who seem uneasy & anxious.'[8] He preached twice in Birmingham, performing the whole service both morning and afternoon before a congregation of fourteen hundred people. His sermons were largely extempore, and *'preciously peppered with Politics'*. 'My *Sermons*', wrote Coleridge, 'spread a sort of sanctity over my *Sedition*.'[9] Writing of this phase in his life in the *Biographia*, he reminisced about the first man he tried to persuade to become a subscriber :

He was a tall dingy man, in whom length was so predominant over breadth that he might almost have been borrowed for a foundry poker. O that face! a face κατ' ἔμφασιν! I have it before me at this moment. The lank, black, twine-like hair, *pingui-nitescent*, cut in a

5*

straight line along the black stubble of his thick gunpowder eyebrows, that looked like a scorched after-math from a last week's shaving. His coat collar behind in perfect unison, both of colour and lustre, with the coarse yet glib cordage that I suppose he called his hair, and which with a bend inward at the nape of the neck (the only approach to flexure in his whole figure) slunk in behind his waistcoat; while the countenance lank, dark, very hard, and with strong perpendicular furrows, gave me a dim notion of someone looking at me through a used gridiron, all soot, grease and iron!

Coleridge argued, described, promised and prophesied; and at length his potential subscriber spoke :

'And what, Sir,' he said, after a short pause, 'might the cost be? 'Only four-pence,' (O! how I felt the anti-climax, the abysmal bathos of that four-pence)! 'Only four-pence, Sir, each number, to be published on every eighth day.' 'That comes to a deal of money at the end of a year. And how much did you say there was to be for the money?' 'Thirty-two pages, sir! large octavo, closely printed.' 'Thirty and two pages? Bless me, why except what I does in a family way on the Sabbath, that's more than I ever reads, Sir! all the year round. I am as great a one as any man in Brummagem, sir! for liberty and truth and all them sort of things, but as to this (no offence, I hope, Sir) I must beg to be excused.'

After being obliged to be the 'figurante of the circle' in whatever group he happened to find himself, he went down with a violent cold in his head and limbs and was confined to his bed for two days before leaving the city with about a hundred subscriptions. He then went on to Derby where he stayed for a weekend, and amongst the 'curiosities' of the city he found Dr Erasmus Darwin, the physician and author of *The Botanic Garden.*

[Dr Darwin, Coleridge reported back to Wade] possesses, perhaps, a greater range of knowledge than any other man in Europe, and is the most inventive of philosophical men. He thinks in a *new* train on all subjects except religion. He bantered me on the subject of religion. I heard all his arguments, and told him that it was infinitely consoling to me, to find that the arguments which so great a man adduced against the existence of a God and the evidences of revealed religion were such as had startled me at fifteen, but had become the objects of my smile at twenty. Not one new objection – not even an ingenious one. He boasted that he had never read one book in defence of *such stuff*, but he had read all the works of infidels![10]

Summing up his total impression of the Doctor, he later said, 'He was like a pigeon picking up peas, and afterwards voiding them with excremental additions.'

On reaching Nottingham he was overcome once again with weariness : 'Ah, what a weary way ! My poor crazy ark has been tossed to and fro on an ocean of business, and I long for the Mount Ararat on which it is to rest.' He was entertained by all the 'first families' and 'marvellously caressed',

> but to tell you the truth [he wrote to Wade], I am quite home-sick – aweary of this long long absence from Bristol. – I was at the *Ball*, last night – and saw the most numerous collection of handsome men & Women, that I ever did in one place – but alas ! the faces of Strangers are but moving Portraits – and far from my comfortable little cottage I feel as if I were in the long damp Gallery of some Nobleman's House, amused with the beauty or variety of the Paintings, but shivering with cold, and melancholy from loneliness.[11]

And it was just as well that he expressed his distaste for the Ball and the beautiful people at it, for the following week a letter came from Bristol reporting that Mrs Coleridge, now pregnant, had been in bad health.

But Nottingham afforded at least one amusing incident. A friend of Coleridge's, a Mr Fellowes, happened to give a prospectus to an Aristocrat, who glancing at the motto – 'That All may know the Truth, and that the Truth may make us free' – said, 'A *Seditious* beginning !'

'Sir' ! said Mr Fellowes, 'the motto is quoted from another Author.'

'Poo !' said the Aristocrat. 'What Odds is it whether he wrote it himself or quoted it from any *other seditious Dog*?'

'Please,' replied Fellowes, 'to look into the 32nd (verse of the 8th) Chapter of John, and you will find, sir, that that *seditious Dog* was JESUS CHRIST!'

He then proceeded to Sheffield, writing as he went the lines *On Observing a Blossom On The First Of February*:

> Sweet flower! that peeping from thy russet stem
> Unfoldest timidly, (for in strange sort
> This dark, frieze-coated, hoarse, teeth-chattering month
> Hath borrow'd Zephyr's voice, and gazed upon thee
> With blue voluptuous eye) alas, poor Flower!
> These are but flatteries of the faithless year.

He was well received in Sheffield, but there was a snag. James Montgomery, the editor of the *Iris*, one of the liberal papers of the provinces, was in prison for libel. His friends felt that the presence of another paper might injure Montgomery's, so Coleridge gracefully withdrew. He then went on to Manchester, and from there to Lichfield where he seems to have done well. He was then due to come south to London to make the necessary arrangements for a publisher there, but Sara's illness, and probably his exhaustion, brought him swiftly home. Wade and Allen took over the London publishing arrangements, and advertisements were placed in the *Morning Chronicle* and the *Star*.

So Coleridge returned to Bristol to find Sara, whose pregnancy was going badly, living with her mother on Red Cliff Hill. He moved in with them, and immediately descended into a mood of despondency and remorse. For he found himself suddenly responsible not only for his wife, but his mother-in-law, a young brother-in-law and George Burnett. Sara groaned and complained without ceasing, and was hourly expected to miscarry; his mother-in-law, also ill, was daily expected to die; the prospect of dire poverty, starvation even, seemed to hover over the family – not altogether an exaggerated anxiety, for food was still at exorbitant famine prices, and the prisons were full of debtors.

So Coleridge became the victim of one of the writer's greatest enemies : '. . . my happiest moments for composition are broken in on by the reflection of – I *must* make haste – I am too late – I am already months behind ! I have received my pay before hand – O way-ward and desultory Spirit of Genius ! ill canst thou brook a task-master ! The tenderest touch from the hand of *Obligation* wounds thee, like a scourge of Scorpions !'[12] It was in these 'brain-crazing' circumstances that Coleridge prepared the first number of the *Watchman* and completed his first edition of the *Poems*, frequently being obliged to take to the fields for the tranquillity necessary for composition.[13] And in this 'quickset hedge of embarrassments', with a 'cold thick darkness' lying before him, with a lapse even in his strong trust in divine providence, Coleridge took to the consolation of drugs.

On 12 March he wrote to John Edwards, the Unitarian minister who had entertained him in Birmingham : 'Such has been my situation for this last fortnight – I have been obliged to take Laudanum almost every night.' It is the first mention Coleridge makes of using drugs as a tranquillizer rather than an analgesic. In 1791, shortly after arriving at Jesus College, he had suffered violent attacks of rheumatism – probably a recurrence of the condition brought on by his night out in the open as a child ; he had reported the illness to his brother George, adding this comment : 'Opium never used to have any disagreeable effects on me – but it has upon many.' This implies that he had probably used opium in the past for similar attacks, and we know that he had suffered a particularly severe bout of rheumatic fever when at Christ's Hospital. It is difficult to estimate how often, and in what quantities, Coleridge was taking the drug at this time, but we know for certain that later in the year, during an attack of neuralgia, he took between '60 & 70 drops of Laudanum'. With such a large tolerance, and in view of the continual domestic miseries of 1796, and the onset of tell-tale health complaints, it seems likely that the drug was taking a strong hold during this year.

And as spring approached, things did not improve. There were problems with the printers, problems with distribution, problems with George Burnett – whose political reports had to be rewritten. Sara's pregnancy sickness seemed to get worse, and on one occasion both she and Coleridge were convinced that she had miscarried – only to discover that she was as big and as pregnant as ever as the days went by. But the train of misery reached its climax at the beginning of May.

My house is at present a house of Mourning. My Wife's Mother has *lived dying* these last six weeks, and she is not yet dead – & the Husband of my Wife's Sister, Robert Lovell . . . died on Tuesday Morning of a putrid fever, & has left an Infant & a Widow. All Monday Night I sate up *with her* – she was removed to the Kitchen, the furthest room in the House from her Husband's Bed-chamber – there being a Court-yard between the two. – It was, you know a very windy night – but his loud, deep, unintermitted groans mingled audibly with the wind, & whenever the wind dropt, they were very horrible to hear, & drove my poor young Sister-in-law frantic. I prayed by her with fervor & very frequently – it soothed her with almost miraculous consolation – At one o'clock the Clock in the Kitchen went down – 'Ah !' (said she) 'it is stopt – Now it clicked & told the hour & did all it's Maker willed it to do – and now it is stopped.' – (A long pause) 'O God ! O God ! my poor Love will stop' – . – Here her agonies became wild – I hastened out, knocked up a Chairman, & had her conveyed to my House – . . . With regard to my own affairs they are as bad, as the most Trinitarian Anathemizer, or rampant Philo-despot could wish in the moment of cursing . . . Meantime Mrs Coleridge asks about baby-linen & anticipates the funeral expenses of her poor Mother – 14

It seems extraordinary that Coleridge managed to proceed with the *Watchman* in spite of these setbacks. Naturally, he must have felt obliged to the many friends and new acquaintances who had invested so much time and money in the scheme. But later, in the *Biographia*, he explained that a compulsion towards duty led him to abandon all self-interest ; that he was so 'completely hag-ridden by the fear of being influenced by self motives, that to know a mode of conduct to be the dictate of *prudence* was a sort of presumptive proof to my feelings, that the contrary was the dictate of *duty*'.

That the *Watchman* would not fulfil all the brave promises laid out in the prospectus was not entirely due to the miserable circumstances in which its author now languished. Between the time that it was planned and its publication there were important changes in political affairs that robbed the periodical of much of its point and sting. Early in December of 1795 Pitt announced that the king was prepared to enter into negotiations to end the war with France. Meanwhile the Whig Club met to deliberate ways of repealing the Two Bills, and rescue freedom of speech and of the press. In February there was still no apparent improvement between France and England, and Pitt was equivocating about the precise moves that had been made towards a peace settlement. Yet the very anticipation of an end to the war had taken much of the momentum out of the present movement, and with it the agitation against the Two Bills. In the first number of the *Watchman* Coleridge actually makes a swift *volte-face* in order to meet the new mood, saying that the Two Bills, repressive as they were upon constitutional freedoms, 'will not have been entirely useless if they should render the language of political publications more cool and guarded, or even confine us for a while to the teaching of first principles, or the diffusion of that general knowledge which should be the basis or substratum of politics'.[15] Parliamentary reform, also an objective heralded in the prospectus, received only scanty treatment, probably because Coleridge had little interest in the forms of government as such.[16]

In view of the fact that Coleridge was running the *Watchman* almost singlehanded it is surprising how many topics it managed to cover : from the permanent barracking of troops, to the abolition of the slave trade, from the Irish question, to the relief of poverty. Yet his most constant theme was France, 'the nation of patriots'. Convinced that the continuance of the war and the atrocities in France were the result of Pitt's base reactionary politics, Coleridge tended to regard the French with benevolence. For Coleridge, patriotism took on a special meaning that transcended nationalism. In an essay entitled 'Modern Patriotism' in *Watchman* No. III, he explains : 'If I might presume so far, I would inform *how* you might become a Patriot. Your *heart* must believe that the good of the whole is the greatest possible good of each individual : that *therefore* it is your *duty* to be just, because it is your *interest*.'[17] This extended notion of 'patriotism' allowed Coleridge to praise the French when they rebuffed the British war aims, especially when such aims consisted in fomenting further rebellion in France in the hopes that the revolution would collapse, he also applauds French resistance to British attempts to destroy the French economy, and elsewhere actually praises French prowess at sea.

Yet Coleridge's shouldering of so much of the burden also resulted in the paper's rather idiosyncratic flavour, which might have been avoided had there been more cor-respondents and something approaching an editorial board. There were essays on such subjects as 'The Maypole – as a type of Liberty Tree'; and a 'New Mode of Warfare', in which Coleridge recommends the substitution of cockfight-ing for real battles. But above all there was the essay on 'Fasts' in which he scoffs at the Church's practice of fast days in order to make the point that a meal of an upper class per-son on such a day would be a feast for a poor man. The essay produced a stern reaction from the more pious of his readers – who resented the frivolous tone in a religious theme. He claims to have lost five hundred subscribers as a result.

Most of the news items Coleridge drew from the London

newspapers – notably the *Morning Chronicle* and the *Star* because of their sympathetic politics, but also from the *Gazetteer* and the *Morning Post* – and even pro-government papers, the *Oracle*, and *The Times*.[18] In spite of his promise that he would give news unadulterated with political comment Coleridge succumbed at once to editorial intervention, particularly by employing the devices of capitals, italics and exclamation marks. Good in terms of wide national and foreign coverage, there was an absence of local news that tended to vex the large number of Midland subscribers; at the same time he opened himself to the accusation of being a 'Newspaper-paragraph-thief' by a scathing anonymous correspondent.

Like most magazines of its kind the *Watchman* was doomed to run for a short time, then disappear under a heap of debts and disillusionment. Early in May, on the day that the ninth number was published, Coleridge wrote to Poole:

It is not pleasant, Thomas Poole! to have worked 14 weeks for nothing – *for nothing* – nay – to have given the Public in addition to that toil five & 40 pounds! – When I began the Watchman, I had forty pounds worth of paper *given me* – yet *with this* I shall not have received a farthing at the end of the Quarter of the Year ... In short, my tradesman's Bills for the Watchman, including what Paper I have bought since the seventh number, the Printing, &c – amount to exactly five pounds more than the whole amount of my receipts.[19]

Yet there was a deeper disillusionment towards the end. As can be seen in the Wickham-Barthélemy correspondence in numbers VII and VIII. It became clear that France was not all she seemed to be. The British Government, having attempted negotiations with France, was rebuffed. This coincided with restrictions being placed on assemblies and the press in France, not unlike the Two Bills which Coleridge had so vehemently deplored in England. Later he would write to his friend Benjamin Flower of the *Cambridge Intelligencer*:

'Indeed, I am out of heart with the French. In one of the numbers of my Watchman I wrote 'a remonstrance to the French Legislators': it contain'd *my* politics, & the splendid Victories of the French since that time have produced no alterations in them. I am tired of reading butcheries and altho' I should be unworthy the name of Man, if I did not feel my Head & Heart awefully interested in the final Event, yet, I confess, my Curiosity is worn out with regard to the particulars of the Process.'[20]

It is likely too that the fate of the *Watchman* describes a characteristic contour in Coleridge's activities; for he seemed to throw himself into energetic extrovert activity for a while — only to retreat into retirement after a period to take stock of his position. There is a poem in the first number which aptly describes this process — 'To a Young Lady. With a Poem on the French Revolution.' It is addressed to Sara in the *Watchman*, but he had originally dedicated it to Ann Brunton in 1794. He begins by describing the sense of gentleness and pity with which he responds to even one natural death:

> No knell that toll'd, but fill'd my anxious eye,
> And suffering Nature wept that *one* should die.

He then proceeds to describe the effect that the war for freedom has upon him.

> Then EXULTATION wak'd the patriot fire
> And swept the wilder hand th' Alcaean lyre:
> Red from the tyrants' wound I shook the lance,
> And strode in joy the reeking plains of France.

But after the fierce activity of political conflict the need for contemplation and retirement reasserts itself:

> In ghastly horror lie th' Oppressors low
> And my heart aches, tho' MERCY struck the blow
> With wearied thought once more I seek the shade,
> Where peaceful Virtue wears the Myrtle braid.

Just as Coleridge was obsessed with the intellectual

conflict between the transcendental and materialist spheres, so he seemed to swing between the polarities of contemplative and active states. Not for long could he be happy with the hectic life of business and editorial anxieties. With the tenth issue of the *Watchman*, publication ceased, and he wrote the epitaph to the venture :

Henceforward I shall cease to cry the State of the political Atmosphere . . . I have endeavoured to do well. And it must be attributed to defect of ability, not of inclination or effort, if the words of the Prophet be altogether applicable to me, 'O Watchman! thou has watched in vain!'[21]

7

In Search of a Role

In the meantime, amidst heavy editorial distractions, Coleridge's long awaited volume – *Poems* – had been published by Cottle. By 13 April he could write his gratitude to this strange young man who had intrepidly seen the collection through all the vicissitudes of the past months : 'On the blank leaf of my poems, I can most appropriately write my acknowledgements to you, for your too disinterested conduct in the purchase of them. Indeed, if ever they should acquire a name and character, it might be truly said, the world owed them to you. Had it not been for you, none perhaps of them would have been published, and some not written.' With the exception of *Religious Musings* it contained about fifty short poems. About half of these are sonnets, the rest lyrics and elegaics ; three of them written in the relaxed conversational manner in blank verse which, excepting the ballad poems, are associated with that handful of fine poems for which Coleridge is remembered. The reception of the volume was encouraging. 'The Reviews have been wonderful,' wrote Coleridge, 'The Monthly has *cataracted* panegyric on my poems ; the Critical has *cascaded* it ; and the Analytic has *dribbled* it with very tolerable civility. The Monthly has at least done justice to my Religious Musings – They place it "on the very top of the scale of Sublimity".'

A short notice in the *British Critic* observed that the collection was 'marked by tenderness of sentiment, and elegance of expression, neither however sufficiently chastened by experience of mankind, or habitude of writing'.[1] The critic, however, singled out the *The Sigh* as a specimen of special merit. And the same poem was cited by the *Analytic Review*, which found the general character of the poems surprisingly unpolitical in view of Coleridge's reputation. 'The numbers are not always harmonious,' pronounced the reviewer, 'and the language, through a redundancy of metaphor, and the frequent use of compound epithets, sometimes becomes turgid: But everywhere the writer discovers a lively imagination, and a ready command of poetical language.' The *Critical Review* likewise found that much of the work 'by not having the pause and accent in the proper place, grates upon the correct ear'.[2] But Mr Coleridge had a 'luxuriant imagination' and time and experience would improve him. John Aiken, however, gave the highest praise in the *Monthly Review*: 'The manner of an original thinker is predominant; and as he had not borrowed the ideas, so he had not fashioned himself to the polish and correctness of modern verse. Such a writer may occasionally fall under the censure of criticism: he will always be, what so few proportionally are, an interesting object to the genuine lover of poetry.'[3] *Religious Musings*, the most ambitious poem of the collection, and the most political, was mostly passed over. Even the sympathetic *Monthly Review* qualified its praise, finding it 'obscure, uncouth and verging to extravagance'. Writing to Thomas Poole in May, Coleridge admitted that while the poem 'was not written for common Readers' there were instances of 'vicious affectation in the phraseology'. The comment was followed by the reflection: 'Good Writing is produced more effectually by rapidly glancing thro' language as it already exists, than by an hasty recourse to the *Mint* of invention.'[4] Coleridge also found himself obliged to offer a defence to a letter of 'violent opposition' from John Thelwall, the famous radical speaker. 'Why pass an act of *Uniformity* against Poets?' asked Coleridge. 'That Poetry pleases which interests — *my* religious poetry interests the *religious*, who read it with rapture – why? because it awakes in them all the associations connected with a love of future existence.' But the most heartening praise came from Wordsworth. 'A very dear friend of mine,' Coleridge wrote to Thelwall, 'who is in my opinion the best poet of the age . . . thinks that the lines 364 to 375 & from 403 to 428 the best in the Volume – indeed worth all the rest – And this man is a Republican and at least a *Semi-atheist.*'5

The unlikely correspondence with John Thelwall, who had been imprisoned in the Tower for high treason in 1794 and was a professed atheist, demonstrates Coleridge's resilience during the depressing aftermath of the *Watchman*. They exchanged letters that were friendly but full of energetic polemic after Thelwall had accused Coleridge of being deluded, of treating 'systems and opinions with the furious prejudices of the cynic', of having branded the 'presumptious children of scepticism with vile epithets and hunted them down with abuse'. Their main disputes were over questions of love, marriage and religion, Coleridge taking a line that was not likely to impress his tough correspondent: 'Observe the face of an whoremonger or intriguer,' argued Coleridge 'and that of a married man – it would furnish physiognomic demonstration.' But Coleridge mainly harangued on his old theme: 'The real source of inconstancy, & prostitution, is *Property*, which mixes with & poisons everything good – & is beyond doubt the origin of all Evil.'6

There was also a flourishing correspondence between Coleridge and Poole in whom he confided his new plans. Once again he was thinking of establishing a school. In preparation for this task he wished to spend six weeks learning German until he could read it with 'tolerable fluency'. Then he would embark on translating the works of Schiller which would pay for a trip to Germany with Sara. In Germany he would study chemistry and anatomy and return to England with all the works of the theologians

Semler and Michaelis, and the metaphysician Kant. It would then be appropriate to found a school for eight young men at 100 guineas each. The studies of this ideal school would produce scholars – one of whom 'would make a better Senator than perhaps one Member in either of our Houses'. The curriculum would be as follows :

1. Man as Animal : including the complete knowledge of Anatomy, Chemistry, Mechanics & Optics.

2. Man as an *Intellectual* Being : including the ancient Metaphysics, the systems of Locke & Hartley, of the Scotch philosophers and the new Kantian System.

3. Man as a Religious Being : including an historic summary of all Religions & the arguments for and against Natural & Revealed Religion. Then proceeding from the individual to the aggregate of Individuals & disregarding all chronology except that of mind I should perfect them 1. in the History of Savage Tribes. 2. of semi-barbarous nations. 3. of nations emerging from semi-barbarism. 4. of civilized states. 5. of luxurious states. 6. of revolutionary states. 7. of Colonies. – During these studies I should intermix the knowledge of languages and instruct my scholars in Belles Lettres & the principles of composition.

Finding young men who could absorb such a wide-ranging syllabus might have proved difficult ; but it demonstrates the polymath tendencies of Coleridge himself, and an early desire to take all manner of disciplines within his scope, however mutually exclusive. As Lamb would write later in the year : 'You seem to have been straining your comparing faculties to bring together things infinitely distant and un-like ; the feeble narrow-sphered operations of the human intellect and the everywhere diffused mind of Deity ; the peerless Wisdom of Jehovah.'[7] At the same time, both the idea of the school and the huge scope of erudition envisaged suggest that he was again emulating Milton. But Coleridge felt sceptical about the realization of the plan even at the moment of its inception : he was, at last, becoming a little more circumspect. How could any scheme be realistic that relied solely on a publisher's whim to accept or refuse the initial scheme of translating Schiller – which was to finance the school? Was it all no more than 'Bright Bubbles of the aye-ebullient brain !'?

There was a second plan, however : that he should become a 'Dissenting Parson', and entirely 'abjure Politics & carnal literature'. It still went much against the grain to 'preach for hire', but 'neediness & Uncertainty' seemed to offer him no alternative – as his improvidence laid him open to temptation ; although he offers no clue as to what such a temptation might be.

Poole now made a move to release Coleridge from his financial difficulties. Early in May he organized a fund of seven or eight friends who promised to contribute five guineas annually 'as a mark of their esteem, gratitude, and admiration'. Coleridge was deeply moved by the gesture but initially begged leave to consider the offer. Mrs Coleridge, however, was in no doubt about the propriety of accepting the timely assistance. 'Mrs Coleridge', he wrote, 'Loves you – & says, she would fall on your Neck & kiss you.' In the event, Coleridge accepted the gift and by the end of May his financial situation improved in other ways. George Dyer lent money to cover the *Watchman* debts, and a number of 'Ladies' subscribed to the *Poems* at a guinea each to compensate 'for his disappointment in the *Watchman*'. Then John Fellowes of Nottingham, who had been kind on the prospectus tour, came forward with a suggestion that he should become a private tutor to a family in Darley. Coleridge welcomed the idea provided that the circumstance of his being married should provide no impediment. The following week came another surprise, when he was awarded ten guineas from the Royal Literary Fund resulting from the following application by James Martin :

Having been informed, that Mr Coleridge, a man of genius and learning, is in extreme difficulties, proceeding from a sick family, his wife being ready to lie in, and his mother in law, whom he has supported, being, as is supposed, on her death-bed, I undertake to lay his case before you. Mr Coleridge is of that description of persons, who fall within the notice of your benevolent Institution. He is a man of undoubted talents, though his works have been unproductive, and, though he will in future be able to support himself by his own industry, he is at present quite unprovided for, being of no profession.[8]

Things looked much improved. Then at the end of June he received a letter from Perry, editor of the *Morning Chronicle*, offering work if he could come to London. Urged by a Bristol friend and close confidant, Dr Beddoes, Coleridge immediately wrote back to accept the proposal, but he had reservations about leaving Bristol of which he had now grown fond. The desire to seek retirement was still strong: 'Local and temporary Politics are my aversion,' he wrote to John Prior Estlin, ' — they narrow the understanding, they narrow the heart, they fret the temper. But there are two Giants leagued together whose most imperious commands I must obey however reluctant — their names are, BREAD & CHEESE.'[9] One of the strongest incentives to go to London was that one of the editors of the Paper, Grey, had just died, and Beddoes thought there might be a possibility of Coleridge's early promotion. Coleridge, however, was rightly sceptical: as he wrote to Poole, 'I rather think, that Perry means to employ me as a mere Hireling, without any *proportionate* Share of the Profits'.

Leaving the job with the *Morning Chronicle* still hanging in the balance, he set off with Sara for Darley to explore the possibility of becoming a private tutor to the children of a Mrs Evans, a wealthy widow. Mrs Evans immediately took to Coleridge, but the final decision to employ him lay with the senior members of the family who held her money in trust; and they, it seems, found many objections to the scheme. Nevertheless the widow initially won the day, and a salary of £150 a year was to be settled on him for educating her children.

At last he seemed to have a certain career, and on the

strength of it he returned south and went to visit his family at Ottery, 'where I was received by my mother with transport, and by my Brother George with joy and tenderness, & by my other Brothers with affectionate civility'.[10] It was very much the return of the prodigal, but their congratulations were sadly premature, for on returning to Bristol he received a letter from Mrs Evans in which the offer was revoked : 'The new and accummulated objections which have arisen to our plan since your departure', she wrote, '. . . are so overwhelming that I think the future happiness of the children as well as my own will be ruined by resistance.' Once again Coleridge's hopes were dashed, and for a time he even seemed to lose trust in divine providence : 'but in no after emotion of vain regret,' he confided to Poole, 'have I apostatized from the divine philosophy, which I profess.'[11] Bachelor Poole's reaction to the sudden reversal was rather less exalted : 'I am now convinced of what I doubted before,' he wrote to Coleridge, 'that woman is inferior to man. No man who is capable of willing as ardently as she willed, who had the heart and head she possesses, and understood the object to be attained so well, would vacillate. Woman, thou was destined to be governed. Let us then bow to destiny.' But it was not entirely the end of the school plan. In the middle of August he went north again to stay in Derby for two days, then proceeded on a tour in Mrs Evans's carriage. He visited Matlock, Oakover and Ilam, and at Dovedale 'dined in a cavern, by the side of a divine little spring'. While most of these days were filled with 'seeing the country, eating, concerts, &c', he spent at least one day drawing up his 'sketch of education' which he meant to publish to try to get a school. On returning the carriage to Mrs Evans, she put in his hand 'a number of bank notes, which amounted to 95£, and gave Mrs Coleridge all her baby clothes'. Providence was not dealing with him so badly after all.

Returning to Derby, he was approached by a Dr Crompton who offered that if he would take a house in

Derby and open a day school, confining the number of pupils to twelve, he would send his three children to him for their education. Until Coleridge had acquired his twelve pupils Crompton undertook to offer 100 guineas a year; and thereafter 20 guineas for each child. 'He thinks there is no doubt but that I might have more than 12 in a very short time, if I like it,' he reported back to Wade enthusiastically. 'If so, twelve times twenty guineas is two hundred and fifty guineas per annum.' With the money that Mrs Evans had given him he could start at once; indeed, that Coleridge did not become a schoolmaster in Derby in 1796 was solely due to a housing shortage there that summer. No suitable property could be found, so he engaged to rent a house that was to be completed in October and returned to Bristol where he continued an intimate correspondence with Poole. 'My Soul seems so mantled & wrapped round by your Love & Esteem,' Coleridge wrote to him, 'that even a dream of losing but the smallest fragment of it makes me shiver – as tho' some tender part of my Nature were left uncovered & in nakedness.'[12] By the second week of September, however, yet another tutorship presented itself. Charles Lloyd, a young man with literary aspirations, just three years younger than Coleridge, was eager to take up residence with him and study under his supervision. They had met in Mosely when Coleridge had gone North to see Mrs Evans. With this new prospect Coleridge once again travelled up to Birmingham to meet Lloyd's father – 'a mild man, very liberal in his ideas, and in religion an *allegorising Quaker*'. An agreement was accordingly made whereby Lloyd was to pay £80 a year in return for board, lodging and friendly, instructive companionship.[13]

Meantime Mrs Coleridge, who had wisely remained in Bristol, was delivered of her child at half past two in the morning, the midwife arriving just in time to take away the after-birth. Coleridge hastened home again, bringing Lloyd with him. On the journey he composed a sonnet which finds its echoes in Wordsworth's *Lucy* poem – 'Strange fits of passion have I known', and the reflections on pre-existence in the *Immortality Ode* :

> Oft of *some unknown Past* such Fancies roll
> Swift o'er my brain, as make the Present seem,
> For a brief moment, like a most strange dream
> When, not unconscious that she dreamt, the Soul
> Questions herself in sleep! and Some have said
> We liv'd ere yet this *fleshly* robe we wore.
> O my sweet Baby! when I reach my door,
> If heavy looks should tell me, thou wert dead,
> (As sometimes thro' excess of Hope, I fear)
> I think that I should struggle to believe,
> Thou wert a spirit to this nether sphere
> Sentenc'd, for some more venial crime to grieve –
> Didst scream, then spring to meet Heaven's quick Reprieve,
> While we wept idly o'er thy little Bier!

With Mrs Coleridge's difficult pregnancy, and the sense that he was fated to be dogged by one disappointment after another, it is not surprising that he expected a tragedy on arriving in Bristol.

'When I first saw the Child,' wrote Coleridge, minutely examining his state of inner feeling, even at this important moment of his life, 'I did not feel that thrill & overflowing of affection which I expected – I looked on it with a melancholy gaze – my mind was intensely contemplative & my heart only sad. – But when two hours after, I saw it at the bosom of its Mother ; on her arm ; and her eye tearful & watching it's little features, then I was thrilled & melted, and gave it the Kiss of a FATHER.' The child was a boy, its name David Hartley Coleridge. 'I hope', declared Coleridge, 'that ere he be a man, if God destine him for continuance in this life, his head will be convinced of, & his heart saturated with, the truths so ably supported by that great master of *Christian* Philosophy.'[14]

Now a father, and mentor of Charles Lloyd, Coleridge

seemed to assume a more sober attitude towards life. At this time too he received news of Charles Lamb's tragic loss of his mother : 'My poor dear dearest sister, in a fit of insanity has been the death of her own mother. I was at hand only time enough to snatch the knife out of her grasp. She is at present in a mad house, from whence I fear she must be moved to an hospital.'[15]

Lamb begged of Coleridge : 'Write as religious letter as possible.' And Coleridge rose to the occasion. In a letter of Christian consolation, which made no pretence that it could alleviate Lamb's present sufferings, he urged him to come to Bristol : 'I wish above measure to have you for a little while here ; no visitants shall blow on the nakedness of your feelings ; you shall be quiet, and your spirit may be healed.'[16] At the same time, Lamb consistently exhorted Coleridge to join him in spiritual renewal : 'Let us learn to think humbly of ourselves, and rejoice in the apellation of "dear children", "brethren", and "co-heirs with Christ of the promises", seeking to know no further.' And again, 'Cultivate simplicity, Coleridge, or rather, I should say, banish elaborateness ; for simplicity springs spontaneous from the heart, and carries into daylight its own modest buds and genuine sweet, and clean flowers of expression.'

Lamb was labouring under a double strain at this time, for he was suffering not only from the loss of his mother but he was obliged to nurse his father who had himself only narrowly missed being murdered by the same knife. The father demanded that Lamb play cards with him night after night when he returned tired and hungry from his office at 7 o'clock. Coleridge was his only outlet. '. . . you are the only correspondent,' he told Coleridge, 'and, I might add, the only friend I have in the world ; I go nowhere, and have no acquaintance. Slow of speech, and reserved in manners, no one seeks or cares for my society, and I am left alone. . . . I can only converse with you by letters, and with the dead in their books.' In his eagerness to shed all aspects of his life which lacked religious simplicity he had even burnt his verses, his notebooks, and 'a little journal of my foolish passion which I had a long time kept'.[17] It seems clear that he also wished Coleridge to join him in these fevid self-denials. Was it that he feared for his own soul? Or Coleridge's soul? It seems more likely that he feared for the sanity of both of them. Writing of himself and his sister on 3 October, he tells Coleridge, 'I must be serious, circum-spect, and deeply religious thro' life : by such means may *both* of us escape madness in future, if it so please the Almighty.' Indeed, earlier in the year he had spent six weeks in an insane house, and the phase of madness had been strongly linked with Coleridge's influence. His own brother, Lamb told him, had said 'you [Coleridge] were the cause of my madness – you and your dammed foolish sensibility and melancholy – and he lamented with a true brotherly feeling that we ever met'. Lamb may have spoken jestingly, but there was perhaps a grain of truth in what he said. While Coleridge never manifested signs of insanity, he no doubt put a great strain on his intimates when he was in a depressed or agitated mood. As has been seen, his brother George had been convinced of his instability, and letters were frequently exchanged between other members of his family on the same theme. It is more than likely, more-over, that he had a detrimental effect on Charles Lloyd, his new pupil, who was to suffer severe fits while living with Coleridge.

Whatever the case, Coleridge seems to have entered into Lamb's circumspect mood and adopted a mode of austerity and seriousness. In the first place he renounced his political activities, and determined on seeking permanent retirement away from cities. Just two weeks after Lamb's mother had been killed he reported to Charles Lloyd's father :

Indeed, If I live in cities, my children (if it please the All-good to preserve the one I have, and to give me more), my children, I say, will necessarily become acquainted with politicians and politics – a set of men and a kind of study which I deem highly unfavourable to all Christian graces. I have myself erred greatly in this respect; but, I trust, I have now seen my error. I have accordingly snapped my squeaking baby-trumpet of sedition, and hung up its fragments in the chamber of Penitences.

Coleridge had certainly changed. His thoughts tended more and more towards religion as the year wore on, both in his reading and his literary plans : 'I affirm that, after reading Isaiah, or St Paul's Epistle to the Hebrews, Homer and Virgil are disgustingly *tame* to me, and Milton himself barely tolerable.' He was determined to publish an answer to Godwin – its 'absurdities and wickedness', and in the last chapter he would 'attack the credulity, super-stition, calumnies, and hypocrisy of the present race of infidels'. His thoughts continually ran on death, and he even seems to have contemplated becoming a vegetarian.[18] In a practical way he seemed to be exclusively absorbed in his school plan and the prospect of bringing up a large family. 'I am anxious that my children should be bred up from earliest infancy in the simplicity of peasants, their food, dress and habits completely rustic, I never shall, and never will, have any fortune to leave them : I will leave them therefore hearts that desire little, heads that know how little is to be desired, and hands and arms accustomed to earn that little.'[19] Little wonder that even the solemn Charles Lamb of this period should later write of little Hartley, 'I did not distinctly understand you, – you don't mean to make an actual ploughman of him?' At the same time, writing to Cottle, who was planning a second edition of the *Poems* – he asks that everything political should be omitted in order to widen his readership.

But this determination to seek retirement seemed to occasion all the old anxieties, disappointments and changes of plan ; at times due to his own vacillation, at times, no doubt, due to the unreliability of others. Already he had decided to reject the plan to take a house in Derby ; instead he wished to live close to Poole at Adscombe near Nether Stowey in Somerset. As Lamb wrote to him on 17 October :

My dearest friend, I grieve from my very soul to observe you in your plans of life veering about from this hope to the other, and settling no where. Is it an untoward fatality (speaking humanly) that does this for you, a stubborn irresistible concurrence of events? or lies the fault, as I fear it does in your own mind? You seem to be taking up the schemes of fortune only to lay them down again, and your fortunes are an ignus fatuus that has been conducting you, in thought, from Lancaster Court, Strand, to somewhat near Matlock, then jumping across to Dr somebody's whose son's tutor you are likely to be, and would to God the dancing demon *may* conduct you at last in peace and comfort to the 'life and labors of a cottager'.[20]

As it happened a suitable cottage was found by an agent, but by November it looked as if there had been a snag. Coleridge wrote to Poole : 'My heart has been full, yea, crammed with anxieties about my residence near you. I so ardently desire it, that any disappointment would chill all my faculties, like the fingers of death.' A few days later the depression occasioned by the uncertainty about the move to Stowey seems to have brought on a painful nervous attack. He provided Poole with a powerful description of his symptoms ; and his recourse to laudanum :

On Wednesday night I was siezed with an intolerable pain from my right temple to the tip of my right shoulder, including my right eye, cheek, jaw, & that side of the throat – I was nearly frantic – and ran about the House naked, endeavouring by every means to excite sensations in different parts of my body, & so to weaken the enemy by creating a division. It continued from one in the morning till half past 5, & left me pale & fainty. – It came on fitfully but not so violently, several times on Thursday – and began severer threats towards night, but I took between 60 & 70 drops of Laudanum, and *sopped* the Cerberus just as his mouth began to open. On Friday it only *niggled*; as if the Chief had departed as from a conquered place, and merely left a small garrison behind, or as if he evacuated the Corsica, & a few straggling pains only remained; but *this morning* he returned in full force, & his Name is Legion! – Giant-fiend of an hundred hands! with a shower of arrowy Death-pangs he transpierced me, & then he became a Wolf & lay gnawing my bones – I am not mad, most noble Festus! – but in sober sadness I have suffered this day more bodily pain than I had before a conception of – . My right cheek has certainly been placed with admirable exactness under the focus of some invisible Burning-Glass, which concentrated all the Rays of a Tartarean Sun. – My medical attendant decides it to be altogether nervous, and that it originates either in severe application, or excessive anxiety. – My beloved Poole! in excessive anxiety, I believe, it might originate! ... With a gloomy wantonness of Imagination I had been coquetting with the hideous *Possibles* of Disappointment – I drank fears, like wormwood; yea, made myself drunken with bitterness! for my ever-shaping & distrustful mind still mingled gall-drops, till out of the cup of Hope *I almost poisoned myself with Despair!*[21]

At last he buried his pride and asked Poole outright if his brother would allow them rooms in his large house for the winter, at least until the cottage at Adscombe had been finalized. Two days later he wrote again, reporting that his pains had lessened, but that he had no appetite. He apologized for the former '*flighty*' letter, written 'under the immediate inspiration of Laudanum'. The drug now left him languid, and he had the 'wind and the hiccups'.

Meanwhile he continued anxious about his chosen course of career: he could think of nothing other than school-mastering or retirement into the country. Yet already he had doubts about teaching: 'educating children suits not the activity of my mind ...' If he was to run a school it would have to be in rural surroundings; the exertions and confinement must find adequate compensation in a more healthy situation. By December, indeed, the desire to run a school would have completely vanished. 'I could not love the man, who advised me keep a School or write for a Newspaper. He must have a hard Heart!'[22] What he really longed for was to be 'an Agriculturist', and a '*hireless* Priest', Charles Lloyd's mentor, and in his spare time to study and

6

write. But the presence of Charles Lloyd, in fact, had only
increased his anxieties, for although he liked him for his
'delicate affections' and 'enlivened benevolence', the young
man began to suffer alarming nervous fits during November.
Coleridge described the symptoms to Poole :

His distemper (which may with equal propriety be named either
Somnambulism, or frightful Reverie, or *Epilepsy from accumulated
feelings*) is alarming. He falls all at once into a kind of Night-mair;
and all the Realities round him mingle with, and form a part of, the
strange Dream. All his voluntary powers are suspended; but he
perceives every thing & hears every thing, and whatever he perceives
& hears he perverts into the substance of his delerious Vision.

Soon he would seek to drop Lloyd, even, from his scheme
of things ; first, by offering only lodgings without tuition,
then by advising him to return home to Mosely. But
Lloyd was greatly attached to the Coleridges, and by his
insistence would remain part of the household for some time
to come.

Coleridge now seemed to be paring away all those aspects
of his life which might prove unreliable ; he wished to
enter on a 'severe process of simplification'. As he wrote to
Poole in mid-December : 'I mean to work *very hard* – as
Cook, Butler, Scullion, Shoe-cleaner, occasional Nurse,
Gardener, Hind, Pig-protector, Chaplain, Secretary, Poet,
Reviewer, and omnium-botherum shilling-scavenger – in
other words, I shall keep no Servant, and will cultivate my
Land-acre, and my wise-acres, as well as I can.' But all
hung upon finding a suitable habitation near Stowey. The
cottage at Adscombe was still unsettled, and in the meantime
Poole had spoken of a house, probably the one next door,
'not a Beauty to be sure ; but its vicinity to you, shall over-
balance its defects.' He asked Poole to rent it for at least a
year, and all seemed certain at last.

But this was not to be. By 12 December Poole had written
dissuading him from coming at all, recommending that he

should take up his abode near friends of his at Acton. Poole had evidently written that the Coleridges would not be comfortable in the cottage, it having only three rooms, and being difficult to heat. There was talk too of a ghost. He also mentioned that in taking the house near his friends at Acton, his removal expenses would be three guineas cheaper. Coleridge wrote two replies to Poole's letter; the first short and deeply distressed, the second long and hysterical. He suspected that Poole's mother had dissuaded him from taking them, and worse still that Poole had, on reflection, cooled in his friendship. With Sara watching the 'workings' of his face, and entreating him to say what was the matter, Coleridge wrote: 'O my God! my God! when am I to find rest! Disappointment follows Disappointment; and Hope seems given to me merely to prevent my becoming callous to Misery! – Now I know not where to turn myself.'[23] One by one he dismissed Poole's objections. With a 'little green List', a carpet, and slight alteration in the fireplace, the cottage could be made habitable; he could send a perfect copy of his manuscripts, and proof work, to Cottle. As for ghosts: 'I should be haunted with Ghosts enough – the Ghosts of Otway & Chatterton, & the phantasms of a Wife broken-hearted, & a hunger bitten Baby!' For this was, indeed, the root of his deepest anxiety, how to make a certain living as a writer:

O Thomas Poole! Thomas Poole! if you did but know what a Father and Husband must feel, who toils with his brain for uncertain bread! I dare not think of it – The evil Face of Frenzy looks at me! – The Husbandman puts his seed in the Ground and the Goodness, Power, & Wisdom of God have pledged themselves, that he shall have Bread, and Health, & Quietness in return for Industry, & Simplicity of Wants, & Innocence. The AUTHOR scatters his seed – with aching head, and wasted Health, & all the heart-leapings of Anxiety – & the Folly, the Vices, & the Fickleness of Man promise him Printers' Bills, & the Debtors' Side of Newgate, as full & sufficient Payment.[24]

Predictably enough, for Poole was a kind-hearted man,

Coleridge received another letter on 18 December saying that he was welcome at Stowey. Immediately, Coleridge began to make the necessary arrangements, but the actual move was delayed until early January by the recurrence of illness, probably due to the anxieties he had experienced on reading Poole's reservations. 'I am very poorly; not to say ill. My face monstrously swoln; my recondite Eye sits quaintly behind the flesh-hill; and looks as little, as a Tomtit's. And I have a sore throat that prevents me from eating aught but spoon-meat without great pain – & I have a rheumatic complaint in the back part of my head & Shoulders.'[25] But in the midst of his worries and illness he managed to write (at the invitation of the *Cambridge Intelligencer*) the *Ode on the Departing Year*. And if there was fault to be found in its lines, Coleridge added – identifying himself again with Milton – minuter criticisms should be disarmed 'by the reflection, that these Lines were conceived "not in the soft obscurities of Retirement, or under the Shelter of Academic Grove, but amidst inconvenience and distraction, in sickness and in sorrow"'.[26]

In *Ode to the Departing Year* Coleridge speaks with the voice of the prophet, predicting the downfall of England. Once more he employs the image of music, addressing 'Divine Providence that regulates into one vast harmony all the events of time, however calamitous some of them may appear to mortals'.[27]

> Spirit who sweepest the wild Harp of Time!
> It is most hard, with an untroubled ear
> Thy dark inwoven harmonies to hear!
> Yet, mine eye fix'd on Heaven's unchanging clime
> Long had I listen'd, free from mortal fear,
> With inward stillness, and a bowéd mind;
> When lo! its folds far waving on the wind,
> I saw the train of the Departing Year!
> Starting from my silent sadness
> Then with no unholy madness,

Ere yet the enter'd cloud foreclos'd my sight,
I rais'd the impetuous song, and solemnis'd his flight.

He contemplates the privileged and safe situation of England:

(Those grassy hills, those glittering dells
　　Proudly ramparted with rocks)
And Ocean mid his uproar wild
　　Speaks safety to his Island-child!
Hence for many a fearless age
　　Has social Quiet Lov'd thy shore;
Nor ever proud Invader's rage
Or sack'd thy towers, or stain'd thy fields with gore.

But the British had shown their gratitude to Providence, comments Coleridge in a footnote to the poem in 1797, 'by eagerness to spread those horrors over nations less happily situated. In the midst of plenty and safety we have raised or joined the yell for famine and blood. Of the one hundred and seven last years, fifty have been years of War. Such wickedness cannot pass unpunished.'[28]

Abandon'd of Heaven! mad Avarice thy guide
At cowardly distance, yet kindling with pride –
Mid thy herds and thy corn-fields secure thou hast stood,
And Join'd the wild yelling of Famine and Blood!

He ends with a determination to seek retirement in the gathering gloom, and contemplate higher things while working the soil: it was an anticipation of the life he sought in Stowey:

Away, my soul, away!
In vain, in vain the Birds of warning sing –
And Hark! I hear the famish'd brood of prey
Flap their lank pennons on the groaning wind!
Away, my soul, away!
I unpartaking of the evil thing,
　　With daily prayer and daily toil
Soliciting for food my scanty soil,
Have wail'd my country with a loud Lament.

> Now I recentre my immortal mind
> In the deep Sabbath of meek self-content;
> Cleans'd from the vaporous passions that bedim
> God's Image, sister of the Seraphim.

The retreat to Stowey seems to have been anticipated with the deep anxiety of a man fearful for his own survival: anything less than this would hardly explain the frenzy with which he regarded any obstacle or delay in his plans. There were a number of contributory factors. It is clear, in the first place, that he wished to free himself from his financial dependence on friends in Bristol: 'What had I to ask of my friends? Not money – for a temporary relief of my Wants is nothing – removes no gnawing of anxiety, & debases the dignity of the Man.' He wished, too, to live alone with Sara, to escape the domestic situation in Bristol where he was enforced to live with his mother-in-law while providing for her; as it was, he settled £20 a year on her. But more than this, he was making an important decision about his future activities, and this involved shedding the life he had lived for the past three years, in order to seek a new inner freedom: 'I am not *fit* for *public* Life; yet the Light shall stream to a far distance from the taper in my cottage window.' It has the ring about it of the dedicated poet; perhaps, even, the dedication of the epic poet. Lamb, indeed, had written to him saying: 'Coleridge, I want you to write an Epic poem. Nothing but it can satisfy the vast capacity of the true poetic genius. Having one great End to direct all your poetic faculties to, and on which to lay out your hopes, your ambition, will show you to what you are equal.' And again, 'You have learning, you have fancy, you have enthusiasm – you have strength and amplitude of wing enow for flights like those I recommend. In the vast unformed and incultivated; search there, and realize your favourite Susquehana scheme.' The *Gutch Notebook* entries record many ideas, in fact, for work of epic dimensions.[29] There is talk of an epic on the Origin of Evil, and a sequence of six 'Hymns to the Sun, the Moon and the Elements'. There is also the idea of a romance on 'The Wandering Jew'. There is little doubt that Coleridge had been feeling the creative stirrings of some great literary achievement within him, and he knew only too well that to realize his true potential he must be free of anxiety.

Moreover, in the latter part of 1796 he had been revealing signs of liberation in his philosophical speculations. Thelwall had written to him in December, objecting that his sonnet *Composed on a journey homewards* was obscure. He seems to have found fault with the following lines, in particular:

> Oft o'er my brain does that strange fancy roll
> Which makes the present (while the flash doth last)
> Seem a mere semblance of some unknown past.

Commenting on these lines Coleridge says: 'I meant to express, that oft times, for a second or two, it flashed upon my mind, that the then company, conversation, & every thing, had occurred before, with all the precise circumstances; so as to make Reality appear a Semblance, and the Present like a dream in Sleep.'[30] The notion is not unlike a passage in *Religious Musings* evidently entered into a later draft before publication in 1796 where he says:

> Believe thou, O my soul,
> Life is a vision shadowy of Truth;
> And vice and anguish, and the wormy grave,
> Shapes of a dream!

Coleridge added a footnote to these lines, saying, 'This paragraph is intelligible to those who, like the Author, believe and feel the sublime system of Berkley [*sic*]; and the doctrine of the final Happiness of all men.' In the letter to Thelwall he also states, 'I am a Berkleian'. He had, in fact, borrowed the second of a two-volume *Works* of Berkeley from the Bristol Library in February. This professed shift in philosophical emphasis is even more surprising than his metaphysical explorations earlier in the summer; for

Berkeley's main tenet – that phenomena perceived by the senses have no absolute existence independent of the mind – runs counter not only to the empiricists, but also to the more traditional schools of metaphysics as represented by Cudworth. Perhaps, more than anything else, however, it reveals the nature of Coleridge's use of philosophy at this time : 'My philosophical opinions,' says Coleridge later in the same letter, 'are blended with, or deduced from, my feelings', and 'I judge of all things by their Utility'. An example of this was his reference to another theory in the above-mentioned poem : 'and Some have said / We liv'd ere yet this *fleshly* robe we wore'. Commenting on these lines to Thomas Poole on 1 November, Coleridge had said, 'Almost all the followers of Fénelon believe that *men* are degraded Intelligencies, who had once all existed, at one time & together, in a paradisiacal or perhaps heavenly state.' The theory 'may be very wild philosophy', he told Thelwall 'but it is very intelligible poetry'.

It seems from this that he had begun to give free scope to his mental experiences and intuition, and subordinate philosophy to a supporting role ; he was clearly enjoying a variety of insights which could be labelled with various, and contradicting philosophical schools of thought, but he was not at this time concerned with the epistemological implications. Importantly, too, it reveals a departure from the political direction of his philosophical allegiance in the preceding three years : no longer was he so concerned with adhering to a set of premises which enabled him to believe in human perfectibility.

By 6 January then Coleridge had at last settled into the cottage at Stowey. There were four bedrooms upstairs, and on the ground floor 'two small and rather dark little parlours, one on each side of the front door, looking straight into the street, and a small kitchen behind, destitute of modern conveniences, and where the fire was made on the hearth in the most primitive manner conceivable'.[31] Although the house was plagued by mice, he claims that they were more comfortable than they had expected. 'Before our door,' he wrote, 'a clear brook runs of very soft water; and in the back yard is a nice *Well* of fine spring water. We have a very pretty garden, and large enough to find us vegetables & employment. And I am already an expert gardener – & both my Hands can exhibit a callum, as testimonials of their Industry.' He was busy raising two pigs, and ducks and geese, and in the garden he was growing 'potatoes & all manner of vegetables'. Beyond the garden there was a 'sweet Orchard' and at the end of it a gate which led into Thomas Poole's garden. He described his new life to Thelwall:

> I never go to Bristol – from seven to half past eight I work in my garden; from breakfast till 12 I read & compose; then work again – feed the pigs, poultry &c, till two o'clock – after dinner work again till Tea – from Tea till supper *review*. So jogs the day; & I am happy. I have society – my *friend*, T. Poole and as many acquaintances as I can dispense with – there are a number of very pretty young women in Stowey, all musical – & I am an immense favorite: for I pun, conundrumize, *listen*, and dance.

Coleridge has, in fact, left a good many of his puns and conundrums on record, of which the following should suffice as specimens: 'If a woman had murdered her cousin, and there were no other proof of her guilt except that she had an *half-barrel cask* in her possession – how would that convict her? Answer. It would be evident, that she had kild-er-kin.' Or again, 'Why Satan sitting on a house-top would be like a decayed merchant? Answer. Because he would be imp-over-i-shed.' Such was the humour of the 1790s.

To supplement his income he had started to review for the *Critical Review* and was reading a batch of gothic novels – Ann Radcliffe's *The Italian*, M. G. Lewis's *The Monk*, and

6*

Mary Robinson's *Hubert de Sevrac* – 'in all of which dun-
geons, and old castles, & solitary Houses by the Sea Side,
& Caverns, & Woods, and extraordinary characters, & all
the tribe of Horror & Mystery, have crowded on me – even
to surfeiting'. He continued to work on the preparation of
the second edition of his *Poems* which was to be published
in collaboration with Charles Lloyd and Lamb, and was
obliged to send printer's corrections by post to Cottle. Early
in February he received an invitation from Richard Sheridan
to write a popular tragedy, a challenge that he readily
accepted, but not with high hopes of success : 'Indeed I
have conceived so high an idea of what a Tragedy ought to
be,' he wrote in his reply, 'that I am certain I shall myself
be dissatisfied with my production ; and I can therefore
safely promise, that I will be neither surprised or wounded,
if I should find *you* of the same opinion.' He renewed his
correspondence with Thelwall, and they continued to dispute
the old questions of morality and marriage. And although
Thomas Poole was accessible through the gate in the wall
that divided their homesteads, and he often sat in Poole's
armchair in the 'great windy parlour' over 'strong beer',
Coleridge embarked on a series of long autobiographical
letters to his friend, which he began by writing : 'I could
inform the dullest author how he might write an interesting
book – let him relate the events of his Life with honesty,
not disguising the feelings that accompanied them.' In this
way he passed the time busily and uneventfully as the
winter wore into the spring of 1797.

Alfoxden

'W E both have a distinct remembrance of his arrival. He did not keep to the high road, but leaped over a gate and bounded down a pathless field by which he cut off an angle.'[1] Thus William Wordsworth recollected Coleridge's first visit to Racedown on 6 June 1797. Since the autumn of 1795 Wordsworth had been living in a secluded house between Crewkerne and Lyme forty miles distant across rough roads from Stowey, where he was recovering from a barren and depressing period spent in London. With him lived his sister Dorothy who was unobtrusively fostering his literary talent, constantly at hand as companion, secretary and copyist.

Wordsworth was eighteen months Coleridge's senior, and a native of Cumberland. Like Coleridge he had suffered the early loss of a parent, his mother dying when he was only eight years of age. He was subsequently sent to Hawkshead Grammar School where he stayed until his eighteenth year, then spent three and a half years at Cambridge, three terms ahead of Coleridge, where he claims to have neglected his studies. Since then he had travelled extensively on the continent and in England, with occasional periods spent in London.

For Dorothy, especially, Racedown was the realization of a life long ambition – to make a home with her brother. 'Racedown was the first home I had,' she wrote, 'I think it is the place dearest to my recollections upon the whole surface of the island.'[2] They had a kitchen garden where

they raised cabbages, a 'pleasure garden' with painted and
gilded 'images', and a sight of the sea from a hill just a
hundred and fifty yards from the door.

Coleridge's exuberant arrival at Racedown in June was,
in fact, a return visit. Wordsworth had already made a brief
call at Stowey in March when returning from a journey to
Bristol. It had been a timely call, for Coleridge had been in a
deep depression 'too dreadful to be described'. It was the
usual anxiety over money : 'I am not the man I have been –
and I think never shall. A sort of calm hopelessness diffuses
itself over my heart. – Indeed every mode of life which has
promised me bread and cheese, has been, one after another
torn away from me.'³ Wordsworth might well have com-
miserated with him for things had not been going so well at
Racedown either. Few escaped the privations of those war
years. In February Wordsworth had complained, 'I have
been lately living on air and the essence of carrots, cabbages,
turnips and other esculent vegetables, not excluding parsley,
the produce of my garden.' And later, in the spring,
Dorothy would be asking her brother Richard to save his
old clothes for them.

Wordsworth had managed to revive Coleridge's spirits
on that occasion at Stowey, and he seems to have left his
mark in other ways. Writing to Cottle after Wordsworth
had left, there is a distinctly Wordsworthian ring about
some of his remarks. Commenting on Southey's recently
published volume of poetry, he writes : 'I am fearful that
he will begin to rely too much on *story* & *event* in his poems
to the neglect of those *lofty imaginings*, that are peculiar to,
& definitive of, *the* POET.' The observation finds its echoes
in the 1800 Preface to the *Lyrical Ballads* where Wordsworth, with Coleridge's full endorsement, castigates the
modern trend in popular poetry – claiming, by implication,
for his own and Coleridge's verse that 'the feeling therein
developed gives importance to the action and situation and
not the action and situation to the feeling'. Yet while Words-

worth's poetry would be increasingly identified with this quality of permanence in terms of feeling – as Hazlitt was to remark, 'The common and the permanent . . . are his only realities' – the tendency no doubt owed much to the influence of Milton. In fact, their common admiration for Milton probably provides us with a major clue to the source of the spontaneous and ardent friendship between the two young poets. As Coleridge wrote to Cottle in the same letter, emphasizing the paucity of 'plot' in *Paradise Lost*: 'The *story* of Milton might be told in *two pages*. It is this which distinguishes *an* EPIC *Poem* from a *Romance in metre*.'[4] Coleridge's '*lofty imaginings*' are similarly an unmistakable blend of the Wordsworthian and the Miltonic; and here he was, immediately after Wordsworth's visit, bent on ordering his life to the exacting standards and disciplines of the epic poet:

> I should not think of devoting less than 20 years to an Epic Poem. Ten to collect materials & warm my mind with universal Science – I would be a tolerable Mathematician, I would thoroughly know Mechanics, Hydrostatics, Optics, and Astronomy, Botany, Metallurgy, Fossilism, Chemistry, Geology, Anatomy, Medicine – then the *minds of man* – in *all* Travels, Voyages & Histories. So I would spend ten years – the next five to the composition of the poem – and the five last to the correction of it.

Anticipating several years – to the period when Coleridge would devote himself to psychology and philosophy in earnest – this confident planning of the great literary epic has a poignant note. Had he no misgivings at all about the possibility of achieving the epic of total, all-embracing vision? Did it at no point occur to him that one man could no longer, even with the wide-ranging genius of a Milton, totally grasp the proliferating knowledge of the sciences, still less reconcile the warring conflicts which had arisen in philosophy, psychology and theology? Even so, to have grasped man's 'total' vision at the turn of this century, to have seized upon the momentous changes at a definite point in time would have implied being left behind. One finds oneself returning again and again to this early formulation of his life's ambition, not only for an understanding of the startlingly cosmic tendencies in his thinking, but for one of the major clues of his later suffering. If there was a tragic flaw in Coleridge's mind it existed perhaps in his inability to understand the impossibility of this main quest of his life. By the same token it helps us get into perspective the later suggestion that he was a 'failure'. Almost without exception, Coleridge's contemporaries were to see the fulfilment or the disappointment of his promise in terms of the great epic or total philosophical system that was to flow from his pen. Of course, it was not to be expected that they should congratulate him on failing to achieve the impossible ; yet it was to be left to subsequent generations to acknowledge the residual value of his endeavour.

On arriving at Racedown for a longer more leisurely period, the mutual respect increased to intense admiration. 'In Wordsworth', enthused Coleridge, 'there are no *inequalities*.' Wordsworth was, indeed, the greatest man he had ever known. 'I speak with heart-felt sincerity and (I think) unblinded judgment, when I tell you, that I feel myself a *little man by his* side ; and yet do not think, myself the less man, than I formerly thought myself.'5 His admiration for Dorothy was equally enthusiastic : 'She is a woman indeed ! – in mind, I mean, and heart – . . . her manners are simple, ardent, impressive . . . Her information various – her eye watchful in minutest observation of nature – and her taste a perfect electrometer – it bends, protrudes, and draws in, at subtlest beauties and most recondite faults.'

And Dorothy was, indeed, exercising that ever watchful eye on Coleridge himself. Writing to their friend Mary Hutchinson, who had left Racedown the day before Coleridge arrived, she records her initial impressions :

He is a wonderful man. His conversation teems with soul, mind, and spirit. Then he is so benevolent, so good tempered and cheerful, and, like William, interests himself so much about every little trifle. At first I thought him very plain, that is, for about three minutes: he is pale and thin, has a wide mouth, thick lips, and not very good teeth, longish loose-growing half-curling black hair. But if you hear him speak for five minutes you think no more of them.

Once again the magic of Coleridge's eloquence was weaving its spell.

Unfortunately Coleridge has left no record of the Wordsworths' appearance on his early acquaintance with them, but Hazlitt, who came to stay at Stowey in 1798, found William quaintly dressed '(according to the *costume* of that unconstrained period) in a brown fustian jacket and striped pantaloons'. He went on :

There was something of a roll, a lounge in his gait, not unlike his own Peter Bell. There was a severe, worn pressure of thought about his temples, a fire in his eye (as if he saw something in objects more than the outward appearance), an intense high narrow forehead, a Roman nose, cheeks furrowed by strong purpose and feeling, and a convulsive inclination to laughter about the mouth) a good deal at variance with the solemn, stately expression of the rest of his face.

There is no very vivid description of Dorothy during these early years, but she could not have altered so very much before De Quincey's first impression of her ten years later. He found her short, slight, and very dark :

Rarely, in a woman of English birth, had I seen a more determinate gipsy tan. Her eyes were not soft, . . . they were wild and startling, and hurried in their motion. Her manner was warm and ever ardent; her sensibility seemed constitutionally deep; and some subtle fire of impassioned intellect apparently burned within her, which, being alternately pushed forward into a conspicuous expression by the irrepressible instincts of her temperament, and then immediately checked, in obedience to the decorum of her sex and age, . . . even her very utterance and enunciation often, or rather generally, suffered in point of clearness and steadiness, from the agitation of her excessive organic sensibility, and, perhaps, from some morbid irritability of the nerves.

De Quincey also noticed a 'stooping attitude' when she walked, which gave 'an ungraceful, and even an unsexual character to her appearance when out of doors'.

On that first visit to Racedown Coleridge listened to Wordsworth reading an early draft of his *Ruined Cottage*.[6] It is the tale of an abandoned mother told to the narrator by a pedlar. The pedlar periodically visits Margaret's cottage after her husband has disappeared during a time of war and famine to join the army. He witnesses her deterioration as her anguish at the loss of her husband gradually destroys her spirit. Her subsequent moral and physical degeneration ending in the deaths of her children and her own death is paralleled by the deterioration of her garden and home ; and yet the pedlar observes a sense of sustained hope in the woman in proportion to the growing unlikelihood of the husband's return. At the same time he realizes that this senseless tragedy occurs within the eternal circuit of Nature, which is aloof from, and independent of transient human events, which is neither wholly beneficent nor malefic, which is both the source of the life from which man creates his suffering and joy, and their final assimilator. It is an extraordinarily mature and moving poem, in which the problem of suffering has been fully acknowledged without any sense of false consolation or morbid despair. For Coleridge it became 'one of the most beautiful poems in the language'.

Wordsworth also read his tragedy *The Borderers* – which is an unactable, and not particularly readable study of utter depravity in a young man. Coleridge found it 'absolutely wonderful'. In turn, Wordsworth thought '*very* highly' of Coleridge's tragedy *Osorio*, and considering Wordsworth a 'strict and almost severe critic' this gave him a boost of much needed confidence.

Coleridge lingered on at Racedown for almost a month,

returning to Stowey on 28 June. But almost immediately he
set out again to bring the Wordsworths back with him by
the 2 July. They were delighted with the surrounding
countryside of the Quantocks : 'There is everything here,'
wrote Dorothy, 'sea, woods wild as fancy ever painted,
brooks clear and pebbly as in Cumberland, villages so
romantic ; and William and I in a wander by ourselves,
found out a sequestered waterfall in a dell formed by steep
hills.'[7]

Two days after the Wordsworths arrived Sara accidentally
spilt a skillet of boiling milk over Coleridge's foot. No doubt
she was in a considerable fluster with so many people
crammed into the tiny household. The accident prevented
Coleridge walking with his guests in the surrounding
country, but it proved a fortunate circumstance from a
literary point of view for it resulted in the composition of
This Lime Tree Bower. Shortly after the Wordsworths'
arrival, Charles Lamb also came to stay. One afternoon
when the three visitors had gone out for a walk, to revisit the
'sequestered dell', Coleridge remained behind in the arbour
in Tom Poole's garden, nursing his foot and musing about
his friends.

Sitting in the arbour he follows them in his imagination,
while contemplating his garden imprisonment and Charles
Lamb's enforced exile in London — which has deprived them
of the sights of Nature, Lamb in the past and Coleridge in
the present. Thus the poem opens with the contrast between
Coleridge's confinement and his friends' freedom as they
'wander in gladness' – 'On springy heath, along the hill-
top edge'. Yet having imagined them high in the sunlight,
he accompanies them down into the deep sunless gorge of
the dell where they will experience a deprivation analogous
to his own. But not without consolation :

> that branchless ash,
> Unsunn'd and damp, whose few now yellow leaves
> Ne'er tremble in the gale, yet tremble still,

> Fann'd by the water-fall! and there my friends
> Behold the dark green file of long lank weeds,
> That all at once (a most fantastic sight!)
> Still nod and drip beneath the dripping edge
> Of the blue clay-stone.

Here, even in the sterility and darkness of the dell with its suggestion of death, a vital beauty is to be found in the motion of the leaves and the weeds.

He then emerges with his friends to view again the magnificent landscape, then the sea —

> With some fair bark, perhaps, whose sails light up
> The slip of smooth clear blue betwixt two Isles of purple shadow!

And by association with the lonely voyage of a single object of light in the opposing shadows, he thinks of Charles Lamb, and addresses him, — 'winning thy way/With sad yet patient soul, through evil and pain/And strange calamity'. Thus he is encouraged to search for redeeming signs of life and beauty in his own garden imprisonment:

> and I watch'd
> Some broad and sunny leaf, and lov'd to see
> The shadow of the leaf and stem above
> Dappling its sunshine!

He is moved by the beauty of the play of light on darkness and darkness on light, blended with subtle motion. The 'ancient ivy' making the 'black mass' of the elms 'gleam with light hue'. And he ends with a restrained passage in which the tensions between light and shadow, motion and rest, sound and silence are delicately reconciled in the flight of a rook across the sunset.

> My gentle-hearted Charles! when the last rook
> Beat its straight path along the dusky air
> Homewards, I blest it! deeming its black wing
> (Now a dim speck, now vanishing in light)
> Had cross'd the mighty Orb's dilated glory,

> While thou stood'st gazing; or, when all was still,
> Flew creeking o'er thy head, and had a charm
> For thee, my gentle-hearted Charles, to whom
> No sound is dissonant which tells of Life.

The coincidence of Wordsworth's and Coleridge's feeling and preoccupation at this time is emphasized by the close parallels which exist between *This Lime Tree Bower* and a poem of Wordsworth's which was read at Stowey this July, *Lines Left upon a Seat in a Yew-Tree*. Just as Coleridge finds consolation in the movement of the weeds in the dark and gloomy dell, so Wordsworth writes:

> Nay, Traveller! rest. This lonely Yew-tree stands
> Far from all human dwelling: what if here
> No sparkling rivulet spread the verdant herb?
> What if these barren boughs the bee not loves
> Yet if the wind breath soft, the curling waves,
> That break against the shore, shall lull thy mind
> By one soft impulse saved from vacancy.

At the same time the loose meditational style of *This Lime Tree Bower* would find its echoes the following year in Wordsworth's *Tintern Abbey*. While Coleridge finds a source of 'sweet . . . remembrance' in the 'beauties and feelings' of Nature, so William will see in them a source of 'tranquil restoration'. Coleridge's mood of trance is described as gazing 'till all doth seem/Less gross than bodily', and Wordsworth talks of being 'laid asleep/In body', of becoming 'a living soul'. Both find in Nature a sense of beneficence which is so closely parallel as to be almost a paraphrase of the other; Coleridge writes:

> Henceforth I shall know
> That Nature ne'er deserts the wise and pure;
> No plot so narrow, be but Nature there . . .

And Wordsworth:

> And this prayer I make,
> Knowing that Nature never did betray

> The heart that loved her; 'tis her privilege,
> Through all the years of this our life, to leap
> From joy to joy . . .

The mutual advantage gained from this growing friendship between the two poets is naturally difficult to assess. So much of *Tintern Abbey* seems to pay tribute to *This Lime Tree Bower*, and yet one feels that *This Lime Tree Bower* might never have been written but for Wordsworth's *Lines*. One sees in these early days at Stowey that total sharing of the inner space of two artists : so extraordinary, so rare, and, in the long run, so dangerous. In time it would become increasingly apparent that Coleridge regarded Wordsworth as the master; but as one Wordsworthian scholar has put it, Coleridge 'gave Wordsworth a philosophical basis for his response to Nature, and in doing so made available to him much of his greatest poetry'.[8] At the same time it is difficult not to read into that simple, negative reflection in Wordsworth's *Lines* –

> he, who feels contempt
> For any living thing, hath faculties
> Which he has never used . . .

The remote origins of the powerful, pervasive impetus of *The Ancient Mariner*. On the other hand, the extent to which Wordsworth's call for 'lowliness of heart' assisted Coleridge in adopting a less arrogant attitude, as some have suggested, is not so easy to determine. Any influence in this regard would be no more than a reinforcement of the lesson Charles Lamb had been impressing on Coleridge for the past nine months. Yet in one respect we know that Dorothy certainly had a part to play in curbing his flashy severity in reviewing. Coleridge recalled many years later, probably of this period, that he had written 'some half a score or more of what I thought clever and epigrammatic and devilishly severe reviews . . . but a remark made by Miss Wordsworth to whom I had, in the full expectation of gaining a laugh of

applause, read one of my judgments occasioned my committing the whole batch to the fire'.[9]

It is difficult not to believe that much of the conversation
during these early days of July must have centred on the
second edition of Coleridge's poems which had just been
printed with contributions by Lamb and Charles Lloyd.
Yet while Lamb's poems were ready to hand he seems to
have been more of a listener than a contributor to the discussions. Later he wrote to Coleridge: 'I could not talk
much while I was with you, but my silence was not sullenness, nor I hope from any bad motive, but in truth disuse
had made me feel awkward at it. . . . It was kind in you all to
endure me as you did.'[10]

Lamb too, quite understandably, was impressed with
Wordsworth's *Lines*, and he asked Coleridge for a copy of
the poem when he returned to London: 'I feel improvement', he wrote, 'in the recollection of many a casual conversation . . . but above all, that *Inscription*! – It will recall
to me the tones of all your voices – and with them many a
remembered kindness to one who could and can repay you
all only by the silence of a grateful heart.'

Another visitor at this time was Cottle, who has left an
amusingly characteristic description. It deserves quoting,
not only as it controverts the commonly held opinion of
biographers that Coleridge's garden was a permanent mass of
weeds, but because it so aptly portrays the Coleridges' happiness and well-being during this summer at Stowey. On
arriving at the cottage some time during the third week of
July, Coleridge first took his guest on a tour of the property:

exhibiting, successively, his house, his garden, his orchard, laden with
fruit; and also the contrivances he had made to unite his two neighbours' domains with his own.

After the grand circuit had been accomplished, by hospitable
contrivance, we approached the 'Jasmine harbour', when, to our
gratifying surprise, we found the tripod table laden with delicious
bread and cheese, surmounted by a brown mug of the true Taunton

ale. We instinctively took our seats; and there must have been some downright witchery in the provision which surpassed all of its kind; nothing like it on the wide terrene, and one glass of Taunton, settled it to an axiom. While the dappled sun-beams played on our table, through the umbrageous canopy, the very birds seemed to participate in our felicities and poured forth their selectest anthems. . . . While thus elevated in the universal current of our feelings, Mrs Coleridge approached, with her fine Hartley; we all smiled, but the father's eye beamed transcendental joy.[11]

The atmosphere of domestic happiness which pervades Cottle's quaint account is borne out by a yet later summer visit of one Richard Reynell. He provides us with one of the most attractive descriptions of Mrs Coleridge on record. Rising in the morning after spending the night in a bedroom where the window was a pane of glass 'made to slide in and out by a piece of wire', he came down and found Mrs Coleridge,

. . . as I have continued to find her, sensible, affable and good-natured, thrifty and industrious, and always neat and prettily dressed. I here see domestic life in all its beauty and simplicity, affection founded on a stronger basis than wealth – on esteem. Love seems more pure than it in general is to be found, because of the preference that has been given, in the choice of a life-friend, to mental and moral rather than personal and material charms, not that you are to infer that Coleridge and his wife have no *personal* recommendation. Mrs Coleridge is indeed a pretty woman.[12]

Coleridge's happiness this July had been made complete, in fact, by the Wordsworths' sudden decision that their visit must be extended to permanent residence. Finding a large house on the northern edge of the Quantocks, Poole negotiated a lease and stood guarantor. The rent was £23 a year, the house was called Alfoxden. 'Our principal inducement in coming here was Coleridge's society,' wrote Dorothy. And writing to Mary Hutchinson shortly after they had taken it she could dwell on the magnificent view from the window where she sat; the splendid walks whichever direction they turned from the house : 'Wherever we turn we have woods, smooth downs and valleys with small brooks running down them through green meadows, hardly ever intersected with hedgerows, but scattered over with trees. The hills that cradle these valleys are either covered with fern and bilberries or oak woods which are cut for charcoal.'

They signed the lease on 14 July and moved in immediately, the Coleridge's accompanying them for 'a change of air'. The contrast with the dingy Stowey cottage must have been great indeed. And a few days later they were joined by another acquaintance, when on 17 July John Thelwall turned up, with white hat, spectacles and stentorian voice, having walked all the way from London. Naturally he went first to Stowey where luckily he found Sara in the cottage who had returned 'to superintend the wash-tub'. 'I slept at Coleridge's cot,' he recorded in his journal, 'and this morning we rose by times and came here time enough to call Samuel and his friend Wordsworth up to breakfast. Faith, we are a most philosophical party . . . the enthusiastic group consisting of C. and his Sara, W. and his sister, and myself, without any servant, male or female. An old woman, who lives in an adjoining cottage, does what is requisite for our simple wants.'[13] After three days they all returned to Stowey where the conversation, not surprisingly, ranged across the political scene, but mainly on the 'moral character of Democrats, of Aristocrats'.[14]

Coleridge sent a description of his radical visitor to Josiah Wade back in Bristol : 'He is a great favourite with Sara. *Energetic Activity*, of *mind* and of *heart*, is his Master-feature. He is prompt to *conceive*, and still prompter to *execute* – . But I think, that he is deficient in that *patience* of mind, which can look *intensely* and *frequently* at the *same subject*.' Coleridge could claim that they got on 'uncommonly well' since they disagreed on every point of religion, morals, politics and philosophy. But he impressed on Wade that their most emphatic differences were political. Thelwall was, he said, 'Perhaps the only *acting* Democrat, that *is* honest for the *Patriots* are ragged cattle – a most execrable herd – arrogant because they are ignorant, and boastful of the strength of reason, because they have never tried it enough to know its *weakness*.' The comment gives rise to an interesting discrepancy between Coleridge's avowed rejection of the extreme radical position by the time he had settled at Stowey, both then and later in life, and continuing reports that he was as revolutionary as ever. The most interesting evidence for the latter comes from Thelwall himself. When Thelwall's personal copy of the *Biographia* recently came to light we were provided with a commentary on Coleridge's view of himself during the Stowey days in the form of marginal glosses. Where Coleridge claims in Chapter X to have retired to Stowey with his 'eyes thoroughly opened to the true character and impotence of the favorers of revolutionary principles ... principles which I held in abhorrence ... ' Thelwall has noted: 'Where I visitted [*sic*] him & founded him a decided Leveller – abusing the democrats for their hypocritical moderation, in pretending to be willing to give the people equality of privileges & rank, at the same time, they would refuse them all that the others could be valuable for – equality of property – or rather abolition of all property.'[15] And where Coleridge, referring to his earlier and admitted radicalism, says, 'O! never can I remember those days with either shame or regret ... ' Thelwall comments: 'Does he forget the letters he wrote to me (& which I believe I yet have) acknowledging the justice of my castigation of him for the violence, and sanguinary tendency of some of his doctrines.'[16] Perhaps Coleridge felt he had fully acquitted himself by the assertion that his opinions were 'almost equidistant from all parties during these times, the Pittites, the Foxites, and the Democrats'.[17]

Another prominent theme of their discussions at Stowey was the 'pursuits proper to literary men – unfit for manage-

ment of pecuniary affairs', a subject naturally applicable to
Coleridge. The question of rural retirement must have been
a central theme, and there are two versions of a conversation
which took place between Thelwall and Coleridge that sheds
light on the style of their discussions at this time. 'I
remember once,' wrote Wordsworth, 'when Coleridge and
Thelwall and I were seated upon the turf on the bank of the
stream, in the most beautiful part of the most beautiful
glen of Alfoxden, Coleridge exclaimed, "This is a place to
reconcile one to all the jarrings and conflicts of the wide
world." "Nay," said Thelwall, "to make one forget them
altogether."'[18] Coleridge's crisp, and possibly more factual,
rendering was: 'Citizen John,' I said to him, 'This is a
fine place to talk treason in!' 'Nay! Citizen Samuel,'
replied he, 'it is rather a place to make a man forget that
there is any necessity for treason.'[19]

Enchanted by this 'most philosophical party' and the
peace and beauty of their surroundings Thelwall was
tempted to join the two poets. In fact he recorded his desire
in some verses – *Lines written at Bridgwater, in Somerset-
shire, on the 27th of July, 1797*

> [Then] by our sides
> Thy Sara, and my Susan, and, perchance,
> Allfoxden's musing tenant, and the maid
> Of ardent eye, who, with fraternal love,
> Sweetens his solitude.[20]

For a long time now, Thelwall had been seeking a place of
retirement, and Coleridge had frequently encouraged him to
emulate his own mode of living. But after he had arrived
it became obvious that persecution and suspicion would
dog him to such an extent that his settling at Stowey might
prove a threat not only to Coleridge and Wordsworth but
also to Thomas Poole who was seen to be 'harbouring' them.
Above all it was feared that Thomas Poole's Benefit Club,
or Poor Man's Club, 'would be materially affected by any

favour of T[helwall].'[21] Already Poole had suffered the alienation of his relatives by assisting Coleridge, and it did not seem possible to procure a place for Thelwall without Poole's further assistance. Coleridge sought in vain for a solution, but eventually he was obliged to write to Thelwall and put him off. He must have remembered with sadness his own disappointment in the previous winter when Poole had tried to dissuade him too from coming to Stowey.

The whole Malignity of the Aristocrats will converge to him [explained Coleridge] as to *one* point – his tranquility will be perpetually interrupted – his business, and his credit, hampered and distressed by vexatious calumnies – the ties of relationship weakened – perhaps broken – and lastly, his poor Mother made miserable – the pain of the stone aggravated by domestic calamity and quarrels betwixt her son and those neighbours with whom and herself there have been peace and love for these fifty years.[22]

There was little Thelwall could do except acquiesce in the face of this kind of pressure. And yet Coleridge was probably describing more or less accurately the consequences of holding radical opinions in England at this time, even in the remote countryside. As for being suspected of something more dangerous than mere opinions, who knew what sinister repercussions might lie in store? – as the peculiar episode which followed on Wordsworth's arrival in the district illustrates. 'You cannot conceive the tumult, calumnies and apparatus of threatened persecutions which this event has occasioned round about us,' wrote Coleridge, referring to the episode of 'the Spy' which occurred after Wordsworth had settled at Alfoxden. Apparently a former servant of Alfoxden, called Mogg, had complained of the stranger Wordsworth to a woman in Bath who had also been a former member of the staff at Alfoxden. She reported the matter to her new employer, a Dr Lysons, who dutifully communicated the following to the then Home Secretary, the Duke of Portland :[23]

11th Aug. My Lord Duke – On the 8th instant I took the liberty to acquaint your grace with a very suspicious business concerning an emigrant family, who have contrived to get possession of a Mansion House at Alfoxton, late belonging to the Revd Mr. St. Albyn under Quantock Hills. I am informed that the Master of the house has no wife with him, but only a woman who passes for his Sister. The man has Camp Stools which he and his visitors take with them when they go about the country upon their nocturnal or diurnal excursions and have also a Portfolio in which they enter their observations which they have been heard to say were almost finished. They have been heard to say they should be rewarded for them, and were very attentive to the River near them. . . . These people may *possibly* be under-agents to some principal in Bristol.

Cottle, whose information originally came from Coleridge, talks of the wild rumours that were being spread about the countryside. However cautious one must be about Coleridge's, or Cottle's, anecdotes, the general drift of his account rings true. He says that the villagers had made Wordsworth the subject of their 'serious' conversation. One had seen him wandering about by night, looking 'strangely at the moon!', and roaming 'over the hills like a partridge'. Another said he had heard him muttering 'in some outlandish brogue that nobody could understand!' He was a conjuror, a smuggler, an illicit brewer, or perhaps – worst of all – 'a desperate French Jacobin, for he is so silent and dark that no one ever heard him say a word about politics'.

The Wordsworths' north-country accent, and what De Quincey referred to as a 'pronounced gipsy tan' accounts for their being taken for 'emigrants'. The credulous neighbours only had to link the strangers' weird activities with current invasion rumours to pronounce them French. The poet's innocent rambles, which were taken for something more sinister, are described by Coleridge in the *Biographia*. He had been planning a long poem on a theme which would 'give equal freedom for description, incident and impassioned reflections on men, nature and society, yet supply a natural connection to the parts and units to the whole'. He explored the idea of following a stream from its source in the hills down through villages, market towns and manufactories, to the seaport: 'My walks therefore were almost daily on the top of Quantock, and among its sloping combes. With my pencil and memorandum-book in my hand I was *making studies* as artists call them, and often moulding my thoughts into verse, with the object and imagery immediately before my senses.'

Through Alfoxden's ex-cook, then, the Home Office came to learn of the strange goings-on in Somerset, and an agent was duly sent to check Mogg's story. On 11 August this agent, Walsh, could report back to the Home Office that Charles Mogg had now heard that some French people 'had got possession of the Mansion House and that they were washing and mending their cloaths all Sunday'. Moreover, a neighbour, Christopher Trickie, who lived at the 'Dog pound' at Alfoxden claimed that the 'French people' had taken a plan of their house, and made maps of all the places round that part of the country. Trickie had been asked whether the brook in front of his house was navigable to the sea, and although he answered to the contrary the 'French' were afterwards seen following the brook down to the sea. Many other people had reported the 'French people very suspicious persons and that they were doing no good there'. It was also considered strange that they 'kept no servant, but they were visited by a number of persons'.

This interrogation of Mogg seemed to substantiate the first report. Consequently Walsh was given £20 and told to proceed to Alfoxden immediately. He was advised to conduct his enquiries in secrecy, and 'narrowly watch their proceedings'. 'Above all,' warned the Permanent Under-Secretary at the Home Office, 'you will be careful not to give them any cause of alarm, that if necessary they may be found on the spot.'

Three days later Walsh sent in his second report from the

Globe Inn at Nether Stowey. He had discovered from the landlord and a customer that Thelwall was at the bottom of these goings-on.

I then asked if they meant the famous Thelwall. They said yes. That he had been down some time, and that there was a Nest of them at Alfoxton House who were protected by a Mr Poole a Tanner of this town, and that he supposed Thelwall was there (Alfoxton House) at this time. I told Woodhouse that I had heard somebody say at Bridgewater that they were French people at the Mansion House. The Landlord and Woodhouse answered No, No. They are not French, but they are people that will do as much harm as all the French can do . . . I think this will turn out no French affair, but a mischevous gang of disaffected Englishmen. I have procured the name of the person who took the House. His name is Wordsworth a name I think known to Mr Ford.

Further information followed the next day. The inhabitants at Alfoxden, Walsh could verify, were a 'set of violent democrats'. Thomas Poole, their protector, was a 'violent member of the Corresponding Society' and he had been harbouring a 'Mr Coldridge and his wife both of whom he has supported since Christmas last'. 'This Coldridge,' continued Walsh, 'is reckoned a man of superior ability. He is frequently publishing, and I am told is soon to produce a new work. He has a press in the house and I am informed he prints as well as publishes his own productions.' Dark and dangerous activities indeed. But Poole was even more to be feared, 'having established in this town, what he stiles *The Poor Man's Club*, and placing himself at the head of it, by the title of the *Poor Man's Friend*.' It was said that a hundred and fifty men belonged to this club, and that Poole had the instant command of every one of them.

This was the last report to appear in the Home Office records. The file was closed, the matter was not pursued any further. But how it came to end so abruptly is uncertain. If Coleridge is to be believed all suspicions of espionage, and even Jacobinism, evaporated after a conversation took place between the agent and himself on the road between Alfoxden and Stowey : 'passing himself off as a traveller,' remembered Coleridge in the *Biographia,* 'he had entered into conversation with me, and talked of a purpose in a democrat way in order to draw me out. The result, it appears, not only convinced him that I was no friend of Jacobinism ; but (he added) I had "plainly made it out to be such a silly as well as wicked thing, that he felt ashamed, though he had only put it on".' Only after a tip off from Poole had Coleridge realized that he and his friends were being watched ; yet his own account includes a good deal of retrospective anecdote, highly amusing but probably apocryphal, including the episode of the agent snooping on his seaside conversations with Wordsworth from behind a sand-dune and mistaking their references to Spinoza for 'Spy Nozy'.

Unlike Coleridge, who relished a good many stories connected with this incident down the years, unlike Poole, Cottle and even Southey, who heard of the matter independently, the only person who seems to have survived the excitement without being even remotely aware of it was Wordsworth himself, the very centre of suspicion. As Peggy, the Wordsworths' maid, reported to the neighbour Mr Jones, who passed on the information to Agent Walsh – her master was 'a Phylosopher', and his total ignorance of the matter until after it was all over gives us a measure of his philosophical insulation.

A direct consequence of the upset, however, was the final decision with regard to Thelwall. Writing to him on 21 August, Coleridge suggested that the only possibility of his taking up residence in the area was to do it gradually :

– come! but not yet! – come in two or three months – take lodgings at Bridgewater – familiarize the people to your name & appearance – and when the *monstrosity* of the thing is gone off, & the people shall have begun to consider you, as a man whose mouth won't eat them – & whose pocket is better adapted for a bundle of sonnets than the

transportation or ambush-place of a French army – then you may take
a *house* – but indeed – I say it with a very sad, but a very clear conviction – at *present* I see that much evil & little good would result
from your settling here.

Later in the summer another visitor arrived in the district
of a rather different distinction than Thelwall's. He was
Tom Wedgwood, member of the wealthy industrialist
family, and brother of John and Josiah. This brilliant
'independent child of the enlightenment', who has gone
down in history as the father of photography, had been
practically raised in the laboratories of his father's potteries
in Etruria. Now at the age of twenty-six he was searching
for suitable men to assist him in a scheme for the amelioration of mankind, namely, a 'master-stroke' which was to take
the form of financing the education of a 'genius'.[24] Writing
to Godwin on 31 July, he had expressed his ambition to
'anticipate a century or two upon the large-paced progress
of human improvement' :

> Let us suppose ourselves in possession of a detailed statement of the
> first twenty years of the life of some extraordinary genius; what a
> chaos of perceptions! . . . How many opposing tendencies which have
> negatived each other. . . . How many hours, days, months have been
> prodigally wasted in unproductive occupation! How many false and
> contradictory ideas imprinted by authority!

The notion illustrates the strong hold of the necessitarian
doctrines of the day, and the rage for educational experiments. Explaining his well-meaning, if odd, theories,
Wedgwood goes on to say: 'The practice should be to
simplify and render intense the first affection of Sense, and
secondly to excite those affections under every possible
favourable circumstance of pleasure.' The most important
of the senses, he insisted, were 'Sight and Touch', consequently special care should be taken in the construction of
the child's nursery. 'Should not the nursery, then, have
plain, grey walls with one or two vivid objects for sight and

touch? Could not the children be made to acquire manipula-
tion sooner? Let hard bodies be hung about them so as
continually to irritate their palms.' And in order to regulate
the process of development and provide a balanced diet of
impressions, 'The child must never go out of doors or leave
his own apartment.' To complete this scheme, so compact
with sadism and good sense, Wedgwood proposed that
there should be none of the usual frivolity of 'romping,
tickling and fooling'. The child should be held strictly to
'rational objects' with no time allowed for daydreaming. 'In
the best regulated mind of the present day, has not there
been, and is not there some hours every day passed in
reverie, thought ungoverned, undirected? How astonish-
ingly the powers and produce of the mind would be increased by a fixed habit of earnest thought. This is to be
given.'

The overseers of this seminary for infant prodigies would
be a committee of 'philosophers', amongst them, Godwin,
Thomas Beddoes – the Bristol physician, Holcroft, Horne
Tooke and Wedgwood himself. The practising superinten-
dents would be difficult to find: 'the only persons that I know
of as at all likely for this purpose', wrote Wedgwood, 'are
Wordsworth and Coleridge.' He expected Wordsworth to
come forward with great alacrity on hearing of the plan, but
held some reservations about Coleridge, fearing that he
might be 'too much of a poet and religionist to suit our
views'. Clearly he had no conception of the unsuitability of
his views for either of the poets. Coleridge's theories, of
course, were moving in the opposite direction. Just the year
before he had told Charles Lamb of his determination to
bring up his own children from earliest infancy 'in the
simplicity of peasants', their habits 'completely rustic'. And
early in the following year he would write of his own child:

> But *thou*, my babe! shalt wander like a breeze
> By lakes and sandy shores, beneath the crags
> Of ancient mountain, and beneath the clouds,

> Which image in their bulk both lakes and shores
> And mountain crags.

On the other hand, Coleridge's interest in the nature of 'genius' was entirely divorced at this stage from any sense of public utility. In this sense he would have reacted vehemently, particularly against Wedgwood's suggestion that the child should be held strictly 'to rational objects'. In the following month on 16 October he wrote to Poole criticizing this very tendency in education.

> Should children be permitted to read Romances, & Relations of Giants & Magicians, & Genii? – I know all that has been said against it; but I have formed my faith in the affirmative. – I know no other way of giving the mind a love of 'the Great', & 'the Whole'. – Those who have been led to the same truths step by step thro' the constant testimony of their senses, seem to me to want a sense which I possess – They contemplate nothing, but *parts* – and all *parts* are necessarily little and the Universe to them is but a mass of *little things*.[25]

Just two days before writing this letter he had written to Thelwall saying how much he longed for an experience that lay beyond the 'immense heap of *little* things' of which the universe seemed to be constituted : 'My mind feels as if it ached to behold & know something *great* – something *one* & *indivisible* – and it is only in the faith of this that rocks or waterfalls, mountains or caverns give me the sense of sublimity or majesty ! – But in this faith *all things* counterfeit infinity !'

We shall see later how this was leading towards a remarkable act of artistic expression. But for the moment it illustrates the huge gap that lay between Coleridge's thinking and Wedgwood's. It was not in the close confines of a specially devised nursery, nor in the strict and 'rational' channelling of a child's reading, that Coleridge believed the mind could flourish, but in the reading of works of Romance and in the presence of natural forms. For Wordsworth too there could be no substitute for Nature, who toiled with

7

'unwearied passion' to 'win us to herself, and to impress/
our careless hearts with beauty and with love'. Wordsworth's
riposte to Wedgwood's system and all that it stood for would
be embodied in the fifth book of the *Prelude* which he began
in the following year.

In fact during Tom Wedgwood's visit in September it
seems likely that Wordsworth may have drawn considerable
fire. Wedgwood was to retain a somewhat jaundiced view
of Wordsworth in the future, whereas Coleridge won unqualified admiration from the rich industrialist. Perhaps
Coleridge realized that Wedgwood's first impressions might
prove important : the financial situation at Stowey was still
far from healthy ; the reviewing was not prospering – as we
have seen, one batch had already been committed to the fire –
and he could hardly hope for too much from his tragedy
Osorio. He was still receiving payments from Tom Poole's
fund, but it never seemed sufficient. Acquaintance with
wealthy philanthropists like Wedgwood might be to his
advantage. We do not know whether Coleridge actually
restrained his opinions on meeting Wedgwood in September,
or later, in November, when he stayed at the Wedgwoods'
home at Cote House near Bristol. But then, Wedgwood
may have found that flow of Coleridgeian eloquence – as
many had done – completely irresistible whatever the
opinion expressed.

In the meantime, however, the anxieties posed by an uncertain future did exist. Coleridge could not continue to
depend on Tom Poole's charity for ever. Yet how could he
be depressed for very long now that he had met Wordsworth? And who knew? Together, they might achieve a
popular literary success which would enable them to finance
their serious, less profitable writing. There was, after all,
plenty of money in the world of books, provided that they
catered for the right market. And what category of literature

more than the 'prose-tale' or the 'verse-romance' was likely
to score a success?

The discussions about reading this autumn, which seemed
to have arisen so naturally from the vexing questions posed
by Wedgwood's quest – the foundation of genius – merge
with Coleridge's literary activities in the second half of 1797.
Of romances Coleridge had written – 'I know no other way
of giving the mind a love of "the Great", and "the Whole"'
and in his longing for something *one* & *indivisible*', he
found in the natural forms of rocks, waterfalls, mountains or
caverns a 'sense of sublimity or majesty!' For Coleridge, the
ultimate grandeur and ennobling of the mind and heart
consisted in breaking through the 'parts', the 'rational
objects' the 'little' things, to the transcendental realities that
lay beyond. 'But in this faith *all things* counterfeit infinity!'

Yet from the very start his close association with Wordsworth determined the shape of his productions throughout
this year. Together, they decided to collaborate in the writing
of a prose-tale, 'The Wanderings of Cain'. Primarily the
purpose was to earn some money, yet the theme naturally
arose from longstanding preoccupations. Already Wordsworth had been dwelling on the theme of psychological
guilt in *The Borderers* and *Salisbury Plain*, and for Coleridge
there was a deeply personal fascination with guilt that went
back to his childhood.

In November 1797 the two poets went on a walk during
which this piece was planned, yet the deeper stirrings, which
Coleridge had expressed in those letters during October,
were also gaining in strength at this time. On this same
walk it seems likely that Coleridge composed *Kubla Khan*.[26]
Dorothy Wordsworth describes the circumstances of their
journey:

[From Porlock] we kept close to the shore about four miles. Our
road lay through wood, rising almost perpendicularly from the sea,
with views of the opposite mountains of Wales: thence we came by
twilight to Lynmouth, in Devonshire. The next day we were guided

to a valley at the top of one of those immense hills which open at each end to the sea, and is from its rocky appearance called the Valley of Stones. We mounted a cliff at the end of the valley, and looked from it immediately on to the sea.[27]

Coleridge told Hazlitt when he met him the following summer that he and Wordsworth were to have made this valley 'the scene of a prose-tale, which was to have been in the manner of, but far superior to, Gessner's Death of Abel, but they had relinquished the design.' Hazlitt who visited the Valley of the Rocks the following summer described it as 'bedded among precipices overhanging the sea, with rocky caverns beneath, into which the waves dash, and where the sea-gull for ever wheels its screaming flight. On the tops of these are huge stones thrown transverse, as if an earthquake had tossed them there, and behind these is a fretwork of perpendicular rocks, something like the *Giant's Causeway*.'[28] Here were the sublime 'rocks', 'mountains', 'caverns' – here too was a setting which may have assisted Coleridge in the writing of *Kubla Khan*. The likely reconstruction of events is that when they were on their way to Culbone, having left the Valley of the Rocks, Coleridge was seized with severe dysentery. One is reminded of Wordsworth's descriptions of Coleridge's attacks which were sometimes so acute that he would 'throw himself down and writhe like a worm on the ground'. He was forced to rest in a farm-house while his companions continued on their way, probably to fetch provisions. Sitting in a room in this secluded house, Coleridge says that he took two grains of opium to check his illness, and eventually fell asleep while reading a passage from *Purchas his Pilgrimage*: 'In Xamdu did Cublai Can build a stately Palace, encompassing sixteene miles of plaine ground with a wall, wherein are fertile Meddowes, pleasant Springs, delightfull Streames, and all sorts of beasts of chase and game, and in the middest thereof a sumptuous house of pleasure.'[29]

Coleridge later wrote that he continued for about three

hours in a profound sleep 'at least of the external senses', during which time he composed between two and three hundred lines – 'if that indeed can be called composition in which all the images rose up before him as *things*, with a parallel production of the correspondent expressions, without any sensation or consciousness of effort'. On waking, and distinctly recollecting the whole, he 'instantly and eagerly' wrote out fifty-four of the lines, before being interrupted 'by a person on business from Porlock' who detained him for over an hour. On returning to his room he found that though he still retained 'some vague and dim recollection of the general purport of the vision, yet, with the exception of some eight or ten scattered lines and images, all the rest had passed away like the images on the surface of a stream into which a stone has been cast, but alas! without the after restoration of the latter!'[30]

Kubla Khan is a controversial poem, both in terms of the circumstances of its composition, its interpretation, and its evaluation. Coleridge preferred to think of it as a 'psychological curiosity', and claimed that it was for this reason alone that he allowed Byron to prevail upon him to publish it, rather 'than on the ground of any supposed *poetic* merits'. The poem is unfinished, a 'fragment'; much of the 'vision' or sequence of 'images' had faded from his mind after the interruption, and he cast doubts on whether the writing of it could properly be called composition. In our own day, of course, it has come to be regarded as one of Coleridge's most important poems, indeed, one of the most remarkable poems in the language. With the aids of scholarship critics have encouraged the modern reader to delve more deeply into the poem's remote origins, to explore the allusive qualities suggested by our knowledge of Coleridge's wide-ranging reading. As John Beer writes: 'For the practical critic it presents in an extreme form a problem which must often greet him in reading romantic poetry – that the total poem may not be readily available in the immediate verbal

structure which appears on the page.' There is little doubt
that this approach has produced intriguing interpretations
and has enriched our response. Yet in spite of this *Kubla
Khan* still retains its essential mystery. In fact, the successive
attempts to pluck out the heart of the mystery are in themselves a tribute to the poem's abiding fascination. This is not
the place to embark on a recapitulation of the many interpretations that have been put forward, but it is, perhaps, a
suitable occasion to oppose the suggestion, implicit in the
proliferation of theorizing, that one should be on one's
guard against a straightforward reading. A more simple
reading does not necessarily render the poem less enigmatic.
To accept the mystery and respond fully to those elements
which seem to elude us, those features which seem to
suggest something which we are always about to understand
but never quite do, is surely an approach that is not to be
despised. As Coleridge himself wrote in his notebook the
following year : 'When no criticism is pretended to, & the
Mind in its simplicity gives itself up to a Poem as to a work
of Nature, Poetry gives most pleasure when only generally
& not perfectly understood. . . . From this cause it is what *I*
call metaphysical poetry gives me so much delight.'[31]

In *Kubla Khan* there is neither narrative nor event, but
rather a series of interrelated and opposing images which
always seem to elude the mind's eye when one is on the
point of achieving a total picture. What is immediately
arresting about these images, and what explains their
elusiveness as a total vision is the sense of polarity between
their groupings, exerting a powerful tension. In the first
stanza, Alph the sacred river is seen to connect the 'stately
pleasure dome' with 'caverns measureless to man' and the
'sunless sea'. There are powerful suggestions in the latter
images – of eternity, the imponderable mystery of the
labyrinth, darkness, death and dissolution : suggestions
which are immediately counteracted by a fuller description
of the pleasure dome and its gardens. The 'fertile ground' is

limited and confined – 'girdled round' – there is light, growth, blossoming, colour, warmth, the sensuousness of the incense-bearing trees, the lyrical beauty of the 'sunny spots of greenery'. There is an atmosphere of artefact, of landscaped gardens, of man taming and shaping the forests 'ancient as the hills'.

But the 'pleasure dome' stands midway between 'the fountain and the caves'. And just as the caverns and the sunless sea seem to symbolize the eternity of things passing away, the fountain suggests the infinite energy of things coming into being – 'counterfeit infinity'. The fountain describes three distinct impressions of motion and energy in three powerful images : fragments rebounding like hail, as of bodies falling, and rising on meeting a stationary surface ; then, 'like chaffy grain beneath the thresher's flail', the motion of bodies forced by an outside agent ; and, finally, 'dancing', as by their own motion. These varying impressions of motion seem to suggest a sense of ambiguity between passive and active states. Are the rocks, or frag-ments, stationary? Are they only *seen* to acquire motion from the 'half-intermitted' burst of the water? Or are they moving freely in the force of the torrent?

Similarly there is an attempt to express the opposing states of permanence and change in a single image '*one and indivisible*' by the movement of the water, the 'ceaseless' turmoil 'momently' forced, 'at once and ever'.

Then, tracing the river down through the pastoral scene of woods and meadows to the caverns and the 'lifeless ocean', he returns once more to the poem's starting point –

> The shadow of the dome of pleasure
> Floated midway on the waves ;
> Where was heard the mingled measure
> From the fountain and the caves.
> It was a miracle of rare device,
> A sunny pleasure-dome with caves of ice!

The source of life and its passing away are finally brought together in the 'mingled measure' from the fountain and the caverns where the reflection of the dome 'floats' on the water. Each group of images, while being in powerful conflict with the other is brought into harmony, and the finite limited area of the pleasure garden enjoys the echoes of infinity and eternity. Within the shadow of this finite, limited artefact the infinite source of life's energy and the imponderable mysteries of eternity are isolated and captured. And yet the achievement of such a vision is not without its dangers ; the closeness of the artist to the sources of Life and Death places him within the circle of initiation, frenzy and madness ; brings him in contact with the ominous voices of the 'Ancestral' dead – voices 'prophesying war'.

At the same time the last line of the above quotation flings an abrupt surprise purely on the level of the finite, and direct sense perception : 'A sunny pleasure-dome with caves of ice.' The origin of this phrase, culled from *Maurice's History of Hindostan* is interesting, but its origin does not seem to help. Does Coleridge mean that the caves of ice form the interior structure of the dome ? Or does the reflected image of the dome on the water suggest the caves of ice ? The ambiguity is in itself intriguing, but more than this there is the shock of a final tension within the realms of the finite : the smoothness, warmth and light of the dome – the rough, dark, subterranean coldness of the 'caves of ice'. It is as if he is destroying the fleeting sense of harmony achieved in the 'mingled measure' with an irreconcilable fusion of opposite images.

For Coleridge the extremes of heat and cold, embodied in the images of sun and ice, had a special significance. At the end of *Religious Musings*, addressing the 'Contemplant Spirits' of the universe in a final, Miltonic address to his Muse, he talks of

> ... Love, omnific, omnipresent Love,
> Whose day-spring rises glorious in my soul

> As the great Sun, when he his influence
> Sheds on the frost-bound waters –

The inspirational implications are clear enough, but he was to continue to explore and develop the expression of the image for many years to come, as one of the supreme examples of the meeting of extremes. As he later observed in his notebook:

> I have repeatedly said, that I could have made a volume, if only I had noted down, as they occurred to me my recollections or observations, the instances of the Proverb, Extremes Meet...
>   The parching Air
>   Burns frore, and Cold performs the Effect of Fire.
>   Par. Lost, Book 2. 594.[32]

Whatever else one might say about *Kubla Khan*, it seems to be expressing in metaphorical form Coleridge's consistent preoccupation with the tension and reconciliation of polarities. One is again reminded of Charles Lamb's comment the year before: 'You seem to have been straining your comparing faculties to bring together things infinitely distant and unlike.' We have seen that this had been a general frame of mind, both in his philosophy and poetry, and here at last it is expressed in terms of an extended, if perplexing, metaphor. Yet by the very extravagance of its tensions, the scale of its significance, the radical mode of its expression, the poem suggests that he was on the brink of a new understanding. It is this aspect of the poem that throws into relief those letters to Poole and Thelwall in October, and his longing to behold and know 'something *one and indivisible*', his discovering in 'rocks or waterfalls, mountains or caverns' a sense of counterfeit infinity. The letter clearly anticipates the frame of mind in which he wrote *Kubla Khan*. The phrase 'counterfeit infinity', borrowed from Cudworth, must have seemed so right in its suggestion of the latent power of natural forms and images to express transcendental ideas, that there was no reason to

7*

expound any further. But writing some years later about the way in which 'waterfalls' gave him a sense of the infinite, he says this :

What a sight it is to look down on such a Cataract! – the wheels, that circumvolve in it – the leaping up & plunging forward of that infinity of Pearls & Glass Bulbs – the continual *change* of the *Matter*, the perpetual *Sameness* of the *Form* – it is an awful Image & Shadow of God & the world.[33]

Similarly in 1805, on a tour of Italy, he was astonished by the fountains in St Peter's Square :

The quiet circle in which Change and Permanence *co-exist*, not by combination or juxtaposition, but by an absolute annihilation of difference/column of smoke, the fountains before St Peter's, water-falls/God! – Change without loss – change by perpetual growth, that ⟨once constitutes & annihilates change⟩ the past, & the future included in the Present//oh! it is aweful.[34]

The extent to which *Kubla Khan* is a self-authenticating manifestation of the marriage of finite and infinite, permanence and change, expressed in forms or images '*one and indivisible*' is at once the source of the poem's artistic success and abiding mystery.

At the same time there is a very special atmosphere about this poem that connects it with the realms of the dream, the trance, and opium states. On 17 December 1796 Coleridge had written to Thelwall about the nature of 'obscurity' in poetry :

You ought to distinguish between obscurity residing in the un-commonness of the thought, and that which proceeds from thoughts unconnected & language not adapted to the expression of them. When you *do* find out the meaning of my poetry, can you (in general, I mean) alter the language so as to make it more perspicuous – the thought remaining the same? – By 'dreamy semblance' I *did* mean semblance of some unknown Past, like to a dream – and not 'a semblance presented in a dream'.

He had been discussing, in fact, his sonnet *Composed on a*

journey homewards, in which he expresses the strange experience of 'Reality' appearing as a 'Semblance, and the Present like a dream in Sleep'. Coleridge's attempts to capture these dreamlike states in his poetry, and his plea for the consequent and intentional obscurity, clearly has a special relevance in any discussion of *Kubla Khan*. Again, he raised this topic in the letter to Thelwall on 14 October, 1797. He has been talking of trance states, and quotes from *This Lime Tree Bower* to illustrate a specific experience:

> Struck with the deepest calm of Joy I stand –
> Silent, with swimming sense; and gazing round
> On the wide Landscape gaze till all doth seem
> Less gross than bodily, a living Thing
> Which acts upon the mind, & with such Hues
> As cloath th' Almighty Spirit, when he makes
> Spirits perceive his presence! –

He follows this with a description of another trance like state which is clearly associated with the after effects of opium:

> It is but seldom that I raise & spiritualize my intellect to this height – & at other times I adopt the Brahman Creed, & say – It is better to sit than to stand, it is better to lie than to sit, it is better to sleep than to wake – but Death is the best of all! – I should much wish, like the Indian Vishna [Vishnu], to float about along an infinite ocean cradled in the flower of the Lotos, & wake once in a million years for a few minutes – just to know that I was going to sleep a million years more.

One sees here the connection between natural forms and the enticing images raised by his drug. And the allurement of that boundless sea again finds expression, this time in a recently composed passage of *Osorio*, where he puts the following words into the mouth of his Moorish Woman:

> – O would to Alla,
> The Raven & the Seamew were appointed
> To bring me food – or rather that my Soul
> Could drink in life from the universal air!

It were a lot divine in some small skiff
Along some Ocean's boundless solitude
To float for ever with a careless course,
And think myself the only Being alive!

The close approximation of the above states to the atmosphere of timeless 'Reverie' in *Kubla Khan*, together with Coleridge's remarks on the special nature of dreamlike states in his poetry should encourage us to respond as fully as possible to the obscurity itself before destroying the full impact of such impressions by searching too hastily for significances that lie beyond 'the verbal structure that appears on the page'. We shall see later how Coleridge defended the indefinite and the obscure in poetry precisely because of its special power to evoke deep feeling and subconscious resonances – 'that shadowy half-being, that state of nascent Existence in the Twilight of the Imagination, and just on the vestibule of Consciousness'.[35] If we are to follow Coleridge in his conviction that in certain circumstances images lacking in clarity or explicit utterance are 'far more incendiary, stir up a more lasting commotion, & leave a deeper stain' we should be encouraged to 'keep the mind passive ... submit to an impression ... keep the mind steady in order to *receive* the stamp', rather than looking beyond the poem 'in order by means of some *other* thing analogous to understand the former'.[36]

But what became of that prose-tale, *The Wanderings of Cain*? The scheme went forward, Coleridge drawing up the outline and contents for each of the three books or cantos which were to be completed in one night! Whoever had completed their canto was to proceed to the third. Writing at a distance of some thirty years after the event, Coleridge was amazed at the impracticability of the task, especially for a poet like Wordsworth – 'for a mind so eminently original to compose another man's thoughts, or for a taste so austerely simple to imitate the Death of Abel'. He was referring, in fact, to Gessner's version of the story widely read in Mrs Collyer's translation. He goes on to recollect the outcome of this impractical scheme, which gives us a fleeting but vivid impression of Wordsworth's personality :

Methinks I see his grand and noble countenance as at the moment when having despatched my own portion of the task at full finger-speed, I hastened to him with my manuscript, – that look of humorous despondency fixed on his almost blank sheet of paper, and then its silent mock-piteous admission of failure struggling with the sense of the exceeding ridiculousness of the whole scheme – which broke up in a laugh : and the Ancient Mariner was written instead.

Again, Dorothy records another walk, taken on 13 November : 'we set out last Monday evening at half past four', she wrote, 'The evening was dark and cloudy : we went eight miles, William and Coleridge employing themselves in laying the plan of a ballad, to be published with some pieces of William's . . .' Once again the motive was money. 'As our united funds were very small,' wrote William, 'we agreed to defray the expense of the tour by writing a Poem, to be sent to the new Monthly Magazine set up by Phillips the bookseller and edited by Dr Aiken. Accordingly we set off and proceeded along the Quantock Hills, towards Watchet, and in the course of this walk was planned the Poem of The Ancient Mariner.'

Wordsworth goes on to describe his own particular contributions to its inception, which were by no means inconsiderable.

Much the greatest part of the story was Mr Coleridge's invention ; but certain parts I myself suggested, for example, some crime was to be committed which should bring upon the Old Navigator, as Coleridge afterwards delighted to call him, the spectral persecution, as a consequence of that crime, and his own wanderings. I had been reading in Shelvock's *Voyages* a day or two before that while doubling Cape Horn they frequently saw Albatross in that latitude, the largest sort of sea-fowl, extending their wings 12 or 13 feet. 'Suppose' said I, 'you represent him as having killed one of these birds on entering the South Sea, and that the tutelary Spirits of these regions take upon them to avenge the crime'. The incident was thought fit for the purpose and adopted accordingly. I also suggested the navigation of the ship by the dead men, but do not recollect that I had anything more to do with the scheme of the poem . . . We began the composition on that, to me, memorable evening. I furnished two or three lines at the beginning of the poem, in particular :

> And listened like a three years' child;
> The Mariner had his will.

These trifling contributions, all but one (which Mr C. has with unnecessary scrupulosity recorded) slipt out of his mind as they well might.[37]

Wordsworth goes on to describe how this second attempt at collaboration failed. It was much the same story as the case of *The Wanderings of Cain*. He says that on that same evening their respective 'manners' of composition 'proved so widely different that it would have been quite presumptuous in me to do anything but separate from an undertaking upon which I could only have been a clog'. Perhaps the most ready explanation for the breakdown of the experiment was that Wordsworth's interest in the theme of crime, guilt and expiation was mainly psychological, whereas Coleridge was beginning to move in a supernatural ambit that was peculiarly his own. In *The Ancient Mariner* Coleridge had, in fact, found the suitable vehicle for the direction in which his feelings and thoughts had been tending; for many more months he would become absorbed in the poem, developing it well beyond their original intention – a popular ballad for a magazine.

During November the Wordsworths were visited by Basil Montagu, the father of Basil Montagu junior, a child they had in their care. Unable to pursue the profession of law at the Bar due to Godwinian scruples, and having recently lost a lawsuit, he was now seeking a means of livelihood. He came to Alfoxden in the hopes of persuading Coleridge to join him in the founding of a school, and for Coleridge, who desperately needed a more certain income, the project seemed initially promising. 'Our scheme was singular and extensive,' he wrote.

Extensive, for we proposed in three years to go systematically, yet with constant reference to the nature of *man*, thro' the mathematical Branches, chemistry, Anatomy, the laws of Life, the laws of Intellect, and lastly thro' universal History, arranging separately all the facts that elucidate the separate states of Society, savage, civilized and luxurious: singular, for we proposed ourselves, not as Teachers, but only as Managing Students.

Coming so shortly after the establishment of Wedgwood's fund, and the meeting in September, it is not unlikely that Coleridge and Montagu (also known to Wedgwood) were hoping to attract the rich industrialist's attention. The students' fees were noticeably high, and it was perhaps thought that Wedgwood would provide 'bursaries' or 'scholarships'.

In the meantime another slender possibility of financial gain came to nothing. On 14 October he completed his tragedy *Osorio* and immediately sent off two copies, one to William Linley, Sheridan's brother-in-law, the other to Sheridan via William Bowles. The tragedy had become a distasteful chore, and Coleridge expressed his relief at having rid himself of it in a letter to Bowles: 'In truth, I have fagged so long at the work, and see so many imperfections in the original and main plot, that I feel an indescribable disgust, a sickness of the very heart, at the mention of the Tragedy.' Not the least of his difficulties had been the pressure of working under financial anxiety. Coleridge was never happy about writing for money, although he seldom managed to avoid it. 'I could not avoid attaching a pecuniary importance to the business,' he wrote, 'and consequently became anxious: and such anxieties humble and degrade the mind.' By 20 November, however, Coleridge had still not heard from Sheridan. Since so much seemed to depend on the outcome, and since Sheridan had virtually commissioned the work, Coleridge's indignation was understandable. 'Sheridan, most certainly, has not used me with common Justice,' he wrote to Cottle. 'The proposal came from himself – and altho' this circumstance did not bind him to accept the Tragedy, it certainly bound him to pay every and that the earliest, attention to it. – I suppose, it lies snugly in his green Bag – if it have not emigrated to the kitchen or the cloaca.' The 'cloaca', of course, in eighteenth-century parlance, was the lavatory.

By 2 December it had been rejected. Later there came a suggestion that certain alterations might make it more suitable for the stage, but Sheridan had failed even to return the manuscript, and Coleridge had lost his only copy. He had never expected much from it, but he was embittered by the delay, the loss of the manuscript, and, above all, by some gossip going the rounds at the expense of both the play and its author. There was a scene set in a cave in which occurred the lines –

> Drip! drip! drip! – in such a place as this
> It has nothing else to do but drip! drip! drip!

Sheridan had parodied them as 'Drip! drip! drip! there's nothing here but dripping!'

When Coleridge was in Germany the following year he was to give a companion, Clement Carlyon, the following abstract and verdict on the play, accurately outlining its defects :

In this sketch of a tragedy, all is imperfect, and much obscure. Among other equally great defects (millstones round the slender neck of its merits) it presupposes a long story; and this long story, which yet is necessary to the complete understanding of the play, is not half told. Albert had sent a letter informing his family that he should arrive about such a time by ship; he was shipwrecked; and he wrote a private letter to Osorio, informing him alone of this accident, that he might not shock Maria. Osorio destroyed the letter, and sent assassins to meet Albert. . . . Worse than all, the growth of Osorio's character is nowhere explained – and yet I had most clear and psychologically accurate ideas of the whole of it. . . . A man who, from constitutional calmness of appetites, is seduced into pride and love of power, by these into misanthropism, or rather contempt for mankind; and from thence, by the co-operation of envy, and a curiously modified love for a beautiful female (which is nowhere developed in the play), into a most atrocious guilt. A man who is in truth a weak man, yet always duping himself into the belief that he has a soul of iron. Such were some of my leading ideas.[38]

At this same time Wordsworth's *Borderers* was rejected, perhaps more predictably. Wordsworth realized that its failure was more or less inevitable. He had not originally intended it for the stage; in fact, only Coleridge's encouragement had led him to alter it for production. 'If ever I attempt another drama,' he wrote 'it shall be written either purposely for the closet, or purposely for the stage. There is no middle way.'

But Coleridge's disappointment over *Osorio* was to be speedily compensated. Early in November he was invited to Cote House, home of John Wedgwood the banker. Here he met Tom again, and probably Josiah; James Mackintosh, philosopher, politician, and historian, was also there. It seems that Coleridge's eloquence 'rivetted' Tom Wedgwood, but Danial Stuart, editor of the *Morning Post*, and Mackintosh's brother-in-law, later claimed that Mackintosh, himself no mean speaker, was set upon Coleridge by the others, who were bored, and reduced him to confusion. Stuart's information, of course, came from Mackintosh himself, decked out with the comment that they had been arguing about Locke, an author whom Mackintosh claimed he had not read. Admittedly Coleridge's *forte* was the monologue, and it is very likely that he may have been at least reduced to silence by Mackintosh's cut and thrust. Perhaps this first clash explains Coleridge's later attitude towards Mackintosh, for as the years passed, he viewed him with increasing distaste: among the many jaundiced comments about his mind and person, Coleridge wrote this in 1801:

In no one moment did any particle of his face from the top of his forehead to the half of his neck, *move*. His face has no *lines* like that of a man – no softness, like that of a woman – it is smooth, *hard*, motionless, *a flesh-mask*! – As to his conversation, it was all uncommonly *well-worded*: but not a thought in it worthy of having been worded at all.

Coleridge's response to this other great talker of his times is interesting – particularly when one remembers the comments of Robert Owen about Coleridge himself. Yet it is unlikely that Mackintosh so outshone Coleridge that he did not at first, at least, acquit himself with his usual eloquence – for as we shall see, he had talked himself into the Wedgwoods' patronage. The effect of Coleridge's conversation both in its power to astonish, or to disgust, deserves a digression at this point.

Of Coleridge's extraordinary eloquence there is no lack of testimony. 'He talks very much like an angel', said one of his listeners. 'When in company, his vehemence of manner and wonderful flow of words and ideas, drew all eyes towards him, and gave him pre-eminence', said another. Frequently his acquaintance were urged to resort to imagery to give an impression of his effect. 'Coleridge,' enthused De Quincey, 'like some great river, the Orellana, or the St Lawrence, that had been checked and fretted by rocks or thwarting islands, and suddenly recovers its volume of waters, and its mighty music, – swept at once, as if returning to his natural business, into a continuous strain of eloquent dissertation, certainly the most novel, the most finely illustrated, and traversing the most spacious fields of thought, by transitions the most just and logical, that it was possible to conceive.' And for Hazlitt, 'In digressing, in dilating, in passing from subject to subject, he appeared to me to float in air, to slide on ice . . .'

His voice was said to be 'broad *Devonshire*' (at least, for a

'Gentleman'), its inflection 'particularly plaintive'. There was
a 'superabundance of words', and as Carlyle put it, 'a
forest of thoughts'. In the space of a two mile walk he could
broach 'a thousand things', according to Keats. And on one
point all seemed to be in agreement: he evidently felt
obliged to 'play first Violin'. He was 'an incomparable
declaimer and speech-maker' commented Crabb Robinson,
but 'he has neither the readiness nor the acuteness required
by a colloquial disputant'. 'Pourtant, pour M. Coleridge, il
est tout à fait un monologue', judged Mme de Stael with
finality. Or as Coleridge himself liked to put it, his talk was
'*one*-versazione' rather than '*con*-versazione'.

The impression, particularly on those who liked to hold
forth themselves, was not always favourable, even though
they might be astonished at the sheer force of the torrent.
As Carlyle wrote, 'it was talk not flowing anywhither like a
river, but spreading everywhither in inextricable currents
and regurgitations like a lake or sea; terribly deficient in
definite goal or aim, nay often in logical intelligibility . . .'
In any case, 'to sit as a passive bucket and be pumped into,
whether you consent or not, can in the long-run be ex-
hilarating to no creature; how eloquent soever the flood of
utterance that is descending.' Another listener who could
not choose but hear, was Joseph Farrington, 'It was all
metaphysical,' he complained, 'frequently perplexed, and
certainly at times without understanding His subject.
Occasionally there was some brilliance, but I particularly
noticed that His *illustrations* generally disappointed me, &
rather weakened than enforced what He had before said.'
On coming away from his first inundation, he remarked to
a companion that the sheer 'confinement' was downright
fatiguing. Crabb Robinson, on the other hand, found that
the flow could be stemmed: 'Tho' he practises all sorts of
delightful tricks and shows admirable skill in riding his
hobbies, yet he may be easily unsaddled.'

Henry Nelson Coleridge, however, felt that a defence

could be mounted both against the charge of meandering and the easy unsaddling: 'He took so large a scope,' says the dutiful nephew in his preface to Coleridge's *Table Talk*, 'that, if he was interrupted before he got to the end, he appeared to have been talking without object; although, perhaps, a few more would have brought you to a point, a retrospect from which would show you the pertinence of all he had been saying. . . . Hence that exhaustive, cyclical mode of discoursing in which he frequently indulged; unfit, indeed, for a dinner-table, and too long breathed for the patience of a chance visitor.'

Yet Coleridge himself would have endorsed the impression of many of his hearers. But if only they would *stop* him! he complains.

'I am most conscious that I hurry forwards, *run over* and tread upon my own arguments . . . And even in conversation, I can affirm most sincerely that any interruption, or admonition that I have lost the bit and curb, and am reducing the conversation to a mono-drama, or dialogue (in which one of the two *dramatis personae* is forced to act the mute) of tongue *versus* ear, is received by me not only thankfully, but with unfeigned pleasure. I wish from my very heart that every one of my acquaintance, not to say my friends, made a point of doing this. "*Lente!* ferruminandus est!" '[39]

And yet, another piece of self-analysis seems to agree with Carlyle's verdict:

There are two sorts of talkative fellows whom it would be injurious to confound/& I, S.T. Coleridge, am the latter . . . Now this is my case – & a grievous fault it is/my illustrations swallow up my thesis – I feel too intensely the omnipresence of all in each, platonically speaking – or psychologically my brain-fibres, or the spiritual Light which abides in the brain marrow as visible Light appears to do in sundry rotten mackerel & other *smashy* matters, is of too general an affinity with all things/and tho' it perceives the *difference* of things, yet is eternally pursuing the likenesses, or rather that which is common/ bring me two things that seem the very same, & then I am quick enough to shew the difference, even to hair-splitting – but to go on

from circle to circle till I break against the shore of my Hearer's
patience, or have my Concentricals dashed to nothing by a Snore –
that is my ordinary mishap.[40]

Yet what lay behind his insistence on taking the lead in
whatever company he happened to find himself? Did he
truly feel, as some observed, that he had nothing to learn
from others? Was it, as the psychologists might suggest,
some pathological urge to rid himself of a primal oral
irritation – such as one finds in the 'word-push' or 'ver-
bigeration' of the manic-depressive; some compensa-
tory realization of that childhood fantasy when he ate a
room and furniture out of a mountain of plum pudding?
Perhaps a more simple answer exists in Dorothy Wordsworth's comment that one forgot his unpleasant exterior
the moment he began to speak. Perhaps it was, after all, a
sense of inferiority that led him to overplay the one external
feature of his character that abounded in excellence. It was
Clement Carlyon who noted how he had heard Coleridge
say 'fixing his prominent eyes upon himself (as he was wont
to do, whenever there was a mirror in the room), with a
singularly coxcomical expression of countenance, that his
dress was sure to be lost sight of the moment he began to
talk'. But then, it may have been, as Coleridge himself
remarked, in part from a 'constitutional temperament not
duly disciplined'; in part from his own habitual inner
communings – 'my thoughts, all born and shaped inwardly
in consequence, and in solitary meditation, communicate
their own continuity, and (to use a phrase of Jeremy Taylor's)
agglomeration, to my conversation'.[41] We shall never
know. One would like to think that the following notebook
reflection had at least a grain of truth in it: 'Egoistic Talk
with me very often the effect of my Love of the Persons to
whom I am talking / My Heart is talking of them / I cannot
talk continuously of them to themselves – so I seem to be
putting into their Heart the same continuousness as to me,
that is in my own Heart as to them.'[42] Yet he was not

entirely unaware of the insidious dangers which are supposed to lie in store for all eloquent writers who dissipate their energies and talents in holding forth rather than putting it on paper. As he once wrote to Southey : 'It is not *thinking* that will disturb a man's morals, or confound the distinctions, which to *think* makes. But it is *talking – talking – talking – that* is the curse & poison.'[43] The curious fact is, however, the comment was directed at somebody else.

Whatever passed between Coleridge and Mackintosh during their first meeting, Mackintosh acted kindly on his behalf by writing to Stuart to see if some work could be found for him on the *Morning Post*. By 17 November Mackintosh had written to Coleridge inviting him to communicate with Stuart who was willing to take him on in a small way. 'In common with every man of taste and feeling,' wrote Mackintosh, 'I have long been an admirer of your genius, but it was not till my late visit to Mr Wedgwood's that I felt an interest in your character almost equal to my admiration of your extraordinary powers.'

The arrangement was that Coleridge would receive a guinea a week in return for agreed contributions. The first, a poem, appeared on 7 December ; but as so often with his journalistic enterprises, he immediately began to fall behind with his contributions, and by January Stuart was getting impatient with him.

Yet another possibility presented itself in the form of taking over the ministry of the Unitarian chapel in Shrewsbury, due to the retirement of one John Rowe. Already there had been an offer from the Unitarians in Norwich, but Coleridge had rejected it, because he did not like the town. Shrewsbury seemed to him a far better proposition : there was a larger salary, the country was more delightful, and provisions of all kinds were much cheaper. Yet he felt that his chances of being offered the position at Shrewsbury were somewhat remote, as the town was so 'violently aristocratic', and he feared that 'the notoriety of my *political conduct*', and the 'peculiarities of my religious creed', would disqualify him.

Throughout December things were held in the balance. No word came from Wedgwood about the idea for a school, and the congregation remained uncommitted. But finally, on Christmas Eve, he received a letter from Josiah Wedgwood, which threw him into a quandary. It was a gift of £100. The following letter accompanied the draft:

Dear Sir,
    My Brother Thomas, and myself had separately determined that it would be right to enable you to defer entering into an engagement, we understand you are about to form from the most urgent of motives. We therefore request, that you will accept the inclosed-draft with the simplicity, with which it is offered to you –
                I remain, dear Sir sincerely your's
                        Josiah Wedgwood

As it happened, Coleridge had not actually been offered the 'engagement' that they spoke of, nor was he very confident that the offer would be made. Consequently, generous as the gift seemed, it threw him into a state of perplexity. For to accept the money would imply relinquishing the Shrewsbury appointment if it were eventually offered. In the meantime he must make some reply to the Wedgwoods.

After three 'nights', he eventually sat down and wrote to the brothers.

You have relieved me from a state of hesitation & perplexity; and have given me the tranquillity and leisure of independence for the next two years. – I am not deficient in the ordinary feelings of gratitude to you and Mr T. Wedgwood; but I shall not find them oppressive or painful, if in the course of that time I shall have been acquiring knowledge for myself, or communicating it to others; if either in act or preparation I shall have been contributing my quota to the cause of Truth and Honesty. –

The extent to which the Wedgwood draft had actually

relieved him of 'hesitation and perplexity' can be judged by his response to a new turn in events. Having sent his letter of acceptance in the morning, he received that very evening a letter from Shrewsbury inviting him to take over the congregation. The permanent security of the Shrewsbury offer was, of course, a better proposition than £100, and he must accept it. But what would he now say to the Wedgwoods. 'It will appear to them that I had accepted the draft in words which implied that it had relieved me from a state of great uncertainty – whereas in truth, I had accepted it to console myself for a disappointment.' The real disappointment, perhaps, was that the Wedgwoods had not seen fit to offer him some kind of permanent patronage.

Coleridge's reasoning throughout these events was based on a growing knowledge of himself : 'a permanent income not inconsistent with my religious or political creeds, I find necessary to my quietness – without it I should be a prey to anxiety, and anxiety, with me, always induces sickliness, and too often sloth : as an overdose of stimulus proves a narcotic.'[44] It would have proved only too easy, in fact, to accept the money and buy two years of freedom. There was every motive for staying on at Stowey ; not the least Tom Poole, 'a friend whose sympathies were perfect with my manners, feeling and opinions'. In fact Poole thought it most inexpedient that he should leave. Then there were the Wordsworths : well might he anticipate the misery of separation. 'The first sunny morning that I walk out, at Shrewsbury, will make my heart die away within me – for I shall be in a *land of Strangers* !' But Coleridge felt that he was acting for the future ; he was convinced that children would 'come fast' upon him, and he seemed determined to dedicate himself '*to some one work* which *may be* of benefit to society', a work upon which he could afford to spend 'three or twice three years'. And there were other practical reasons for going to Shrewsbury, as he carefully explained to Josiah Wedgwood in a letter on 5 January.

I shall have at least five days in every week of perfect leisure – a good house, valued at £30 a year – and if I should die and without any culpable negligence or extravagance have left my family want, congregations are in the habit of becoming the guardians. Add to this, that by Law I shall be exempted from military service – to which, Heaven only knows how soon we may be dragged.

The decision, however, had not been an easy one. How he extricated himself from the thicket of scruples is interesting. In the first place, he rejected the extremes of idealism in which a man might 'abstain from all modes of conduct, the general practice of which was not permanently useful, or at least absolutely harmless : his furniture, his servants, his very cloathes are intimately connected with Vice and Misery'. Some compromise was necessary – simply to live : 'we *must* compound with a large quantity of evil – taking care to select from the modes of conduct, which may be within our choice, those in which we can do the most good with the least evil.' There were, of course, palpable disadvantages in entering the ministry. It made one's livelihood hang upon the profession of '*particular opinions*', opinions which tended to 'warp the intellectual faculty'. Furthermore, relying on one's congregation induced a minister to 'adapt his moral exhortations to their wishes rather than to their needs'. Finally, routine might bring on a certain sectarian manner-ism, which 'generally narrows the intellect itself, and always narrows the sphere of it's operation'.

Yet he was confident, he could assure the Wedgwoods, that he had sufficient insight to guard against these snares. In any case, the freedom of his own particular sect would ease the pressure of undue conformity. 'The *necessary* creed in our sect is but short – it will be necessary for me, in order to my continuance as an Unitarian Minister, to believe that Jesus Christ was the Messiah – in all other points I may play off my intellect ad *libitum*.' And if he were not to accept the offer, he would be forced to continue with

journalism, a course of career that held far more dangers
for the mind and the spirit than the ministry indeed :

The few weeks that I have written for the Morning Post, I have
felt this – Something must be written and written immediately – if
any important Truth, any striking beauty, occur to my mind, I feel a
repugnance at sending it garbled to a newspaper: and if any idea of
ludicrous personality, or apt antiministerial joke, crosses me, I feel a
repugnance at rejecting it, because *something must be written*, and
nothing else suitable occurs. The longer I continue a hired paragraph-
scribbler, the more powerful these Temptations will become: and
indeed nothing scarcely that has not a *tang* of personality or *vindictive*
feeling, is pleasing or interesting, I apprehend, to my Employers. Of
all things I most dislike party politics – yet this sort of gypsie jargon I
am compelled to fire away.

Reading between the lines, it is difficult not to interpret
these carefully balanced sets of disadvantages, whichever
course he took, as a plea to the Wedgwoods that they should
make a new, more permanent, proposition. The palpable
bait, of course, was contained in the expression of intention
to dedicate himself '*to some one work* which *may be* of benefit
to society', a work upon which he could afford to spend
'three or twice three years'. The phrasing was of the sort
that would have appealed to Wedgwood. Yet if Coleridge
was being financed by the Shrewsbury congregation there
would be no necessity to accommodate himself to any of
Wedgwood's aspirations. On the other hand, should
Wedgwood take the bait Coleridge would find himself more
or less committed to being as good as his word. From the
very day, early in January of 1798, that Coleridge wrote this
letter to Wedgwood he had put his career as a poet in
jeopardy.

So after rejecting the £100 Coleridge set off for Shrewsbury
on 13 January. He arrived late on the Saturday afternoon,
the day before he was due to give his inaugural sermon, and

Mr Rowe, whom he was going to succeed, was astonished to find 'a round-faced man, in a short black coat (like a shooting jacket) which hardly seemed to have been made for him, but who seemed to be talking at a great rate to his fellow passengers'. Hazlitt says that Mr Rowe returned to his house disappointed not to find Mr Coleridge, 'when the round-faced man in black entered, and dissipated all doubts on the subject, by beginning to talk. He did not cease while he stayed ; nor has he since, that I know of.'

Coleridge preached the next day both in the morning and afternoon, and he wrote a brief and despondent letter to his Unitarian friend, Estlin : he had arrived, he was well, but had nothing to say : '. . . why should I stand wringing my dish clout of a brain in order to squeeze out a few dirty drops not worth having.' He found the people of Shrewsbury 'dressy and fond of expense – and the women very handsome – the Parsons of the Church of England, many of them, Unitarians and Democrats – and the people hot-headed Aristocrats.'[45] Coleridge gave the impression, in fact, that he was depressed. But to one of his young listeners, William Hazlitt, son of the Unitarian minister at Wem, he gave a far different impression. Walking ten miles in the mud from Wem, Hazlitt attended the Sunday morning service at Shrewsbury :

When I got there, the organ was playing the 100th psalm, and when it was done, Mr Coleridge rose and gave out his text, 'And he went up into the mountain to pray, *himself, alone.*' As he gave out this text, his voice 'rose like a steam of rich distilled perfume,' and when he came to the two last words, which he pronounced loud, deep, and distinct, it seemed to me, who was then young, as if that prayer might have floated in solemn silence through the universe. The idea of St John came into my mind. . . . The preacher then launched into his subject, like an eagle dallying with the wind. The sermon was upon peace and war; upon church and state – not their alliance but their separation – on the spirit of the world and the spirit of Christianity, not as the same, but as opposed to one another. He talked of those who had 'inscribed the cross of Christ on banners dripping with human gore.' He made a poetical and pastoral excursion – and to show the fatal effects of war, drew a striking contrast between the simple shepherd boy, driving his team afield, or sitting under the hawthorn, piping to his flock, 'as though he should never be old,' and the same poor country lad, crimped, kidnapped, brought into town, made drunk, at an alehouse, turned into a wretched drummer boy, with his hair sticking on end with powder and pomatum, a long cue at his back, and tricked out in the loathsome finery of the profession of blood.

The effect on the young Hazlitt was stunning : 'I could not have been more delighted if I had heard the music of the spheres. Poetry and Philosophy had met together. Truth and Genius had embraced, under the eye and with the Sanction of Religion.'

The following Tuesday Coleridge came out to Wem to visit Hazlitt's father, and for two whole hours conversed with 'W. H.'s forehead!' Old Hazlitt was surprised and pleased, and pushing back his spectacles, a 'smile of delight beamed across his rugged cordial face, to think that truth had found an new ally in Fancy!'

The next day, on coming down to breakfast, Hazlitt says that Coleridge had just received a letter from Tom Wedgwood, 'making him an offer of 150 l. a year if he chose to waive his present pursuit, and devote himself entirely to the study of poetry and philosophy'. His letter to the rich brothers had worked, his rejection of the £100 had now landed him an income. But what of the Unitarian ministry at Shrewsbury? 'Coleridge seemed to make up his mind to close with this proposal,' says Hazlitt, 'in the act of tying up one of his shoes.'

On the 17 January, he replied accepting the offer :

Your benevolence appeared so strange and it came upon my mind with such suddenness, that for a while I sat and mused on it with scarce a reference to myself, and gave you a moral approbation almost wholly unmingled with those personal feelings which have since

filled my eyes with tears – which do so even now while I am writing
to you.

Within a few days Coleridge could return to Stowey,
'Disembarrassed from all pecuniary anxieties yet un-
shackled by any regular profession, with powerful motives
and no less powerful propensities to honourable effort.' Or
would he? It seemed a remarkable gift. Yet was it so
fortunate after all? Is one to feel with one of Coleridge's
past biographers, that 'the worst possible thing had
happened to him'? That he was shirking his 'share of the
economic burden which is, or ought to be, the common
lot of humanity'?[46] One might just as well say that rich
industrialists ought not to give away their money. Although,
of course, it seems ironic that Coleridge, usually so scrupulous
about his connections, never questioned the remoter origins
of Wedgwood's wealth. Some years later, certainly long
after Tom Wedgwood's 'Master-Stroke' for the improvement of mankind had been forgotten, Josiah Wedgwood
was called before Robert Peel's Committee on the conditions
of children in factories. Wedgwood had to admit that
children were employed for over twelve hours a day in his
potteries, and that whatever wages they received were spent
not in giving the children improved clothing and food but
on procuring liquor for the parents. When asked whether
he objected to Legislative interference with the factories,
he replied : 'I have a strong opinion that, from all I know at
present of manufactories in general, and certainly from all I
know of my own, we had better be left alone.'[47] But then, as
Coleridge observed just a fortnight before accepting the
annuity, a man's 'furniture, his servants, his very cloaths are
intimately connected with vice and misery'.

Undoubtedly the gravest disadvantage consisted in the
sense of obligation that such a gift would generate. Wedgwood had, of course, fixed no conditions to the annuity, but
Coleridge had made it clear that if he had the leisure he
would devote himself exclusively to a work which would

benefit mankind. And such a work, as we shall see in the following year, would be envisaged as a prose critique of philosophy and psychology rather than the great epic he had conceived early in 1797. Not that Coleridge would immediately abandon all ideas of writing an epic; the question was, could he combine the two disciplines successfully?

Apart from this consideration there was perhaps another which arises from the vantage point of hindsight. By his own admission much of the distress in his life arose from financial anxiety. The annuity, however generous, was still only a modest sum. In fact, within two or three years it would almost halve in value through the excessive inflation of the war years. After deducting the £20 a year which he had settled on his mother-in-law, it could only prove an advantage if he managed his household with great care. Yet the very freedom it allowed (as Coleridge himself put it, his 'tether' had been lengthened) threatened the benefit that it brought. Such an income could not support the subsequent journeys he made in England and abroad (the latter, precisely to equip himself for the great work of benefit to mankind), with all the added expense of living separately from his family and the purchase of large numbers of books. Naturally, Coleridge's genius would never have developed in the way it did had he not done these things, and it is useless to speculate what he might have achieved had he been anchored in Shrewsbury; but the annuity was undoubtedly a mixed blessing, and its results shed an interesting light on the perennial problem of artistic patronage. Curiously enough Coleridge's acceptance was not altogether greeted with the unanimous approval of his own intimate circle. Estlin was 'ardent' for his declining the offer, and wrote a long letter 'at' him to persuade him to change his mind. And Wordsworth commented wryly to his friend Tobin: 'No doubt you have heard of the munificence of the Wedgwoods towards Coleridge. I hope the fruit will be good as the seed is noble.' Wordsworth for one, it seems, was not too enthusiastic about the origin of Coleridge's good fortune.

At the beginning of February Coleridge made his way back to Stowey, Hazlitt accompanying him six miles along the road. 'It was a fine morning in the middle of winter,' remembered Hazlitt, 'and he talked the whole way . . . I observed that he continually crossed me on the way by shifting from one side of the foot-path to the other.' At the time it struck him as an odd movement; 'but I did not at that time connect it with any instability of purpose or involuntary change of principle, as I have done since'.

Coleridge returned to his family now confident in his future and determined to lay down the foundations of that work of permanent value. He was still only twenty-five, and he must have felt that the years of fulfilment were only just beginning. How could he possibly have guessed that during the next few months he would be at the high point of his poetical powers, the high point of his happiness? The ease and delight of those early months of 1798 are recorded in Dorothy Wordsworth's journal. Her entries mainly describe the simple joys of walking to and fro between Alfoxden and Stowey, observing the subtle alteration in the woods, the hills, the sky and the sea, as the days slipped by and the spring approached.

By 3 February Coleridge was in Stowey and from now until May he was seldom absent from daily entries :

A mild morning, the windows open at breakfast, the redbreasts singing in the garden. Walked with Coleridge over the hills. The sea at first obscured by vapour; that vapour afterwards slid in one mighty mass along the sea-shore; the islands and one point of land clear beyond it. The distant country (which was purple in the clear dull air), overhung by straggling clouds that sailed over it, appeared like the darker clouds, which are often seen at a great distance apparently motionless, while the nearer ones pass quickly over them driven by the lower winds. I never saw such a union of earth, sky, and sea. The clouds beneath our feet spread themselves to the water, and the clouds of the sky almost joined them. Gathered sticks in the wood; a perfect stillness. The redbreasts sang upon the leafless boughs. Of a great number of sheep in the field, only one standing. Returned to dinner at five o'clock. The moonlight still and warm as a summer's night at nine o'clock.

In so many of her observations one detects the unspoken sharing of experiences with Coleridge. How typical of him it would have been to remark on the 'union of earth, sky and sea'. Then again, visiting the dell described in *This Lime Tree Bower*, she remarks on the 'perpetual motion from the current of air; in summer only moved by the drippings of the rocks', a clear echo from Coleridge's —

> and there my friends
> Behold the dark green file of long lank weeds,
> That all at once (a most fantastic sight!)
> Still nod and drip beneath the dripping edge
> Of the blue clay-stone.

There are passages too which seem to suggest the setting of one of Coleridge's finest poems. On 17 February Dorothy wrote:

The sun shone bright and clear. A deep stillness in the thickest part of the wood, undisturbed except by the occasional dropping of the snow from the holly boughs; no other sound but that of the water, and the slender notes of a redbreast, which sang at intervals on the outskirts of the southern side of the wood. There the bright green moss was bare at the roots of the trees, and the little birds were upon it.

For the next few days it was 'sharp and frosty' — and it may have been during this time that Coleridge wrote *Frost at Midnight*.

The poem begins with the silence of the world outside the poet's cottage at night. There is a suggestion of darkness, silence, stillness, as the frost performs its 'secret ministry/ Unhelped by any wind'. Then the 'owlet's cry' breaks in on the silence, 'loud — and hark, again! loud as before', and the setting changes to within the cottage where the writer sits

awake while the inmates of his cottage are at rest, and by
his side his 'cradled infant slumbers peacefully'. Yet the
calmness of the situation informs his mind with an opposite
mood of disturbance and vexation –

> 'Tis calm indeed! so calm, that it disturbs
> And vexes meditation with its strange
> And extreme silentness.

The setting changes again to the world outside – 'Sea,
hill, and wood,/This populous village!' – and 'all the
numberless goings-on of life' seen in his mind's eye 'in-
audible as dreams'. Again the poet returns to the interior of
his cottage to contemplate the 'thin blue flame' on the fire
in the grate; and the careful observation of the 'film'
fluttering on the grate in contrast to the 'low-burnt' fire that
'quivers not' :

> Only that film, which fluttered on the grate,
> Still flutters there, the sole unquiet thing.
> Methinks, its motion in this hush of nature
> Gives it dim sympathies with me who live,
> Making it a companionable form,
> Whose puny flaps and freaks the idling Spirit
> By its own moods interprets, every where
> Echo or mirror seeking of itself,
> And makes a toy of thought.

The subtle contrasts and parallels have built up a series of
tensions and reconciliations, culminating in this explicit
statement of the recognition of an active self in the solitude,
a sense of lonely consciousness in the midst of unconscious-
ness. And yet he finds 'companionable' forms – the 'mirror'
or 'echo' – seeking of itself. Every transition in the poem
has strengthened this contrast between active and passive
phenomena, 'the ministry' of the frost, the sound of the
owlet in the silence, the waking poet in a sleeping household,
the mind of the poet creating as it were concentric distur-
bances moving outwards then returning to himself.
8

Now enacting the restless yet volitional movement, in contrast to the purely passive objects about him, the poet again journeys outwards in time and space, to his school-day's, when he remembers a similar film in the grate of his schoolroom. And he recollects the sense of trepidation as he waited for a visitor : thus the film in the grate is invested with special significance by the association of a feeling of expectancy and restlessness rooted in his past. Then he moves even farther back in time to his home life as a child ; and the scene is one of daylight, warmth and sound—in contrast to the night, the frost and the silence of the present. And so returning once more to his schooldays, and back to the present, he again contemplates the sleeping baby at his side—

> Whose gentle breathing, heard in this deep calm,
> Fill up the interspersèd vacancies
> And momentary pauses of the thought.

Now he moves forward in time, where he promises the child a boyhood quite different from his own 'pent mid cloisters dim'.

> But *thou*, my babe! shalt wander like a breeze
> By lakes and sandy shores, beneath the crags
> Of ancient mountain, and beneath the clouds,
> Which image in their bulk both lakes and shores
> And mountain crags.

It is a world in which the same 'dim sympathies' recognized by the poet in the darkness of winter, imprisoned in his cottage, are displayed in more majestic form. And if the poet himself could learn from the 'sky and stars' at school in the city, how much more sublime will be the child's response !

> so shalt thou see and hear
> The lovely shapes and sounds intelligible
> Of that eternal language, which thy God

> Utters, who from eternity doth teach
> Himself in all, and all things in himself.
> Great universal Teacher! he shall mould
> Thy spirit, and by giving make it ask.

Like the 'echo' and 'mirror', and the clouds 'which image in their bulk both lakes and shores', this consciousness is at once both active and passive, ever increasing by the measure of its giving and seeking.

He returns again across time and the seasons in a gradual transition to the winter, with the implication that the child will be capable of discovering a sense of universal beauty in every situation :

> Whether the summer clothe the general earth
> With greenness, or the redbreast sit and sing
> Betwixt the tufts of snow on the bare branch
> Of mossy apple-tree, while the night hatch
> Smokes in the sun-thaw ; whether the eave-drops fall
> Heard only in the trances of the blast,
> Or if the secret ministry of frost
> Shall hang them up in silent icicles,
> Quietly shining to the quiet Moon.

Thus the poem ends in the delicately stated tensions of warmth and cold, night and day, motion and rest ; the most subtle suggestions of sound and silence—'Heard only in the trances of the blast'. Images which suggest these tensions without obtrusive and obvious juxtaposition. And clearly the most arresting of these is the fusion of sun and snow

> while the nigh thatch
> Smokes in the sun-thaw

It points back to the 'Sunny pleasure dome and caves of ice' in *Kubla Khan*, twice echoed in notebook experiments since, but now in a rustic setting :

> The reed-roof'd village, still bepatch'd with snow
> Smok'd in the sun-thaw –

and again—

> The Sun-shine lies in the cottage-wall
> Ashining thro' the snow –

But here he manages the interpenetration without the explicit juxtaposition, quietly achieving the reconciliation of opposites in an 'indivisible' image.

Throughout much of the early part of 1798 Coleridge was alone with the Wordsworths—'Tho we were three persons, it was but one God.'[48] A typical day was 26 February. 'Coleridge came in the morning,' records Dorothy. '. . . walked with Coleridge nearly to Stowey after dinner. A very clear afternoon. We lay sidelong upon the turf, and gazed on the landscape till it melted into more than natural loveliness. The sea very uniform, of a pale greyish blue, only one distant bay, bright and blue as a sky; had there been a vessel sailing up it, a perfect image of delight.' The passage has almost an early eighteenth-century ring about it, leisured, dilettante, deliberately pastoral; as if consciously applying Coleridge's lines—'as I have stood/Silent with swimming sense'—to their situation; as if applying art to life.

At the same time their relationships were undergoing a gradual readjustment as Coleridge increasingly subordinated himself to his new friend. 'The Giant Wordsworth—God love him!—even when I speak in the terms of admiration due to his intellect, I fear lest those terms should keep out of sight the amiableness of his manners,' he wrote to Cottle in March. And as Wordsworth took up more and more of the centre of his life he retreated further from 'ephemera'. 'I have for some time past withdrawn myself almost totally from the consideration of *immediate* causes,' he told his brother George, 'which are infinitely complex and uncertain, to muse on fundamental and general causes—the "causae causarum."'

He now dissociated himself entirely from the French

'Philosophers and Friends of Freedom'. Indeed, there was
nothing to recommend the French government. 'History
has taught me,' he told George, 'that RULERS are much the
same in all ages and under all forms of government : they
are as bad as they dare to be.' As for revolutions—they are
pointless unless 'individuals will see the necessity of individual effort ; that they will act as kind neighbours as good
Christians, rather than as citizens and electors.' This was
the only way, Coleridge contended, that society could purge
itself of the old error of 'attributing to Governments a
talismanic influence over our virtues and happiness—as if
Governments were not rather effects than causes'.

His renewed invective against the French was probably
stimulated by the French invasion of Switzerland which
had received a great deal of hysterical coverage in the press.
In February he wrote *The Recantation: an Ode*, which later
appeared in the *Morning Post*. Here he acknowledges his
former joy in the Revolution :

> With what a joy my lofty gratulation
> Unawed I sang, amid a slavish band –

But now he hears the 'loud lament' from Switzerland's
'icy caverns'—

> O France, that mockest Heaven, adulterous, blind,
> And patriot only in pernicious toils !
> Are these thy boasts, Champion of human kind ?
> To mix with Kings in the low lust of sway,
> Yell in the hunt, and share the murderous prey ;
> To insult the shrine of Liberty with spoils
> From freemen torn ; to tempt and to betray ?

It seems strange that he should be capable of writing this
sort of inflated rhetoric during the very month in which he
wrote *Frost at Midnight*, yet such was the obligatory mode of
political effusions, the favoured style of editors. The Ode
was printed a second time in the *Morning Post*.

As for politics at home, both parties were to him equally

distasteful. In fact, he would prefer Pitt and the Tories to stay in power : then, extraordinary as it may seem, he claims, 'I think very seldom on the subject; but as far as I have thought, I am inclined to consider the Aristocrats as the more respectable of our three factions, because they are more decorous ... I am no Whig, no Reformist, no Republican.'[49] Again, it seems, he was appeasing George.

But what of more positive aspirations? 'I devote myself to such works as encroach not on the antisocial passions,' he wrote. In poetry his purpose was to 'elevate the imagination and set the affections in right tune by the beauty of the inanimate impregnated, as with a living soul, by the presence of Life'. 'I love fields and woods and mountains with almost a visionary fondness—and because I have found benevolence and quietness growing within me as that fondness has increased, therefore I should wish to be the means of implanting it in others—and to destroy the bad passions not by combatting them, but by keeping them in inaction.' In all this one can see the pervasive influence of Wordsworth :

> Not useless do I deem
> These quiet sympathies with things that hold
> An inarticulate language ...

—continued Coleridge, quoting in the letter to his brother a passage from an early conclusion to Wordsworth's *Ruined Cottage*, spelling out in plodding fashion the more subtle, exemplified sense of his own *Frost at Midnight* :

> Methinks, its motion in this hush of nature
> Gives is dim sympathies with me who live,
> Making it a companionable form ...

It is equally indicative of his increasing homage that he should prefer Wordsworth's 'He seeks for Good & finds the Good he seeks', rather than his own theistic 'Himself, in all, and all things in himself,/Great universal Teacher! he shall mould/Thy spirit, and by giving make it ask'.

He could also report to brother George that he was

becoming more tolerant, more peaceable with his fellow human beings : 'With regard to others, I never contravert opinions except after some intimacy and when alone with the person, and at the happy time when we both seem awake to our own fallibility – and then I rather state *my* reasons than argue against his. – ' In conversation and in company, he claims, it is now his habit to find out 'the opinions common to us', and with regard to himself he was now disciplining his mind to 'long meditation'.

Ironically enough, at the very time when he was congratulating himself on an improvement in his relationships he found himself drawn into a strange squabble – 'a long and odd story', as Southey put – involving Charles Lloyd, Lamb, Southey, Cottle, and in its final stages the Wordsworths. The circumstances found their origin in the spring of 1797, but the complicated bickering did not burn itself out until July of 1798. In the minds of some of the participants the matter would be brooded on for many years to come.

Lloyd had returned to the Coleridge family in February of 1797. He had brought his poems with him and they were to be included in the second edition of Coleridge's *Poems*, along with contributions from Lamb. Just two weeks after arriving he was again taken ill with the same fits that he had suffered in the previous year. So he returned home in the third week of March to recuperate. In the course of the summer he fell in love with a Sophia Pemberton, but his family opposed the match and he went to London in August to seek consolation of Charles Lamb. Lamb, who had his own store of anxieties, nursing his sister and his father, presently took him down to Southey, who was now living at Bruton in Hampshire. Lamb stayed just one night before leaving his lovesick charge and escaping back to London. At this stage Coleridge became indirectly involved, when Lamb sent him a letter saying, 'You use Lloyd very ill, never writing to him. I tell you again that he is not a mind with which you should play tricks. He deserves more tenderness from you.' Probably Coleridge was expected to communicate, advise and sympathize – as Lloyd's father-figure; and, of course, we do not know how often Lloyd had in fact written to Coleridge.

Meanwhile, Southey, never indecisive when it came to marriages, now hauled Lloyd back to Birmingham from Hampshire to confront Sophia with the proposition of a Scottish wedding; we may take it that Southey lectured the couple at length on the subject of his own clandestine nuptials. But Sophia was not to be persuaded; so the two men returned to Bruton early in September.

By November Coleridge had contributed three 'mock sonnets' to the *Monthly Magazine*, signing himself Nehemiah Higginbottom. He told Cottle that he had attempted to parody his own, Lamb's and Lloyd's verses. But the parodies were more obviously aimed at Lloyd's alone, their target being 'doleful egotism', and 'low, creeping language and thoughts, under the pretence of *simplicity*'. Southey, still delicate from his quarrel with Coleridge in 1795, was convinced that they were aimed at himself, seizing upon the line 'Now of my false friend, plaining plaintively'. Thus Coleridge was obliged to write a strenuous denial. Yet in the very letter which was intended to heal a possible breach, there lay a sting which would wound Southey more than any parody. 'I am sorry,' wrote Coleridge, 'that I wrote them [the sonnets]; because I am sorry to perceive a disposition in you to believe evil of me, and a disposition to teach others to believe evil.'[50] Coleridge then proceeded to write to Lamb denying the reference to Southey: but Lamb was convinced that the denial 'was a lie too gross for the grossest ignorance to believe!' Meanwhile, reacting indignantly on his own behalf, Lloyd wrote to Cottle asking that his contributions to the collected edition of poems should be withdrawn from any future edition. Coleridge was upset by this, but sustained a philosophical front. 'By past experiences we build up our moral being,' he observed sorrowfully.

Matters might have ended there. But in April Cottle now published *Edmund Oliver*, a novel by Charles Lloyd which had been completed in November at the very time when the Nehemiah Higginbottom sonnets had been published. It was a work of blatant calumny which could only inflict the cruellest possible wound on Coleridge – who had so lately begun to put behind him the chaotic indiscretions of his youth. Edmund Oliver, the hero of the novel, has a 'large glistening eye' and 'dark hair'. His is in love with Gertrude, but has a rival in Mr D'Oyley to whom he loses, and he runs away to the army in a frenzy of passion. He has a friend Charles Maurice with whom he corresponds, and Maurice's letters are full of uplift and reproof ; he also has a sister who sends 'prodigal-son' letters. Edmund resorts to opium, of course, when things get too much for him, and he writes letters with such extraordinary sentences as, 'I have some Laudanum in my pocket. I will quell these mortal up-braidings ! – I cannot endure them.' On 14 May, on the very day that his second child, Berkeley, was born, Coleridge wrote to Estlin deep in misery : 'I have had many sorrows and some that bite deep ; calumny and ingratitude from men who were fostered in the bosom of my confidence.'

Naturally Coleridge knew that Southey was involved, for there was little doubt that whatever gaps there had been in Lloyd's knowledge of the details of Coleridge's mis-adventures could be supplied by his old friend. In fact, Southey himself records in his common place book 1798–99 an intention to publish a three-volumed novel with an army hero called Oliver Elton. And in 1801, still playing with the idea, he notes that he should omit 'the soldier part'. One is tempted to wonder just how sincere Southey's and Lloyd's indignation over the paltry, dubiously wounding Higgin-bottom sonnets could have been, knowing all the while that the brazen and libellous text of *Edmund Oliver* was being prepared for publication in Bristol.

Yet even after publication, the matter did not end there
8*

for Lloyd. He now wrote to Dorothy Wordsworth engaging
her to tell Coleridge that Lamb no longer intended to write
to him. We also know that Lloyd tried to alienate Dorothy
herself. Still mulling over the affair twelve years later
Coleridge remembered, 'He even wrote a letter to D.W.,
in which he not only called me a villain, but appealed to a
conversation which passed between him and *her*, as the
grounds of it – and as proving that this was her opinion no
less than his – She brought over the *letter* to me from
Alfoxden with tears – I laughed at it.'⁵¹ [51]

From this point onwards the quarrel gradually burnt
itself out. Coleridge wrote to Lamb requesting him to
summon Lloyd to a tête-à-tête meeting, or a general
meeting with all affected parties present. The request was
characteristic as it was unlikely. Then, the Wordsworths
and Coleridge decided to set out and 'reclaim' Lloyd of their
own initiative while he was staying in Bristol : but by the
time they arrived he had gone.

By June, however, Lloyd proclaimed with largesse that
he would forget the whole matter. 'I love Coleridge and can
forget all that has happened,' he told Cottle. 'At present I
could not well go to Stowey . . . I shall write to Coleridge
today.' Lamb, curiously enough, was slow to forget, although
we cannot be sure to what extent Lloyd had poisoned his
mind. On hearing that Coleridge was departing for Germany
in the autumn, he sent him some burlesque scholastic
theses, with the strong implication that he was a hypocritical
liar, sneerer, and egotist. The self-congratulation of the
spring had reached a sorry conclusion. Coleridge showed
Cottle the letter, and assuming his philosophical front,
commented, 'These young visionaries will do each other
no good'. In time the breach with Lamb would be healed
as if there had been no enmity at all ; and Lamb would
write to Coleridge of Lloyd : 'He almost alienated you from
me, or me from you, I don't know which. But that breach is
closed. The dreary sea is filled up.'

Coleridge would not forget so easily. In 1810, sitting in the loneliness of an hotel in London, after he had broken with the Wordsworths in the Lake District, he pondered on Lloyd's treachery with all the sad confabulation of a para-noiac: Lloyd's conduct, he confided to his notebook, 'was not that of a friend, only because it was that of a madman – on my side, patience, gentleness, and good for evil – yet this supernatural effort injured me – what I did not suffer to act on my mind preyed on my body'. He went on to blame Lloyd for the formation of his opium habit, his inability to finish *Kubla Khan,* and the failure (as well as the inability to complete) his *Christabel.* But worst of all, he had spoiled his friendship with Wordsworth:

Well! he [Wordsworth] settled in the North – and I determined to leave all my friends and follow him – Soon after came – Lloyd and settled at Ambleside – a thick acquaintance commenced between him and W – so that the fear of *his* coming in and receiving an unpleasant agitation occasioned such Looks and hurry and flurry and anxiety that I should be gone from Grasmere, as gave me many a heart ache – It was at this time that speaking of C.Ll.'s conduct to me and others I called him a rascall – *DW* fired up, and said, *He was no rascall* – in short, acted with at least as great warmth on his behalf, as she ever could have done on mine – even when she had known me to have acted the most nobly – At length, a sort of reconciliation took place between me and C.Ll – – about six or 8 months after, some person told *D.W.* that C.Ll. in a public Company had given it as his opinion, that *Coleridge* was a greater poet, and possessed of more genius by nature, than *W.W.* Instantly, D.W. pronounced him a VILLAIN. And thenceforward not a good word in his favor! ![52]

Coleridge never did voice these wholesale allegations in public, but it is clear that he had Lloyd in mind when he wrote the epigraph *To one who Published in Print what had been entrusted to him by my Fireside.*

> Two things thou has made known to half the nation,
> My secrets and my want of penetration:
> For oh! far more than all which thou hast penn'd,
> It shames me to have call'd a wretch, like thee, my friend!

The Freudian slip should delight the psychologically inclined. In our own day, of course, Coleridge might have earned himself a fortune in a libel case.

The Ancient Mariner

COLERIDGE had completed *The Rime of the Ancient Mariner* by March 1798, but he left for Germany before its publication in the *Lyrical Ballads* in September. That he was out of England at that time may have softened the blow of its unsympathetic reception. 'The Lyrical Ballads are laughed at and disliked by all with very few excepted,' Mrs Coleridge informed Poole; above all *The Ancient Mariner* was singled out for scorn.

The extent to which *The Ancient Mariner* constitutes a departure from the accepted literary norms of the eighteenth century can be ascertained from the initial reaction of perplexity. Having found the connexion between the stanzas absurd or unintelligible, Southey pronounced in the *Critical Review*, 'we do not sufficiently understand the story to analyse it'.[1] Charles Burney in the *Monthly Review* felt much the same. It was a 'rhapsody of unintelligible wildness and incoherence (of which we do not perceive the drift), unless the joke lies in depriving the wedding guest of his share of the feast'.[2] An anonymous reviewer in the *British Critic* went on to find a 'kind of confusion of images, which loses all effect, from not being quite intelligible'.[3] And, later, Wordsworth himself could not resist publishing a note in the second edition of the *Lyrical Ballads* about the poem's 'great defects', among which, 'that the events having no necessary connexion do not produce each other'.[4] Even Lamb, who thought highly of the poem, and criticized Southey for his biting review, spoke of the 'spectre bark' passage as 'fertile in unmeaning miracles'. One is reminded of the bewilderment with which Turner's paintings were greeted a decade later, long before the period in his development when such remarks would begin to seem justified in modern eyes: they were a 'waste of morbid strength' commented Hazlitt, 'because of the painter's apparent inability to draw a distinct line'; and there was Hoppner's dismissive sneer, that 'so much was left to be *imagined* that *it was like looking into a coal fire, or upon an old wall, where from many varying & undefined forms the fancy was to be employed in conceiving things*'.[5] It was precisely that special quality of involving the reader in an experience requiring a deeply personal response that Henry Nelson Coleridge remarked upon in his famous review of Coleridge's poetry in 1834:

... it is rarely or never exclusively objective; that is to say, put forward as a spectacle, a picture on which the mind's eye is to rest and terminate. You may if your sight is short, or your imagination cold, regard the imagery itself and go no further; but the poet's intention is that you should feel and imagine a great deal more than you see.

Lamb would imply much the same thing in a letter to Wordsworth about the note in the Preface to the *Lyrical Ballads*: 'I am hurt and vexed that you should think it necessary, with a prose apology, to open the eyes of dead men that cannot see.'

The fact was that Coleridge had presented his readers with a powerful literary experiment that far outstripped the innovations Wordsworth would outline in his 1800 preface. Significantly the initial bewilderment was associated with the poem's lack of 'drift', 'coherence' and 'connexion' both in the 'story' and its 'images', an indication of an inflexible critical attitude, a severely limited response, even on the part of Coleridge's more sympathetic contemporaries. As Henry Nelson Coleridge would say: 'You must think with him, must sympathize with him, must suffer yourself to be lifted

out of your own school of opinion or faith, and fall back
upon your own consciousness, an unsophisticated man.' In
private, at least, the poem had its admirers : although the
praise was more a concession to some undefinable and
hidden power than any explicit merit. Lamb talked of its
'fifty passages as miraculous as the miracles they celebrate',
and Francis Jeffrey, later to become editor of the *Edinburgh
Review* and one of Coleridge's sharpest critics, claimed that
it had 'more new images than in all the German ballads and
tragedies, that have been holding our hair on end for these
last three years'. In time of course this response to the
discreet power and originality of the poem would gather
momentum, but at this early stage, perhaps, it would have
taken a critical intelligence as subtle and as unusual as
Coleridge's to appreciate the poem's worth; in fact, the
growing awareness of its special qualities is surely owed in
part to the influence of his own criticism.

Above all Coleridge would attack the misleading tendency
to apply a familiar and rigid logic to a work of art, to
abstract meaning, or to describe a work in terms of something
other than itself. In his notebook he would later write that
one of the main obstacles to grasping 'transcendent or
genetic' qualities arises in the 'tendency to look abroad, *out*
of the thing in question, in order by means of some *other*
thing analogous to understand the former'. In fact he might
have been referring specifically to his own poetry when he
spoke of the necessity to hold in the mind the 'act we are
describing – Cohesion, for instance – and by this all co-
herents & particular forms of cohesion are to be rendered
intelligible, not it by them'.[6] Consonant with this attitude
was his idiosyncratic regard for allegory. The idea of
allegory he certainly favoured, but not if it meant a rigid
pattern of abstractions. 'Now an allegory,' he wrote in the
Statesman's Manual, 'is but a translation of abstract notions
into a picture-language which is itself nothing but an
abstraction from objects of the sense; the principal being

more worthless even than its phantom proxy, both alike unsubstantial, and the former shapeless to boot.' In *The Ancient Mariner* transcendental significances are firmly rooted in direct sensory experience, and the 'connexions' are found here rather than in a set of coldly representative images conducting themselves within the rules of an inflexible logic. Coleridge was a 'philosophical' poet, a metaphysician – certainly, but this by no means implied that he dealt in abstractions in his finest poetry :

. . . a great Poet must be, implicitè if not explicitè, a profound Meta-physician. He may not have it in logical coherence, in his Brain & Tongue; but he must have it by *Tact*/for all sounds, & forms of human nature he must have the *ear* of a wild Arab listening in the silent Desart, the eye of a North American Indian tracing the foot-steps of an Enemy upon the leaves that strew the Forest – ; the Touch of a Blind Man feeling the face of a darling Child – /⁷

It was in just such terms as these that he liked to describe his own poetic activity. Many years later he recollected a conversation with Southey which summed up his own peculiar mode of work :

Southey once observed to me – I (said he) hunt by the eye, like a Grey-hound. I see what my Object is : and dash in a strait line towards it. But you hunt with your nose to the earth : track the Prey thro' every bend & zigzag, in and out thro' the whole maze of Puss' or Renyard's Feet – and at the end what do you catch? – Why, the *Scent*, perhaps, of the Hare or Vermin which I had killed an hour before, after a five minutes run.⁸

Or as Coleridge put it in a notebook entry : 'I value most highly the excellencies of scent, patience, discrimination, free Activity ; and find a Hare in every Nettle I make myself acquainted with. I follow the Chamois-Hunters, and seem to set out with the same Object.'⁹ To follow Coleridge in a work like *The Ancient Mariner* demands the same 'free Activity', the same attentiveness to sound and to '*scent*'. 'In ATTENTION,' he wrote, 'we keep the mind *passive* . . . we submit to an impression – we keep the mind steady in order to *receive* the stamp.' Only then was the mind ready for thought, where 'we seek to imitate the artist, while we ourselves make a copy or duplicate of his work'.[10]

It is not surprising that in concentrating on plot and logical connexions Coleridge's contemporaries missed the most immediate and connecting impact of the poem – above all, the sense of motion with the closely cohering qualities of sound and light. Nor is it surprising that they missed, or resisted, the invitation to subordinate themselves in a deeply personal way to the elements which stir the subconscious, the glimpses and echoes of 'nascent existence'. It is curious that one of the few contemporary critics who noticed the former clue to Coleridge's poetry merely mentioned it in a pejorative way. 'In his poetry nothing in nature is dead. Motion is synonymous with Life', wrote the anonymous reviewer in the *Quarterly Review* (XII).

With the reservation that one finds a whole variety of 'coalescent' sensory experience in *The Ancient Mariner*, one is tempted to say that it is as much *about* motion as, say, Turner's *The Shipwreck* (1804) or his *Calais Pier* (1803): the immediate, all-pervasive 'texture' through which the inner meaning shines forth is primarily expressed in the sense of movement. The fact that this was, and is, overlooked has much to do with the poem's seeming simplicity on the level of the immediate senses. There is not space here to enter upon a detailed appreciation of *The Ancient Mariner*, but an illustration of that deceptive simplicity in just two early stanzas should suffice.

> The ship was cheered the harbour cleared
> Merrily did we drop
> Below the kirk, below the hill,
> Below the light-house top.
>
> The sun came up upon the left,
> Out of the sea came he!

> And he shone bright, and on the right
> Went down into the sea.

The proportion of these lines is almost naïve, yet in terms of motion a sense of ambiguity is immediately created in the first stanza between 'we' and the objects on the horizon line. The confusion is just, for while in fact the kirk, the hill, the lighthouse are literally descending, it is the ship that is in motion and the illusion of dropping is 'lent' from the objects on the horizon. It is an effect similar to Wordsworth's 'huge peak, black and huge' in the first book of *The Prelude,* which 'As if with voluntary power instinct / Upreared its head'; and one is reminded of 'those thin clouds above' in Coleridge's *Dejection Ode,* 'that give away their motion to the stars', or the icebergs, later in *The Ancient Mariner,* which 'came floating by', 'lending' the *absence* of motion to the ship.

There is ambiguity in another sense; for while we understand that the ship moves across the sea in a horizontal plane, the repetition of 'drop' and 'below' gives a powerful impression of vertical progression downwards, preparing the way for the rising and again falling sun in the second stanza. And yet the sun's vertical course is only superficially so: we understand that its movement is semielliptical, or semicircular. We have simultaneously, then, horizontal progression, the vertical rising and falling, and the semi-elliptical movement from side to side. It is exactly that multidimensional sense of movement we experience out at sea, expressed in an unobtrusive and coherent pattern. Meanwhile the sense of the lengthening journey is also implied, and the rising and falling of the sun mark the passage of diurnal time, to the quiet transition :

> Higher and higher every day,
> Till over the mast at noon –

The cosmic latitudinal and longitudinal movements are brought in line with the human sense of motion on the sea, creating a total picture of interaction and expansion. Writing of this sense of 'blended' motion some years later Coleridge remarked :

One of the most noticeable and fruitful facts in Psychology is the modification of the same feeling by difference of form/The heavens lift up my soul, the sight of the Ocean seems to widen it. We feel the same Force at work, but the difference from Body & Mind both that we should feel in actual travelling horizontally or in direct ascent, that we feel in fancy – for what are our feelings of this kind but a motion imagined? with the feelings that would accompany that motion less distinguished more blended, rapid, confused, & thereby coadunated – as white is the very emblem of one in being the confusion of all.[11]

It is precisely the reduction of complexity to 'coaduna-tion', as he calls it, that is the brilliant success of these stanzas. But the underlying complexity does not end there. Although the stanzas are rhythmically identical, there is a different momentum between the first and the second. The first stanza seems to express an increasing sense of lightness – a rising effect produced by the long vowel sounds 'cheered' and 'cleared', followed by the short 'did', 'drop', 'kirk', 'hill', 'top', all coming on the heavy stresses. Paradoxically the lightening effect to the culminating 'top' enacts the very reverse of the 'dropping' motion expressed in the stanza's meaning. In the following stanza we find the opposite procedure : 'up' and 'left' are stressed, but light and short-vowelled, and the stressed syllables throughout the rest of the stanza are long and ponderous – 'sea', 'he', 'bright', 'right', 'sea'. In other words, not only does he employ a metrical pattern to *rise* against the 'dropping' ship, but he works that same pattern against itself in the second stanza, producing the delightful, if subliminal, experience of simultaneously conflicting patterns of metre and rhythm, as if using them as separate instruments. Again it was H. N. Coleridge's review that first paid tribute to Coleridge's extraordinary powers of versification : 'The verses seemed as if *played* upon some unseen instrument.' His poetry was distinguished he wrote, 'in a remarkable degree by the perfection of the rhythm and metrical arrangement'.

But there are more instruments yet. Significantly the finest passage in the outward journey was written in 1800 after he had been to Germany and made his first sea voyage :

> With *sloping* masts and *dipping* prow
> As who *pursues* with yell and blow
> Still treads the *shadow* of his foe
> An *forward* bends his head,
> The ship drove fast *loud roared* the blast
> And *southward* aye we fled.

My italics draw attention to the disyllables which naturally create a syncopating effect along the iambic line. They are noticeably balanced in the first line, then swing to and fro in a pitching and heaving motion to the end. To demonstrate the powerful rhythmic effect of these disyllables, it is worth anticipating the manner in which he isolates them after the first syllable in the line when the ship is becalmed, giving the right sense of monotony :

> The *very* deep did rot : O Christ!
> That *ever* this should be
> Yea, *slimy* things did crawl with legs
> *Upon* the *slimy* sea.

Furthermore, the disyllables give rise to yet more complex and subtle sound effects. While 'sloping' and 'dipping' follow the same stress pattern, they work against each other metrically : 'sloping' and 'dipping', achieving that opposing impression of steady, tangential movement against the pressure of the wind, and the short plunging of the ship as it meets the waves. Meanwhile 'pursued' and 'shadow' balance up 'sloping'; and in the final three lines the echoing 'forward', 'loud roared', 'southward' aptly express the remorseless chase across the wide expanse of ocean.

And yet to leave matters here, even, is to over simplify : the '*s*loping ma*st*s and *d*ipping prow' anticipates an alliterative pattern of *s*, *st d* and *dr* sounds, finding their culminating force in –

> The ship *dr*ove fa*st*, lou*d r*oare*d* the bla*st*

The fractional pause between the second *d* and *r* in 'lou*d r*oared', (which becomes a disyllable by analogy with 'forward' and 'southward'), expresses the hesitation between the ship's hurtling course and the pursuing wind, so beloved of Coleridge ('half-intermitted burst', 'traces of the blast', 'interspersed vacancies'). It is important to stress, moreover, the introduction of further 'dimensions' of motion : the wind having 'struck' and 'chased', is seen both to propel the ship and at the same time to harass it so fearfully that it flees of its own motion, moving as if by repulsion.

With the advent of the land of mist and snow, and the Albatross, this orchestration of motion enacting the movement of the ship in fair passage and storm – moving from expanding harmony to a crescendo of tension and suspense in the chase and race of foe and victim – now enters a new sphere of significance. The natural forms and the ship are seen to be engaged in an intricate dance. The atmosphere of the dance has already been anticipated by the 'pacing' of the bride, the 'nodding' of the ministrelsy at the wedding feast : it has found a remote outlet in the 'sun came up upon the left . . . and he shone bright and on the right . . .', and there has been the regular skipping measure of the ballad rhythm : if music appeals to the head, the heart and the feet, *The Ancient Mariner* is surely no exception.

In the land of mist and snow, the ice, like the sun, not only takes up its station both on the right and the left, 'The ice was here the ice was there', but also forms a circle, 'The ice was all around'. The Albatross *'crosses'* then itself enters the circular movement, 'And round and round it flew'. At this point the ship repeats the crossing movement in 'the helmsman steered us through', closely followed by the south wind, and yet again the Albatross :

> And a good south wind sprung up behind
> The Albatross did follow.

The dance seems to enact the fearful storm, the hurtling and pursuing, in ritualistic and benevolent form, reducing and assimilating the fear and tension. The sense of dance or game at this point anticipates similar movements later in the poem, more particularly and explicitly the 'death-fires':

> About, about, in reel and rout
> The death-fires danced at night . . .

And the stars in a later passage –

> The upper air burst into life!
> And a hundred fire-flags sheen,
> To and fro they were hurried about!
> And to and fro, and in and out,
> The wan stars danced between.

At the same time the poem has been resonant with sound. 'The merry din' of the wedding feast gives way to the *cheering* of the ship as it leaves the harbour; the 'loud bassoon' and the 'merry minstrelsy' to the *yelling* and *roaring*, the *splitting* with 'thunder-fit' of the ice, the 'hollo' of the mariner. And there has been a corresponding transition and balancing with light and colour; the brightness of the sun in the early passages is contrasted with the mysterious 'dismal' sheen and *glimmering* moon-shine in the polar regions, pointing back to the initiated 'glittering eye' of the Mariner. And the primary colour simile 'red as a rose is she' finds its counterpart in the ice-bergs – 'as green as emerauld'. In effect one has all the rowdiness and gaiety of a fiesta, giving way to the noise of battle and storm and ending with the strange dreamlike noises ('like noises in a swound') in the ghostly land of mist and snow. The transitions clearly bring a different emphasis, yet each stage seems to connect or 'coadunate' with the others. It is difficult not to think of that late addition to *The Eolian Harp* :

> O ! the one Life within us and abroad
> Which meets all motion and becomes its soul
> A light in sound, a sound-like power in light,
> Rhythm in all thought, and joyance everywhere.

Motion, sound and light. The theme of motion has been constant up to this point in Coleridge's poetry. It has been an essential way of looking at the world for Priestley, a way of identifying the basis of unity in Nature : 'Suppose then,' he had written in *Matter & Spirit*, 'that the Divine Being, when he created *matter*, only fixed *certain centres of various attractions and repulsions*, extending indefinitely in all directions, the whole effect of them to be upon each other.' In *Destiny of Nations* Coleridge had expressed this Priestleian notion of a unifying principle when he wrote :

> Nature's vast ever-acting energy
> In will, in deed, Impulse of All to All !

Again, in *Religious Musings* he had addressed the Spirit of the Universe :

> And ye of plastic power, that interfused
> Roll through the grosser and material mass
> In organizing surge !

In *The Eolian Harp* he had developed a stage further, in an attempt to describe the active self working within this material unifying principle – drawing an analogy between motion and music :

> And what if all of animated nature
> Be but organic Harps diversely fram'd . . .

Yet in his more recent poetry while retaining its central importance the theme had become less obtrusive. In *This Lime Tree Bower* motion becomes synonymous with beauty and life, and it is the redeeming feature of the gloomy dell, where the reeds

> Ne'er tremble in the gale, yet tremble still
> Fann'd by the water-fall.

And in *Frost at Midnight* motion is seen as an image of
self-conscious awareness, connecting with the vibrant but
inarticulate world by 'dim sympathies'

> Methinks, its motion in this hush of nature
> Gives it a companionable form . . .

In one sense the all pervasive movement up to part III of
The Ancient Mariner is more discreet than it had been in the
poems cited above, and yet it is more powerful. The
essential difference is that the significance of motion is
enacted rather than stated, presented, as in *Kubla Khan*, as a
self-authenticating experience, rather than the explicit
affirmation of a cosmological or philosophical theory. And
the power of this experience of an 'active Universe' achieves
its greatest impact at the point where the huge reversal
takes place, the Mariner having shot the Albatross and the
crew having shared in his guilt.

Coleridge told a friend many years later that before his
visit to Germany in 1798 he had been soaking himself in
Boehme's *Aurora* where he learnt the interconnection
between gravitation, light and sound. And there he would
have read a captivating vision in which the realms of matter,
spirit and the interior life of man reflected each other. Of the
natural Forms, Boehme wrote :

> When thou beholdest this World, thou has a *Type* of Heaven. . . .
> The *Elements* signify or denote the wonderful Proportion, Variety,
> *Change* and Alteration of the Form and Position of Heaven : For as
> the Deep between the Stars and Earth always alter and change in their
> *Form*, suddenly it is Fair, Bright and Light, suddenly it is Lowery and
> Dark, now Wind, then Rain, now Snow, suddenly the Deep is Blue or
> Azure, suddenly Greenish, by and by Whitish, then suddenly again
> Dusky.[12]

It was a world order at once more mystical, more visionary,
more suited to the direction in which Coleridge was developing his poetry than the scientific attractions and repulsions of
Priestley ; and essentially it was a universe which connected

directly with the interior life of man. It is precisely this visionary freedom which is being invoked when the great reversal in Nature follows on the Mariner's crime, and the wonderful variety, change and alteration of the elements ceases.

There is a *dropping* of the sails, as with the ship and the sun at the beginning of the voyage, but there is no rising. There is silence where there had been riotous sound. And where there had been expansion dilation and progression, the sun now *stands*, and contracts – 'no bigger than the moon,' ; the ship is *stuck* and the boards 'shrink' ; there are signs of death : the sea *rots*, the mariners' tongues are *withered*. At this point the 'revenge' of the sun seems to give rise to one of the chief sources of ambiguity in the poem. When Coleridge's contemporaries spoke of the lack of connection between the images, or Wordsworth of the events not producing one another, they may have had in mind the sun's sudden alteration from beneficence to maleficence. In its very simplest form, the argument could run in two ways : one could say that the sun is acting out the 'revenge' of Nature on the Mariner's crime : or, to take a more psychological view, that the state of 'fixedness', thirst and burning heat is a manifestation of the dislocated state of the mariner's soul. But to make the 'connexion' in either of these ways is unsatisfactory. For the poem neither settles entirely in the objective or subjective spheres, but merges the two states undefinably. Up to the point where the Mariner kills the Albatross the sense of the 'real' objective world has been uppermost, and yet it is a tale told by a wild man with a 'glittering eye', a man who seems to have suffered a terrifying initiation, who, the wedding guest suspects, might be mad. But it is only with the lightest stroke – 'like noises in a swound' – that the poet suggests he is talking of anything but the real world.

Once the ship is becalmed, however, that 'real' world blends with the suprasensory realms of the dream, the

trance, the nightmare ; then comes a whole train of supernatural reference points, of spirits, daemons, angels ; it is a
twilight world of sleeping and waking, Life and Death,
Heaven and Hell, loneliness in the expanse, imprisonment
with the multitude : a strange no-man's-land, suspended
between the spheres of Matter and Spirit, Faith and Reason,
the subconscious and the conscious, the subjective and the
objective. Again we might return to Coleridge's description
of 'that shadowy half-being, that state of nascent Existence
in the Twilight of the Imagination, and just on the vestibule
of Consciousness'.[13] In charting such ambiguous and
shadowy regions of experience, there can be no such thing
as a neat interpretation of images or symbols. Once again, in
Boehme's *Aurora* we find the strangely ambiguous interpenetration of the 'Self of every creature' and the natural
forms, with reference to the soul of a sinning man and the
sun. In the margin of his copy of the *Aurora* Coleridge
later wrote :

Boehme might have & probably had, thought of a Central Fire,
which radiating to all points of the circumference was the genial
warmth of the Globe, and above the warmth rising cloathed it with
Light. But yet to such as sunk down, & seeking a centre of all, it must
be a very horrible Fire, which no creature can endure. Now the Self
of every creature should be the Light or Glory of God, even his
Word & co-eternal Son – in whom is *Life* & that Life the Creature's
Light – and not in the abysmal Will.[14]

Similarly the Mariner's duality of vision in terms of good
and evil are connected with the disposition of his will, until
his spiritual journey leads him to subordinate himself to the
divine purpose. For the rest, however, the apparitions and
'supernatural' events seem to defy any kind of single,
exact, or final interpretation. They are like the images which
form our 'manifest dream content', which do not end in
themselves but give rise both to permanent and universal
processes of the psyche, and associations that are deeply
personal and subjective. Particularly enlightening in this

latter regard are those discussions of the associations that these images may have held for Coleridge, for they reveal by analogy a leading variation amongst the many possibilities inherent in a subjective response without dictating an inflexible reading of the poem. A distinguished example of this approach is Professor George Whalley's *The Mariner and the Albatross*[15] where he links the emotional content of the images and events with, for example, the powerful sense of loneliness and its manifold associations in Coleridge's life. Professor Whalley has called the poem a 'personal allegory', a reading that was in fact anticipated by Rowland Prothero, in the *Edinburgh Review* (162) in 1885, who saw *The Ancient Mariner* as Coleridge's prophetic expression of the deepest fears in his nature. Professor Whalley rightly adds the warning – 'no specialized interest – moral, biographical, or allegorical – can be allowed to assail the integrity to which, as a poem, it is entitled'. Yet the poem is only 'assailed' when such a reading carries the implication that the 'specialized interest' will find no corresponding echoes in the hearts of its readers. What redeems the highly emotive and subjective elements from the status of merely 'local' or biographical interest is the extent to which they are variations on fearful spiritual and emotional 'constants', which speak to all of us, which are as universal and permanent in their own way as hope, love and joy are in theirs. At the same time the unique status of the poem consists in the marriage of these intuitive and deeply personal resonances with the immediate, positive, and disciplined qualities, the brilliant virtuosity of its versification and the powerful and immediate appeal to the senses. If Coleridge was ever successful in reconciling the conflicting tendencies of his age as represented by 'positivism' and Romantic idealism, he achieves it here in *The Ancient Mariner*.

There is not space here to add to the many interpretations of *The Ancient Mariner*, but I should like to describe briefly an aspect of the poem that I personally find deeply interesting and moving – an aspect that is perhaps appropriate in a biographical study. From his very childhood Coleridge was what some people might call a 'religious' person. The term 'religious' carries the unfortunate overtones of sectarian involvement, idiosyncratic piety, righteousness, and orthodox propensities ; but here it is meant in its fundamental sense – an awareness of the mystery of human existence, an urgent need to understand man's purpose and role, a restless curiosity about his affinity with the rest of the universe. But above all, a quality which only Coleridge himself can describe. In his notebook he says how he 'Saw in early youth as in a Dream the Birth of the Planets' :

& my eyes beheld as *one* what the Understanding afterwards divided into 1. the origin of the masses, 2. the origin of their motions, and 3. the site or position of their circles and Ellipses – all the deviations too were *seen* in one intuition of one, the self-same, necessity – & this necessity was a Law of the Spirit – & all was Spirit – and in matter all beheld the past activity of others or their own – this reflection, this Echo, is matter – its only essence, if essence it be – and of this too I saw the necessity and understood it – but I understood not, how infinite multitude and manifoldness could be one. Only I saw & understood, that it was yet more out of my power to comprehend how it could otherwise – & thus in this unity I worshipped in the depth of knowledge that passed all understanding the being of all things – and in Being their sole Goodness – and I saw that God is the one, the Good – possesses it not, but is it.[16]

In many respects Coleridge's quest was similar to that of the young Augustine of Hippo who expressed his youthful aspiration in this way : 'I was left with an unbelievable fire in my heart, desiring the deathless Qualities of Wisdom.'[17] Like Augustine, he found himself pondering the relationship between the one and the manifold in regard to good and evil. Like Augustine, his constant preoccupation was, 'From what cause do we do evil?' Coleridge actually recorded the title 'Origin of Evil' as a projected subject of an epic poem in 1796, but it seems that he had been considering this idea as far back as 1794. Charles Lamb wrote to Coleridge in February of 1797 saying, 'I have a dim recollection that, when you were in town you were talking of the Origin of Evil, as a most prolific subject for a long poem. Why not adopt it, Coleridge? There would be room for Imagination.'[18] The epic was never realized; *The Ancient Mariner* was written instead.

The Mariner's dilemma aptly illustrates the working out of the Augustinian problem of the existence and experience of evil in the mind of a man who tends towards Pantheism. If God is all – then God too must be evil – naturally, an unacceptable conclusion; the alternative is a rigid dualism – a universe in which pure evil coexists with pure goodness, in which man is subsumed by the one or totally enveloped and imprisoned by the other.

As we have seen, in the first stage of the Mariner's suffering the whole of nature seems to undergo a momentous reversal: the motion and alteration of the elements gives way to stagnation, sterility and death. At the same time the very effects of these sufferings, dumbness and thirst, imply an awakening of desire and a need for self-expression. And yet the Mariner and the crew immediately favour the superstitious and terrifying conclusion that they are the victims of the instruments of darkness – the return of the motion of the dance with the 'death-fires' and the lurid burning of the waters is associated with witchery, and the crew are assured in dreams that the Spirit from the 'land of mist and snow' has pursued to 'plague' them. Significantly the sense of paranoia and superstition towards their environment is attended by 'evil looks', cast on the Mariner by the rest of the crew as he becomes the guilty one, the Jonas, or like that most guilty figure in history – the Wandering Jew.

An optimistic view of death, both in spiritual and psychological terms, might imply rebirth, or assimilation into the unity of God or Nature, but the startling appearance of the death ship plays on the hideous associations of death as the final triumph of the powers of evil.

> And straight the Sun was flecked with bars,
> (Heaven's Mother send us grace!)
> As if through a dungeon-grate he peered
> With broad and burning face.

The image seems to suggest the confinement of life through a death that can only be viewed with despair and hopelessness. At the same time it qualifies the later self-encaged nature of the Mariner's loneliness. Nobody more than Coleridge understood this horrifying sense of claustrophobic solitude, and later we shall see how he cries out against his isolated predicament in real life as a 'prison without ransome, anguish without patience'.

Yet it is noticeable that in his very terror and solitude there is a gradual awakening. He becomes more conscious of himself and his own responses – 'Alas! (thought I, and my heart beat loud)'. He begins to think and reflect, and his apprehensions become *purposive*, he begins to 'listen' where he had merely heard, to 'watch' and 'behold' where he merely saw. Ironically the 'game' played between the Albatross and the Mariner with its fatal outcome is now repeated in the playing of dice between Death and her Mate, encouraging the Mariner's superstitious view of the fortuitousness and futility of life and death. The horrid figure of Death's Mate is a mockery of the bride at the wedding feast – 'red as a rose is she' – 'her skin as white as leprosy', and the suggestion of the sterility and disease of the whore who brings death in life offers a sharp and dualistic contrast to the Virgin Mary on whom the Mariner calls in vain for life and grace.

The departure of the death ship and the startling descent

of thick night brings with it a sense of ignorance, fear and total abandonment, yet under the cloak of this darkness there are hints of salvation at hand, hints that as yet lay buried in the Mariner's absorption with evil. By 1817 Coleridge would add the sacramental and sacrificial suggestion of the chalice in 'Fear at my heart, as at a cup / My life-blood seemed to sip !', reinforcing the baptismal significance of cleansing and quenching in the forming of dew on the sails. It is as if the very descent of night will bring some form of redemption of which he is as yet unaware. But the greatest agony is yet to come. With the death of the crew he shoulders the unbearable guilt of their murder, and he is left totally alone. And in his solitude the deep fears return in excess. There is a sense of complete spiritual abandonment – 'never a saint took pity on / My soul in agony', of despair in the inability to pray ; and an identification of his own evil with all of creation : 'And a thousand, thousand slimy things / Lived on and so did I.'

Again in the midst of the terror and loneliness the motion and light of the natural forms, while conducting themselves in patterns of great beauty, merely mock him – and that earlier sense of witchcraft and menace is intensified –

> Her beams bemocked the sultry main,
> Like April hoar-frost spread;
> But where the ship's huge shadow lay
> The charméd water burnt alway a
> Still and awful red.

Again the Mariner, *watches*, and contemplates the movement of the water snakes – still connecting them with the elfish realms of evil, but as he continues to watch he is absorbed by the sheer apprehension of their motion light and colour, without personal judgment or interpretation as to their quality or origin – until :

> O happy living things! no tongue
> Their beauty might declare:

> A spring of love gushed from my heart,
> And I blessed them unaware:

There is a passage in the *Confessions* where Augustine refers to the serpent, the universal symbol of evil, reproach and horror as good, and not only good but beautiful – in that the creature corresponds to the order of the divine will. And he comments that the life in the body of such a creature gives it a transcendental claim to beauty for it 'hints much more clearly than its body at the unity which creates all natures'.[19] It is surely no coincidence that Coleridge chose the contemplation of the water snakes, creatures to be cursed and reviled, as the Mariner's moment of release from his imprisoned soul and vision, or that the lesson he has learnt is in all respects similar to Augustine's comment that the 'worm' enjoys its instinctual fulfilment of God's will while man suffers the anguish of dislocation through sin. Where the Mariner had before identified his state of misery with an existing state of horror and evil outside himself – 'a thousand, thousand slimy things Lived on ; and so did I' – he now discovers that good and evil exist in proportion to a creature's self-surrender to the love of God through the beauty of all his creatures.

Clearly the Mariner's redemption is achieved by his recognition of the beauty of the watersnakes, and in this sense the poem stands well within familiar Coleridgian themes ; but there is a striking simultaneous event which takes the poem into areas that are unusual for Coleridge, although hardly unexpected. It is the reception of 'grace' which enables the Mariner to bless the creatures and to pray, releasing him from his living hell. This blatant introduction of a theological mechanism into the poem, rather than restricting its universality and power, paradoxically increases it. Just as the poem demonstrates that all that exists does not involve a sharp separation of Good and Evil ; so the path to the Mariner's redemption does not merely involve the right attitude or the correct aesthetic apprehension of the universe, even though this is a precondition. This would be to throw the acquisition of happiness and goodness entirely on human nature (which is the reverse of the poem's tendency), clearly an implausible proposition. Nobody more than Coleridge would have been conscious of the existence of personal suffering, anguish and evil in spite of the right attitude, and the right aspirations.

But as tempting as it may be to interpret *The Ancient Mariner* as a commentary on the theology of Original Sin and Coleridge's later development of orthodox religious belief, he was too fine a poet in 1798 to have fallen into such a trap. In placing the context of the ballad in a deliberate medieval setting, the operation of Catholic symbolism acquires a poetic rather than an 'apologetic' reference, and the more diffuse sense of 'grace' or beneficence from without is gained by the continuous and gentle, yet by no means unobtrusive, natural imagery : 'A noise like of a hidden brook / In the leafy month of June' and the mild influence of the moon : for Boehme the symbol of regeneration, and for Coleridge the auspices of the imagination.

Yet the sacramental elements are sustained until the very conclusion of the poem, and continue to exemplify the operations of the 'supernatural' on the Mariner's soul beyond the limits of his vision and will. In 1803 Coleridge would say that his life's ambition was to provide a solution to the 'two grand Problems' – 'how, being acted upon, we shall act ; how, acting, we shall be acted upon'.[20] While he had little relish for the 'superstitions' of Catholicism, he was fascinated by the way in which the Catholic liturgy exemplified the seasons of nature,[21] and more particularly how the sacrament of the Eucharist (specifically in terms of transubstantiation) reconciled the 'two grand Problems' outlined above :

Were one a Catholic, what a sublime oration might not one make of it! – Perpetual, παντopical – yet offering no violence to the Sense, – exercising no domination over the free will – a miracle

9

always existing, yet perceived only by an act of the free will – the beautiful Fuel of the Fire of Faith / the fire must be pre-existent, or it is not fuel – yet it feeds & supports, & is necessary to feed & support, the fire that converts it into its own nature.[22]

The passage indicates the extent to which the symbolism of the Christian sacrament exemplified for Coleridge the force of a conviction only blandly and vaguely realized in *Frost at Midnight*, written during the very months when he was engaged on *The Ancient Mariner*, 'Great Universal Teacher! he shall mould / Thy Spirit, and by giving make it ask'. But more than this, the operation of theological symbolism – particularly in the Lenten and ascetic suggestion of continued penance, confession and pilgrimage emphasizes man's tendency to evil in spite of the redemptive powers of 'grace' or Nature. Yet here again the points of reference extend beyond the 'doctrinal'. The feature of original sin that lends itself most readily to universal implications is the idea of man carrying the inescapable mark of death, and it is this that Coleridge emphasizes throughout the poem. Like the spectre bark the Mariner's ship had brought death to the polar regions, and when they return to the home country they strike terror into the hermit and pilot's boy. Like the death ship they will drive fast across the ocean 'without a breeze', and their sails, like the spectre-bark's gossamers will become thin and sere. Yet unlike the spectre bark the mariner's ship is associated with life and Death in Nature rather than the life *in* Death of the powers of evil. Their sails sigh 'like sedge'; they are like 'brown skeletons of leaves that lag / My forest-brook along . . .', and the Mariner himself, while taking on the skeleton appearance of death is by virtue of Wordsworth's contribution 'long, and lank, and brown / As is the ribbed sea-sand'.

For the dead crew there is the hope of resurrection suggested in the rising and clustering round the mast. But in what sense can the Mariner, death-stricken but remaining in life, aspire to the goodness and beauty of heaven as revealed in nature and his visions? Writing of the angels in the *Aurora* Boehme describes how 'they take one another by the *Hand*, and walk together in the curious *May* of Heaven. . . . Here is nothing but a cordial and gentle Love, a friendly, courteous Discourse, a gracious, amiable, and *blessed* Society.' At that point in the poem where the motion of the elements is re-established, a troop of 'angelic spirits' sing in wonderful harmony, the oneness and manifoldness. The alteration and permanence of nature is manifested in their music – and at the beginning of their song the motion of the 'dance' of the Albatross, the 'fire-flags' and the 'water-snakes' return : 'Around, around, flew each sweet sound . . .'

> Sometimes a-dropping from the sky
> I heard the sky-lark sing;
> Sometimes all little birds that are,
> How they seemed to fill the sea and air
> With their sweet jargoning.
>
> And now 'twas like all instruments,
> Now like a lonely flute;
> And now it is an angel's song,
> That makes the heavens be mute.

There is a marriage of Nature and Heaven in the parallel of the nightingale and the Angels, 'When thou beholdest this World, thou hast a *Type* of Heaven', but for the Mariner and for mankind it would be premature to emulate the rejoicing of Heaven in its human, ritualistic form – the wedding feast – as if the battle were already won. For the Mariner there is no abiding place ; the 'woful agony' of his fallen nature must return again 'at an uncertain hour', and he must 'pass, like night, from land to land.' For him, the '*Type* of Heaven', the closest he can arrive at the perfection and happiness of the Angels, is to emulate their harmony in the watchful spirit of Christian love, to subordinate his will to the divine purpose in the manner of Christian worship

— the human and visible acknowledgment of those supernatural forces of redemption in the poem.

> O sweeter than the marriage-feast,
> 'Tis sweeter far to me,
> To walk together to the kirk
> With a goodly company! —
>
> To walk together to the kirk
> And all together pray,
> While each to his great Father bends,
> Old men, and babes, and loving friends
> And youths and maidens gay!

But again the Christian 'message' is invested with the
force of analogy — as the Mariner's final utterance extends
the 'precept' of love and the acknowledgment of the
Mariner's affinity to Nature :

> but this I tell
> To thee, thou Wedding-Guest!
> He prayeth well, who loveth well
> Both man and bird and beast.

Do these closing lines, simple to the point of bathos,
disintegrate under the burden of the poem's anguish,
grandeur and complexity? Surely it is the lightest twist that
invites the mind to wind and unwind again the golden
thread that has led the way through so many secret and
mysterious places. Who can resist the allurement of
embarking again and again on that strange journey? How
can there be arrival or conclusion?

Germany

COLERIDGE had contemplated the idea of a visit to Germany as far back as the Spring of 1796, and in the Autumn of that year had formulated his expectations from such a trip. He would study chemistry and anatomy, and return with all the works of Semler, Michaelis and Kant. By the end of 1797, moreover, his resolve to 'complete' his education in Germany had been strengthened by his association with the Wedgwoods and the consequent determination to embark on a great work for the improvement of mankind; it was now unthinkable that he should be 'compelled to fag on in all the nakedness of Talent without the materials of Know-ledge or systematic Information'.[1] Originally he had planned to attain a 'tolerable' grasp of German before departing, and he had also hoped to take Sara with him. But by the summer of 1798 his domestic situation had altered considerably: Sara's second child, Berkeley, was barely three months old, and they would be obliged to organize their lives on a certain, but restricted budget. It became clear that Sara could not accompany him. Yet in spite of objections from both Estlin and Poole, he was determined to set off. 'I still think the scheme of high importance to my intellectual utility; and of course to my moral happiness,' he told Poole. Undoubtedly one of the most attractive features of the plan was Words-worth's and Dorothy's decision to accompany him, and he would also have the benefit of the companionship of John Chester, a neighbour at Stowey.

The party embarked for Germany on 16 September,

Coleridge dressed 'all in black with large shoes and black worsted stockings'. And as the ship sailed out from Yarmouth, he was seized with a fit of patriotism, one might almost say chauvinism: 'For the first time in my life I beheld my native land retiring from me – my native land to which I am convinced I shall return with an intenser affection – with a proud Nationality made rational by my own experience of its Superiority.' And when the land had at last disappeared, he experienced a vivid, curiously ominous, vision. 'When we lost sight of land, the moment that we quite lost sight of it, and the heavens all around me rested upon the waters, my dear Babies came upon me like a flash of lightening – I saw their faces so distinctly!' In another account he wrote, 'they came upon my eye as distinctly as if they had that moment died and were crossing me in their road to heaven!'

Out at sea Chester began to look 'Frog-coloured and doleful', and Dorothy retired to the cabin in confusion, soon to be followed by Wordsworth. But Coleridge could boast good sea legs and was 'gay as a lark'. At once he became the centre of attraction as he talked and laughed amongst the passengers. Later he fell in with a party of Danes who at first took him for a priest because of his dress, but he quickly disabused them, informing them that he was 'un Philosophe'. They took to drinking, and in a short while were 'spouting, singing, laughing, fencing, dancing country dances', all within earshot of his bilious companions below. Eventually one of the Danes, by now tipsy, cornered Coleridge to himself and embarked on a broken conversation which, Coleridge tells us, began thus:

'Vat imagination! vat language! vat fast science! vat eyes! – vat a milk vite forehead! – O my Heafen! You are a God! – oh me! if you should tink I flatters you – no, no, no – I have ten tousand a year – yes – ten tousand a year – ten tousand pound a year! – vell, vat's that? a mere trifle! – I 'ouldn't give my sincere heart for ten times the money. – Yes! you are a God! – I a mere Man! – But my dear

Friend! tink of me as a Man. Is I not speak English very fine? Is I
not very eloquent?'

Coleridge records their absurd conversation at great
length in his journal, obviously intent on treasuring every
moment of his trip with little eye for selection. 'I trust
nothing to memory', he commented. Thus the voyage
passed in revelry until they reached Heligoland, 'an ugly
Island Rock', at four o'clock on 18 September, and a few
hours later saw the mainland, 'which seemed as scarce able
to hold its head above water – low, flat, and dreary – so low
that it edged the water'. They then passed up the Elbe,
reaching Hamburg the next day : an ugly city 'that stinks
in every corner, house, and room worse than cabbin, sea
sickness or bilge water!' He was also astonished by the
great numbers of windows in the buildings ; 'Pitt's tax
would greatly improve the architecture of Hamburg,' he
observed. They found an expensive and filthy room in an
hotel where they settled temporarily, and three days later
obtained an introduction to the elderly Klopstock, famous
for his *Messiah*. Wordsworth did most of the talking,
having the only common language, French. For his part,
Coleridge found Klopstock with his monstrously swollen
legs and black teeth repulsive, nor was he very impressed
with Klopstock's conversation. Not only did the old man
reveal no great depth in anything he said, but he seemed to
know nothing of the older German poets, 'and talked a
great deal of nonsense about the superior power of con-
centering meaning in the German language'. Yet the man's
goodness and cheerfulness moved Coleridge almost to tears.
'Honour to poets and great men', he recorded in his notebook. 'You think of them as parts of nature / and anything of
tuck and fashion wounds you as if you were to see epaulettes
dangling from an orange tree.' Interestingly enough
Klopstock told Wordsworth that Kant was a 'Mounteback &
the disgrace of Germany – an unintelligible Jargonist. – And
that his New Lights were going out very fast in Germany.'

A short time afterwards Coleridge and Chester set about finding lodgings in Ratzeburg, and by 30 September had moved in with a pastor there. But the Wordsworths moved on to Goslar, hoping that it would be cheaper than the Hamburg area. The main difference in their intentions was that the Wordsworths wished to travel and compensate the expense by finding a cheaper place to live ; whereas Coleridge had decided to settle immediately and apply himself to his studies. Back in England, however, the early separation gave considerable satisfaction to their mutual friends and acquaintances, although not in all cases from the best motives. 'I think you both did perfectly right,' wrote Poole, ' – it was right for them to find a cheaper situation, and it was right for you to avoid the expense of travelling, provided you are where *pure German* is spoken.' Josiah Wedgwood was similarly pleased for Coleridge's sake : 'I hope that Wordsworth and he will continue separated. I am persuaded that Coleridge will derive great benefit from being thrown into mixed society.' But Lamb seemed to relish the separation with malicious glee. 'I hear that the two noble Englishmen have parted no sooner than they set foot on German earth,' he remarked to Southey, 'but I have not heard the reason – possibly, to give novelists an handle to exclaim, "Ah me ! what things are perfect ?" '

The house at Ratzeburg was peaceful and situated in 'wholesome air' with a splendid view of the town, woods and lake from the window. Ratzeburg had the advantage of being a place where German was spoken with 'utmost purity' and the Pastor's children used to stand about the sofa correcting Coleridge's pronunciation. As usual he became the object of 'adulatory attention' from the local nobility and gentry. His translations into German of his own poetry were much admired, and he claimed that he was working hard to 'shorten the time of absence'. He soon discovered a 'ridiculous partiality or rather madness for the English' ; for example, he found playing cards, albeit of

German manufacture, sold in a packet on which was written 'Genuine *English* Cards', and a packet of sticking plaster – 'Royal Patent *English Ornament* Plaster'. There were 'English' signs over shops and boarding houses, and medicines boasted essences from the 'English Oaks'. On attending a concert, the band struck up 'Rule Britannia' as Coleridge entered, and at a dinner given in honour of Nelson's victory in the battle of the Nile a twenty-one-gun salute was fired. As Coleridge noted, 'to be an English man is in Germany to be an Angel'.

It was a fine autumn and Coleridge could enjoy walks in and around the town, but by the beginning of November the mists and rains descended, the lake ran turbid, and the woods 'degenerated into a shabby dirt-colour'. By the end of the month the countryside and the lake was in the grip of hard frost. But with the coming of winter Coleridge was already depressed, mainly because he had not been receiving letters regularly. 'Am I not a friend, a husband, or father? – and do there not belong to each of these it's own inquietude?' he wrote to Sara. He could report that he was doing little else but working at his German. 'It is very difficult to combine and arrange the German sentences,' he confessed ' – and I make miserable havoc with the genders – but yet my progress is more repaid than I could myself have believed.' And by December he was also missing the Wordsworths:

William, my head and my heart! dear William and dear Dorothea! You have all in each other; but I am lonely, and want you!

But he was cheered by transcriptions of *The Prelude* which Wordsworth was sending him, and he was immensely pleased with the passage *There was a boy*. Of the lines – 'uncertain heaven received Into the bosom of the steady lake' he wrote: 'I should have recognized it anywhere; and had I met these lines running wild in the deserts of Arabia, I should have instantly screamed out "Wordsworth!"' Again he wrote in December: 'I am sure I need
9*

not say how you are incorporated into the better part of my being ; how whenever I spring forward into the future with noble affections, I always alight by your side.'

By 4 January he claimed that he could read German as well as English. Curiously enough he could talk 'tolerably well' on trivial or deep metaphysical subjects – 'but in that conversation, which is between both, I bungle most ridiculously'. By this time he had decided to proceed to Göttingen and embark on a work that would make the visit pay for itself. He planned to write a life of Lessing, the German dramatist and poet, 'and interweaved with it a true state of German Literature, in its rise and present state'. Lessing was born in 1729 and had, like Coleridge, received his education from charity. His youth was marked by a tendency to read out-of-the-way books, and a brief interest in chemistry and botany encouraged him to contemplate medicine as a career. His parents had intended him to be a clergyman, but he broke away on a rebellious course of his own and became involved in magazines and the theatre. Self-identification was not far to seek. Yet Coleridge seemed to be aware of a danger that would threaten the fulfilment of his plan even at this early stage. 'That is the disease of my mind – it is comprehensive in its conceptions and wastes itself in the contemplations of the many things which it might do ! – I am aware of the disease, and for the next three months, if I cannot cure it I will at least suspend its operation.' Yet the stay in Germany, he felt, had improved him considerably in this regard, 'my habits are less irregular ; and my *mind* more in my *own power*! But I have much still to do!' He had actually disciplined himself sufficiently to 'very *modestly*' refuse constant invitations to attend balls throughout the winter. 'They dance a most infamous dance called the Waltzen – There are perhaps 20 couple – the man and his partner embrace each other, arms around waists, and knees almost touching, and then whirl round and round, the whole 20 couple, 40 times round at least, to lascivious music.' There was no country on earth where the women were as chaste as in England, he was convinced. In Germany, he observed, the married men intrigue and whore. 'I am no Puritan,' he told Poole, 'but yet it is not customs or manners that extinguish in me the sacredness of a married woman, or quench the disgust I feel towards an adultress.'

One recreation he did allow himself was to be drawn across the frozen lake on a kind of toboggan. 'It is a pleasant amusement to sit in an ice-stool (as they are called) and be driven along the ice by two skaters – I have done so, faster than most horses can gallop.'

In the intense cold of early February he set of with Chester for Göttingen in a stage coach that was a 'temple of all the winds of Heaven ! !' The second night of their journey, he claimed, was the coldest night of the century. They had arrived in Göttingen by 12 February and the next morning found four neat rooms, but to their annoyance discovered that they had been cheated in the price. 'Every human being from the highest to the lowest is in a conspiracy against you,' reflected Coleridge. 'Commercial integrity is quite unknown in Germany, and cheating in business is a national, and therefore not an individual crime / for a German is educated to consider it as *right*.'

He matriculated at the university mainly to gain access to the library, and was actually given permission to 'send to' the library for an indefinite number of books in his own name. Shortly after settling in he met three Englishmen who gave him a very melancholy picture of the place, 'of its dullness – of the impossibility of being introduced into mixed societies, etc. etc.' He visited the library which impressed him with its grandeur, and that same evening he met Antony Hamilton of St John's College, Cambridge, who took him to the 'Saturday Club', where they met up with more Englishmen – 'Such an evening I never passed before – roaring, kissing, embracing, fighting, smashing bottles and glasses against the wall, singing – in short, such a scene of uproar I never witnessed before, no not even at Cambridge. – I drank nothing – but all, except two of the Englishmen were drunk.' Casting his mind back to what he had been at Cambridge, then considering his 'total inability now to do ought *but meditate*' the feeling of 'deep alteration' in his moral being gave the scene a 'melancholy interest' to him.

Coleridge also met two other Englishmen, George Greenough and Clement Carlyon–who has left reminiscences of their relationship in Germany. He tells us how Coleridge was never without his pocket dictionary, 'and there was something inexpressibly comic in the manner in which he dashed on, with fluent diction, but with the worst German accent imaginable'. He also noted how affectionately Coleridge spoke of his wife and children, and recollected that Coleridge once said that 'there was no reward so gratifying to him as the approving smiles of his wife'. Amongst Coleridge's many peculiarities he noted his habit of fixing his eyes on his person whenever there happened to be a mirror in a room. Together they attended lectures on natural history given by Professor Blumenbach, who liked to exhibit his collection of skulls and was in the habit of asking his visitors to point out the skull of a Jew.

In the meantime there had been a sad occurrence back in Stowey. While Coleridge had travelled that cold and tiresome journey to Göttingen, on the 10 February, little Berkeley had died. In November the child had been inoculated for smallpox, and appeared to remain healthy, although Coleridge had wept over the news. But by January it became apparent that he was suffering from consumption. Little Berkeley's death was at first concealed, but fearing that Coleridge might hear the news from some other source, Poole wrote a tender letter which Coleridge did not receive until early April. In his reply he wrote :

I read your letter in calmness and walked out into the open fields, oppressed, not by my feelings, but by the riddles, which the thought so easily proposes, and solves – never! . . . But I cannot truly say that I grieve – I am perplexed – I am sad – and a little thing, a very trifle would make me weep; but for the death of the body I have *not* wept! Oh! this strange, strange, strange scene-shifter, Death! that giddies one with insecurity, and so unsubstantiates the living things that one has grasped and handled! –

Many years later he wrote on the flyleaf of his copy of the Works of Boehme how he wrote the following lines, 'then blind from weeping about little Berkely . . . ':

O what a Life is the Eye! What a fine and inscrutable Essence!
Him that is utterly blind nor glimpses the Fire that warms him,
Him that never beheld the swelling Breast of his Mother
(Smiling awake at the bosom as a Babe that smiles in its Slumber)
Even for Him it exists! It stirs and moves in its Prison,
Lives with a separate Life: and 'Is it a Spirit?' he murmurs:
'Sure, it has Thoughts of it's own, and *to see* is only a Language?'[2]

Writing to Sara he comforts her and himself with the thought that there was a distinction between 'the revealing voice of our most inward and abiding nature', and 'when we sport and juggle with abstract phrases': the agonizing question in his mind was whether a child was capable of future existence. 'I will not believe that it ceases – in this moving stirring and harmonious Universe I *cannot* believe it!'

The tragedy at home served to draw Coleridge closer to his wife and prompted him to make resolutions about his relationship with her:

When in moments of fretfulness and imbecillity I am disposed to anger or reproach, it will, I trust, be always a restoring thought – 'We have wept over the same little one – & with whom am I angry?' – with her who so patiently and unweariedly sustained my poor and sickly infant through his long pains – with her – who, if I too should be called away, would stay in the deep anguish over my death-pillow! Who would never forget me!

And yet in this same month his letters to the bereaved mother display an extraordinary lack of tact ; it was one of his unfortunate characteristics, particularly in his relationship with his wife, that he seemed incapable of judging the natural response that many of his remarks would evoke. There were descriptions of the Christmas customs amongst parents and children in Germany, along with various superstitions, including one that 'if any one die before the performance of his vow, they believe that he hovers between Heaven and Earth'. There were lengthy descriptions of graves, with such quotations as Jeremy Taylor's 'and the summer brings briars to bud on our graves'. There was a description of a gallows at Göttingen with the remark that he mistook animal bones for human ones : ' . . . the grass grows rank, and yet the bones overtop it. – The fancy of human bones must, I suppose, have arisen in my ignorance of comparative anatomy.' And yet it was all well-meaning.

The death of his child also produced a querulous and reactionary note in his correspondence with Poole about the necessity of religion : 'Without religious joys and religious terrors,' wrote Coleridge, referring to the people Poole assisted in Stowey, 'nothing can be expected from the *inferior* classes in society – whether or no any *class* is strong enough to stand firm without them, is to me doubtful. – There are favoured *individuals*, but not *classes*.'[3]

Just a week after the news of Berkeley's death the Wordsworths passed through Göttingen on their way home : 'had I followed my impulses,' he wrote on 23 April, 'I should have packed up and gone with Wordsworth and his sister. . . . If they burn with so much impatience to return to their native country, they who are all to each other, what must *I* feel, with every thing valuable, and every thing dear to me at a distance.' He was still transcribing from eight to ten hours a day, but could not think of returning home for another six weeks. The point was that he now saw the German trip as an investment that might fail unless he managed to collect sufficient material for his life of Lessing. 'Nothing could support me but the knowledge that if I return now we shall be embarrassed and in debt; and the moral certainty that having done what I am doing, we shall be more than *cleared*.' It is ironic that the stay in Germany from which he had hoped for so much had turned into little more than a scholarly chore, while Wordsworth, whom he had criticized for his '*unseeking* manners' up in Goslar, seemed to have gained by burying himself away to write *The Prelude*. The fact of the matter was that Coleridge had made more than a financial investment: he was staking his literary future on erudition and had become bogged down in the seemingly endless and unsavoury process of acquiring it.

'Transcription is such a body-and-soul-wearying Purgatory!' he complained to Josiah Wedgwood; and again, to Poole, 'I believe my late proficiency in learning has somewhat stupified me . . . ' And he seemed to have few illusions about the profit of what he was doing. 'With the advantages of a great library,' he told Poole, 'learning is nothing, methinks – merely a sort of excuse for being idle – yet a man gets a reputation by it; and reputation gets money – and for reputation I don't care a damn, but money – yes – money I must get, in all honest ways . . . '

One would have thought it more congenial for him to have followed up the promise to contribute reports of his stay in the *Morning Post*. Not only had he failed to fulfil this promise, he had also neglected his journal, and seemed unwilling to envisage any kind of publication of his 'travels' (although portions of the journal did eventually appear in *The Friend*). His journal had started well enough at the beginning of the trip, although it seemed curiously unselective. As much, and even more, space was given to details of German prices, menus, recipes and trivial conversation as to description and reflection; and his descriptions are frequently tedious, lacking in power and interest, in fact at times his descriptive entries degenerate into mere 'directions'. Coleridge was acutely conscious of this lack of vitality in his notebooks and letters and continued to be anxious about it throughout the year. In November he wrote to Sara : 'I recommense my Journal, but with feelings that approach to disgust – for in very truth, I have nothing interesting to relate.' And again : 'I will endeavour to give you some idea of Ratzburgh ; but I am a wretched describer.' In January he closes his journal saying, 'After this time one day is like another.' And in March he wrote, 'Description is not my fort ; but descriptions of towns and cities – I abhor even to *read* them !' Eventually, in May, he openly discussed the problem with Sara :

These letters, and the descriptions in them . . . must be insupportably unmeaning – accumulated repetitions of the same words in almost the same combinations – but how can it be otherwise? In Nature all things are individual; but a word is but an arbitrary character for a whole class of things; so that the same description may in almost all cases be applied to twenty different appearances – and in addition to the difficulty of the thing itself I neither am or ever was a good hand at description. – I see what I write/but alas! I cannot write what I see.

It was an awful admission, and it must have depressed him deeply to make it. It was also one of the first occasions in his life when his confidence in his literary powers had been shaken. Two days later he returned to the problem. He had been striving to describe to Poole the appearance of a group of women walking in the mountains – when he suddenly breaks off –

The thick mist, thro' which their figures came to my eye, gave such a soft *unreality* to them! These lines, my dear Poole, I have written rather for my own pleasure than your's – for it is impossible that this misery of words can give to you, that which it may yet perhaps be able to recall to me. – What can be the cause that I am so miserable a describer? Is it that I understand neither the practice nor the principles of painting? – or is it not true, that others have really succeeded? – I could half suspect that what are deemed fine descriptions, produce their effects almost purely by charm of words, with which and with whose combinations we associate *feelings* indeed, but no distinct *Images*.

He is falling back on the emphasis on feeling so frequently made by Wordsworth, and it is possible that he and Wordsworth actually discussed the problem of prose descriptions when they met early in April. Yet the half-suggestion that perhaps nobody had ever succeeded in descriptive writing reveals a deep reluctance to accept his own difficulties as a lack of personal ability. In a sense, of course, he was right not to do so : for while he was no doubt suffering from a temporary personal failure, he is amongst the finest descriptive prose writers of his age, and he was surely conscious of this in his better moments. Hence his bafflement and unwillingness to accept that he was at fault. Unfortunately the analysis of his difficulties at this time was rather inflexible, and it seems that he overlooked the powerful effect of striking and fresh associations of images. He had revealed his extraordinary associative powers again and again in his poetry, yet he seemed unable to recognize its importance consciously in prose. As it is there are some rare glimpses of his brilliant talents during his time in Germany which contradict his confession of failure and redeem the general flatness of his notebooks and letters.

On the voyage out, for example ; he is sitting up on deck alone in the middle of the night :

The ocean is a noble thing by night; a beautiful white cloud of foam at momently intervals roars and rushes by the side of the vessel, and stars of flame dance and sparkle and go out in it – and every now and then light detachments of foam dart away from the vessel's side with their galaxies of stars, and scour our of sight, like a Tartar troop over a wilderness ![4]

Or a description of ice-skating on the lake at Goslar ; although it is difficult not to believe that this piece was stimulated by a letter from Wordsworth who was at this time engaged on the first book of *The Prelude* :

In skating there are three pleasing circumstances – the infinitely subtle particles of ice, which the skate cuts up, and which creep and run before the skater like a low mist, and in the sun rise or sun set become coloured; 2nd the shadow of the skater in the water seen thro' the transparent ice, and 3rd the melancholy undulating sound from the skate not without variety; and when very many are skating together, the sounds and the noises give an impulse to the icy trees, and the woods all round the lake tinkle.[5]

Then again when he was walking on the Brocken in the Spring :

We reached the top – and behold! now and again the spring meets us! I look back and see the snow on the Brocken, and all between the black *mineral*-green of pine-groves, wintry, endlessly wintry/and the beach and the birch, and the wild ash all leafless – but lo! before us – a sweet spring! not indeed in the full youthful verdure as on our first day's journey, but timidly soft, half-wintry and with here and there spots and patches of Iron brown.[6]

Finally, this remarkable description of his beloved waterfalls also written on the Brocken walk :

Now again is nothing but Pines and Firs, above, below, around us! – How awful is the deep Unison of their individable murmur – What a *one* thing it is – it is a sound that impresses the dim notion of the omnipresent! In various parts of the deep vale below us we behold little dancing waterfalls gleaming thro' the branches; and now on our left hand from the very summit of the hill above us a powerful stream flung itself down, leaping and foaming, and now concealed, and now not concealed, and now half-concealed by the fir trees, till towards the road it became a visible sheet of water, within whose immediate neighbourhood no pine could have permanent abiding place! – The snow lay every where on the sides of the roads, and glimmered in company with the waterfall-foam – snow-patches and water breaks glimmering thro' the branches in the hill above, the deep bason below and the hill opposite.[7]

Yet these are brief flashes in long passages of dullness. Somehow the visit to Germany had not proved congenial to his talents. The first and most obvious conclusion one might draw is that his daily 'purgatory' of scholarly transcription, and his deep preoccupation with the language had, indeed, 'stupified' him, blunted those delicate powers of observation, that brilliant associative facility. There is another conclusion, equally substantiated by Coleridge himself throughout that year. He was quite plainly homesick. In March he wrote to his wife : 'I have thought and thought of you, and pictured you and the little ones so often and so often, that my imagination is tired, down flat and powerless ; and I languish after home for hours together, in vacancy ; my *feelings* almost wholly unqualified by *thoughts*.' Indeed he was convinced that if he were to remain a few years among 'objects for whom I had no affection' he would wholly lose his powers of intellect : 'love is the vital air of my genius, and I have not seen one human being in Germany, whom I can conceive it *possible* for me to *love* — no, not one.' This homesickness was not simply a sense of absence but a very palpable dislike of both Germany and the Germans. He despised their manners, their morals, and their lack of taste, and his letters are full of unqualified disgust : a typical observation is this made in a letter to Sara in November :

All the men have a hideous custom of picking their teeth with their forks – some hold up their napkins before their mouths while they do it – which is shocking – and adds a moral filth to the action by evidencing that the person is conscious of the filth of the action. – And the top of their teeth, the breadth of the top, is commonly black and yellow with a life's smoking –

But undoubtedly the news of Berkeley's death exacerbated his sense of misery and loneliness, and even served to induce in him a sense of guilt. As he told Poole, 'There are moments in which I have such a power of Life within me, such a conceit of it, I mean – that I lay the blame of my child's death to my absence – not *intellectually* ; but I have a strange sort of sensation, as if while I was present, none

could die whom I intensely loved.' The consequent misery
drove him deeper into the mindless, routine chore of transcription. Again he wrote to Poole in May, 'My dear Poole!
I am homesick. – Society is a burthen to me; and I find
relief only in labour. So I read and transcribe from morning
to night – and never in my life have I worked so hard as this
last month . . . '

At least while the Wordsworths were still in Germany he
had derived some comfort from their frequent correspondence, hearing from them as often as 'letters can go backward and forward in a country where 50 miles in a day and
night is expeditious travelling !' But even his regard for
Wordsworth seemed to be assuming an ominous note.
Writing of the mistake it was for Wordsworth to have taken
his sister with him – 'Sister here is considered as only a
name for a mistress' – he goes on to say, 'Still however *male*
acquaintance he might have had – and had I been at Goslar,
I *would* have had them – but W., God love him ! seems to
have lost his spirits and almost his inclination for it.'* And
later in May he told Poole how Wordsworth appeared to
have 'hurtfully segregated and isolated his being/doubtless,
his delights are more deep and sublime ;/but he has likewise
more hours, that prey on his flesh and blood'.

At this very time, in fact, Coleridge's attachment to
Wordsworth was being put severely to the test. Unable to
return to Alfoxden, Wordsworth now felt drawn to the
North, and he told Coleridge that he could no longer live
in Stowey for lack of books ; in Cumberland, at least, he
would have access to the libraries of Sir Wilfred Lawson
and Sir Frederick Vain. Whatever the truth about Wordsworth's need for libraries (as far as Coleridge was concerned
the above collections were merely fashionable), he clearly
longed to return to the countryside of his childhood. Matters
had come to a head, however, in April when the Wordsworths passed through Göttingen, for they had tried to

---

* The MS of this letter is blurred, see *C.L.* I, 459–60.

persuade Coleridge to come north with them, and there was every chance that they might succeed, since he had been determined for many months now to leave the cramped and uncomfortable cottage in Stowey. But still he could not envisage a separation from Poole ; at least, not for the time being. He reported to Poole how he had explained his dilemma to a tearful Wordsworth :

I told him plainly that *you* had been the man in whom *first* and in whom alone I felt an *anchor* ! With all my other connections I felt a dim sense of insecurity and uncertainty, terribly incompatible. W. was affected *to tears*, very much affected ; but he deemed the vicinity of a library absolutely *necessary* to his health, nay to his existence. It is painful to me, too, to think of not living near him ; for he is a *good* and *kind* man, and the only one whom in *all* things I feel my superior – and you will believe me when I say that I have few feelings more pleasurable than to find myself, in intellectual faculties, an inferior. But my resolve is fixed, *not to leave you till you leave me* !

Yet still undecided about his future residence, Coleridge at last made ready for the homeward journey in June. At the last minute, however, he spoke of returning via Denmark, Sweden and Norway, but his companions delayed their departure until he decided that it was too late. Carlyon and Greenough accompanied him and Chester to Brunswick ; they climbed the Brocken for a second time, and from here they went on to Wolfenbättel, where Coleridge wished to collect further material for his life of Lessing. But although it was material 'which it would be criminal to neglect' Coleridge was so affronted by the rudeness of the librarian that he neglected it all the same. At last he reached Cuxhaven on 18 July, and he was home in Stowey by the end of the month.

Apart from his learning of German and the acquisition of a quantity of information on Physiology, Anatomy and Natural History, he had brought little home with him of value. The real fruit of his stay in Germany lay in a box, which was to follow later after his arrival, of '30 pounds worth of books (chiefly metaphysics, and with a view to the one work, to which I hope to dedicate in silence the prime of my life)'. Yet what he had lost in terms of the neglect of his poetical powers was incalculable.

On arriving in England Coleridge's first act was to try to re-establish his relationship with Southey, although his feelings towards him were still decidedly ambivalent. To the accumulation of enmity occasioned by the Pantisocracy débâcle and the Lloyd affair, he could now add the severity of Southey's review of *The Ancient Mariner*. Already Lamb had confronted Southey with an accusation of treachery on this score :

If you wrote that review in 'Crit. Rev.', I am sorry you are so sparing of praise to the 'Antient Marinere'; so far from calling it, as you do, with some wit, but more severity, 'A Dutch Attempt', etc, I call it a right English attempt, and a successful one, to dethrone German sublimity.... You allow some elaborate beauties – you should have extracted 'em.

Wordsworth's response came to much the same thing; writing to Cottle, he says :

He knew that I published those poems for money and money alone. He knew that money was of importance to me. If he could not conscientiously have spoken differently of the volume, he ought to have declined the task of reviewing it. The bulk of the poems he had described as destitute of merit. Am I recompensed for this by vague promises of my talents? I care little for the praise of any other professional critical, but as it may help me to pudding.

For his part, Coleridge vented his feelings in an epigram addressed 'to a Critic who extracted a passage from a poem without adding a word respecting the context, and then described it as unintelligible'.

However wounded Coleridge may have felt as a result of the review, Southey had shown kindness to Sara and Hartley after Berkeley's death, and there must have been strong arguments from Sara to patch up the old quarrels on account of Southey's wife, her own sister Edith. 'I am perplexed what to write, or how to state the object of my writing,' Coleridge eventually wrote to him.

Any participation in each other's moral Being I do not *wish*, simply because I know enough of the mind of man to know that is impossible. But, Southey, we have similar talents, sentiments nearly similar, and kindred pursuits – we have likewise in more than one instance common objects of our esteem and love – and I pray and entreat you, if we should meet at any time, let us not withold from each other the outward Expressions of daily kindliness; and if it be no longer in your power to soften your opinion, make your feelings at least more tolerant towards me – / a debt of humility which assuredly we all of us owe to our most feeble, imperfect and self-deceiving Nature. –

Southey's response to this was a letter of self-justification, dwelling on Coleridge's supposed slander of his character, which only elicited yet another self-absolving letter from Coleridge : 'I never charged you with aught but your deep and implacable enmity of me.' And to offer conclusive proof of his assertion an accompanying letter was enclosed from Poole, who had written :

Without entering into the particulars, I will say generally that in the many conversations I have had with Coleridge concerning yourself, he has never discovered the least personal enmity against, but on the contrary the strongest affection for you ; stifled only by the untoward circumstances of your separation – such has been the general impression I have received from him – and from him alone I have been acquainted with your intellectual and moral character.[8]

This second appeal worked, and Southey who had been walking through the West Country with Edith, came over to Stowey by 12 September and spent 'some days wholly immersed in conversation'. The two poets were once again working 'at the same table', and Southey could write that the 'hours slip away and the ink dries upon the pen in my hand'. Two weeks later the reconciled families went off to Ottery St Mary together to visit Coleridge's family, followed by a tour in South Devon.

At home Coleridge was shocked to discover how reactionary his brothers had become. Of George, and of James, who was now a Colonel, he wrote : 'In all they speak and all they do not speak, they give good reasons for the opinions which they hold – viz. they hold the propriety of Slavery – an opinion which being generally assented to by Englishmen makes Pitt & Paul the first among the moral Fitnesses of Things.' Coleridge avoided argument at table by finding 'preoccupation for his *mouth*' with 'Roast fowls, mealy potatoes, pies and clouted cream'. He even met their mischievous challenge and drank to the toast – 'Church and King !' It was worth burying his scruples, he told Poole, to live in peace. Later, in Exeter, he dined at the house of Thomas Northmore, where he met Hucks, his companion on the Welsh Tour. Northmore was himself a Greek scholar and became the occasion of one of Coleridge's vigorous and idiosyncratic descriptions; he was, said Coleridge, 'an honest vehement sort of fellow, who splutters out all his opinions, like a Fizgig made of Gunpowder not thoroughly dry/sudden and explosive yet even with an adhesive blubberliness of elocution – shallow, shallow – a man who can read Greek well, but shallow'.

Coleridge had returned to Stowey by 25 September. The breach with Southey now seemed completely healed, and they continued to correspond. Now would have been the time to settle down to his life of Lessing, but he appeared to embrace further distractions as the winter wore on. He was deep in his beloved travel books again ; at the same time sending out requests for Bacon's *Works* and Milton's prose from Southey, William Morice's *Coena Quasi* Κοινη from his brother, and buying the works of Sennertus ('which I mean to cite in a future work'). He was dipping into William

Taylor, Herder and Zimmerman, but all the time could claim to be 'sunk in Spinoza . . . as undisturbed as a toad in a rock'. Yet there was no lack of external distractions. 'Our little hovel is almost afloat – poor Sara is tired off her legs with servanting – the young one fretful and noisy from confinement exerts his activities on all forbidden things – the house stinks of sulphur.' Hartley had returned from Exeter with the itch, or so it was diagnosed ; anxious to avoid the complaint themselves, Sara and Coleridge were suffering from the drastic prophylactic of those times : 'You must know that our apothecary persuaded me & Sara to wear mercurial girdles, as preventives – accordingly Sara arrayed herself with this cest of the Caledonian Venus, and I eke/– On the first day I walked myself into a perspiration, and O Christus Jesu ! – how I stunk !' Nothing by halves – he promptly caught a cold which degenerated into rheumatism : the relished, mock-humorous description of his symptoms would become a characteristic of his letters in future years :

Since my rheumatic fever at School I have suffered nothing like it ! – Of course I threw off my girdle – for such damned twitches ! I would rather have old Scratch himself, whom all brimstone in Hell can't cure, than endure them ! – . . . and by way of a clincher, I am almost certain that Hartley has not had the itch.

There were troubles too from a neighbouring family, the Riches. This elderly couple had a son who had been sent away to the Navy at considerable personal sacrifice to the parents. This autumn the boy returned home 'discharged as an ideot', and promptly set about his father. Coleridge rushed into the house to find the boy beating the old man unmercifully with a stick, his 'physiognomy truly *hellish*'. Coleridge pinned the young man to the wall until a peace officer came. But that was not the end of the matter ; the wretched young man was still allowed to run free. 'He vows vengeance on me,' Coleridge told Southey, 'but what is really shocking he never sees little Hartley but he grins with hideous distortions of rage, and hints that he'll do him a mischief.'

'I am not', he emphatically assured Southey, 'in a poetical mood.' He was determined to publish nothing till his 'Great Work', but he had a 'lucrative speculation' on hand in the form of a 'school book'.

In the middle of October he took off for Bristol with the idea of proceeding to London to retrieve his luggage which had followed him from Germany. But instead of going to London he rushed up to Sockburn in the North, taking Cottle with him, to see Wordsworth because of 'alarming accounts' of his health, which turned out to be 'little more than alarms'. He met up with Wordsworth in the home of one Thomas Hutchinson who had a farm there, and whose household was kept for him and his son George by his daughters Mary, Sara and Johanna. Unfortunately Coleridge did not see fit to inform his wife of these moves, and she returned from Watchet where she had been staying with friends to find the cottage shut up. In fact he did not write to her until December, she expecting all the time that word would come from Bristol, where she imagined he was, for her to join him – 'for as I have no maid I cannot remain in the house alone'. Coleridge, then, arrived at Sockburn on 26 October, and the next day set out for the Lakes with Wordsworth, leaving Cottle to return to Bristol by way of London. He had evidently had enough of his publisher's companionship : 'his timidity is indeed not greater than is easily explicable from his lameness and sedentary STATIONARY occupations.'[9] This excursion with Wordsworth was Coleridge's introduction to the Lake District ; meeting with John Wordsworth, William's seafaring brother, they went on to Hawes Water, Windermere, Ambleside, Rydal and Grasmere, where they stayed for two days. Immediately Coleridge was impressed with John. Writing to Dorothy he says, 'Your Br. John is one of you ; a man who hath solitary usings of his own Intellect, deep in feeling, with a subtle tact, a swift instinct of Truth and Beauty. He interests me much.'

Together they climbed over the fork of Helvellyn on a day, says Coleridge, 'when light and darkness coexisted in contiguous masses, and earth and sky were but *one*! Nature lived for us in all her grandest accidents'.[10]

To Dorothy he wrote of the powerful impression this new country had made on him :

You can feel what I cannot express for myself – how deeply I have been impressed by a world of scenery absolutely new to me. At Rydal and Grasmere I recd I think the deepest delight, yet Hawes Water thro' many a varying view kept my eyes dim with tears, and this evening, approaching Derwentwater in diversity of harmonious features, in the majesty – O my God! and the black crags close under the snowy mountains, whose snows were pinkish with the setting sun and the reflections from the sandy rich clouds that floated over some and rested upon others! It was to me a vision of a fair country.[11]

Yet even in these times unpleasant incursions had been made on the beauty of the area, and Coleridge had to complain of a 'bitch' of a house, a 'white Palace' built by one Mr Law at the head of Lake Windermere, and there was a Mr Partridge who had built a house and barn to 'represent a chapel'.

On 11 November they left Keswick and continued their tour for another week before parting on the 18th, when Coleridge returned to the Hutchinsons at Sockburn to stay for another week. And it was during this second visit that Coleridge came to know Sara Hutchinson, the second daughter, better ; indeed to fall in love with her. Sara, who was three years younger than Coleridge, is almost as unknown to us as Coleridge's first love Mary Evans. His own fullest description of her was made in 1808 in a letter to Daniel Stuart, when he wrote : 'If Sense, Sensibility, Sweetness of Temper, perfect simplicity and unpretending Nature, joined to shrewdness and entertainingness make a

valuable Woman, Sara Hutchinson is so.' Coleridge's
daughter, Sara, did not meet her until 1808 herself but she
has left this physical description of her : 'She had fine, long,
light brown hair, I think her only beauty, except a fair skin,
for her features were plain and contracted, her figure
dumpy, and devoid of grace and dignity. She was a plump
woman, of little more than five feet.' Coleridge bears out the
fact that her attraction was of a quiet and subtle kind : 'Can
see nothing extraordinary in her – ', he commented in his
notebook in 1802, ' . . . all the virtues of the mild & retired
kind'. Once again it was the magnetism of the affectionate
circle of sisters, with the enhancing complication that
Wordsworth was deeply attached to them, especially to the
eldest sister, Mary. To a man like Coleridge, who tended to
be entirely engrossed with the environment of the moment,
it would not have been difficult for him to forget his wife ;
indeed he had no idea even where Mrs Coleridge was at
that time. Eventually, the contrast between Mrs Coleridge's
faults and drawbacks and Sara Hutchinson's advantages
would become clear ; although, of course, the very presence
of Sara would be a factor in the deterioration of his relationship with his wife. But in what ways must Sara Hutchinson
have appeared to be all that Mrs Coleridge was not at this
early stage? Perhaps the strongest impression of their
separate personalities is gained from their correspondence,
and Professor Coburn who has edited Sara Hutchinson's
letters provides us with a character sketch of the two women
as it appears to her there :

In Mrs Coleridge's letters, whether the matter is cheerful or
'vexatious', all is in disorder. Everything tumbles out, helter-skelter,
dropped and picked up again, repeated, apologized for, till we do not
know whether to laugh, cry, or scream. Her words come freely but
out of a state of perpetual consternation. Her stream of words is a
cheerful but agitated and muddy one ('forgive all blunders'), full of
rocks and holes, constantly swinging around corners very quickly and
meeting the unexpected, picking up debris here and there, often

doubling back on itself. Asra's [Sara Hutchinson's] letters flow evenly, steadily, making for their destination, showing a ripple here and there, occasionally a rock below the surface, sometimes making an interesting change of level, but always clear, under command, bringing us into a sweet vista now and then. With Mrs Coleridge there is no time to attend to the banks that fly past – the waters themselves are too troubled. With Asra we pause occasionally, perhaps for a person to be described: – Lady Farquhar 'has a countenance so benign and expressive of enjoyment that it is evident in a moment that you must love her sometime or other' – for a quiet evening to be spent – a serious problem in someone's life to be discussed – a joke, for its own sake, like a letter from Lamb – or for some general reflection on life – 'The painters who flatter are quite in the right. Truth gives no satisfaction.'[12]

All we know of the week that Coleridge spent with the Hutchinsons is that it passed with fireside happiness – 'Conundrums and puns and stories and laughter' – but there was a moment when Coleridge took Sara's hand, and he recorded later in his notebook: 'et Sarae manum a tergo longum in tempus presabam, and tunc temporis, tunc primum, amor me levi spiculo, venenato, eheu! & insanabili, &c.'[13] Which may be translated: 'And pressed Sara's hand a long time behind her back, and then, then for the first time, love pricked me with its light arrow, poisoned alas! and hopeless.'[14]

Leaving Sockburn on 25 November Coleridge started out for London to take up an offer 'of a pleasant kind' on the staff of the *Morning Post* which had been offered him in Keswick. On the journey down his notebook records some of the lyricism of former days:

Nov. 27th, Awoke from the uneasy doze-dream of the coach / a rich orange sky like that of a winter evening save that the fleecy dark blue that rippled above showed it to be morning / – soon became a glowing brass colour, fleeces of brass like sand – convolves high up in to the sky – the sun rose o'er the plain like a kite / rose wholly, and in a Column in the waters, and soon after, a hill meeting with it, rose thro' other clouds – with a different glory – Starlings – [15]

Later in the day he was distressed to see signs of abandoned houses and farmland : 'Wretched hovels, half roof of rotten thatch, wholly swamped by weeds – where vegetable life prospered, not animal.' He arrived in London at midnight on 27 November taking up lodgings at 21 Buckingham Street, and no doubt still under the enchantment of Cumberland he was at once appalled by the city – which in these days numbered 700,000 inhabitants : 'The immoveableness of all things thro' which so many men were moving – harsh contrast compared with *the universal motion, the harmonious system of motions, in the country and everywhere in nature*. – In this, dim light London appeared to me as a huge place of Sepulchres thro' which hosts of spirits were gliding.'[16]

The main purpose of Coleridge's settling in London was to earn as much money as possible as quickly as possible. He had anticipated his annuity from Wedgwood until the end of 1800, and he hoped to earn enough money by April to make up for this deficit. In the mornings he claims to have been employed in the writing of 'booksellers' compilations', though there is no evidence that he actually did so ; in the afternoons and evenings he wrote for the *Morning Post*, and made at least forty contributions between the beginning of December and April of 1800.[17] His pieces were lucid and elegant, but dealt in the entertaining juxtaposition of ideas rather than in the retailing of hard fact ; they are certainly in the best tradition of 'leader' writing, but hardly more than that. Here is a typical flourish when he is discussing the French Constitution and the right of the Senate to make a final selection after the vote : 'If the French people accept, or rather submit to, this constitution, all danger from French principles is passed by ; the volcano is burnt out, and the snow has fallen round the crater.' Or again when he is arguing the pros and cons of the Act of Union : 'A question the most important that can occur in the annals of nations is to be decided ; it will be lost or won

by half a neck. But whether lost or won, depends not so
much on the justice of the case, as on the success of the
previous intrigues among the jockies.' But undoubtedly he
rose to his height when dealing with Pitt – a figure who at
once attracted and repelled him :

Mr Pitt built up his periods, as usual in all the stately order of
rhetorical architecture; but they fell away at once before that true
eloquence of common sense and natural feeling which sanctifies, and
renders human, the genius of Mr Fox. Like some good genius, he
approached in indignation to the spell-built palace of the state-
magician, and at the first touch of his wand, it sunk into a ruinous and
sordid hovel, tumbling in upon the head of the wizard that had
reared it.

From this winter of 1799 until the spring of 1800
Coleridge seems to have existed in a state of strange suspension, cut off from the Wordsworths and Poole alike, and
deeply involved in the tiring, time-consuming business of
'Grub Street'. It was to Southey that he wrote more than
any body else, as if he had returned to the Bristol days and
the hectic task of lecturing that was to precede the glorious
departure for America. In fact, there were moments when he
tentatively suggested a revival of the old scheme : 'I would
accompany you,' he told Southey, ' – and see no impossibility
of forming a pleasant little colony for a few years in Italy or
the South of France.' And perhaps Tom Wedgwood and
even Wordsworth might be interested in such a venture?
But he knew even in the moment of suggesting it that it was
'Precious stuff for dreams – and God knows I have no time
for them !' At the same time there is a bias for the Mediterranean in his suggestions; all thoughts of a politically
orientated commune have disappeared, neither is there a
hint of the Grand Tour motive : the paradisal dream of
southern Europe with its glow of warmth, health, leisure
and inspiration was beckoning as it would to future generations of English Romantics. In the meantime he lived the
hectic life of a political journalist. And we get glimpses of

the strain of such a life in hurried letters to his friends during that period. In January : 'my occupations have swoln above smothering point – I am over mouth & nostrils.' In February : 'I have attended the Debates twice, & the first time I was 25 Hours in activity, & that of a very unpleasant kind – and the second Time from 10 in the morning to 4 o/clock the next morning.' As he wrote to Josiah Wedgwood ; 'We Newspaper scribes are true Galley-Slaves – when the high winds of Events blow loud & frequent, then the Sails are hoisted, and the Ship drives on of itself – when all is calm & Sunshine then to our oars.' And not unlike the journalists of every generation, we hear of him getting drunk of an evening and having to write a letter of apology to his hosts of the evening before – in this case, Godwin.[18]

Coleridge was a good journalist, and it is certain that Daniel Stewart, the *Morning Post*'s editor, who eventually made a fortune out of the newspaper world, got his money's worth from the hard-up poet. And yet Coleridge had to face what it all meant in the long term. At the time he could not help displaying a kind of pride in what he was doing : 'It is not unflattering to a man's vanity,' he wrote to Josiah Wedgwood, 'to reflect that what he writes at 12 at night will before 12 hours is over have perhaps 5 or 6000 Readers !' Certainly a much larger audience than he could reach with his poetry. Nor was he unconscious of the value of what he was doing. Of his contributions he wrote : 'they are important in themselves & excellent Vehicles for general Truths. I am not ashamed of what I have written.'

When Coleridge came to write the *Biographia* he tended to distort and exaggerate his own importance on the *Morning Post* and later on the *Courier*. In a sense this was an understandable rebuff to answer those who had accused him of dreaming away his life to no purpose. This was clear to Stuart the editor, who put the record straight after Coleridge's death. 'Coleridge had a defective memory for want of interest in common things', said Stuart kindly, closing the long dead squabble over Coleridge's claim to have made the fortunes of the *Morning Post* by improving its editorial policies. The fact of Coleridge's dishonesty in this matter, however, tended to overshadow the more important issue of his desperate attempts to justify his becoming a journalist in the first place. 'To have lived in vain,' he wrote in the *Biographia*, 'must be a painful thought to any man, and especially so to him who has made literature his profession.' But just as he had insisted with Southey, that one cannot measure a man's literary worth by the number of lines he wrote, he continually hammered home the same point in relation to journalism : 'are books the only channel through which the stream of intellectual usefulness can flow?' he asks. He had no doubt of the answer in 1800. In a letter to Poole on 21 March, after he had ceased to work regularly for Stuart, he supplied his own answer : 'I think there are but 2 good ways of writing – one for immediate, & wide impression, tho' transitory – the other for permanence – / Newspapers the first – the best one can do is the second – that middle class of translating Books &c is neither the one or the other.[19] Subject to the chaotic exigencies of his life and the stormy times in which he lived, it was a faith to which he could cling. Again in the *Biographia* he would reveal an extraordinary insight into what would eventually emerge as his own value :

Would that the criterion of a scholar's utility were the number and moral value of the truths which he has been the means of throwing into the general circulation; or the number and value of the minds whom, by his conversation or letters, he has excited into activity and supplied with the germs of their after-growth! A distinguished rank might not indeed, even then, be awarded to my exertions, but I should dare to look forward with confidence to an honourable acquital.

In February there was an interesting example of Coleridge's new and commonsense attitude towards his literary
10

life. For some time he had been encouraging Southey to write an educational book purely for money. Southey evidently needed the money to finance a trip abroad, but he was reluctant to allow his own name to appear on any 'popular' book. Coleridge was dismissive of this attitude : 'I do not see,' he wrote, 'that a book said by you in the Preface to have been written merely as a Book for young Persons could injure your reputation more than Milton's Accidence injured *his* – I *would do* it – because you can do it so easily.' Then, as he also pointed out, there was the question of the facts of the publishing world. It was, after all, the name which sold a book, and by way of illustration he could report an interesting comment of Thomas Longman's :

But it is *the name* / Longman remarked acutely enough – We Booksellers scarcely pretend to judge the merits of the *Book*, but we know the saleableness of the name ! & as they continue to buy most books on the calculation of a *first* Edition of a 1000 Copies, they are seldom much mistaken : – for the name gives them the excuse of sending it to all the Gemmen in Great Britain & the Colonies, from whom they have standing Orders for new books of reputation. This is the secret, why Books published by Country Booksellers, or by Authors on their own account, so seldom succeed.[20]

In fact Coleridge himself had undertaken a translation of Wallenstein's trilogy of plays for Longman. Once again it was a question of money : Longman had offered £50 in advance, and it was a way of speeding up his release from London. Remarkably, in the space of about six weeks Coleridge translated *The Piccolomini* and *The Death of Wallenstein*, at the same time keeping Stuart at bay with occasional pieces and frequent apologies. The frenzied life of a jobbing author in London during those times is well illustrated by a letter he sent to Stuart on 1 March :

I consider myself as two full week's Work in your Debt for that which I have already received – – These cursed Plays play the Devil

with me – I have been working from morning to night, & almost half
of the night too, & yet get on too slowly for the Printer – & Mr Longman is kept in constant dread that some rival Translation may pop
out before mine. [21]

To Poole he wrote : 'positively for the last week have worked
with my pen in my hand 14 hours every day.' No doubt he
had these hectic weeks in mind when he wrote his 'affectionate exhortation' in the *Biographia* to the 'youthful literati' :
'*never pursue literature as a trade.*'

And yet there is ample evidence that even during these
busy times the centre of his interest was taken up with preoccupations that were more permanent and universal than
politics at the turn of the century. In the New Year he
described himself to Josiah Wedgwood, shivering over a
fire in a 'rug great coat' : '*Now* I make up my mind to a sort
of heroism in believing the progressiveness of all nature,
during the present melancholy state of humanity – and on
this subject I am now writing/and no work, on which I
ever employed myself, makes me so happy while I am writing.' It was always in the fundamental and wideranging
speculations that his inquiring, penetrating mind found its
vitality and interest. Here was the true source of his 'Enthusiasm'. 'Life were so flat a thing without Enthusiasm,'
he wrote on that day, ' – that if for a moment it leave me, I
have a sort of stomach-sensation attached to all my thoughts,
like those which succeed to the pleasurable operation of a
dose of opium.' And in a piece of self-analysis which was to
become so characteristic as he got older he tries to diagnose
the cause of his own strange propensity towards meditating
questions which 'are perhaps disproportionate to our
faculties and powers'. It was, he conceded, a kind of
disease. 'But I have had this disease for so long, and my
early education was so undomestic, that I know not how to
get rid of it ; or even wish to get rid of it.'[22]

His enthusiastic curiosity, anxiety, almost, was extraordinarily discursive and mercurial. Just the day before

writing to Wedgwood he had sent off a list of queries to the young Humphry Davy. The coalescing of extremes that had excited his imagination, 'the burning ice', was now fascinating him in scientific terms. How was it he asked that there was a similarity in the initial sensation between extremes of heat and cold? Furthermore, 'How is this explained in a philosophical Language divested of corpuscular theories?' Then, with a leap, to a minor application of a similar question : 'What is the cause of that sense of cold, which accompanies inhalation, after having eat peppermint Drops?' Then, with another bound, 'I wish in your Researches that you & Beddoes would give a compact compressed History of the Human Mind for the last Century – considered simply as to the acquisition of Ideas or new arrangement of them.'

Considered simply ! And yet there was a sense in which Coleridge was showing ominous signs of atrophy. Once again the occasion was the appalling confusion of his finances, although there was evidently a more fundamental cause at work. Writing to Poole towards the end of March about his future plans and the settlement of debts, he says : 'I am sure, if God give me health, to make all even before the End of this year – & I find that I can without any straining gain 500 guineas a year, if I give up poetry – i.e. original Poetry.'[23] It is perhaps important to point out that Coleridge was in no sense beginning to put money before poetry. As he remarks later in the same letter, Stuart had offered him £2,000 a year if he would take a share in the paper, an offer he promptly rejected : 'I told him, that I would not give up the Country, & the lazy reading of Old Folios for two Thousand Times two thousand Pound – in short, that beyond £250 a year, I considered money as a real Evil – at which he stared.' The point was that he was obliged to earn sufficient money to see his way clear to the end of the year, and it would be an expensive year if he was to establish a new home – either in the North or back in Stowey : moreover, there were new financial problems in the form of Pitt's Income Tax and steadily rising prices. Even if he managed to set things straight his first duty was to Wedgwood, at least to the extent of seeing through the book on Lessing. For a second year, Coleridge was to relegate poetry to second place. For a poet in his twenty-eighth year, particularly one who relied so much on lyrical feeling, the fact of neglect alone spelt creative suicide.

Since December of 1799 the Coleridges had been to all intents and purposes homeless. Not much is known of Mrs Coleridge during this period. We do know that Coleridge had been obliged to write to Cottle early in December to find out where she was, and later in the month she took up lodgings with Coleridge in London. We may take it that she was far from in good humour. Not only was she 'shockingly uncomfortable' in their present lodgings, she was again expecting a child by January. There were also signs of serious disagreement about their future plans. Writing to Poole in January, Coleridge commented that Sara must have 'neighbours and acquaintances. For my friends form not that society which is of itself sufficient to a woman...' Presumably 'my friends' refers to the Wordsworths with whom, as will be seen, Sara was never particularly at ease. On the other hand she had been happy with Poole. There was probably considerable conflict over any suggestion of going north. 'God knows where we can go,' wrote Coleridge. 'For that situation which suits my wife does not suit me, and what suits me does not suit my wife. However, that which is, is, – a truth which always remains equally clear, but not always equally pleasant...'[24]

It was the first explicit reference to domestic unhappiness, and there is little doubt that his inexplicable neglect of his wife and child for two months, and his recent discovery of Sara Hutchinson, had much to do with it. At the beginning of March Mrs Coleridge left London to stay with friends at Kempsford, and Coleridge moved in with Lamb. Meanwhile he continued to give Poole the impression that he was

longing to return to Stowey. 'I am Stowey-sick', he would
say. But how much was the longing for Stowey a wish to
return to the situation of the year before when Wordsworth
was there? As he put it on another occasion : 'I have a huge
Hankering for Alfoxden.' But all the while he laid down
conditions that would be difficult to fulfil : 'I shall beyond
all doubt settle at Stowey, if I can get a suitable House –
that is – a House with a Garden, & large enough for me to
have a Study out of the noise of Women & children – this is
absolutely necessary for me.' By the end of March, however,
he implied in a letter to Poole that Stowey would be attractive only if Wordsworth were there : although it was now
impossible that Wordsworth would ever consider leaving
the North : 'I would to God, I could get Wordsworth to
retake Alfoxden – the Society of so great a Being is of
priceless Value – but he will never quit the North of
England.' And again he parades the worship of his 'God' :
'Since Milton,' he wrote, 'no man *manifested* himself equal
to him.'

At about this time Poole had written to say that there was
a possibility of renting part of a farmhouse at Stowey,
although they would have to share a kitchen. This Coleridge
seemed to approve for the space of a month, but then
declared the idea unacceptable, for the joint use of the
kitchen would lead to continual squabbles and it would 'be
worse than the old hovel fifty times over'. Perhaps Poole
realized that Coleridge's thoughts tended inexorably
northwards, for he seems to have warned Coleridge about
his excessive regard for Wordsworth. He had considerable
insight into human nature, and a deep regard for Coleridge,
there is every indication that he tried to forestall the dangers
that lay in store should Coleridge subordinate himself
totally to Wordsworth's superiority. The warning, however,
evoked nothing less than a clear confirmation of Coleridge's
hero worship. 'You charge me with prostration in regard to
Wordsworth,' wrote Coleridge :

Have I affirmed anything miraculous of W.? Is it impossible that a greater poet than any since Milton may appear in our days? Have there any *great* poets appeared since him?... Future greatness! Is it not an awful thing, my dearest Poole? What if you had known Milton at the age of thirty, and believed all you now know of him? – What if you should meet in the letters of any then living man, expressions concerning the young Milton *totidem verbis* the same as mine of Wordsworth, would it not convey to you a most delicious sensation? Would it not be an assurance to you that your admiration of the *Paradise Lost* was no superstition, no shadow of flesh and bloodless abstraction, but that the *Man was* even so, that the greatness was incarnate and personal? Wherein blame I you, my best friend. Only in being borne down by other men's rash opinions concerning W.

Before very long the justice of Poole's reservations would become more apparent.

Greta Hall

By 5 April Coleridge had disappeared from London and had repaired to the Lakes. 'Coleridge has left us on a visit to his god Wordsworth,' wrote Lamb who had the Wallenstein proofs dumped on him. The visit in the North was to be followed by a serious attempt at house-hunting in Somerset, but he left Wordsworth early in May having found a house 'of such a prospect, that if, according to [Godwin] & Hume, impressions & ideas *constitute* our Being, I shall have a tendency to become a God'. As he travelled south again it is likely that his mind was already made up. First he visited Humphry Davy in his laboratory at Bristol, with its 'cold bath and Moon light stones', and was intrigued to find that Davy had discovered 'a perfectly new Acid' which was supposed to restore the use of atrophied limbs of rheumatics. By 21 May he was with Poole, searching for a house in Porlock and Stowey, but after two weeks he gave up, and determined finally on the North. So, at last, he parted from Poole 'with pain & dejection'. It was not simply that he could find no suitable house; as he later explained to Josiah Wedgwood : there were more emotional reasons. 'Mrs Coleridge had scarcely any Society there, and inter nos the nearness to Bristol connected me too intimately with all the affairs of her family.' What was more, he claimed that Poole's relatives constantly showed antipathy to himself and had actually insulted Mrs Coleridge. There is no mention of Wordsworth. But his friends in the West Country were under no illusions as to the real motive and its dangers. As Humphry Davy remarked, 'He has done wrong, I think, in removing so far from his other friends, and giving himself wholly to Wordsworth ; it is wrong on his own account, and more so on his wife's, who is now at an unreachable distance from all her sisters.'

The family travelled northwards in a chaise stopping at Chester, where, said Coleridge, 'the Air of the city is thick enough to be edible, & stinks', and Liverpool, where they stayed for a week with the Cromptons who had tried to assist Coleridge with the establishment of a school back in 1796. Finally they moved on to Grasmere to stay with the Wordsworths : but on arrival Coleridge fell ill, having caught a cold in Liverpool, and their stay was extended from 29 June until 24 July. The night before they left Grasmere for their new home at Greta Hall, Keswick, thirteen miles north of Grasmere, they had a picnic on the lake island.

We drank tea the night before I left Grasmere on the Island in that lovely lake, our kettle swung over the fire hanging from the branch of a Fir Tree, and I lay & saw the woods, & mountains, & lake all trembling, & as it were idealized thro' the subtle smoke which rose up from the clear red embers of the fir-apples which we had collected. Afterwards, we made a glorious Bonfire on the Margin, by some alder bushes, whose twigs heaved & sobbed in the uprushing column of smoke – & the Image of the Bonfire, & of us that danced round it – ruddy laughing faces in the twilight – the Image of this in a Lake smooth as that sea, to whose waves the Son of God had said, Peace!

Greta Hall was situated close to Keswick where there were 'respectable & neighbourly acquaintance', and, what was increasingly important for Coleridge, a 'sensible and truly excellent medical man'. Greta Hall was, in fact, two houses built as one, and in the 'Sister house' lived the landlord, Jackson, 'a modest & kind man' who had 'raised himself' by 'the severest economy' from a carrier into the possession of a 'comfortable Independence'. He had a library of five
10*

hundred books, mostly of 'esteemed' modern writers, such as Gibbon, Hume Johnson and Scottish dictionaries, and there was a large kitchen garden which they were allowed to use as their own. But the most attractive feature of the place was its beautiful setting. The room that Coleridge took as a study commanded

> six distinct Landscapes – the two Lakes, the Vale, River, & mountains, & mists, & Clouds, & Sunshine make endless combinations, as if heaven & Earth were for ever talking to each other. – Often when in a deep Study I have walked to the window & remained there *looking without seeing*, all at once the Lake of Keswick & the fantastic Mountains of Borrodale at the head of it have entered into my mind with a suddenness, as if I had been snatched out of Cheapside & placed for the first time on the spot where I stood.[1]

Everybody must come and stay with him; he had 'head room and heart room' for Southey, Davy, Tobin, Henry Howard the painter, Samuel Purkis, Godwin, and of course Poole.

When Coleridge went to Jackson shortly after their arrival, this unusual landlord told him that he did not want any rent at all. 'This I laughed him out of,' Coleridge told Josiah Wedgwood. But, in any case, the landlord absolutely refused to receive any rent for the first six months as he insisted that the house was not completely finished. This act of generosity must have come as an enormous relief. Financial difficulties were, as usual, pressing on him from all sides. Another child was about to be born – Sara in fact gave birth to a boy late in September – whom he named Derwent from 'a sort of sneaking affection . . . for the *poetical* & *novellish*'. Already in the spring he had suffered the embarrassment of settling an old bill with Cottle by overdrawing on Josiah Wedgwood without warning. And throughout the summer we learn of debts to Davy, a Mrs King, Godwin and, as usual, Poole. By the Autumn he would be back in the old situation, 'Dunning

Letters &c &c – all the hell of an Author', and overdrawn on his annuity for 1801 by £40, 'probably more'.

He still had vague hopes of getting on with the Lessing, but the much neglected biography was put aside once again and the pressing obligations evaporated in the excitement of discovering the Lakes and renewing his working friendship with Wordsworth.

Throughout the rest of the summer Coleridge was continually out walking, trying to finish his *Christabel,* and passing to and fro between Grasmere and Keswick. As he wandered he was increasingly engrossed by the idiosyncrasies of colour and light, and it was the momentary, transitory moods of beauty which seized his attention.

> Mountains & mountainous Scenery taken *collectively* & *cursorily* must depend for their charms on their novelty – / they put on their immortal interest then first, when we have resided among them, & learnt to understand their language, their written characters, & intelligible sounds, and all their eloquence so various, so unwearied.[2]

Once as he walked over Helvellyn to Grasmere, probably with *Christabel* in his pocket, he saw the ridge that runs between the vales into Threlkeld as 'raspberry & milk coloured crags'. In the sunset he observed 'smoke flame over Wanthwaite & under that mass a *wedge* of light on the cliff', and later, 'the whole of Wanthwaite drunk with a black-hued scarlet'. Walking with Sara and Hartley one Sunday evening in August, the light was a 'bright Buff', and 'Walla crag purple red, the lake a deep dingy purple blue'. And the following evening he saw the same landscape and skyscape with clouds of 'sandy light –/ now a rich satteny yellow'. The crag above Walla was a 'dusky marone', and above him there was a 'marbled Sky with under clouds of pink'. Standing at his window during a storm in September he saw the lake

> bright silver / over it & intercepting Borrodale a *thick palpable Blue* up to the moon / save that at the very top of the blue the *clouds rolled*

lead-coloured – small detachments of these clouds running in thick flakes near the *moon, & drinking its light in amber & white.* – The Moon in a clear azure sky – the Mountains seen indeed, and only seen – I never saw aught so sublime.

At times, possibly because of a new craze of his for prisms, it seemed as if he was responding like a scientist to the oddities of colour, at times his preoccupation was similar to that of the painter; in fact there were occasions when his fascination with the predominant elements of fire and smoke, or, as in the following passage, with water and mist, is reminiscent of Turner :

Sept 14 to Sept 22 An interval during which I travelled much Sept 1800 Lodore & the fall in Borrodale whiten conspicuously – yet ever and anon the Sun is on the Hills & Mounts, the universal mist not *dissipated* but attenuated – & sometimes the mist will dissolve wholly from some field or eminence, that stands out from the rest of the landscape, bright & newbathed – Now the Hills are all in mist but the Vale all bathed & clean, one column of watry Sunshine falls upon the Grange. – To the inverted arch in Newlands clear; at the Arch a wall of impenetrable Darkness – A pelting shower. – Clear – & a road of silver brightness from the woods far over the Lake to the other side of the Island. – Vanishes – beautiful appearance of moving mist, over Newlands – long dividuous flakes the interspaces filled up by a thinner mist – all in sunlight.[3]

Then there was a night when he observed 'thin scattered rain clouds . . . scudding along the Sky, above them with a visible interspace the crescent Moon . . . her own hazy light fill'd up the concave, as if it had been painted & the colors had run'.[4] And even at night sitting in his armchair he hourly recorded phenomena of shape, motion, light and sound :

11 clock at night – that conical Volcano of coal half an inch high, ejaculating its inverted cone of smoke – the smoke in what a furious wind, this way, that way – & what a noise!

The poet's eye in his tipsy hour
Hath a magnifying power

Or rather his soul emancipates his eyes
Of accidents of size /
In unctuous cones of kindling Coal
Or smoke from his Pipe's bole
His eye can see
Phantoms of sublimity

12 clock at night no moon – Hear a nick! nick! at the window-panes – went with the candle – saw at both windows an amazing of flies or small gnats (very small) and a spider whose web was on the outside, as busy as a successful poacher.[5]

This acute sensitivity to sensory experience suggests that his perception may have been aided by opium, although there is no palpable evidence as to the quantities he was taking. But a remark in a letter to Davy is explicit enough : 'I would that I could wrap up the view from my House in a pill of opium, & send it to you!'

Occasionally Coleridge walked with Dorothy Words-worth, but mainly he clambered dangerously in the mountains by himself, by day and night, turning up at Keswick or Grasmere wet to the skin, with bruised hands or having almost broken his neck. Far from being a resumption of the golden days of Alfoxden, it was as if he was being driven in on himself. For over two years now he had not attempted any serious poetry. Since April he had had the leisure, but he did not seem to have the mood. The Wallen-stein, he told Godwin in May 'wasted and depressed my spirits, & left a sense of wearisomeness and disgust which unfitted me for anything but sleeping and immediate society'. He had one important task : to complete his poem *Christabel* for the second edition of *Lyrical Ballads* which he and Wordsworth were now preparing. On those lonely walks he was striving to regain an inspiration which seemed to have fled : as he wrote to Josiah Wedgwood : 'I tried & tried, & nothing would come of it. I desisted with a deeper dejection than I am willing to remember. The wind from Skiddaw & Borrowdale was often as loud as wind need be

— & many a walk in the clouds on the mountains did I take; but all would not do.'[6] At length, he says that he dined out one evening at the house of a neighbouring clergyman, and drank so much that 'I found some effort and dexterity requisite to balance myself on the hither edge of sobriety'. The next day his 'verse making faculties' seemed to be restored and he proceeded successfully until the poem 'grew so long & in Wordsworth's opinion so impressive, that he rejected it from his volume as disproportionate both in size & merit, & as discordant in its character'.

In that one simple phrase 'disproportionate both in size & merit' lay a tragedy. That the poem was too long was neither here nor there. That is was 'disproportionate' in merit was everything. He had in fact finished the first part before going to Germany, and during the first summer at Keswick he was labouring with the second -- which he completed; but the poem remained unfinished. Yet more than his inability to complete the entire poem he was depressed by his apparent lapse in judgment, and in this the Wordsworths had not been helpful, for during the trial readings at Grasmere it seems that they had been 'abundantly anxious to acquit their judgements of any blindness to the very numerous defects'.[7]

We know of two important occasions when Coleridge walked over to Grasmere to read (or recite) *Christabel*. The first was on the last day of August, when he made a romantic enough appearance out of the night. 'At 11 o'clock Coleridge came when I was walking in the still clear moonshine in the garden,' wrote Dorothy. 'He came over Helvellyn. . . . We sat and chatted till ½ past three, W. in his dressing gown. Coleridge read us a part of Christabel. Talked much about the mountains etc. etc.'

Just two weeks later Wordsworth wrote to Biggs and Cottle, who were printing the second edition of *Lyrical Ballads*, that a new group of his own poems should be printed before *Christabel*, even if *Christabel* had been set up.

And two days later Coleridge wrote to James Tobin of the poem, 'Every line has been produced by me with labor-pangs. I abandon Poetry altogether – I leave the higher & deeper kinds to Wordsworth, the delightful, popular & simply dignified to Southey; and reserve for their writings, as they deserve to be felt and understood.'[8] But the final blow came in October. Once again Coleridge came across the mountains with the poem in his pocket : this time the second part had been completed. Dorothy noted in her journal :

> October 4 *Saturday*. Coleridge came in while we were at dinner, very wet – we talked till 12 o'clock. He had sate up all the night before, writing Essays for the newspaper. His youngest child had been very ill in convulsion fits. Exceedingly delighted with the second part of Christabel.
> October 5 *Sunday Morning*. Coleridge read a 2nd time Christabel; we had increasing pleasure. A delicious morning.
> Oct. 6 *Monday*. A rainy day. Coleridge intending to go but did not get off. We walked after dinner to Rydale. After tea read *The Pedlar*. Determined not to print Christabel with the L.B.

So, exceedingly 'delighted' as they were, the poem was finally rejected. On 6 or 7 October Wordsworth wrote again to the printers :

> It is my wish and determination that (whatever the expense may be, which I hereby take upon myself) such Pages of the Poem of Christabel as have been printed (if any such there be) be cancelled – I mean to have other poems substituted – a sheet of which will be sent by the next Post – and you may now and henceforth *depend* on being supplied without any intermissions.[9]

Later, on 18 December, Wordsworth explained to Longman and Rees, who were to publish the second edition, that 'upon mature deliberation I found that the style of his Poem (Christabel) so discordant from my own that it could not be printed along with my poems with any propriety'. Naturally Wordsworth had every right to reject a poem that he felt to be 'discordant' in this collection ; but

his antipathy towards *Christabel* and, indeed, *The Ancient
Mariner* ran much deeper. In 1818 Coleridge wrote of the
Wordsworth's 'cold praise and effective discouragement of
every attempt of mine to roll onward in a distinct current of
my own'.[10] Coleridge was not above blaming others for his
own shortcomings – but the truth can not be very far off.
Already on Wordsworth's insistence he had been obliged to
alter *The Ancient Mariner* for the second edition, but in
spite of this Wordsworth added what amounted to a
disclaimer at the end of his preface :

> The poem of my Friend has indeed great defects; first, that the
> principle person has no distinct character, either in his profession of
> Mariner, or as a human being who having been long under control
> of supernatural impressions might be supposed himself to partake of
> something supernatural : secondly, that he does not act, but is con-
> tinually acted upon : thirdly, that the events having no necessary
> connection do not produce each other ; and lastly, that the imagery is
> somewhat laboriously accumulated.[11]

This note was probably sent on 2 October while Coleridge
was away from Grasmere, but no doubt Wordsworth had
forewarned Coleridge, or at least told him what he had
written by 4 October. The critical blindness is interesting
enough, but what is more astonishing is that he could not
imagine the damage he was wreaking on Coleridge's
confidence. For Coleridge's part, his idolatry of Wordsworth was such – 'the latch of whose Shoe I am unworthy to
unloose'[12] – that he presumably had little defence to offer
in the face of the 'God's' criticisms. Yet as Poole would have
pointed out, he had nobody to blame but himself. Few
poets of great merit could have sacrificed their own interests
for another artist to the extent that Coleridge had done.
Throughout the summer of 1800 he seems to have given an
inordinate amount of his time to the careful preparation of
the text of the second edition of *Lyrical Ballads*. It is more
than likely too that Coleridge was ever ready to boost his
friend's confidence to even greater heights as Wordsworth

settled into the most creative period of his life. As Coleridge wrote to Godwin the following year: 'If I die, and the Booksellers will give you anything for my Life, be sure to asy – "Wordsworth descended on him, like the Tνῶθι σεαυτόν [the know-thyself] from Heaven ; by showing him what true Poetry was, he made him know, that he himself was no Poet.'[13]

It is worth drawing attention to the fact that Coleridge's first acknowledgement of his failing powers, whether it was justified at this stage or not, came before the enervating illnesses, the constant 'metaphysicizing', or the developing effects of opium addiction of the following year. For two years he had neglected the writing of serious poetry, and the facility with which Wordsworth wrote doubtlessly demoralized him. Yet there was no trace of resentment, simply a reiteration of what seemed to him an obvious truth : 'I would rather have written Ruth and Nature's Lady ['Three years she grew in sun and shower'?] than a million such poems [i.e. poems like *Christabel*]', he wrote to Humphry Davy on 9 October. For the rest he seemed blank and bewildered. He had exerted an almost super-human effort to get *Christabel* right and it had not seemed to work. An entry in his notebook at the end of October must surely be one of the most poignant reflections ever written by a potentially great poet : 'He knew not what to do – something, he felt, must be done – he rose, drew his writing-desk suddenly before him – sate down, took the pen – & found that he knew not what to do. Octob. 30. 1800.'[14] It was the writer's worst enemy – 'self-doubt'. And even as he returned to the miserable business of taking in hand those long neglected money-making projects a bleak despair descended upon him. As he wrote to Daniel Stuart on 7 October :

If I know my own heart, or rather if I be not profoundly ignorant of it, I have not a spark of *ambition* / and tho' my *vanity* is flattered, more than it ought to be, by what Dr Johnson calls 'colloquial prowess', yet it leaves me in my study. This is no virtue in me, but depends on the accidental constitution of my intellect – in which my taste in judging is far, far more perfect than my power to execute – & I do nothing, but almost instantly it's defects & sillinesses come upon my mind, and haunt me, till I am completely disgusted with my performance, & wish myself a Tanner, or Printer, or any thing but an Author.[15]

It will become increasingly apparent as this narrative progresses that Coleridge was prone to psychosomatic disorders. The sad train of illness, depression and inactivity which followed after October of 1800, the vicious circle of debts, anxiety, sleeplessness and further illness all exacerbated by opium, probably followed on the sense of failure he was suffering at that time. The fruitful reunion with the Wordsworths in the 'fair country' had turned to ashes. And as if things were not bad enough already the detestable Charles Lloyd turned up and took a house close to the Wordsworths. There were frequent social visits between the Lloyds and the Wordsworths, Coleridge felt betrayed, and his journeys across the mountains fell off as he became more and more self-absorbed, depressed and hypochondriacal.

There is little doubt that Coleridge tended to over-dramatize his complaints. The frequent references to his shortly expected death (he in fact lived until the age of sixty-two, and probably died of a heart attack),[16] the dark hints that he was suffering from consumption, or some other fatal illness, abound in his letters. A typical example is this in July of 1801 :

As to my health, I am *going*, as I suspect. – My knee & leg remains swoln & troublesome – but that is a trifle. Other symptoms of a more serious nature have lately appeared – a tendency to scrophulous Boils and Indurations in the Neck, a dry husky Cough, with profuse sweats at night confined to the Region of my Chest.

Coleridge's illnesses were never in fact of a dangerous

nature. Yet for all that, the vivid descriptions of pain and
anxiety leave us in little doubt as to his suffering. An example
of this would be his hysterical reaction on the voyage to
Malta in 1804 when he had the convoy's surgeon summoned
and transferred at the peril of the man's life to administer
an enema for his constipation. Yet as with so many of
Coleridge's complaints the intensity of pain and fear are
described with such vehemence that one is forced to
acknowledge that he at least was convinced of his imminent
demise.

The effect of opium as a contributory factor in his frequent
illnesses is difficult to assess, for Coleridge – normally a
veritable walking pharmacopeia – is vague about the
occasions on which he took the drug and the quantities in
which he took it. It seems that he was convinced that his
'addiction' originated in May of 1801, having read of a
laudanum cure for rheumatism. Yet we know that he had
been taking opium in the form of laudanum ever since his
schooldays as an analgesic, and later in Bristol as an anti-
depressant. De Quincey, the self-appointed 'Pope' of opium,
remarks in his *Confessions* that he himself had been taking
opium for eight years before he became addicted. The fact is
that the actual 'dependence' or 'addiction' only seems to be
recognized when the addict realizes that his suffering is
directly attributable to the withdrawal of the drug. The
vicious circle of increased tolerance and exacerbated
symptoms are well known.

Coleridge was used to taking opium in the form of
laudanum, or 'tincture of opium'. The drug in this
modified form is obtained by dissolving opium in spirit,
usually brandy; the advantage of the drug in this form was
its almost immediate effect. The strength of laudanum
naturally depends on the quantity of opium dissolved in
the alcohol, and De Quincey tells us that the common
hospital equation in the early nineteenth century was 25
drops of laudanum to every grain of opium.[17] From this

one can establish that as early as 1796 Coleridge was
capable of taking three or four grains of opium a day
without ill effect, although this was negligible compared to
De Quincey's intake – whose idea of a pleasant evening was
to settle down with a volume of Kant and a *quart* of laudanum
in the decanter at his elbow.

In Coleridge's day opium was both cheap and widely
taken. According to De Quincey the number of people
taking the drug in London was 'immense', and in Manchester he was informed by several cotton manufacturers
that their work-people were rapidly getting in the practice.
'On a Saturday afternoon the counter of the druggists were
strewed with pills of one, two, or three grains, in preparation
for the known demands of the evening.' Opium, it seems, was
a cheaper method of alleviating misery than ale or spirits.
But more significantly, perhaps, it was the only anodyne
for child illnesses, 'pulmonary affections', and tooth-ache ;
moreover, it was actually considered a preventative for
consumption.

The important factor in opium is its ten per cent of
morphine, the principal action of which is to raise the pain
threshold. Morphine, in fact, is still regarded as the most
powerful analgesic known to man. The repression of pain is
accompanied by a sense of contentment and well being,
consequently the tendency to addiction is connected with
the extent of the analgesic and euphorizing effects – the
more successful, the more likely the addiction. In our
own day medical research has found that the incidence of
addiction is great when the drug is used to relieve pain and
discomfort in recurrent illnesses, also in those who are
inclined to depressive reactions, oversensitive to physical
discomfort, easily hurt by the small stings of life. In spite of
De Quincey's contention that it might take anything up to
eight years to form an addiction, it is nowadays held that it
takes a mere twenty to twenty five days' use of the drug to
convert a stable person, less for an unstable. It has also

been found that physical illness is much less often the real reason for beginning dependence than patients claim it to be.[18] While addiction in no way affects mental changes there are certain well defined psychological reactions: 'increasing inactivity and laziness, the wasting of time in day-dreams, indecisiveness, and the paralysis of the ability to make any strong persistent efforts'.[19] The 'withdrawal symptoms', which sufferers are often loath to admit as resulting directly from the drug are depression, restlessness, and physical and mental irritability. Habitual constipation changes to diarrhoea, and there are other unpleasant symptoms such as anorexia, retching, vomiting, trembling, yawning, sweating, pains in any part or all parts of the body, a profound malaise and anxiety. Distorted vision and hallucinatory experience are common, also 'pin-point' pupils, slow pulse, increased salivation and sweating'.

In the readiness of some biographers and critics to wag the moral finger and stress Coleridge's moral laxity, sloth and hypochondria, or, at the opposite extreme, to ignore completely the less attractive side of his character, the plain physical and psychological facts of opium addiction seem often to be overlooked. In the light of so many of Coleridge's symptoms which coincide with the above descriptions, and which started in 1800, it is almost certain that he was falling under the permanent tyranny of opium during that year.

The first bout of illness which put Coleridge in bed that summer started when he arrived at Grasmere with his family. It was, he says, 'a sort of rheumatic fever' resulting from a 'cold from wet'. He had a 'Head into which on the least agitation the blood felt as rushing in & flowing back again like the raking of the Tide on a coast of loose stones', and swollen and inflamed eyelids. The illness lasted about a month, and he felt more unwell, he said, 'than I have ever been since I left school'. By November the inflamed eyes had returned – 'they are so blood-red, that I should make

a very good Personification of Murder.' Once again, he
blamed the condition on a cold made worse by a long walk
in the wind, and writing late at night. He also had large
boils on his neck, possibly due to vitamin deficiency, a
common addict's condition. Ominous too at this time is the
recording of a nightmare in his notebook. It is characteristic
of many of the frightful dreams that were to follow in
subsequent years. The dream occurred on a visit to the
Wordsworths, and brief as the description is one can
imagine the chill of horror his cries sent through the cottage:

Friday Night, Nov. 28, 1800, or rather Saturday Morning – a
most frightful Dream of a Woman whose features were blended with
darkness catching hold of my right eye & attempting to pull it out –
I caught hold of her arm fast – a horrid feel – Wordsworth cried
out aloud to me hearing my scream – heard his cry & thought it
cruel he did not come / but did not wake till his cry was repeated a
third time – the Woman's name Ebon Thalud – When I awoke,
my eyelid swelled – [20]

Throughout November he had been 'tumbling on
through sands and swamps of Evil, & bodily grievance'. He
could scarcely write; and he describes a strange visual
phenomenon – 'the act of poetic composition, as I lay in bed,
perceptibly affected them [his eyes], and my voluntary
ideas were every minute passing, more or less transformed
into vivid spectra.' And again, 'I have made some rather
curious observations on the rising up of Spectra in the eye
in its inflamed state, & their influence on Ideas &c'. It is
reminiscent of De Quincey's observation: 'I feared lest some
dropsical state or tendency of the brain might thus be
making itself (to use a metaphysical word) objective, and
that the sentient organ might be projecting itself as its own
object.'

Terrified, yet fascinated, he witnessed his own body
becoming a 'crazy machine', sensitive to every change in
weather, or alteration in his own emotional state. For three
weeks over Christmas and the New Year he was in bed at

Grasmere with 'rheumatic fever'. And on his return to Keswick in the first week of January he developed a hydrocele. From a 'foolish shamefacedness almost peculiar to Englishmen' he delayed showing it to the doctor, but carried out his own experiments, applying to his scrotum 'Fomentations & fumigations of Vinegar', the 'Sal ammonica dissolved in verjuice'. As one might expect the result was dramatic : 'I am convinced it is the identical Torment which the Damned suffer in Hell.' The excruciating smarting was followed by five 'angry ulcers', and further experiments – 'three leaches', 'hot cloaths' and poultices 'of bread grated & mixed up with a strong solution of Lead'.

Having recovered from the hydrocele by the end of January, Coleridge says that he exerted himself with greater intensity of thought and application than he had ever done in all his former life, and as a result believed that he had injured his nervous system. In March there was a relapse, 'irregular Gout' as he called it, and 'frequent nephritic attacks' in his fingers, toes, ankle and right knee. But 'All this was mere nothing' to the 'stomach fits – they were terrible ! – The Disgust, the Loathing, that followed these fits & no doubt in part too the use of Brandy & Laudanum which they rendered necessary.' The symptoms are familiar, De Quincey tells of an acquaintance whose opium addiction began with a feeling 'as though rats were gnawing at his stomach', and remarks that he himself suffered 'a most appalling irritation of the stomach' at the onset of his own habit.

From May onwards he was suffering many of the characteristic symptoms of the addict. There were 'shivering fits and sleepless nights', 'confusion in the Head, or sensations of Disgust in the stomach', 'Forms which struck terror into me in my fever-dreams', 'profuse sweats at night confined to the Region of my chest'. It would affect his work, his relationships and ultimately his place of abode, as he planned an escape to a better climate – convinced that the root cause was rheumatism or 'irregular gout'. There is little doubt that he *did* suffer from rheumatism, but the multitude of symptoms pointed to an even more tragic affliction.

During this first long period of illness, from the autumn of 1800 to the summer of 1801, Coleridge began to concentrate on psychology and philosophy in earnest. It is not altogether true to say that he had abandoned the idea of serious poetry, or that his philosophical ponderings were merely an anodyne for his sufferings. However far he seemed to wander from the sphere of imagination, the way back was always open. At least, so he thought in his better moments. As he wrote to Josiah Wade : 'If I can hereafter do good to my fellow creatures, as a poet, and as a metaphysician, they will know it.' The decision to put philosophy at the centre of his life, in fact, dates back to at least 1799, long before the self-doubt or long illnesses began, and it was clearly connected with a sense of obligation arising from Wedgwood's annuity. In Germany, as we have seen, he had talked of buying thirty pounds worth of books, 'chiefly metaphysics / and with a view to the one work, to which I hope to dedicate in silence the prime of my life'. By the winter of 1800 he was getting down to the job ; as for poetry, whether he entertained a lingering faith in his powers, or fatalistically abandoned all hope, the fact remained that it was of secondary importance. The most he could hope for was that metaphysics and the Muse might not be mutually exclusive. Or, as he told Poole, 'I hope, Philosophy and Poetry will not neutralize each other, and leave me an inert mass'. By his own admission, however, he was more often and more vehemently convinced that the one was ousting the other. Although the famous letter to Godwin describing the death of his imagination, is paradoxically zestful and highly imaginative :

In my long Illness I had compelled into hours of Delight many a sleepless, painful hour of Darkness by chasing down metaphysical Game – and since then I have continued the Hunt, till I found myself unaware at the Root of Pure Mathematics – and up that tall smooth Tree, whose few poor Branches are all at it's very summit, am I climbing by pure adhesive strength of arms and thighs – still slipping down, still renewing my ascent... The Poet is dead in me – my imagination (or rather the Somewhat that had been imaginative) lies, like a Cold Snuff on the circular Rim of a Brass Candle-stick, without even a stink of Tallow to remind you that it was once cloathed & mitred with Flame. That is past by! – I was once a Volume of Gold Leaf, rising & riding on every breath of Fancy – but I have beaten myself back into squat and square on the earth amid the hurricane, that makes Oaks and Straws join in one Dance, fifty yards high in the Element.[21]

Twice in December he again suffered a total loss of confidence in his creative powers. 'As to Poetry, I have altogether abandoned it,' he told Thelwall, 'being convinced that I never had the essentials of poetic Genius, & that I mistook a strong desire for original power.'[22] To Francis Wrangham he wrote, 'He [Wordsworth] is a great, a true Poet – I am only a kind of Metaphisician.' And he records in his notebook the sad reflection, 'Into a *discoverer* I have sunk from an *inventor*.'[23] But his conviction on this score tended to alter with the state of the weather and the condition of his demoralizing symptoms.

Yet pain, sleeplessness and exhaustion did not prevent him from embarking on several lines of intellectual inquiry which imposed a severe strain on his nervous system. In December he told Poole: 'I have not been altogether idle, having in my own conceit gained great light into several parts of the human mind which have hitherto remained either wholly unexplained or most falsely explained.' In the following months as he increased the 'austerity' of his speculations, his behaviour must have appeared very strange indeed to Mrs Coleridge; to Wordsworth it actually seemed dangerous. Night after night he kept vigil in his room, appearing at breakfast with scarred hands – 'scratches from a Cat, whose back I was rubbing in the Dark in order to see whether the sparks from it were regragible by a Prism' ; his jowls caked with soap and blood having allowed his attention to stray from the shaving mirror to another of his beloved prisms as it caught the rays of the rising sun. During the day he was absorbed in optical and chemical experiments, lost in trancelike observation of objects ; preoccupied with the motion of Derwent's gums, deep in conversation with little Hartley about the nature of perception and 'Life'. And when his sore eyes permitted he was gutting Descartes, Hobbes, Newton, Locke, Hume, Leibnitz, Lambert, Wolff, and above all, Kant.

At first sight his inquiries seem confused and haphazard, yet there is a general theme of communication, perception, and the 'Relation of Thoughts to Things'. As random notebook entries show, he was asking basic questions, making his own personal observations :

It seems to elucidate the Theory of Language, Hartley, just able to speak a few words, making a fire-place of stones, with stones for fire. – four stones – fire-place – two stones – fire – / – arbitrary symbols in imagination / Hartley walked remarkably soon / & *therefore* learnt to talk re. late.[24]

Babies touch *by taste* at first – then about 5 months old they go from the Palate to the hand – & are fond of feeling what they have taste – / Association of the Hand with the Taste – till the latter by itself recalls the former – & of course with volition.[25]

Abed – nervous – had noticed the prismatic colours transmitted from the Tumbler – Wordsworth came – I talked with him – he left me alone – I shut my eyes – beauteous spectra of two colors, orange and violet – then of green, which immediately changed to Peagreen, & then actually *grew* to my eye into a beautiful moss, the same as is on the mantle-piece at Grasmere. – abstract Ideas – & unconscious Links!![26]

But where was it all leading? For his own part he was convinced that he was shedding new light on important questions, although he laments in December that he had not 'evidenced a more tangible utility'.[27] Unfortunately, as the months passed we are left with no more than stray hints at this early, and probably most intuitive stage. The starting point seemed to be in September of 1800 when he wrote to Godwin, suggesting that he write a book in which certain questions are to be answered:

I wish you to write a book on the power of words . . . Is *thinking* impossible without arbitrary signs? & – how far is the word 'arbitrary' a misnomer? Are not words &c parts & germinations of the Plant? And what is the Law of their Growth? – In something of this order I would endeavor to destroy the old antithesis of *Words & Things*, elevating, as it were, words into things, & living Things too. All the nonsense of vibrations etc you would of course dismiss.[28]

The proposition was both psychological and epistemological. He was penetrating the heart of the eighteenth- and nineteenth-century controversy over nominalism and universal concepts, and introducing leading questions on the nature of perception, ideas, feeling and language. Significantly he has totally dismissed the 'nonsense of vibrations' – or Hartley. In view of the fact that these are questions to which there cannot be clear and scientific answers, particularly in relation to 'morals and politics', his early, more reticent propositions are of great importance.

Some time in early January he wrote in his notebook: 'To *think* of a thing is different from to *perceive* it, as "to walk" is from "feel the ground under you" – perhaps, in the same way too – namely, a succession of perceptions accompanied by a sense of *nisus* & purpose.'[29] He was answering, in fact, a question he had posed Godwin in the previous Autumn, 'whether there be reason to hold, that an action bearing all the *semblance* of pre-designing Consciousness may yet be simply organic, and whether a *series* of such actions are possible'.[30] By organic, Coleridge meant mechanical in a Hartleian sense; and the question would seem to be probing the empirical proposition that it is only the repetition of an act that makes us look for a cause, or a predesigning purpose. He is making a distinction between simple sense impressions and the complex, self-conscious act of contemplation, so absent in the reasoning of the empiricists. And in talking of a *series* of seemingly self-conscious and predesigning acts, it sounds as if he is reducing the empirical contention to absurdity by the mere suggestion of such a phenomenon in their terms.

Not long after this he records another distinction, this time in relation to simple impressions themselves :

> Objects, namely, Fire, Hobs, and Kettle, at the first Look shone apparently upon the green Shrubs opposite to the Parlour, but in a few seconds acquired *Ideal* Distance by, the Shrubbery limiting the view, yet it appeared *indefinitely* behind the Shrubbery – / I found in looking an unpleasant sensation, occasioned as I apprehend from the distinctness of the Shrubbery, & the distinct shadowyness of the Images / [31]

Even on the level of simple perception, images might appear shadowy, indefinite, 'Ideal'. Nor was there any mistake about the distinction – it was 'unpleasant' to concentrate simultaneously on the peripheral, or out-of-focus, images and on the in-focus images.

The relevance of these reflections seems to appear in another notebook entry, made later in the year, when he tries to explain the significance of the central 'spot of time' in Wordsworth's *Tintern Abbey* :

> – and the deep power of Joy
> We see into the *Life* of things –
>
> i.e. – By deep feeling we make our *Ideas dim* – & this is what we mean by our Life – ourselves. I think of the Wall – it is before me, distinct Image – here. I necessarily think of the *Idea* & the The Thinking I as two distinct & opposite Things. Now ⟨let me⟩ think of *myself* – of the thinking Being – the Idea becomes dim whatever it be – so dim that I know not what it is – but the Feeling is deep & steady – and this I call *I* identifying the Percipient & the Perceived. [32]

The volitional, self-conscious, contemplation of an idea renders the impression dim and indistinct, as opposed to the direct and simple awareness of ideas, observed without reflection. He is establishing an unfamiliar polarity, setting aside the old debate of the particular and the general, the individual and the universal. But what is of more importance, he associates the purposive act of contemplation with deep and steady feeling. The consideration must have arisen quite naturally from the central experience of his own and Wordsworth's poetry, their conversations, and even Dorothy's journal : one is reminded of such phrases as 'melted into more than natural loveliness', 'Silent with swimming sense, gaze till all doth seem / Less gross than bodily – ', 'dim sympathies with me who live'. It involved the high-point of their poetical, even mystical, experiences, and naturally raised a good many important questions. Wordsworth, for his part, had tended to consign such experiences to the mysterious : they were a gift 'Of aspect more sublime', and even the quasiphysical commentaries – 'we are laid asleep / In body' – have the force of metaphor, or, at least, the vaguest approximations to what might be happening on the physical plane.

But the emphasis on a quality of dimness, shadowiness, indistinctness, naturally has a more general aesthetic significance. It was to become, for example, one of the basic features of Hazlitt's aesthetic theory :

Objects of sense are not as it were simple and self-evident propositions, but admit of endless analysis and the most subtle investigation. We do not see nature with our eyes, but with our understandings, and our hearts. To suppose that we see the whole of any object, merely by looking at it, is a vulgar error.[33]

A similar reflection occurs in Ruskin's *Modern Painters* in defence of Turner : 'WE NEVER SEE ANYTHING CLEARLY. . . . We suppose we see the ground under our feet clearly . . . there is literally *no* point of clear sight. . . .

What we call seeing a thing clearly, is only seeing enough of it to *make out what it is*.'[34] And in our own day, in a rather different context, E.H.Gombrich has claimed that 'we learn to articulate, to make distinctions where before there was only an undifferentiated mass'.[35]

For Coleridge the distinction between clarity and obscurity in art was at once associated with the difference between living things and – merely – things. He seems to be claiming that the basis of this living dynamic quality is 'the Thinking I', a reflection that found expression several years earlier in *The Eolian Harp* and which probably owed its origin to Cudworth, and in part at least to Berkeley. The development was naturally a departure from the crude and all-embracing physical analogy of Priestley and Hartley. Yet this same consciousness of a palpable answer to the empiricists also led him away from aesthetic considerations and into the realms of epistemology: not at first sight an unprofitable pursuit, except that it would necessarily affect his return to aesthetics at a later date. The temptation to expand the equations of clarity with thing, and obscurity with *vital* thing, into a general system, are clear from many references in letters and notebook entries early in 1801. For example, in February he tells Davy that his heart *'burns'* to *'concenter'* his mind 'to the affinities of the Feelings with Words & Ideas' under the title of 'Concerning Poetry & the nature of the Pleasures derived from it'. But by the scale of its implications it would 'supercede all the Books of Metaphysics hitherto written / and all the Books of Morals too'.

In Germany, in spite of former metaphysical influences, he had returned to the nominalist position in order to justify his difficulties with prose description. 'In nature', he wrote, 'all things are individual, but a word is but an arbitrary character for a whole class of things ; so that the description may in almost all cases be applied to twenty different appearances.' The answer to the problem at that time seemed to be association, 'I could half suspect that what

are deemed fine descriptions, produce their effects almost
purely by charm of words, with which and with whose
combinations we associate *feelings* indeed, but not distinct
Images.' But now, in the seeming discovery that words
could be both 'things' and 'living things' a new solution was
apparent, and the way seemed open to approach the problem
of empiricism, with all its unsatisfactory moral and aesthetic
implications, from a new angle. The position of the empiricists, the necessitarians, the materialists, was a mistake
about language, a basic mistake about the nature of the
mind : in attempting to simplify and clarify our notions
about the nature of mind they had produced mystification
and confusion. 'Materialists', he recorded in his notebook,
'unwilling to admit the mysterious of our nature make it all
mysterious.' And he adds the sarcastic remark, 'nothing
mysterious in nerves, eyes, &c : but that nerves think
&c ! !'

It is clear from Coleridge's poetry that he had been
disillusioned with the empirical position for several years
now : it was something deeply felt. Yet what could he do
about it? Tracing the origins of the materialist philosophy
back to Newton he could simply assert, 'I believe the Souls
of 500 Sir Isaac Newtons would go to the making up of a
Shakespeare or a Milton'. But the matter could not be left
there. 'Every man asks – how?' he wrote in his notebook.
'This power & instinct is the true substratum of philosophy.'[36] That he was driven to ask continually 'how', was to
be Coleridge's great strength, or weakness, depending on
the extent to which one views the propriety of scientific
questions in the realms of the mysterious – a point on
which he himself could never quite make up his mind.

The basis of the materialists' mistake, he asserted was in
positing a passive nature of mind. '*Mind* in his [Newton's]
system is always passive – a lazy Looker-on in an external
World.' Coleridge's self-active, self-conscious principle in
thought, language and ideas presupposed a far different

situation, a far different 'system'. 'If the mind be not *passive*,' he wrote to Poole in March, 'if it be indeed made in God's Image, & that too in the sublimest sense – the Image of the *Creator* – there is ground for suspicion that any system built on the passiveness of the mind must be false, as a system.'[37] So false, indeed, that 'all the irreligious metaphysics of the modern Infidels' were directly traceable to this mistake, including 'the doctrine of Association, as taught by Hartley', and 'especially, the doctrine of Necessity'.[38] But there was still the question – how? In March Coleridge told Poole that he was on the brink of deducing from '*one sense*' all the five senses, thus solving 'the process of Life & Consciousness'. And it was not surprising that in the absence of tangible arguments and proofs he should try to overwhelm his friend with the sheer vehemence of his conviction – for it sounded dangerously as if he was turning the inductive process completely on its head. The sacred system of Locke was like a triangle with the broad base of sense experience leading up to the general representations enshrined in language at the apex. Since Locke had demolished the notion of innate ideas in Descartes, the primacy of sense experience was held to be incontrovertible. But was it? asked Coleridge. Turning once again to Locke's basic tenets in the *Essay on Human Understanding*, he was convinced that the father of the empirical movement was no more than a plagiarist of Descartes himself. The first task that lay to hand was to undermine Locke's reputation with a frontal attack; in this way he was convinced that the whole empiricist position would collapse.

The fruit of Coleridge's reassessment of Locke, important as he regarded it at the time, was entrusted in a series of letters sent to Josiah Wedgwood in February and March; copies were also sent to Poole. His general argument was that Locke was not so much a critic of Descartes as a distorter: or, as he jotted in his notebook: 'Mr Locke supposed himself an *adder* to Descartes & so he was in the sense of a *viper*.'

Locke claimed to be attacking innate ideas, says Coleridge, but he falls back on Descartes's definition. 'He [Locke] would willingly change the Term 'Idea' for a better, if any one could help him to it. But he finds none that stands so well *"for every immediate object of the mind in thinking, as Idea does"*.'[39] Both Locke and Descartes, according to Coleridge, are in agreement on their use of the term 'Idea' and in their explanations for its origin.

They both taught, nearly in the same words and wholly to the same purpose, that the Objects of human Knowledge are either Ideas imprinted on the Senses, or else such as are perceived by attending to the passions and operations of the mind, or lastly Ideas formed by Help of Memory and Imagination, either compounding, dividing, or barely representing those originally perceived in the aforesaid Ways.[40]

Coleridge goes on to point out that Locke posited three classes of ideas : sensation, reflection, and thirdly, complex ideas, formed by combining, comparing, or separating various simple ideas of sensation or of reflection. In fact, says Coleridge, Descartes's 'innate' ideas were exactly the same as Locke's ideas of reflection ; furthermore, Descartes had emphatically denied innate ideas in Locke's sense.

The main point of Coleridge's argument is not so much to demolish Locke's thesis as to convince himself of Locke's poor claim to genius and originality. Locke, he asserts, is guilty of confusion, and the *Essay on Human Understanding* is 'only a prolix Paraphrase on Descartes with foolish Interpolations of the Paraphrast's'.[41] Yet what had he to put in its place? We have only the random ideas on purposive, self-conscious thought, on obscurity and clarity of impressions, at this stage. And in the letters on Locke he merely poses a vague hypothesis : 'What if instead of innate Ideas a philosopher has asserted the existence of *constituent* Ideas / the metaphor would be not a whit more gross, nor the hypothesis involved more daring or unintelligible, than in the former phrases/and I am sure, it would lead to more profitable Experiments & Analyses.'[42] What is more significant, however, is his conviction at this time that the question of consciousness and will lies outside the area of proof. He sums up his position in this way :

Des Cartes asserted only, that the Will and Reason of Man was a Something essentially distinct from the vital Principle of Brutes / and that we had no *proof* that Brutes are *not* mere automatons. Des Cartes, like Hartley & Darwin, held the possibility of a machine so perfect & susceptible of Impulses, as to perform many actions of apparent Consciousness without consciousness / but the falsehood of a thing possible can never 'be *demonstrated*,' tho' such demonstration may be superseded by intuitive Certainty. I am *certain* that I feel; and when I speak of men, I *imply* in the *word* 'Men' Beings like myself; but in the word 'Brutes' I imply Beings someway or other different from my own species, to them therefore I am not entitled to transfer my intuitive Self-knowlege / consequently, I cannot *prove* i.e. demonstrate, that any consciousness belongs to them.[43]

Ironically Josiah Wedgwood neglected to read or acknowledge the first of Coleridge's 'Locke' letters ; consequently there was a month's delay before Coleridge sent a further two. Wedgwood's eventual reaction reveals his poor interest : 'As to Metaphysics,' he wrote to Poole, 'I know little about them, and my head is at present so full of various affairs that I have not even read the letters Coleridge has written on those subjects, as I have honestly told him. From the cursory view I took of them he seems to have plucked the principal feathers out of Locke's wings.'[44] Poole's reaction was equally dampening. On 14 March he wrote to Coleridge saying, 'think before you join the herd of Little-ists, who without knowing in what Locke is defective, wish to strip the *popular mind* of him, leaving in his place nothing – darkness, total darkness'.[45] No, replied Coleridge, it was Locke himself who was a Little-ist. But there was no fear, in any case, that he would disseminate his view of Locke : 'My dear Friend, how unutterably silly & contemptible these Opinions would be, if written to any but another Self, I assure you, solemnly assure you, that you & Wordsworth are the only men on Earth to whom I would have uttered a word on this Subject.[46]

Yet beyond satisfying himself in his own mind that Locke had 'no honest claim' to high reputation, his positive findings were inconclusive, and it seemed for the time being that his suspicion about '*supposed Discoveries* in Metaphysics' was as applicable to himself as to those he criticized. As the year wore on he turned his attention to the destruction of Hobbes and Hume, and his reading reveals a favourable approach to Kant and the scholastics. In Kant he found 'The excellent distinction between Klar and deutlich (clear and indicable)', which seemed to support his conclusions about obscurity and clarity in relation to consciousness and language, and in the summer he was reading Aquinas, Scotus and Suarez. In the *Biographia* he would later suggest that Hume had plundered Aquinas for the development of his ideas on association, and there is a notebook entry[47] implying that Suarez had combated Descartes and Berkeley by anticipation. 'As to Hume', he wrote to Southey in the autumn, 'was he not – bui non fur, ibi stultus – & often thief & blockhead at the same time?'

Coleridge had been so preoccupied with philosophical ponderings during the early months of 1801 that the matter of earning a living had been put completely aside. In spite of the fact that direct poverty and debt were staring him in the face he felt obliged to continue his speculations to the exclusion of all other tasks 'for it seemed to me a Suicide of my very soul to direct my attention from Truths so important'. Although in March he wrote to Longman claiming that it was his illness that had left him unproductive: 'one feature of it is an extreme Disgust which I feel

at every perusal of my Productions.' In December he had
made another attempt at the German Travels : 'Nothing
but the most pressing necessity for the money could have
induced me & even now I hesitate & tremble.' Nothing
came of it. With the bookseller Phillips too he was engaged
to write a school book, but in spite of receiving an advance
he had done nothing : eventually he received an attorney's
letter for the £25 he owed the man, which at first amused
him but later made his 'heart ache'.

Meanwhile the debts mounted. Wordsworth had assumed
a debt of £30 on his behalf with Longman ; he owed £25 to
shopkeepers in Keswick and his landlord ; to Poole he owed
£30, or at least thought he did – the actual sum was sub-
stantially more. To Lamb he owed £13, and he was £15
behind in his obligations to his mother-in-law. In the
meantime his only asset by January was 'a Drama, and a sort
of Farce', he told Poole,' written wholly *for* the Theatre, &
which I should be ashamed of in any other view – works
written purposely vile'. But again nothing came of them.

Yet his increasing poverty and debt urged him to do little
beyond raising his head occasionally to denounce the government for the sorry state of affairs in England. 'I am assured,
that such is the depravity of the public mind, that no literary
man can find bread in England except by misemploying &
debasing his talents,' he told Poole in March. The contention was no doubt supported by Longman's remark that 'the
chief Buyers of Books were the Wealthy who bought them
for furniture'. The annuity which he felt he held 'by a very
precarious Tenure' would shortly be worth less than one
half of its value when first allowed him. At the same time
there were heavy impositions from the government to
counteract the cost of the war. Pitt's Income Tax, which
stood at two shillings in the pound and 'that brutal Tax upon
the understanding', the Postage Tax, which was a shilling
for a single letter sheet in 1800. It horrified Coleridge to
think of 'all the domestic affection that had been stifled, all

the intellectual progress that would have been, but is not'.

As he viewed the state of the country from the remoteness of Greta Hall he felt further and further removed in sympathy from any of the figures or parties on the political stage. 'Change of Ministry interests *me* not', he wrote in February. And again in April,

Our enormous Riches & accompanying Poverty have corrupted the *Morals* of the nation. All *Principle* is scouted – : by the Jacobins, because it is the death-blow of vainglorious Scepticism – by the Aristocrats, because it is visionary & theoretical. . . . Property is the bug bear – it stupifies the heads & hardens the heart of our Councellors & Chief Men! – They know nothing better than Soup-shops – or the boldest of them push forward for an abolition of Tythes!

As for revolution – there was little hope in that direction either. 'Revolutions bring forward the conscious distinct attention to *Power*,' he wrote in his notebook, 'by change in power/Hence weaken the sense of Right.'[48]

That he had retired to a remote part of the country did not mean, of course, that he had escaped the bitter reality of poverty in England during these days. 'I am oppressed at times with a true heart-gnawing melancholy when I contemplate the state of my poor oppressed country,' he wrote in March. ' – God knows, it is as much as I can do to put meat & bread on my own table ; & hourly some poor starving wretch comes to my door, to put in his claim for part of it.'[49]

According to Patrick Colquhoun, the economist, there were at the turn of the century over one and a half million paupers in England, and well over 300,000 vagrants (amongst whom a large proportion of 'vicious and criminal individuals'), and this in a population of only nine and a half million people.[50] With a million members of the armed forces involved in a war which extended from the West Indies to the Nile, it is not surprising that there was an extraordinary rise in vagrancy in the 1790s due to the return of the wounded and the discharged ; there was also, of course, the added problem of unemployment due to the depression in the manufactories. Yet in Colquhoun's view, which no doubt reflected government policy, the large numbers of poor made good economic sense: 'It is at the same time equally true,' he says on the question of the unemployed, 'that every state is supported *by the poverty of the community* composing the body politic. Without a large proportion of poverty there could be no riches in any country; since riches are the offspring of labour, which labour can result only from a state of poverty.'

The large number of destitute people on the roads even in the Lake District is well attested by Dorothy Wordsworth's journal in the previous year: 'A young woman begged at the door. . . . She had buried her husband and three children within a year and a half . . . '; ' . . . I met a half crazy old man. He shewed me a pincushion and begged a pin . . . '; 'A little girl from Coniston came to beg. She had lain out all night . . . '. All these were within five days. As one of her neighbours, John Fisher, remarked, 'in a short time there would be only two ranks of people, the very rich and the very poor'.

Coleridge's reaction to the constant presence of these sad vagrants was curiously impractical in one who had displayed such a keen sense of social conscience in his early manhood. On 23 March in an outburst against 'our pestilent Commerce, our unnatural Crowding together of men in Cities, & our Government by Rich Men', he told Poole that the fact that the 'laborious Poor [were] dying with Grass within their Bellies' was a manifestation of 'offended Deity'. For his own part he only wished to get away from it all. 'Not any romantic scheme, but merely because Society has become a matter of great Indifference to me – I grow daily more & more attached to Solitude – but it is a matter of the utmost Importance to be removed from seeing suffering and *Want*.' Not only was the desire to be far away impractical in the wider sense, it was totally out of the question domestically.

In April, reporting his periodic symptoms to Poole, he says that he screams mechanically on the least motion: ' . . . it is not my bodily Pain – but the gloom & distresses of those around me for whom I ought to be labouring and cannot.' Pipe dreams, or not, Coleridge began to scheme for a removal to a distant and warmer climate in earnest.

Once again his thoughts turned to Southey and the dream of living together in the sun. In the previous year he had written, 'The time returns upon me, Southey! when we dreamt one Dream, & that a glorious one – when we eat together, & thought each other greater and better than all the World beside, and when we were bed fellows.' Alas, Southey only remembered Coleridge as a 'vile bed-fellow', but there were more reasons than that for his scepticism about Coleridge's plans to escape *en famille* to freedom and the sun, not the least of them being Coleridge's inability to make a decision and stick to it.

In March of 1801 Coleridge seriously considered going out to America, there were even political undertones here, 'a Land where human Life was an end, to which Labour was only a Means'.[51] And it would be all the better 'if Wordsworth would go with me, & we could persuade two or three Farmers of this Country who are exceedingly attached to us, to accompany us'. Three weeks later, convinced that he was destined for an early grave in the English climate, he wrote to Greenough, the old Göttingen friend, saying that he considered 'visiting the Azores, in order to ascertain the effect which a mere continuing summer may have'. In fact the Azores scheme took such a hold that, according to Coleridge, Wordsworth and Dorothy had agreed by May that they too would settle there with him, after he had given it a fair trial.[52] He learnt that he could go from Whitehaven for a mere 'trifle', that his expenses for the whole winter would be no more than £10. But there were the usual volatile reservations: 'When I am sick or in pain, I look forward to this Scheme with a comforting satisfaction – but whenever

I am quite at ease, I cannot bear even to think of it.' So convinced was Wordsworth both of Coleridge's need and purpose that he actually wrote to Poole asking for £50 to pack him off. But it was an act of kindness that would recoil. The Stowey days of easy, intimate, generosity were over : Coleridge had opted for Wordsworth and the North : in any case, the times were harsh, and £50 was a great deal of money. Instead of replying to Wordsworth – the mediator, in the bland, confidential style of days gone by, Poole wrote directly to Coleridge. In the first place he proposed that he should accompany Tom Wedgwood who was bound for convalescence in Sicily, a suggestion that had originally come from Coleridge himself at an earlier date. Secondly, he urged that he should try borrowing from his brothers, who were by Coleridge's own admission 'rich men'. Finally, if all else failed he could offer no more than £20. He also felt it incumbent on him to add the stinging reminder that Coleridge's debt to him amounted to £52 and not, as Wordsworth seemed to imagine, £37.

But even as Poole wrote the letter, the Azores scheme had passed into oblivion. In May Coleridge once again wrote to Southey. 'I am willing to believe that the blessed dreams, we dreamt some 6 years ago may be augeries of something really noble which we may yet perform.' And now a palpable opportunity seemed to present itself, although its nobility and approximation to those former 'blessed Dreams' was rather doubtful. Here was the latest scheme of the one time founding Pantisocrat, who just four years earlier had eschewed even custard pies on the grounds that they were the product of West Indian slave labour : on 25 July he wrote to Southey :

Now mark my scheme! – St Nevis is the most lovely as well as the most healthy Island in the W. Indies – Pinny's Estate is there – and he has a country House situated in a most heavenly way, a very large mansion. Now between you & me I have reason to believe that not only this House is at my service, but many advantages in a family way that would go one half to lessen the expenses of living there – and perhaps Pinny would appoint us sine-cure Negro-drivers at a hundred a year each, or some other snug & reputable office – & perhaps, too we might get some office in which there is quite nothing to do, under the Governour. Now I & my family, & you & Edith, & Wordsworth & his sister might all go there – & make the Island more illustrious than Cos or Lesbos. A heavenly climate – a heavenly country, – & a good House. The Sea shore so near us – dells & rocks, & streams – / Do now think of this! But say nothing about it – on account of Old Pinny. – Wordsworth would certainly go, if I went. By the living God, it is my opinion, that we should not leave three such men behind us.[53]

Of course, he might have been joking, but the suggestion was repeated on 7 September to Poole (mercifully without the 'sine-cure Negro-driver' aspiration), again to Godwin on 22 September, and yet again to Poole on 5 October.[54] On all three occasions he talks of Pinney procuring for him 'the means' of living on St Nevis, and Pinney's business, indeed – the entire economy of St Nevis – being what it was, Coleridge could have been under no illusion as to what he might be associating himself with. Foremost amongst the great plantation owners, John Pinney has since gone down in the history of anti-slavery as a veritable blue-beard : 'But surely God ordained them for use and benefit of us,' he once said with wide-eyed ingenuousness, 'otherwise his Divine Will would have been manifest by some particular sign or token.' For some years he had been a close friend and bene-factor of Wordsworth ; it was certainly no moral scruple that prevented Coleridge from enjoying similar auspices.

The need to escape, whatever the consequences or cir-cumstances, seems to have hounded Coleridge throughout the spring and summer of 1801. His illness naturally had much to do with it. But simply to escape seemed in itself imperative. His sense of imprisonment is dramatically recorded in a notebook entry at this time, 'A prison without ransome, anguish without patience, sick bed in the house of

11*

contempt.' Similar expressions were to be repeated in the following year : he was 'a creature robbed on his free agency', 'a starling self-incaged'. There is little doubt that this feeling of being trapped had much to do with increasing domestic unhappiness. As early as February of the previous year he had talked of his unhappiness to Southey :

> My wife is a woman of absolutely pure mind and considerable intellect . . . [he wrote in Latin], but her everyday self and her minor interests, alas, do not at all harmonize with my occupations, my temperament, or my weaknesses – we cannot be happy in all respects. In my early married life I was often almost miserable – now (as everything mellows) I am content, indeed, thankful!

The uneasy contentment, we may take it, evaporated on each occasion that he came in close contact with Sara Hutchinson. At Christmas and New Year of 1800–1 he had been ill at the Wordsworths for three weeks where Sara had been staying, and again in March he saw more of her, a period which coincided with renewed attempts to complete *Christabel* and a return to Bartram's *Travels*, a book which had provided him with so much poetic sustenance in the past.[55]

In the following month Dorothy Wordsworth provides the first vivid picture of discord in the Coleridge household. Writing to Mary Hutchinson of Coleridge's illness she adds the following comments :

> She is indeed a bad nurse for C., but she has several great merits. She is much very much to be pitied, for when one party is ill matched the other necessarily must be so too. She would have made a very good wife to many another man, but for Coleridge!! Her radical fault is want of sensibility and what can such a woman be to Coleridge? She is an excellent nurse to her sucking children (I mean to the best of her skill, for she employs her time often foolishly enough about them). Derwent is a sweet lovely Fatty – she suckles him entirely – he has no other food. She is to be sure a sad fiddle faddler. From about $\frac{1}{2}$ past 10 on Sunday morning till two she did nothing but wash and

dress her two children and herself, and was just ready for dinner. No doubt she suckled Derwent pretty often during that time.[56]

In time Mrs Coleridge's inadequacies would be aired more frequently and openly; but as each domestic crisis arose Sara Hutchinson would be there in the background – no doubt both the occasion of Coleridge's growing dissatisfaction, and a disturbing factor in Mrs Coleridge's worsening humour.

At length, when Coleridge did get away for a summer holiday in the third week of July, it was on the pretext of reading the scholastics in the library of Durham Cathedral, but predictably enough Sara Hutchinson was not far away. First he went to stay with Sara's brother George who had a farm at Middleham, then moved on to Durham. Writing on 25 July to Southey, he was in high spirits :

I am in Durham at an Inn – & that too I do not like – & have dined with a large parcel of Priests all belonging to the Cathedral – thoroughly ignorant & hard hearted. I have had no small trouble in gaining permission to have a few books sent to me 7 miles from the place, which nobody has ever read in memory of man. – Now you will think what follows a Lie – it is not. I asked a stupid haughty fool, who is the Librarian of the Dean and Chapter's Library in this city, if he had Leibnitz. He answered – 'We have no Museum in this Library for natural curiosities ; but there is a mathematical Instrument-seller in the town, who shews such animalcula thro' a glass of great magnifying powers.' Heaven & Earth! he understood the word 'live Nits.'

At the same time he could inform Southey that he was about to return to Middleham the next day – 'to a quiet good family, that love me dearly – a young farmer, & his Sister & he makes very droll verses in the northern dialect & in the metre of Burns, & is a great Humourist; & the woman is so very good a woman, that I have seldom indeed seen the like of her.' On the way back from Durham he had a relapse of 'gout' and his left knee 'swelled "*pregnant* with agony"'. A Doctor Fenwick 'earnestly persuaded' him to try 'horse-exercise & warm Sea-bathing'; so he could later report that he had been riding with Sara Hutchinson – on the way to Gallow Hill. In spite of the fact that the said doctor had warned him against bathing in the open sea – he found he could not resist it. 'I came out all at once on the Beach, and had Faith in the Ocean. I bathed regularly, frolicked in the Billows, and it did me a proper deal of good.' The frolick resulted in the lines 'God be with thee, gladsome ocean' – which he sent to Southey, 'which will please you as a symptom of convalescence – for alas ! it is a long time since I have cropt a flowering weed on the sweet Hill of Poesy.'

By 7 September he had returned to Greta Hall where he was visited by Southey who was about to depart for Ireland to take up a government post. Once again the two poets were sitting at the same table. 'I once said – that I *missed* no body,' Coleridge had written to Southey, 'I only enjoyed the *present*. At that moment my heart misgave me, & had no one been present, I should have said to you – that you were the only exception.' To Daniel Stuart he sent the hopeful news : 'Southey and I do well together in this line ; (a *fair stock in hand*) of poems, serious & ludicrous, tales &c . . . for I have always 50 subjects with all the ideas therunto appertaining, but it is always a struggle with me to execute – and this Southey performs not only with rapidity, but takes great pleasure in doing it.' But while he seemed to long for Southey when he was absent, a few days with his old friend showed the glaring impossibility of their ever enjoying a successful friendship. As he confided in his notebook, 'Talk to a blind man – & he knows, he wants the sense of sight – but has some certain internal senses which a man may want & believe he has them / it is unpleasant to be much in conversation with such men. There is no *reasoning*, of course, with them / nothing is possible but naked Dissent which implies a sort of contempt – or what I am afraid a kindness is very likely to fall into, a sort of acquiescence very like duplicity – Australis'.[57] Australis was Coleridge's private name for Southey, as *Asra* was to be for Sara Hutchinson. Meanwhile the holiday in Durham, Middleham and Gallow Hill, during which he had spent so much time with Sara Hutchinson, had completely unsettled him, or at least exacerbated his growing dissatisfaction with Mrs Coleridge and his general feeling of restlessness. And it is likely that Southey's 'blindness' was in connection with his lack of sympathy towards these growing domestic problems.

'The only time I ever saw S angry with Edith, was on an occasion of her sportfully putting a little milk in his mash which (a drop or two) fell on his jacket & he feared would stain it. "'Twas *wrong*" with a frown (unnoticed – as a beggar's Fiddle on a crowded crossing – as a pompous Funeral in Cheapside at noon, noticed chiefly by those who curse it for going so slow –)'[58]

From this autumn onwards Coleridge tended to identify much of the unhappiness in his life with his wife's un-sympathetic nature. There is no need to anticipate the catalogue of criticisms he would eventually level at her ; but one notebook entry in the late summer of 1801 clearly lay at the root of their incompatability :

Coldness perhaps & paralysis in all *tangible* ideas & sensations – all that forms *real Self* – hence she creates her own self in a field of Vision & Hearing, at a distance, by her own ears & eyes – & hence becomes the willing Slave of the Ears & Eyes of others. Nothing affects her with pain or pleasure as it is but only as other people will *say it is* – nay by an habitual absence of *reality* in her affections I have had an hundred instances that the being beloved, or not being beloved is a thing indifferent; but the *notion* of not being beloved – that wounds her pride deeply. I have dressed perhaps washed with her, & no one with us – all as cold & calm as a deep Frost.[59]

At the same time Sara Hutchinson was constantly in his thoughts and fantasies : 'By thinking of different parts of her Dress I can at times recall her face – but not so vividly as

when it comes of itself – & therefore I have ceased to try it.'
And again : 'Prest to my bosom & felt there – it was quite
dark. I looked intensely towards her face – & sometimes I
saw it – so vivid was the spectrum, that it had almost all its
natural sense of *distance* & *outness* – except indeed that,
feeling & all, I felt her as *part* of my being – twas all
spectral.'[60]

Towards the end of September he was determined to
leave Greta Hall and settle in London again ; but, he told
Godwin, 'If I come, I come *alone*. – *Here* it will be imprudent
for me to stay, from the wet & the cold – even if every
thing within doors were as well suited to my head & heart,
as my head & heart would, I trust, be to every thing that was
wise & amiable.' And as the weeks passed he continually
heralded his immediate departure with warnings about his
imminent death should he stay in the Lakes for another
winter. To Southey he confided the truth of the situation.

... Sara – alas! we are not suited to each other. But the months of
my absense I devote to self-discipline, & to the attempt to draw her
nearer to me by a regular development of all the sources of our
unhappiness – then for another Trial, *fair* as I hold the love of good
men dear to me – patient, as I myself love my own dear children.
I will go believing that it will end happily – if not, if our mutual
unsuitableness continues, and (as it assuredly will do, if it continue)
increases & strengthens, why then, it is better for her & my children,
that I should live apart, than that she should be a Widow & they
Orphans. Carefully have I *thought thro'* the subject of marriage &
deeply am I convinced of it's indissolubleness. – If I separate, I do it in
the earnest desire to provide for her & them; that when I die, something may have been accumulated that may secure her from degrading
Dependence. When I least love her, then most do I feel anxiety for
her peace, comfort, & welfare. Is she not the mother of my children?
And am I the man not to know & feel this?[61]

Finally on 10 November Coleridge made his farewells at
Grasmere. Dorothy Wordsworth for one seemed to guess
that it was the end of an era. 'Every sight and every sound

reminded me of him – ' she wrote on that day, 'dear, dear
fellow, of his many walks to us by day and by night, of all
dear things. I was melancholy, and could not talk, but at last
I eased my heart by weeping – nervous blubbering, says
William. It is not so. O! how many, many reasons have I to
be anxious for him.'

Coleridge left for London in the 'heavy coach' on 13
November. It was evidently an uncomfortable journey with
many delays. On two occasions new horses had to be sent
for, one of the team falling, another plunging and tearing all
the harness. And by the time he arrived at Southey's
lodgings in Bridge Street, Westminster, on 19 November,
he was 'miserably uncomfortable'. It was a traumatic change
from the society of the three persons and the one Wordsworthian God, for in London he was meeting 'Lords many,
& Gods many – some of them very Egyptians, Physio-
gnomes, dog-faced Gentry, Crocodiles, Ibises, &c.' Indeed
he felt like a 'Fish in air, who . . . lies panting & dying from
excess of Oxygen.'

Once again he was taken on by the *Morning Post*, and
Daniel Stuart found him a first floor set of rooms over
Howel's the tailor in King Street, Covent Garden. Howel's
wife, thought Stuart, would nurse Coleridge as kindly as
if 'he were her son'. But on this occasion Stuart was not to
get much work out of his tame poet. Stuart's practice was to
call on him in the middle of the morning, talk over the news,
and project a leading paragraph for the next day, 'but
though he would talk over everything so well, I soon found
he could not write on the daily occurrences of the day'.
Stuart eventually became convinced that Coleridge was one
of those men who 'never could write a thing that was
immediately required of him. The thought of compulsion
disarmed him.' On one occasion at least, however, Coleridge's lack of copy was due to his illness. 'Having arranged

with him the matter of a leading paragraph one day,'
remembered Stuart, 'I went about six o'clock for it ; I found
him stretched on the sofa groaning with pain. He had not
written a word ; nor could he write.'[62] Stuart went away,
wrote it himself and eventually returned so that Coleridge
could correct it, 'and decorate it a little with some of his
graceful touches'. But Stuart having read the piece out loud,
Coleridge exclaimed : 'Me correct that? It is as well written
as I or any other man could write it.'

By mid-December, however, he was again feeling
trapped : 'It is all buz buz buz with my poor Head — & like a
creature robbed of his free agency I do what I *must* not what
I *would*.' Some consolation he found, at least, in 'reading in
the old Libraries' for his 'curious metaphysical work'. This
was no doubt 'the History of the opinions concerning Space
& Time for Mackintosh', a work he would refer to in
February 1802, and which he had mentioned earlier in 1801
when he told Poole, 'if I do not greatly delude myself, I have
not only completely extricated the notions of Time, and
Space ; but have overthrown the doctrine of Association, as
taught by Hartley, and with it all the irreligious metaphysics of modern infidels'. The work evidently involved a
return to Aquinas and Scotus, and occasioned a catty
comment from Southey :

A great metaphysical book is conceived and about to be born.
Thomas Wedgewood the Jupiter whose brain is parturient — Mackintosh the man-midwife — a preface on the history of metaphysical
opinions promised by Coleridge. This will perhaps prove an
abortion. . . . It has, however, proceeded so far as to disturb the
spiders, whose hereditary claim to Thomas Aquinas and Duns
Scotus had not been disputed for many a year before. Time and
Space are the main subjects of speculation.[63]

But Coleridge was restless, and he talked once more of
convalescing with Thomas Wedgwood in spite of his
adamant rejection of any such plan earlier in the summer :
'it is of the first importance to me to make the connection

with the Wedgwoods one of Love and *personal* attachment,'
he now told his wife, 'as well as of moral calculation &
intellectual Hope –which are subject to sad Caprices in this
mortal Life.' The precariousness with which he held his
annuity was obviously preying on his mind.

A more immediate escape presented itself, however. On
Boxing Day he took himself off to spend a holiday with
Poole down in Stowey. Sitting on the top of the coach he
weathered what seemed to him the worst storm he had ever
experienced : 'Rain & Hail & violent wind with vivid
flashes of Lightning, that seemed almost to alternate with the
flash-lie Re-emersions of the Waning Moon, from the ever
shattered ever closing Clouds.' He was protected by a 'huge,
most huge, Roquelaire' which was 'provided for the
Emigrants in the Quiberon Expedition. I dipped my head
down, shoved it up, & it proved a compleat Tent to me. I
was as dry as if I had been sitting by the fire.'

But the holiday did not raise his spirits. During the first
ten days of his stay he had 'every evening a bowel attack –
which layed my spirits prostrate'. Even yet he did not
associate the tell-tale symptoms with opium addiction : any
more than he did a later bowel attack and shivering fits in
the following month, which he blamed on eating greens at
Southey's. He was visited too with unhappy thoughts of his
domestic situation which seemed to permeate his whole
being. 'I would gladly lie down by the side of the road, &
become the country for a mighty nation of Maggots,' he
wrote to Southey on New Year's Eve, ' – for what is life,
gangarened, as it is with me, in it's very vitals – domestic
Tranquillity ?'

He returned to London with Poole on 21 January with
little improvement in health or happiness, and began to sink
even deeper in a slough of ill-health, intoxication and
insomnia. At the same time he began to castigate himself ;
his indolence, he thought, lay at the root of all his ills :

I have not slept two hours for the last three nights. . . . Partly from ill-health, & partly from an unhealthy & reverie-like vividness of *Thoughts*, & (pardon the pedantry of the phrase) a diminished Impressibility from *Things*, my ideas, wishes, & feelings are to a diseased degree disconnected from *motion & action*. In plain & natural English, I am a dreaming & therefore an indolent man – . I am a Starling self-incaged, & always in the Moult, & my whole Note is Tomorrow, & tomorrow, & tomorrow. The same causes, that have robbed me to so great a degree of the self-impelling self-directing Principle, have deprived me too of the due powers of Resistances to Impulses from without. I might so say, I am, as an *acting* man, a creature of mere Impact. 'I will' & 'I will not' are phrases, both of them equally of rare occurrence in my dictionary. – This is the Truth – I regret it, & in the consciousness of this Truth I lose a larger portion of Self-estimation than those, who know me imperfectly, would easily believe – / I evade the sentence of my own Conscience by no quibbles of self-adulation; I ask for Mercy indeed on the score of my ill-health; but I confess that this very ill-health is as much as effect an a cause of this want of steadiness & self-command; and it is for mercy that I ask, not for justice.[64]

Examples of strange spectra and vivid illusions abound in his notebook at this time. On the night of 14 February he had the following experience while lying on his bed :

A luminous cloud interposed between my Limbs & the sheet wherever I drew a figure with my nail on my leg or thigh, the same *appeared* on my limb & all, the path of the nail a luminous white, like phosphorus in oxygen, or the falls which we made in the water in Wales. When I press my thigh a great luminous Mist of White burst out of the spectrum Thigh.[65]

And again he was conjuring Sara Hutchinson's image out of the shadows of the night. 'As I have been falling to sleep, the thought of you has come upon me strongly, that I have opened my eyes as if to look at you.'[66]

As for Mrs Coleridge, he occasionally wrote to her from London ; more than she to him, it seems. He gave her advice about her rheumatism : 'I hope to God, you will make yourself flannel Drawers . . . & that you have already begun to take the Mustard pills'; he chides her angrily for her silence, and writes again to apologize: 'You did very wrong in not writing to me – and I did very wrong in writing to you so angrily.' But he also wrote with gentle affection and hope, particularly during a brief period of wellbeing in mid-November:

I attribute my amendment to the more tranquil State of my mind – & to the chearfulness inspired by the thought of speedily returning to you in love & peace – I am sure, I drive away from me every thought but those of Hope & the tenderest yearnings after you – And it is my frequent prayer, & my almost perpetual aspirations, that we may meet to part no more – & live together as affectionate Husband & Wife ought to do.[67]

He even had new plans for a removal abroad, 'What do you say to a two years' residence at Montpellier – under blue skies & in a rainless air?' And he actually made attempts to amuse her, yet in doing so betrays a pathetic lack of tact. This is how he describes his life in London in a letter to her on 24 February:

On Sunday I dined at Sir William Rush's and on Monday likewise – & went with them to Mrs Billington's Benefit – 'Twas the Beggar's Opera – it was *perfection*! – I seem to have acquired a new sense by hearing her! – I wished you to have been there – / . I assure you, I am quite a man of *fashion* – so many titled acquaintances – & handsome Carriages stopping at my door – & fine *Cards* – and then I am such an exquisite Judge of Music, & Painting – & pass criticisms on furniture & chandeliers – & pay such very handsome Compliments to all Women of Fashion / that I do verily believe, that if I were to stay 3 months in town & have tolerable health & spirits, I should be a Thing in Vogue – the very *ton*ish Poet & Jemmy Jessamy fine Talker in Town / If you were only to see the tender Smiles that I occasionally receive from the Honorable Mrs Damer – you would scratch her eyes out for Jealousy / And then there's the *sweet* (N.B. musky) Lady Charlotte – nay, but I won't tell you her name / you might take it into your head to write an Anonymous Letter to her, & disturb our little innocent amour.[68]

To 'Sally Pally' (as he liked to call his wife in his lighter moments), struggling on desperately in the great damp house at Keswick, with nothing to console her but 'flannel Drawers' and 'Mustard Pills' the letter must have seemed flippant and provoking in the extreme. Yet the pity of it was that Coleridge was almost certainly trying to cheer his much neglected wife. And well might he have tried, for in the same letter, carefully wrapped up in another explanation of the 'Montpellier' scheme, and Wordsworth's anticipated marriage with Mary Hutchinson, he talks of his plan to visit Sara Hutchinson and bring her to Grasmere :

About July we shall all set sail from Liverpool to Bordeaux &c – / Wordsworth has not yet settled, whether he shall be married at Gallow Hill, or at Grasmere – only they will of course make a point that either Sara shall be with Mary, or Mary with Sara*h* / previous to so long a parting. If it be decided, that Sarah is to come to Grasmere, I shall return by York, which will be but a few miles out of the way, & bring her / .[69]

But the urgent arrangements, with the exception of the determination to return home via Sara Hutchinson's, existed purely in Coleridge's head. The Wordsworths professed complete bewilderment, and subsequent events at Greta Hall leave us in little doubt about Mrs Coleridge seeing through the flimsy camouflage.

Eventually, in early March, Coleridge travelled northwards to carry out his plan. He arrived at Gallow Hill on 2 March and stayed until the 13th. Whatever passed during that time, whatever the warmth and consolation of nights spent 'by the low decaying' fire with Sara's eyelash playing on his cheek (see *A Day-dream*), we know that the 'trance-like Depth' of his happiness was brief. At the end of his visit he 'wept aloud' and the next day set off for Keswick in a 'violent storm of snow and wind'. [70]

And on his return home the domestic strife was renewed as never before.

Scarce a day passed without such a scene of discord between me &
Mrs Coleridge, as quite incapacitated me for any worthy exertion
of my faculties by degrading me in my own estimation ... ;[71] Ill
tempered Speeches sent after me when I went out of the House, ill-
tempered Speeches on my return, my friends received with freezing
looks, the least opposition or contradiction occasioning screams of
passion, & the sentiments, which I held most base, ostentatiously
avowed – all this added to the utter negation of all, which a Husband
expects from a Wife – especially, living in retirement – & the consciousness, that I was myself growing a worse man.[72]

One can think of many obvious reasons for this renewal
of hostilities. Foremost among them no doubt was the
jealousy and suspicion occasioned by Coleridge's visit to
Sara on his way home, and the impression that he was putting the Wordsworths and the Hutchinsons before his own
family. Little wonder that his friends were greeted 'with
freezing looks'. Yet Coleridge's implication that he was a
tragic Lear, persecuted by a screeching Goneril was hardly
just. Both were victims of this impossible marriage. Coleridge would have made a difficult husband for any woman : as
Lamb once said, Coleridge should never have been married –
he was more suited to 'diocesan care' than 'parish duty'.
Whereas Sara was a proud and simple woman with narrow
aspirations and restricted talents, incapable of separating the
rare consolations from the manifold disadvantages of
having a genius for a husband. There had been a constant
accumulation of debts and domestic anxieties arising from
her husband's illnesses from the time that they were first
married. There were frequent absences, during which he
was desperately striving to redeem his fortunes ; but it must
have seemed to Sara that he was having rather a good time
of it, hobnobbing with the wealthy and famous, and no
doubt spending money like water, while she bore the burden
of responsibility for the home and the children. One cannot help wondering what it must have been like for Mrs Coleridge, 'Minnow amongst the Tritons', in that impressive

circle of her husband's friends and acquaintances; what feelings of humiliation she must have borne in her own house. We know for a certainty that Dorothy Wordsworth shared Coleridge's view that his wife's mind was 'light' and 'silly'; one wonders what attitudes of patronizing pity Mrs Coleridge may have read in their eyes.

At the same time Coleridge despised her 'external manners & looks & language', her 'inveterate habits of puny thwarting & unintermitting Dyspathy' which he did not hesitate to correct in the presence of others, no doubt in that tone of 'impetous and bitter censure' which provoked even more strident outbursts of anger. Yet the hopeless situation of their 'two unequal Minds', their 'two discordant Wills' is poignantly emphasized on those occasions when they tried to view their situation objectively and dis-passionately, and analyse the root cause of their grievances, not unmixed with an acknowledgement of the other's worth. As Sara once remarked to Southey, her husband was a 'good man' save for his 'prejudices and prepossessions'. 'I should be a very, very happy woman,' she admitted, 'if it were not for a few things – and my husband's ill-health stands at the head of these evils!'[73] On the other hand, Coleridge's verdict tells us much – not only about the force and self-righteousness of his 'bitter censure', but the hope-lessness of raising his wife's standards to his own:

Mrs Coleridge's mind has very little that is *bad* in it – it is an innocent mind – ; but it is light and *unimpressible*, warm in anger, cold in sympathy – and in all disputes uniformly *projects* itself *forth* to recriminate, instead of turning itself inward with a silent Self-question-ing. Our virtues & our vices are exact antitheses – I so attentively watch my own Nature, that my worst Self-delusion is, a compleat Self-knowledge, so mixed with intellectual complacency, that my quickness to see & readiness to acknowlege my faults is too often frustrated by the small pain, which the sight of them gives me, & the consequent slowness to amend them. Mrs C. is so stung by the very first thought of being in the wrong that she never amends because she never endures to look at her own mind at all, in it's faulty parts – but shelters herself from painful Self-enquiry by angry Recrimination. Alas! I have suffered more, I think, from the amiable propensities of my nature than from my worst faults & most erroneous Habits – and I have suffered much from both.[74]

The misery that Coleridge suffered in consequence of these scenes was appalling : 'I can say with strict truth', he told Tom Wedgwood, 'that the happiest half-hours, I have had, were when all of a sudden, as I have been sitting alone in my study, I have burst into tears.'[75] Elsewhere, in his notebooks, he talks of the 'constant dread' in his mind respecting 'Mrs Coleridge's temper',[76] a phenomenon well testified by her younger sister, Martha, who once remarked :

Coleridge would never be able to live with her [Sara] ... for she had the most horrible temper she had ever known or heard of: that she was both irascible and implacable, and when they were girls at a boarding-school they were glad to go back to school, for her temper made the house so uncomfortable to them.[77]

Yet the most ominous note of despair lay in his repeated conviction that these 'private afflictions' led to the consciousness 'that I was myself growing a worse man', and that these scenes 'rendered any subject to me, immediately connected with feeling, a source of pain & disquiet'.[78] The clear implication was that domestic discord was not only destroying the poet in him, but dragging him down to hell. The stern allegation against Mrs Coleridge, however indirect, is hard to accept. And even if it were true, at least to the extent of Dorothy Wordsworth's verdict, 'her radical fault is want of sensibility and what can such a woman be to Coleridge', the remedy lay easily to hand : he could always leave as he had left before. Yet matters were more complex than this : and we must turn to a verse letter to Sara Hutchinson, or *Asra*, that Coleridge wrote at this time, to understand his state of mind more fully.

The circumstances which led to the writing of *A Letter to*

[*Asra*] shed an interesting light on the poem itself. Before he left London for Gallow Hill Coleridge had recorded in his notebook several ideas for love poems. There were plans to write 'a *series*' with a 'large interfusion of moral Sentiment & calm Imagery on love in all moods of the mind'.[79] The ambitiousness of the '*series*' would never be realized ; but he went on to outline a more modest work :

A lively picture of a man, disappointed in marriage, & endeavouring to make a compensation to himself by virtuous & tender & brotherly friendship with an amicable woman – the obstacles – the jealousies – the impossibility of it. – Best advice that he should as much as possible withdraw himself from the pursuits of morals &c – & devote himself to abstract sciences.

Shortly after he returned from Sara Hutchinson's to the scenes of strife at home, he walked over to the Wordsworths one afternoon in the wind and rain. Dorothy records on 19 March : ' . . . Coleridge came in – his eyes were a little swollen with the wind. I was much affected with the sight of him he seem'd half stupified.' After talking with the Wordsworths in the evening, Coleridge went to bed and the others stayed up until four in the morning : 'my spirits were agitated very much,' says Dorothy. There can be little doubt that they discussed the sad alteration in their friend, the alteration that Wordsworth was to portray in his *Castle of Indolence* in May :

Ah! piteous sight it was to see this Man
When he came back to us, a withered flower,
Or like a sinful creature, pale and wan.
Down would he sit : and without strength or power
Look at the common grass from hour to hour.

Coleridge's gloomy plight must have found an echo in Wordsworth's mood at this time, for he too had suffered much from illness during the past three years, and as early as the Goslar days, had told Coleridge how much his sufferings had hampered his writings.[80] In spite of the fact that he was about to embark on a period of unparalleled lyricism the late days of March found Wordsworth in a mood of deep despondency.

During the following week, on 27 March, Dorothy says that William wrote part of an ode, and a week later she herself read this latest effusion to Coleridge while on a visit to Greta Hall. It was the first four stanzas of the *Immortality Ode*. The poem as we now know it, of course, describes the poet's dejection and sense of loss followed by a reaffirmation of faith in Nature and his visionary powers. But on 4 April it ended —

> — But there's a Tree, of many, one,
> A single Field which I have looked upon,
> Both of them speak of something that is gone:
>   The Pansy at my feet
>   Doth the same tale repeat:
> Whither is fled the visionary gleam?
> Where is it now, the glory and the dream?

That Coleridge had long felt a sense of lost vision and that Wordsworth had sympathized and fully shared with his dejection is borne out by the close resemblance of the *Immortality Ode*, to a poem Coleridge had published in the *Morning Post* in October 1800, entitled *The Mad Monk*, the second stanza of which contains the following lines:

> There was a time when earth, and sea, and skies,
> The bright green vale, and forest's dark recess,
> With all things, lay before mine eyes
>   In steady loveliness:
> But now I feel, on earth's uneasy scene,
>   Such sorrows as will never cease; —
>   I only ask for peace;
> If I must live to know that such a time has been!

It was probably on Sunday 4 April, the day when Dorothy had read William's stanzas, that Coleridge sat down in the evening to write a letter in verse to Sara Hutchinson. And

as he sat at his desk beside 'the dull sobbing Draft' of his
Eolian lute, looking out at a 'New Moon, winter-bright!'
the lines of Wordsworth's ode were fresh in his mind, and
before him was a letter which Sara had recently sent him in
reply to a 'complaining Scroll' of his own. Coleridge writes :

> I read thy guileless letter o'er again –
> I hear thee of thy blameless Self complain –
> And only this I learn – & this, alas! I know –
> That thou art weak & pale with Sickness, Grief, & Pain –
> And *I – I* made thee so.

There is little doubt too that he was turning over in his
mind the plan for that 'lively picture of a man disappointed
in marriage'. Thus, taking his cue from Wordsworth, the
letter became a description of his own loss of visionary
power, an *apologia* in reply to Sara's last letter, and a profession of his love against the background of domestic
unhappiness. But it also marked the culmination of a host of
afflictions that stretched back over two years. There is no
need to rehearse the dreary record of long and painful
illnesses, the opium addiction, the insomnia and nightmares ; the conviction that his creative powers were failing ;
the domestic discord and financial anxieties ; the consciousness that his closest friends, the Wordsworths and the
Hutchinsons, were gathering together in a circle of harmony
and love from which he, Coleridge, was excluded by his
coarsening emotions and infectious misery. The importance
of the verse letter to the biographer is the light it sheds on
Coleridge's view of his unhappiness at this time, the extent
to which he had come to terms with it, and the important
role that Sara Hutchinson was now playing in his life.

Halfway through this deeply personal, self-revealing
poem, Coleridge listens to the wind outside, 'Which long
has rav'd unnotic'd', and asks himself what the wind is
saying. At length he hazards :

'Tis of a little Child
Upon a healthy Wild,
Not far from home – but it has lost it's way –
And now moans low in utter grief & fear –
And now screams loud, & hopes to make it's Mother hear!

He is consciously referring to Wordsworth's *Lucy Gray*, and yet one is reminded of that childhood story in which he himself lay out the whole of one night, contemplating how miserable his mother must be, yet crying out unheard ; it is the theme too of several harrowing dreams in the following years – of a child lying on a plain of rubble calling out helplessly. And there is a strong sense in which the verse letter is itself, not only a cry for help from Sara, who is described as 'the conjugal & mother Dove', but an attempt, however unconsciously, to impose the depth of his own misery upon her.

At the outset he describes a state of mind and feeling which has by now become all too familiar : he is like Milton's Samson, not without the implication that he has lost his powers through a woman's treachery :

A Grief without a pang, void, dark, & drear,
A stifling, drowsy, unimpassion'd Grief,
That finds no natural Outlet, no Relief
In word, or sigh, or tear –

Adopting his habitual distinction between head and heart, he can say of the beautiful evening landscape and skyscape

– I see them all, so excellently fair!
– I see, not feel, how beautiful they are.

Here the new emphasis on conscious, purposive, self-active thought, which had been the matter of his philosophical contemplation in the year before finds its expression in the poignant assertion, 'I may not hope from outward Forms to win / The Passion & the Life whose Fountains are within !' It was the complete reversal of his early vision in the days of Priestley's and Hartley's influence – of man shaped by his circumstances, and more particularly of the confidence he had expressed in the beneficence of Nature in the Clevedon days : 'The pleasures, which we receive from rural beauties, are of little consequence compared with the moral effect of these pleasures – the best possible we at last become ourselves the best possible.'[81] Yet even more, it marked a definite breaking of a poetic spell – the delicate interpenetration achieved between man and nature in his finest poetry during 1797–8. It was not simply that he had reversed the substance of his earlier philosophical convictions, such as we find in *The Eolian Harp*, but that he had returned to that earlier manner of statement, rather than losing himself totally in exemplification ; there is again a distinction between the inner and outer man, where he had once achieved reconciliation :

> I may not hope from outward Forms to win
> The Passion & the Life, whose fountains are within!
> These lifeless Shapes, around, below, above,
>   O what can they impart?

At this point he addresses Sara, to tell her that even the thought that she too is gazing on the same 'Heaven' only feebly stirs his heart. Even this sweet thought, of a 'Maiden's quiet Eyes/Uprais'd, and linking on sweet Dreams by dim Connections/To Moon, or Evening Star, or glorious western Skies – ', does not move him. Yet while he seems incapable of feeling the outward-going joy of love, the thought of himself as love's recipient lightens the weight of despair :

> I feel my spirit moved –
> And wheresoe'er thou be,
> O Sister! O Beloved!
> Those dear mild Eyes, that see
> Even now the Heaven, *I* see –
> There is a Prayer in them! It is for *me*
> And I, dear Sara – *I* am blessing *thee*!

The nature of Coleridge's passive, childlike role as one beloved of Sara finds its clearest expression as he recollects an evening spent with Sara and her sister Mary, Wordsworth's fiancée:

> O that affectionate & blameless Maid,
> Dear Mary! on her Lap my head she lay'd –
>   Her Hand was on my Brow,
>   Even as my own is now;
> And on my Cheek I felt thy eye-lash play.
> Such Joy I had, that I may truly say,
> My Spirit was awe-stricken with the Excess
> And trance-like Depth of its brief Happiness.

It is the passive love of domestic, mothered affection. But more than this, it is the love that Wordsworth would inherit on marrying Mary and taking Sara too into his home.

> When thou, & with thee those, whom thou lov'st best,
> Shall dwell together in one happy Home,
> One House, the dear *abiding* Home of all . . .

Yet what part would Coleridge inherit in this loving circle? Already in reply to his 'complaining scroll' Sara had proved the degeneration of his 'better mind', his blighting influence as he sent 'from far both Pain & Sorrow thither'. And the anticipated rejection from the loving circle at Grasmere seems to give rise to a series of self-pitying fantasies – the unwanted child, the leper in exile, the deprived and rejected orphan, the unrequited lover whose love is such that he will sacrifice all self-interest to preserve the happiness of his love object. But the implicit recrimination that is involved is inescapable, for the dramatic expression of his disinterestedness calls attention to itself, cries out for pity.

> Nor shall this Heart in idle Wishes roam
>   Morbidly soft!
> No! let me trust, that I shall wear away
> In no inglorious Toils the manly Day,

> And only now & then, & not too oft,
> Some dear & memorable Eve will bless
> Dreaming of all your Loves & Quietness.

It is a state of mind that approximates closely to the Life-in-Death fantasy of the voluntary exile or the fantasy suicide – the wish that others will feel all the sorrow and remorse of having allowed him to come to this pass, while he is somehow still present to observe them doing it, and yet anticipating their possible accusation of self-pity by assuring them in advance that they are not to mourn his absence.

> Be happy, & I need thee not in sight.
> Peace in thy Heart, & Quiet in thy Dwelling,
> Health in thy Limbs, & in thine Eyes the Light
> Of Love, & Hope, & honorable Feeling –
> Where e'er I am, I shall be well content!
> Not near thee, haply shall be more content!

At the same time, 'if thou pin'd,/Whate'er the Cause, in body or in mind,/I were the miserablest Man alive/To know it & be absent!' In the meantime, however, while he suffers from insomnia – his beloved must enjoy 'her gentle Sleep!' 'Cover her, gentle Sleep! with wings of Healing' – he asks, for he longs to hear that she is well and happy again, it is this alone indeed which can bring a glimmer of happiness to the dispossessed child, more sinned against than sinning:

> For, oh! beloved Friend!
> I am not the buoyant Thing, I was of yore –
> When I like an own Child, I to JOY belong'd;
> For others mourning oft, myself oft sorely wrong'd,
> Yet bearing all things then, as if I nothing bore!

No longer can he endure misfortunes as in the past when 'Hope grew round me like the climbing Vine'. 'Ill Tidings' of his loved one, in fact, threaten to weigh him down with such misery that –

> ... oh! each Visitation
> Suspends what Nature gave me at my Birth,
> My Shaping Spirit of Imagination!

The train of thought is at this point fast degenerating, as he appeals for yet more pity while recoiling from the implied accusations of rejection, or pleas for sympathy. Thus, while he can talk of his 'shaping Spirit of Imagination' given him at birth, he can talk of 'Leaves & Fruitage, not my own seem'd mine!' While Sara is to know that her 'Ill Tidings' suspend his inspiration, she must understand that the original destruction of his powers originates from domestic unhappiness, 'those habitual Ills' —

> That wear out Life, when two unequal Minds
> Meet in one House, & two dicordant Wills.

Yet having made this assertion he then doubles back to insist that his real complaint is not so much that news of Sara's sickness (which he admits is due to his own complaining) destroys his shaping Spirit, but that his 'coarse domestic Life' has robbed him of the 'heart-nursing Sympathy' that would enable him to mourn with her:

> No Griefs, but such as dull and deaden me,
> No mutual mild Enjoyments of it's own,
> No Hopes of it's own Vintage, None, O! none.

Had he already forgotten the affection of the Hutchinson sisters, 'the fair Remembrances, that so revive/The Heart, & fill it with a living Power,'? Could he expect no concern and sympathy from Dorothy and William? He has not so much forgotten them, as anticipated the 'trance-like Depth of it's brief Happiness', and committed a spiritual suicide in advance, while of course withdrawing the implication that his friends are in the least to blame by laying the responsibility at Mrs Coleridge's feet, in the past.

> For not to think of what I needs must feel,
> But to be still & patient all I can:

And haply by abstruse Research to steal
From my own Nature all the Natural Man –
This was my sole Resource, my wisest plan !
And that, which suits a part, infects the whole,
And now is almost grown the Temper of my Soul.

Here is the self-imposed Life-in-Death, uttered not only as a *fait accompli*, but by the subtle qualifications 'haply' and 'now is almost grown', with swift alterations in tense and mood, as an encroaching decision, or threat. Did Coleridge really believe that he was alleviating Sara Hutchinson's sorrow ? How was she supposed to react, other than with renewed and helpless suffering on his behalf ? And had he really come to believe that his 'coarse domestic Life' lay at the root of his recourse to 'abstruse Research' ? That Mrs Coleridge's behaviour lay at the root of all his problems, including his failure as a poet ?

In that notebook entry earlier in the year, when he had planned the 'picture of a man, disappointed in marriage', the 'abstruse Research' was to have played a rather different role ; for the advice that he should 'devote himself to abstract sciences' was seen not merely as an antidote to domestic suffering, but as a mode of palliating his frustrated love for the 'amicable' other woman. Here in the *Letter to* [*Asra*] it is clearly used as a weapon of spiritual self-destruction, to inflict suffering on that 'amicable woman', and at the same time as evidence of Mrs Coleridge's murder of his soul. Thus one finds no simple and sharp delineation of love for Sara, condemnation of Mrs Coleridge, but Sara herself is both the object of love and punishment : she too must share his love song with her 'breast against a Thorn'.

The story of Coleridge's retreat from poetry to metaphysics has been long and involved. Yet a brief recapitulation of that process is necessary at this point to get this latest instance of Coleridge's self-analysis into perspective.

We have seen how he neglected the serious pursuit of poetry for two years, while in Germany and London. In 1799, no doubt under the sense of obligation to the Wedgwoods, he had declared his intention of spending the main portion of his life in the writing of a great single work, clearly philosophical in nature. There was no hint at that time that he begrudged the Wedgwoods this fatal change of course in his energies. On the other hand there was the growing consciousness that erudition and neglect were impairing his creative powers, and even the occasional assertion that home-sickness for his wife and children was playing a part too. Yet in spite of the dangers that the neglect of his craft must pose to a young poet already at the height of his powers, he allowed those two years to pass apparently without realizing the effect of his neglect. By the time he settled in Keswick in 1800 he announced that it was Wordsworth who had made him realize that he was no poet, then, gradually, he put it about that his metaphysical researches (first proposed as a voluntary change of direction, then pursued with all the vigour of a man shedding light on important discoveries) were now no more than an antidote for pain. Throughout the year, from the summer of 1800 to the summer of 1801 his main enemy was sickness, and it was exacerbated by the onset of opium addiction with all its train of mental and physical affliction. There is little in the way of complaint against Mrs Coleridge at this time, except the comments in Latin to Southey, that he had been 'almost' miserable when they were first married, but that he had grown to accept her lack of sympathy with his illness. In fact, domestic distress only begins to loom ominously after his summer holiday with the Hutchinsons, quickly checked by his departure for London, and only to be sharply renewed after his visit to Sara Hutchinson on his way back in March of 1802.

The rationalization that this long process of decline in feeling found its origin in Mrs Coleridge's behaviour

12

towards him is clearly unacceptable. In any case, Coleridge's sense of survival, his 'sheet anchor' in life, existed not so much in his poetry as in his relationships, each successive friendship or network of friendships taking on the significance of a home rediscovered: from the Evans family to Southey, from Southey to Poole, from Poole to Wordsworth. Indeed his true sense of home now existed in the expanding Wordsworth circle in which he saw himself and Sara Hutchinson partaking as spiritual partners (how curious it is that Coleridge seemed to attach himself to the sister, or fiancée's sister of his closest friends!) And the one person who threatened his place in this 'dear *abiding* Home of All' was, of course, his wife, who greeted his friends 'with freezing looks' and constantly reminded him of his duties to his own home. It would not be overstating the case to suggest that what mattered most to Coleridge at this time was his membership of that extraordinary, intimate circle, and in threatening his continued place in it Mrs Coleridge was repeating the story of his childhood. Understandably he had grown to associate his long train of problems with this one threat to his survival. Yet even though his analysis was hardly accurate, even though he had eminently failed to come to terms with his real problems, the 'Grief' which hitherto had no 'natural Outlet, no Relief' had now found a 'timely utterance'.

The desperation of his plight, as he saw it and felt it, is seen with its fullest force in a notebook entry in the following year when he ponders the thought of Mrs Coleridge's death with the following reflection:

There is one thing wholly out of my Power. I cannot look forward even with the faintest pleasure of Hope, to the Death of any human Being, tho' it were, as it seems to be, the only condition of the greatest imaginable Happiness to me, and the emancipation of all my noblest faculties that must remain fettered during that Being's Life. – I dare not, for I can not: I cannot, for I dare not. The very effort to look onward to it with a stedfast wish would be a suicide, far beyond what the dagger or pistol could realize – absolutely suicide, coelicide, not mere viticide.[82]

It was not Mrs Coleridge's temper, her behaviour, her actions – effects he could counteract by absenting himself, it was her very *existence* that fettered him. It was an ominous fixation, and one that was taking a firm hold ; a rationalization that explained away all his difficulties while allowing him to do nothing about them. But what complexities lay beneath the surface? Following the above reflection is a further comment clearly addressed to Sara Hutchinson :[83]

But if I could secure you full Independence, if I could give too all my original Self healed & renovated from all infirm Habits; & if by all forms in my power I could bind myself more effectively even in relation to Law, than the Form out of my power would effect – then, *then*, would you be the remover of my Loneliness, my perpetual Companion?

The entry expresses the agony of mind Coleridge suffered in 1802, and which would remain with him for some years to come. In the first place it explains why Coleridge's departure from Keswick was no simple solution. The fact that Mrs Coleridge was a barrier to his 'greatest imaginable happiness' in Keswick was, of course, because of the 'obstacles – the jealousies – the impossibility of it', as he had noted in the year before. And yet to have left Keswick would have meant a withdrawal from the Grasmere circle to which Sara would now belong. Either way, whether he stayed or left, Mrs Coleridge stood in his way. Her death was quite literally the 'only condition of the greatest imaginable happiness', and as much as he may have buried the idea there was a potential source of guilt that could return to plague him. It is with similar thoughts that he turns to his children towards the close of the letter :

My little Children are a Joy, a Love,
A good Gift from above!

> But what is Bliss, that still calls up a Woe,
>   And makes it doubly keen
> Compelling me to *feel*, as well as KNOW,
> What a most blessed Lot mine might have been.

Better, perhaps, they might never have been born – he suggests, and yet that same ambiguity is implicit : better, for they goad him again to feel with head and heart? Better, because they anchor him to Mrs Coleridge and Keswick? Or, better because their very existence is a barrier to the consumation of his love for Sara Hutchinson?

> There have been hours, when feeling how they bind
> And pluck out the Wing-feathers of my Mind,
> Turning my Error to Necessity,
> I have half-wished, they never had been born!

The note of implied guilt at the thought of wishing his children dead, and surely the powerful subconscious guilt at wishing for his wife's extinction too, takes us back to that original childhood story with which we began the tale of Coleridge's life, and which serves as such an apt parallel with what is happening in the *Asra* letter. The reason that Coleridge ran away from home was that, in his child's mind at least, he had attempted to murder his brother, the brother who had challenged his position as favourite in the family circle, who threatened to oust him from the centre of his parents' affections. In harbouring murderous thoughts against his brother he had naturally acquired deep feelings of guilt and the consequent fear that his mother would punish and reject him. Thus when he lay by the river during the night and thought how miserable his mother must be he was punishing her in anticipation for her rejection of him. And yet, no doubt, he hoped that she would understand that his running away was wholly the fault of his brother Frank who had brought him to this pass. It is precisely this ambivalent sense of love and hatred for Sara, as he yearns for her with all the strength of self-survival, and yet punishes her in anticipation of her rejection of him – a fear that naturally arose from a sense of guilt for his murderous feelings for his wife and children – that one senses in the *Asra* letter. The strong current of imagery associated with infection and disease, so rightly noticed by David Pirie in his recent study of the verse letter,[84] can be clearly associated with his demoralizing illnesses, but it is also consonant with the depressive content of so many of Coleridge's dreams in the following year, a species of dream symbolism which Freud has connected with guilt.

It is in this light that the closing stanzas of the letter make abundant sense, where he addresses himself almost blindly and as by instinct to religious perfection, as if his bewilderment, his sense of guilt and sin that lies beyond conscious understanding is leading him away from that former trust and optimism not only in his own natural powers but in the beneficence of Nature. It is the agonizing sense of guilt, unworthiness and insecurity that explains the shift in emphasis of Coleridge's religious beliefs in the months that lay ahead as he moved inexorably towards an acknowledgement of Original Sin and the Atonement of the Crucifixion, as he lost the artist's urge to perfect the objective and externalized manifestations of his inner tensions and preoccupations, and turned inwards to secure the redemption and salvation of his soul. For 'from the Soul itself must issue forth/A Light, a Glory, and a luminous Cloud/Enveloping the Earth!'

> O pure of Heart! thou need'st not ask of me
> What this strong music in the Soul may be,
>   What, & wherein it doth exist,
> This Light, this Glory, this fair luminous Mist,
> This beautiful & beauty-making Power!
> JOY, innocent Sara! Joy, that ne'er was given
> Save to the Pure, & in their purest Hour,
> JOY, Sara! is the Spirit & the Power,

That wedding Nature to us gives in Dower
A new Earth & new Heaven
Undreamt of by the Sensual & the Proud!
Joy is that strong Voice, Joy that luminous Cloud –
We, we ourselves rejoice!
And thence flows all that charms or ear or sight,
All melodies the Echoes of that Voice,
All Colors a Suffusion of that Light.[85]

No longer could he look on Nature, and say as in *Frost at Midnight*, 'Great universal Teacher! he shall mould/Thy spirit, and by giving make it ask ...' The source of Life and Joy goes out from within, 'O Sara! we receive but what we give,/And in *our* Life alone does Nature live.' Thus the impotence of his active, outward going love in the early stages of the letter; his helpless inability to be anything but a passive recipient of affection and joy, unites with his disillusionment in the role of Nature's active beneficence on the passive soul, and he finds new hope and strength in the self-giving inward dwelling power of moral strength.

A Letter to [Asra] went through a number of drafts throughout the year until it was finally published on 4 October in the *Morning Post*, Wordsworth's wedding day, and the anniversary of his own marriage, as *Dejection: an Ode*. The passages of self-immolating self-pity have been pared away, so too has the implied indictment against his wife and the dark thoughts about his children; so far as Sara Hutchinson is concerned it is a poem that would have given consolation rather than pain. There is a pervasive strength, yet that strength had only been won by gradual stages in the verse letter. The *Dejection Ode* is commonly accepted to be Coleridge's last great poem; and yet, *A Letter to [Asra]* – in so far as it tells us so much more about the agony of Coleridge's inner torments and weaknesses, in so far as it portrays a growing strength which heralded the end of his life as a poet – is at once a more human and poignant poem.

'. . . a little theological'

IN October of 1802 Southey wrote to John Rickman: 'I am the only man among his acquaintance to whom Coleridge does not complain of his wife – and I think that implies some merit on my part.' Strange merit even had it been true: which, in fact, it was not. Coleridge frequently complained of Mrs Coleridge to Southey, and Southey seldom hesitated in offering his diagnosis of the marital ills at Greta Hall. 'It is all from his want of *calculation*,' he liked to point out, 'from that constant sacrifice to present impulse which marks his character and blasts the brightest talents that I have ever witnessed.'[1] All the same, some time early in the summer Coleridge seems to have capitalized on that 'sacrifice to present impulse' as far as his domestic troubles were concerned, and Southey – ever agog at Coleridge's marital saga – could comment from Bristol on 5 May, 'We hear nothing of separation, tho he has unwisely made it the gossip of all his acquaintance here.' Whether he had seriously intended leaving or not, the fact was that Coleridge had imparted the prospect of this 'very aweful step' to Mrs Coleridge herself, which seems to have brought about an immediate and happy 'Revolution' at Greta Hall. Although the precariousness of the new reign can be judged from Coleridge's extraordinary account of it to Southey in July:

It did alarm Mrs Coleridge – the thought of separation wounded her Pride – she was fully persuaded, that deprived of the Society of my children & living abroad without any friends, I should pine away – & the fears of widowhood came upon her. And tho' these feelings were wholly selfish, yet they made her *serious* – and that was a great point gained – . . . and for the first time since our marriage she felt and acted, as beseemed a Wife & a Mother to a Husband, & the Father of her children – She promised to set about an alteration in her external manners & looks & language, & to fight against her inveterate habits of puny Thwarting & unintermitting Dyspathy – this immediately – and to do her best endeavors to cherish other *feelings*. I on my part promised to be more attentive to all her feelings of Pride, &c&c and to try to correct my habits of impetuous & bitter censure – . We have both kept our Promises – & she had found herself so much more happy, than she had been for years before, that I have most confident Hopes, that this happy Revolution in our domestic affairs will be permanent, & that this external conformity will gradually generate a greater inward Likeness of thoughts, & attachments, than has hitherto existed between us.[2]

And well might there be a reconciliation between the Coleridges at this time, for during the very week that Southey observed that the separation was slow in coming, Coleridge reported to his friend William Sotheby, 'Mrs Coleridge is indisposed, & I have too much reason to suspect that she is breeding again'. It was, as he added with tight-lipped understatement, 'an event which was to have been deprecated'.

The domestic peace seems to have continued for many months, Mrs Coleridge receiving fresh stimulus to keep to her resolution in the middle of the summer, according to Coleridge, by the sudden expectation of his death after a violent quarrel. 'She threw herself upon me & made a solemn promise of amendment – & she has kept her promise beyond any hope.'

How much this alteration in their affairs was in fact due to Sara's pregnancy, how much to the fact that Coleridge had released his most agonizing tensions in the timely utterance of the Asra letter, one cannot say, but it seems certain that the loyalty and sympathy of the Wordsworths, who unlike Southey were only too willing to accept Coleridge's account of things did much to sustain him during the weeks of inner torment that spring. At the same time Dorothy Wordsworth would have been extremely sceptical of Coleridge's claim that his wife had become more serious. At the very height of Coleridge's new contentment she wrote, 'Mrs Coleridge is a most extraordinary character – she is the lightest weakest silliest woman!' Ironically enough Dorothy's outburst was occasioned by an instance of the very efforts Mrs Coleridge was making to be a better wife : it was at a period too when there was actually talk of the Wordsworths moving over to Keswick after the marriage with Mary Hutchinson :

She sent some clean clothes on Thursday to meet C. (the first time she ever did such a thing in her life) from which I guess she is determined to be attentive to him – she wrote a note, saying not a word about my letter, and all in her very lightest style – that she was sorry the Wilkinsons were from home etc etc . . . she concludes 'my love to the Ws – ' Is not it a hopeless case ? So insensible and so irritable she never can come to good and poor C. ! but I said I would not enter on this subject and I will not.[3]

Whatever the effectiveness of Mrs Coleridge's attempts to be 'attentive' it is more than likely that the most dramatic improvement in her behaviour consisted in her indulgence towards Coleridge's relationships over at Grasmere. How much Coleridge needed their comfort and understanding can be seen from the poignant notebook entries during this time : 'A poem on the endeavour to emancipate the soul from day-dreams & note the diffcrent attempts & the vain ones.' Only to be followed by the sweetest of all day-dreams, 'Poem on this night on Helvellin / William & Dorothy & Mary / Sara & I'. Was it the vision of living togcther with those loved ones in a mountain fastness of his dreams ?[4] And then, 'Poem on the length of our acquaintance / all the hours that I have been thinking of her &c.'[5] The Wordsworths bore the full brunt of it.

Towards the end of April Coleridge walked to Grasmere, and a little way before Whythburn on thc Keswick–

Grasmere road stopped to carve his own name and Dorothy's 'over the S.H.' on a piece of sheer rock which he came to call 'Sara's Rock'.[6] That evening he turned up at the Wordsworths, and for the next six weeks he was rarely out of their presence or their thoughts. On the following morning as William and Dorothy sauntered in the garden enjoying the spring sunshine, Coleridge came out to them and revealed the depths of his inner torment, and there can be little doubt that they now understood their own part in his misery. 'Coleridge came up to us,' recorded Dorothy, 'and repeated the verses he wrote to Sara. I was much affected with them, and was on the whole, not being well, in miserable spirits. The sunshine, the green fields, and the fair sky made me sadder.' Coleridge stayed on with them for five days, talking, walking, writing and reading. It was as if they were striving to recapture the old days at Alfoxden ; he spoke of planting Laburnum in the woods and they wandered as they had done so often in the past —

We left William sitting on the stones, feasting with silence ; and C. and I sat down upon a rocky seat — a couch it might be under the Bower of William's eglantine, Andrew's Broom. He was below us, and he came to us, and repeated his poems while we sate beside him on the ground. He had made himself a seat in the crumbling ground.

And when Coleridge returned to Keswick their letters went back and forth daily, one letter of Coleridge's, at least, so disturbing as to keep Wordsworth awake for the whole of one night. There were meetings, too, halfway between Grasmere and Keswick. One such was on 4 May. 'We saw Coleridge on the Wytheburn side of the water,' wrote Dorothy, 'he crossed the Beck to us.' They spent the hot and lazy afternoon wandering in the hills, searching in vain for shade, and at length settled by a moss-covered stone where they lay down and picnicked until sunset. Coleridge and Wordsworth recited poetry to each other, Dorothy 'drank a little Brandy and water, and was in Heaven'. They parted, fittingly, at 'Sara's Rock' where Coleridge had carved that very morning the signatures which completed the 'dear Abiding' circle. To those of Sara, Dorothy and his own, he now added William's, Mary Hutchinson's and John Wordsworth's. Dorothy then set her seal upon this strange triste : 'I kissed them all' ; and William, as if to emphasize S. T. C.'s immovable setting in the constellation, 'deepened the T. with C.'s penknife'.

As Coleridge departed from them, Dorothy and William sat on a wall, watching the sun go down and the reflection on the lake. 'C. looked well', wrote Dorothy, 'and parted from us cheerfully, hopping upon the side stones.'

But there were other days when things did not go so well ; days of 'bad news of Coleridge', melancholy letters which sent Dorothy hastening over to Keswick. Or days like those at the end of May. Coleridge sends a letter to Grasmere. They are not to go to Keswick, they are to meet him at 'Sara's Rock'. And there they find him on 22 May. 'He was sitting under Sara's rock when we reached him. He turned with us. We sate a long time under the wall of a sheep-fold. Had some melancholy talk about his private affairs.' Instead of returning to Keswick he goes on with them to Grasmere. He stays the night, and Dorothy sits with him the whole of the next morning ; William is 'nervous', Dorothy takes laudanum. He stays yet another night and returns home on 24 May only to send a letter to Grasmere the moment he arrives. On 25 May Dorothy writes, 'again no sleep for William'.

Could it ever be the same again? Change, separation, ageing and loss were the very atmosphere of that spring of 1802. It was there in small seemingly insignificant comments : Dorothy on 31 May, for example, 'My tooth broke today. They will soon be gone. Let that pass. I shall be beloved – I want no more.' But it was clearly manifest in Coleridge's *Dejection Ode*, in Wordsworth's gradual shaping of the *Imortality Ode*, *The Castle of Indolence* and the *Leech Gatherer* :

> But, as it sometimes chanceth, from the might
> Of joy in minds that can no further go,
> As high as we have mounted in delight
> In our dejection do we sink as low.

The ominous examples from the past merged with the present: Chatterton, Burns, Collins – now Coleridge. And perhaps Wordsworth himself? Could there be any doubt that he had himself and Coleridge in mind when he wrote :

> My whole life have I lived in pleasant thought,
> As if life's business were a summer mood;
> As if all needful things would come unsought
> To genial faith, still rich in genial good;
> But how can he expect that others should
> Build for him, sow for him, and at his call
> Love him, who for himself will take no heed at all?

Yet Wordsworth continued to explore, continued to feel his way towards new areas of the heart in the only way that he knew – as a poet. It is a token of his versatility and dedication that this period of dejection suggested new outlets of feeling – the discovery of the 'peculiar grace' of human solitude, the unearthly atmosphere of 'visionary dreariness' that was to help him towards new possibilities in a year or two. Even had Coleridge possessed Wordsworth's versatility he had long lost that dedication and concentration, and in any case Wordsworth was about to enter a period of great personal happiness where Coleridge felt that he had every reason to suspect that he was 'A wither'd branch upon a blossoming Tree'.

When the time finally came for William and Dorothy's departure for Gallow Hill and the long absence in London and France, Coleridge seemed to accept it with an air of gloomy fatalism. On 12 July he walked with them six or seven miles of the way. 'He was not well,' wrote Dorothy briefly, 'and we had a melancholy parting after having sate together in silence by the roadside.'

And yet the exhausting business of propping up Coleridge during these months had not been in vain, for after they had gone Coleridge seemed to find life without them not quite so empty as he had feared. In the first place, his children were now of an age when he was beginning to find them companionable; and in spite of those unhappy reflections in April ('I have half-wished, they never had been born!'), he began to find them a source of great joy. It was usually to Sara Hutchinson that he wrote of them.

There is something in children that makes Love flow out upon them, distinct from beauty, & still more distinct from good-behaviour / I cannot say, God knows! that our children are even decently well-behaved – Hartley is no beauty – & yet it has been the Lot of the two children to be beloved. They are the general Darlings of the whole Town : & wherever they go, Love is their natural Heritage.

His favourite was indeed his first-born, Hartley. 'That child is a Poet,' he wrote to Southey, 'spite of the Forehead *"villainous low,"* which his Mother smuggled into his Face.' 'Play fellows are burthensome to him . . .' he wrote to Sara, 'excepting *me* / because I can understand & sympathize with, his wild Fancies – & suggest others of my own.' One cannot help wondering what an exhausting experience it must have been to have Coleridge for a father, particularly during periods of stress. We get a hint of it perhaps at the end of July; when he reports Hartley as crying out – 'Don't ask me so many questions, Papa! I can't bear it.'[7]

But while Coleridge's relationship with his children, particularly Hartley, often seemed intense and demanding, his moments of greatest joy were to watch them running wild and free in the fields outside :

. . . as pretty a sight as a Father's eyes could well see – Hartley & Derwent running in the Green, where the Gusts blow most madly – both with their Hair floating & tossing a miniature of the agitated

Trees below which they were playing/inebriate both with pleasure –
Hartley whirling round for joy – Derwent eddying half willingly,
half by the force of the Gust – driven backward, struggling forward,
& shouting his little hymn of Joy.[8]

And if the emotional void left by the Wordsworths could
never be entirely filled, there was always that well-tried
brother-in-law ready to hand. It is perhaps indicative of
Coleridge's character that no sooner had the Wordsworths
gone than he set about enticing Southey up to the Lakes. It
is equally indicative of Southey's character that he never
failed to take the bait, in spite of his stern verdict on
Coleridge's character. 'I never feel so little satisfied with
myself,' he wrote to John Rickman in the autumn, 'as upon
the recollection that my inclination to like him has always
got the better of a judgment – felt at first sight – and
deliberately and perpetually strengthened by every
experience.'[9]

The whole household could be shuffled, enthused
Coleridge, and there would be ample room for Southey's
family, with space enough for two separate studies, and that
necessary extra bedroom 'as I am so often ill'. The incalculable advantage of their coming, he told Southey,
would be 'the services, & benefits, I should receive from
your society & the spur of your example'.[10] Another unspoken advantage, no doubt, was the fact that they would
share the rent of the house. Just the week before this
pressing invitation we learn that Coleridge had already used
up his Wedgwood allowance for the rest of the year.[11]
Whatever work Coleridge had been engaged on since
leaving London it had had little connexion with remunera-
tion. But what *had* Coleridge been doing since he returned to
Keswick?

Writing to Poole in the first week of May he claims to
have been 'far from idle'. He could send the firm assurance,
in fact, that by the end of the year, 'I shall have disburthened
myself of all my metaphysics, &c.' Moreover, looking

forward to the following year, 'I shall, if I am alive & in possession of my present faculties, devote to a long poem.' Was it a reluctance to admit that Poole had been right about the dangers of his worshipping Wordsworth that prevented him from admitting his deepest fears? Writing to Southey in July, he tells a less optimistic story – and, unlike in the past, his disillusionment is expressed at a time of health and virtual happiness: 'As to myself, all my poetic Genius, if ever I really possessed any *Genius*, & -it was not rather a mere general *aptitude* of Talent, & quickness in Imitation / is gone – and I have been fool enough to suffer deeply in my mind, regretting the loss.'[12]

Yet in sickness or in health Coleridge was seldom, if ever, wholly idle. As he commented to his brother George on 1 July, 'It seems as if there were something originally amiss in the constitution of all our family – if that can be indeed without presumption called "amiss" which may probably be connected intimately with our moral & intellectual characters – but we all, I think, carry much passion, & a deep interest, into the business of Life.'[13] It is reminiscent of that earlier remark made to Josiah Wedgwood in the winter of 1799: 'Life were so flat a thing without Enthusiasm – that if for a moment it leave me, I have a sort of stomach-sensation attached to all my thoughts, like those which succeed to the pleasurable operation of a dose of opium.'

Yet while Coleridge seldom enjoyed, or suffered, periods of inactivity, he seems to have found it necessary to invent work completed which he had barely begun. In spite of assertions that summer that he had finished a translation of Salomon Gessner's poem *Der erste Schiffer* (which William Sotheby, whom he met in Keswick, had placed with him) it is clear that he had not got beyond the first half. As with the Wallenstein he later admitted that it was a task of 'double disgust, moral and poetical'. Sotheby too seemed for a time a likely substitute for the absent Wordsworths, and he accordingly received an invitation to come and live at Greta Hall. He declined the offer, but there was a continued correspondence between them throughout the summer that gives us some indication of Coleridge's intellectual preoccupations.

Later, in the autumn, Coleridge described how he had gone about scrutinizing Sotheby's play, *Orestes*, in order to criticize it : he had looked 'at the building', he told Sotheby, 'with something of the eye of an architect, to turn myself into a *fly*, & creep over it with animalcular feet, & peer microscopically at the sand-grit of its component Stones'.[14] The comment sums up the deep and intense interest Coleridge began to take in the art of criticism and in critical theory in the summer of 1802. And from the very outset it was a direction that took him out from beneath the demoralizing shadow of Wordsworth's superiority. It was 'most certain' he confessed to Sotheby, the day after Wordsworth had left for Gallow Hill, that the Preface to the *Lyrical Ballads* had arisen from their mutual conversations : 'the first passages were indeed partly taken from notes of mine'. It was equally true that he agreed with Wordsworth's abhorrence of 'these poetic Licences, as they are called and indeed tricks of Convenience & Laziness'. 'But', went on Coleridge, '*metre itself* implies a *passion*, i.e. a state of excitement, both in the Poet's mind, & is expected in that of the Reader – and tho' I stated this to Wordsworth, & he has in some sort stated it in his preface, yet he has not done justice to it, nor has he in my opinion sufficiently answered it.'

Not only had Wordsworth failed to admit that 'Poetry justifies, as *Poetry* independent of any other Passion, some new combinations of Language', he had moreover in his practice, 'sinned against' the principle 'that *commands* the omission of many others allowable in other compositions'. On this point, Coleridge added, he and Wordsworth had had 'some little controversy'. In fact, 'we begin to suspect, that there is somewhere or other, a *radical* Difference in our opinions'. Out of this *'radical* Difference' there seemed to arise a new confidence and excitement which finds expression in Coleridge's letters throughout July. It was as if he had found a new release, and stood once more at the threshold of new intellectual adventures. If ever we can recapture an impression of his breathless flow of speech in his correspondence it is surely here in a letter to Southey on 29 July :

Of course, Darwin & Wordsworth having given each a defence of *their* mode of Poetry, & a disquisition on the nature & essence of Poetry in general, I shall necessarily be led rather deeper – and these I shall treat of either first or last/But I will apprize you of one thing, that altho' Wordsworth's Preface is half a child of my own Brain/& arose out of Conversations, so frequent, that with few exceptions we could scarcely either of us perhaps positively say, which first started any particular Thought – I am speaking of the Preface as it stood in the second Volume [edition?] – yet I am far from going all lengths with Wordsworth/He has written lately a number of Poems (32 in all) some of them of considerable Length/(the longest 160 lines) the greater number of these to my feelings very excellent Compositions/ but here & there a daring Humbleness of Language & Versification, and a strict adherence to matter of fact, even to prolixity, that startled me/his alterations likewise in Ruth perplexed me/and I have thought & thought again/& have not had my doubts solved by Wordsworth/ On the contrary, I rather suspect that some where or other there is a radical Difference in our theoretical opinions respecting Poetry – / this I shall endeavor to go to the Bottom of – and acting the arbitrator between the old School & the New School hope to lay down some plain, & perspicuous tho' not superficial, Canons of Criticism respecting Poetry. – What an admirable Definition Milton gives quite in an obiter way – when he says of Poetry that it is *'simple, sensous, passionate.'*! It truly comprizes the whole, that can be said on the subject.[15]

Discussion of 'passion' led him to re-examine Bowles, whom he now found to have 'indeed the *sensibility* of a poet ; but . . . not the *Passion* of a great Poet'. Paradoxically enough, Coleridge linked this failure with a deficiency in

thinking — 'he has no native Passion, because he is not a
Thinker' — which similarly gave rise to yet another con-
fusing term in relation to poetry : 'metaphysics'. How often
had Coleridge claimed that he was too much of a thinking
man to be a poet! That he was a kind metaphysician
rather than a poet. The problem was, as he developed his
critical theory there were not words in the language to
describe exactly what he meant. He was referring, if anything, to the very opposite of his own metaphysicizing when
he explains :

. . . a great Poet must be, implicité if not explicité, a profound Metaphysician. He may not have it in logical coherence, in his Brain &
Tongue; but he must have it by *Tact*/for all sounds, & forms of
human nature he must have the *ear* of a wild Arab listening in the
silent Desart, the eye of a North American Indian tracing the foot-
steps of an Enemy upon the Leaves that strew the Forest — ; the
Touch of a Blind Man feeling the face of a darling Child.[16]

At the same time he goes on to say, 'A poet's *Heart* &
Intellect should be *combined*, *intimately* combined & *unified*
with the great appearances in Nature — & not held in
solution & loose mixture with them in the shape of formal
similes.'[17] It is that quality in true poetry which finds it
origin in the 'imagination', and here, in the summer of
1802 he expresses in its simplest form the definition of that
faculty in contradistinction to the 'fancy', anticipating the
convolutions of later years. 'Fancy, or the aggregating
Faculty of the mind,' he writes on 10 September, is to be
distinguished from '*Imagination*, or the *modifying*, and *co-
adunating* Faculty. This the Hebrew Poets appear to me to
have possessed beyond all others — & next to them the
English. In the Hebrew Poets each Thing has a Life of it's
own, & yet they are all one Life. In God they move & live,
& *have* their Being — not *had*, as the cold System of
Newtonian Theology represents — but *have*.'[18] Again he is
returning to those ponderings of the spring of 1801 when
he had written of the difference between 'things' and 'living

things' in Nature and in language. 'Nature,' he says 'has her own proper interest; & he will know what it is, who believes & feels, that every Thing has a Life of its own, & that we are all *one Life.*'

At the same time, while acknowledging that '*Tact* / for all sounds & forms of human nature' is an essential talent in a great poet, he is groping, a little uncertainly, in the realms of the subconscious. Talking of the *Der erste Schiffer* translations he says that Gessner's 'Refinement'

necessarily leads the imagination to Ideas without *expressing them* – Shaped & cloathed – the mind of a pure Being would turn away from them, from natural delicacy of Taste/but in that shadowy half-being, that state of nascent Existence in the Twilight of the Imagination, and just on the vestibule of Consciousness, they are far more incendiary, stir up a more lasting commotion, & leave a deeper stain.[19]

Here one finds a connection with those earlier reflections on the quality of 'dimness' and 'shadowyness' of the year before; and yet he finds it necessary to offer a solemn warning against the operation of such 'twilight' states in matters of religion and morals, for here the 'suppression & obscurity' gives rise to a quality that is 'altogether meretricious', and the 'Conceptions, as they *recede* from distinctness of Idea, approximate to the nature of *Feeling*, & gain therby a closer & more immediate affinity with the appetites'.[20] This distinction seemed to Coleridge of paramount importance in the general campaign against the materialists, 'Hartley, Priestley, & the Multitude'.[21] And yet the ramifications 'of simplicity or manifoldness' and the quest for '*one sense*', were by no means entirely settled in his mind. 'In what sense is it one?' he asks a year later – 'sense, Appetite, Passion, Fancy, Imagination, Understanding, & lastly the Reason & Will?' The superiority of 'a clear or distinct idea over a "Schwankend"' notion was to be seen in the affinity between 'pure Virtue' and those 'Feelings that prompt to action & sustain under Pain / Dignity, Hope

&c.'[22] How much this reflection arose from bitter experience is revealed in the Asra letter. On the other hand, he contends that

the best part of Heaven &c is that being utterly indistinct & dim it acts nothing but a representation of Virtue. But if you make it clearly, it is then just as base as a guinea/ & would be felt as such by any noble minded Child of 7 years old – to whom you told a story of virtuous Action – God = Reason personified Self – Heaven = Complacency & satisfaction.[23]

The conviction no doubt arose out of one of those deep conversations with Hartley, now in his seventh year, whose precocious aptitude for religious speculation serves as an amusing indication of his father's new shift in theological emphasis. When Derwent was scolded for eating too many gooseberries this summer, Hartley promptly piped up : 'He is far over wicked ; but it's all owing to Adam, who did the same thing in Paradise.' As Coleridge confessed to Southey on 29 July, 'I am myself a little theological'. In one sense this naturally meant that he was engaged in an orgy of reading. Yet, as with the pursuit of so many of his leading ideas and interests, the impulse came from a direct conviction of the whole man. The fact was that the swarm of afflictions over the past two years had led him to a state of feeling where, contrary to every instinct and intellectual conviction in the past, he could now wholeheartedly endorse little Hartley's assertion about Adam.

My Faith is simply this [he confided to his brother George on 1 July], that there is an original corruption in our nature, from which & from the consequences of which, we may be redeemed by Christ – not as the Socinians say, by his pure morals or excellent Example merely – but in a mysterious manner as an effect of his crucifixion – and this I believe – not because I *understand* it; but because I *feel*, that it is not only suitable to, but needful for, my nature and because I find it clearly revealed.

There is something impressive about the simplicity and

honesty with which Coleridge returned to the fold of orthodoxy, for he never pretended that it arose from anything other than lived experience and self-knowledge. And while he was to spend the rest of his life exploring the intellectual implications he never lost the original force of the simple faith of his religious conviction, nor did he ever surpass the moving eloquence with which he described it.

... Religion passes out of the ken of Reason [he wrote in 1818], on where the Eye of Reason has reached its Horizon; and Faith is then but its *continuation*, even as the Day softens away into the sweet Twilight, and Twilight hushed & breathless steals into the Darkness. It is Night, sacred Night! The upraised Eye views only the starry Heaven, which manifests only itself – and the outward look gazes on the sparks, twinkling in the aweful Depth only to preserve the Soul steady and concentered in its Trance of inward abstraction.[24]

It was the same kind of self-affirming conviction that Wittgenstein would write of a hundred years later, long after the nineteenth-century battles over empiricism and metaphysics had subsided : 'There are, indeed, things that cannot be put into words. They *make themselves manifest*. They are what is mystical.' How strange, too, that both men should employ even the same image to distinguish between the 'world' and what lies beyond. 'Our life has no end,' writes Wittgenstein, 'in just the way in which our visual field has no limits.'[25] And Coleridge : 'Religion passes out of the ken of Reason on where the Eye of Reason has reached its horizon.' In many respects too it was similar to Newman's view, expressed half a century later in the *Grammar of Assent*, where he repudiated the function of reason in religious belief : 'After proceeding in our investigations a certain way, suddenly a blank or maze presents itself before the mental vision, as when the eye is confused by the varying slides of a telescope.'[26]

In the middle of the summer Coleridge seemed to acquire a

remission from debilitating illness, and regained something of the robust energy of former days. Early in August he prepared to set out on a long walk through Cumberland : 'I had a shirt, cravat, 2 pair of Stockings, a little paper & half a dozen Pens, a German Book (Voss's Poems) & a little Tea & Sugar, with my Night Cap, packed up in my natty green oil-skin, neatly squared, and put into my *net* Knapsack / and the Knap-sack on my back.' Before leaving the house he decided he needed a walking-stick, and finding nothing better to hand he stripped Mrs Coleridge's 'Besom stick' of its twigs, leaving them scattered over the kitchen floor, and set out with his wife's and the servant's voices raised behind him. An account of the walk was written in a series of 'journal letters' to Sara Hutchinson, including a frightening adventure in the mountains when he found himself trapped on a ledge. The passage deserves quoting if only as an example of the riches that lie waiting for the readers of Coleridge's letters :

There is one sort of Gambling, to which I am much addicted; and that not of the least criminal kind for a man who has children & a Concern. – It is this. When I find it convenient to descend from a mountain, I am too confident & too indolent to look round about & wind about 'till I find a track or other symptom of safety; but I wander on, & where it is first *possible* to descend, there I go – relying upon fortune for how far down this possibility will continue. So it was yesterday afternoon. I passed down from Broadcrag, skirted the Precipices, and found myself cut off from a most sublime Crag-summit, that seemed to rival Sca' Fell Man in height, & to outdo it in fierceness. A Ridge of Hill lay low down, & divided this Crag (called Doe-crag) & Broad-crag – even as the Hyphen divides the words broad & crag. I determined to go thither; the first place I came to, that was not direct Rock, I slipped down, in a few yards came to just such another / I *dropped* that too / but the stretching of the muscles of my hands & arms, & the jolt of the Fall on my Feet, put my whole Limbs in a *Tremble*, and I paused, & looking down, saw that I had little else to encounter but a succession of these little Precipices – it was in truth a Path that in a very hard Rain is, no doubt, the channel of a most splendid Waterfall. – So I began to suspect that I ought not to go on / but then unfortunately tho' I could with ease drop down a smooth Rock 7 feet high, I could not *climb* it / so go on I must / and on I went / the next 3 drops were not half a Foot, at least not a foot more than my own height / but every Drop increased the Palsy of my Limbs – and I shook all over, Heaven knows without the least influence of Fear / and now I had only two more to drop down / it was twice my own height, & the Ledge at the bottom was so exceedingly narrow, that if I dropt down upon it I must of necessity have fallen backwards & of course killed myself. My Limbs were all in a tremble – I lay upon my Back to rest myself, & was beginning according to my Custom to laugh at myself for a Madman, when the sight of the Crags above me on each side & the impetuous Clouds just over them, posting so luridly & so rapidly northward, overawed me / I lay in a state of almost prophetic Trance & Delight – & blessed God aloud, for the powers of Reason & the Will, which remaining no Danger can overpower us! O God, I exclaimed aloud – how calm, how blessed am I now / I know not how to proceed, how to return / but I am calm & fearless & confident / if this Reality were a Dream, if I were asleep, what agonies had I suffered! what screams! – When the Reason & the Will are away, what remain to us but Darkness & Dimness & a bewildering Shame, and Pain that is utterly Lord over us, or fantastic Pleasure, that draws the Soul along swimming through the air in many shapes, even as a Flight of Starlings in a Wind.[27]

The final comments on the nature of reason and the quality of 'Dimness' reveal the extent to which he constantly mused on their significance.

After returning from his walk the Lambs came to visit him, and Charles wrote of how Greta Hall was 'quite enveloped on all sides by a net of mountains : great floundering bears and monsters they seemed, all couchant and asleep'. He says that they entered Coleridge's study at dusk, when the mountains were 'all dark with clouds upon their heads'. 'Coleridge had got a blazing fire in his study ; which is a large, antique, ill-shaped room, with an old-fashioned organ, never played upon, big enough for a church, shelves of scattered folios, an Aeolian harp, and an old sofa, half-bed

&c.'[28] Lamb entered into the spirit of Coleridge's mountain expeditions and found himself clambering up to the top of Skiddaw and wading down the bed of Lodore, but there were occasions when he was obliged to think of the ham and beef shop near St Martin's Lane to counteract the 'mental effects' of mountain scenery.[29]

On 25 August Coleridge wrote an account of 'a glorious Walk' to the waterfall that 'divides Great Robinson from Buttermere Halse Fell' – just eight miles from Keswick. Lamb was probably with him on this occasion :

I had a glorious Walk – the rain sailing along those black Crags & green Steeps, white as the wooly Down on the under side of a Willow Leaf, & soft as Floss Silk/& silver Fillets of Water down every mountain from top to bottom that were as fine as Bridegrooms. . . . The thing repaid me amply/it is a great Torrent from the Top of the mountain to the Bottom/the lower part of it is not the least Interesting, where it is beginning to slope to a level – the mad water rushes thro' it's *sinuous* Bed, or rather prison of Rock, with such rapid Curves, as if it turned the Corners not from the mechanic force, but with foreknowledge, like a fierce & skilful Driver/great Masses of Water, one after the other, that in twilight one might have feelingly compared them to a vast crowd of huge white Bears, rushing, one over the other, against the wind – their long white hair shattering abroad in the wind/ the remainder of the Torrent is marked out by three great Waterfalls – the lowermost apron-shaped, & though the Rock down which it rushes is an inclined Plane, it shoots off in such an independence of the Rock as shews that it's direction was given it by the force of the Water from above. The middle, which in peaceable times would be two tinkling Falls, formed in his furious Rain one great *Water-wheel* endlessly revolving/& double the size & height of the lowest – the third & highest is a mighty one indeed/it is twice the height of both the others added together/nearly as high as Scale Force/but it rushes down an inclined Plane – and does not *fall*, like Scale Force/however, if the Plane had been smooth, it is so near a Perpendicular that it would have *appeared* to fall – but it is indeed so fearfully savage & black & jagged, that it tears the flood to pieces – and one great black Outjutment divides the water, & overbrows' keeps uncovered a long slip of jagged black Rock beneath, which gives a marked *character* to the whole force. What a sight it is to look down on such a Cataract! – the wheels, that circumvolve in it – the leaping up & plunging forward of that infinity of Pearls & Glass Bulbs – the continual *change* of the *Matter*, the perpetual *Sameness* of the Form – it is an awful Image & Shadow of God & the World.[30]

Coleridge's robust health of this summer lasted into the autumn, when he could claim to feel better, and look better, than he had done for several years. But with the prospect of another winter in the Lakes, the spectres of pain, depression and restlessness arose before him. By the end of September he had suffered a 'very serious attack of low Fever' which left him weak, and once again he began to think of wintering in a warmer climate. But where could he go? And where would he find the wherewithal? Towards the end of October he wrote to Tom Wedgwood, who was ailing with an incurable disease, inviting him to stay at Greta Hall. The invitation was hardly compelling : 'Our climate is inclement, & our Houses not as compact as they might be / but it is a stirring climate / & the worse the weather, the more unceasingly entertaining are my Study Windows.' Not that Coleridge wished his invitation to be particularly pressing. Knowing that Wedgwood was contemplating a trip abroad and that his intended companion, John Leslie, was unlikely to go, he suggested a hasty alternative to Wedgwood's visit in the North : 'If Leslie could not go abroad with you, & I could in any way mould my manners & habits to suit you, I should of all things like to be your companion.'[31] Two weeks later Coleridge received a letter from Wedgwood. His patron was planning a trip to Wales, then intended to follow the sun : Coleridge was invited to come at once, and they would meet at Cote House near Bristol.

13

'A Comet tied to a Comet's Tail'

COLERIDGE'S decision to become a travelling companion to the rich and ailing Tom Wedgwood can be seen as yet one more fatal step amongst a host of fatal decisions over the past few years. If the attempt to write a grand work of philosophy had taken Coleridge away from his rightful métier, poetry, the long succession of house-parties and travelling that would continue over the next year would hardly fit him for any kind of sustained work, poetical or otherwise.

But he did not hesitate to ponder the distant implications. 'Mrs Coleridge is fully of the opinion that to lose Time is merely to lose spirits,' he informed Wedgwood by return of post. 'Accordingly I have resolved not to look the children in the Face (the parting from whom is the only downright Bitter in the Thing) but to take the chaise tomorrow morning.' Wedgwood had at least anticipated some difficulty in fearing that Coleridge might feel himself at a social disadvantage. But Coleridge, contrary to the opinion of many who knew him, could put Wedgwood's mind at rest on this score :

I regard it among the Blessings of my Life that I have never lived among men whom I regarded as my artificial Superiors; that all the respect, I have at any time payed, has been wholly to supposed Goodness or Talent ... I am anxious that in the event of our travelling together you should feel yourself at ease with me, even as you would with a younger Brother, to whom from his childhood you had been in the Habit of saying, Do this, Col. – or don't do that – .[1]

He set off from Keswick on 4 November, but in spite of the great haste to get to the South, he stayed the night in Penrith, where Sara Hutchinson was now living. At least he had the honesty to give Mrs Coleridge an account of the time he spent with Sara, if not the tact. The result, as one would expect, was renewed hostilities by correspondence. Mrs Coleridge, who was after all expecting another child, and who believed his trip to be one of great urgency and financial necessity, no doubt felt that her efforts of the past months had been scantily rewarded.

He stayed briefly in London, promising Mrs Coleridge that he would see nobody but Stuart and John Wordsworth ; as if in anticipation of reprisals. And already his letters were beginning to tell the sad self-pitying tale of the past : the journey had been uncomfortable, and his 'Limbs were quite crazed & feverous, & my inside hot as fire'. 'My dear Love,' he wrote to her, 'write as cheerfully as possible. I am tenderer, & more fluttery, & bowel-weak, than most – I can not bear any thing gloomy, unless when it is quite necessary. – ' And he adds the timorous reminder – '. . . try to *love* & be *kind* to, those whom I love.'

But the damage was already done and he pleaded in vain, for by the second week in November – after arriving at Cote House, he received a scolding letter from Mrs Coleridge which 'immediately disordered my Heart and Bowels'. Thus he felt it incumbent on him to take up his pen and deliver a sermon by letter to keep his enraged wife to her resolutions :

As I seem to exist, as it were, almost wholly within myself, in *thoughts* rather than in *things*, in a particular warmth felt all over me, but chiefly felt about my heart & breast ; & am connected with *things without* me by the pleasurable sense of their immediate Beauty or Loveliness, and not at all by my knowledge of their average value in the minds of people in general ; & with *persons without* me by no ambition of their esteem, or of having rank & consequence in their minds, but with people in general by general kindliness of feeling, & with my especial friends, by an intense delight in fellow-feeling, by an intense perception of the Necessity of LIKE to LIKE; so you on the contrary exist almost wholly in the world *without*/the Eye & the Ear are your great organs, and you depend upon the eyes & ears of others for a great part of your pleasure.[2]

From Cote House he set off almost immediately with Tom and Sally Wedgwood for South Wales, travelling via Abergavenny and Brecon through the Vale of Usk. His conversations with Wedgwood, who was suffering from a 'thickening gut', must have ranged in the main over their separate illnesses, for Coleridge's letters in the following weeks abound in dietary and symptomatology. At the same time, ironically enough, he started to suffer from acute indigestion. 'All I am troubled with, is a frequent opression, a suffocating weight, of Wind,' he wrote on 16 November. 'Sunday Night I was obliged to *sit up* in my bed, an hour and a half – & at last, was forced to make myself sick by a feather, in order to throw off the Wind from my Stomach.' Moreover, the 'valetudianarians' had been comparing notes, and it seems that Wedgwood advised that opium was far better than stimulants of any kind. Coleridge could also report that he was discovering the marvellous properties of ginger. ' – I take no Tea – in the morning Coffee, with a tea spoonful of Ginger in the last cup – in the afternoon a large Cup of Ginger Tea – / & I take Ginger at 12 o clock at noon, & a glass after supper ... & once in the 24 hours (but not always at the same hour) I take half a grain of purified opium, equal to 12 drops of Laudanum ...'[3] As for the trip abroad, there was talk of going to Italy, but Wedgwood was indecisive : 'His determinations are made so rapidly that two or three days of wet weather with a raw cold air might have such an effect on his Spirits, that he might go off immediately for Naples, or perhaps for Teneriff – which latter place he is always talking about.'

Meanwhile, back in Cumberland, Mrs Coleridge had suffered fainting fits and was desperately short of money. In connection with the latter, Coleridge had bad news : 'I can not ask Wedgwood – & he has not said any thing to me / but merely borrowed from me the money, I had, saying – that it was impossible, we could have any but joint expences.' Of the many disadvantages in store for the poor who hobnob with the rich – this was one he had perhaps least envisaged. Having sent this news, Coleridge got very little sleep that night worrying over Mrs Coleridge's predicament. A little after five in the morning he arose from his bed in the inn where they were staying near Crescelly, and wrote a long letter to her. She was 'INSTANTLY to get a nurse', she was to have a fire in her bedroom, and if she became seriously ill or unhappy, he would return – 'for I know, you would not *will* it, tho' you might *wish* it, except for a serious cause'. But in a short space his concern drifts into the old recriminations. His last letter of criticism, he tells her, was not written 'without much pain, & many struggles of mind, Resolves, & Counter-resolves'. It was not simply her feelings about his stay at Penrith, – 'there was one whole sentence of a very, very different cast'. Whatever Mrs Coleridge had written in her scolding letter, it prompted yet another lecture on the necessity of his being allowed to love his friends without hindrance or criticism ; and it demonstrates again the extent to which one of the root causes of his misery with Mrs Coleridge lay not so much in her actual character as the jealousies and difficulties she posed in his love for Sara and the Wordsworths :

That we can love but one person, is a miserable mistake, & the cause of abundant unhappiness. I can & do love many people, dearly – so dearly, that I really scarcely know, which I love the best. Is it not so with every good mother who has a large number of Children – with many, many Brothers & Sisters in large & affectionate Families? . . . Would any good & wise man, any warm & wide hearted man marry at all, if it were part of the Contract – Henceforth this Woman is your

only friend, your sole beloved! all the rest of mankind, however
amiable & akin to you, must be only your acquaintance! – It were
well, if every woman wrote down before her marriage all, she thought,
she had a right to, from her Husband – & to examine each in this
form – By what *Law* of God, or Man, or of general reason, do I
claim *this* Right? – I suspect, that this Process would make a ludicrous
Quantity of Blots and Erasures in most of the first rude Draughts
of these Rights of Wives – infinitely however to their own Advantage,
& to the security of their genuine Rights.

But the self-righteousness of his case had by now carried
him well beyond the original substance and tone of his letter.
And if there was any truth in his own assertion that Mrs
Coleridge brought out the very worst in him – the perora-
tion of this letter of 'concern' is ample proof.

Permit me, my dear Sara! without offence to you, as Heaven knows!
it is without any feeling of Pride in myself, to say – that in sex,
acquirements, and in the quantity and quality of natural endowments
whether of Feeling, or of Intellect, you are the Inferior. Therefore it
would be preposterous to expect that I should see with your eyes, &
dismiss my Friends from *my* heart, only because you have not chosen
to give them any Share of *your* Heart; but it is not preposterous, in
me, on the contrary I have a *right* to expect & demand, that you should
to a certain degree love, & act kindly to, those whom I deem worthy of
my Love.

Admittedly he attempts to gainsay the inescapable tone of
contempt : but he had a way of bantering that probably did
more damage than his 'bitter censure' : 'If you read this
Letter with half the Tenderness, with which it is written, it
will do you & both of us, G O O D ; (& contribute it's share to
the turning of a mere Cat-hole into a Dove's nest !)* [*inked
out in the MS] You know, Sally Pally ! I must have a Joke –
or it would not be me !'[4] As Dorothy Wordsworth had
commented, it was a 'hopeless case'.

The very next day, having visited the country seat of one
John Allen of Crescelly, Coleridge could report back to his

wife that he was basking in the company of three 'good, kind-hearted Lasses – Jesse, the eldest, uncommonly so'. He was, in fact, having a whale of a time :

I eat sweet meats, & cream, & some fruit, & talked a great deal, and sate up till 12, & did not go to sleep till near 2. In consequence of which I arose sickish, at ½ past 7 – & all the way from Crescelly I was in a very pleasurable state of feeling; but my feelings too tender, my thoughts too vivid – I was deliciously unwell.

But on arriving back at his inn at St Clear's another letter from Mrs Coleridge awaited him, and he had not finished reading it before 'a fluttering of the Heart came on, which ended (as usual) in a sudden & violent Diarrhoea / I could scarcely touch my Dinner, & was obliged at last to take 20 drops of Laudanum'. Mrs Coleridge's distress and Coleridge's violent reaction was no doubt in consequence of further bad news about financial troubles, for by 4 December her request for money and his inability to send any is yet again the leading topic of their letters. He would send money the very next day he promised : 'I have vexed & fretted myself that I did not send it a fortnight ago – there was no earthly reason, why I should not. You know, how hateful all Money-thoughts are to me ! – & how idly & habitually I keep them at arm's length.' He did in fact send a draft on 5 December for fifty pounds. It was dated, however, 13 December – and (the final blow), not payable until two months after that date. 'I have a faith, a heavenly Faith, that our Future Days will be Days of Peace, & affectionate Happiness,' he wrote on 4 December.

Meanwhile he had returned to John Allen's and was writing more of those consoling letters home – 'What sweeter & more tranquillizing pleasure is there, than to feel one's self completely innocent among compleatly innocent young Women – ! Save when I think of home, my mind is calm & soundless.' He wrote of Sally Wedgwood playing the piano '*divinely*', and noted how suited he was to country house living: 'Warm Rooms, warm Bedrooms, Music, pleasant Talking, & extreme Temperance – all this agrees with me – & the best Blessing, that results from all, is a *placid Sleep* – no difficulties in my Dreams, no Pains, (no Desires).'[5] Yet he could assure Mrs Coleridge, whose baby was expected during that very month, that his thoughts were with her during her pregnancy. 'I feel it very, very hard to be from you during this time.' In the meantime he would give her the benefit of his thoughts on the baby's name:

> Don't you think, Crescelly Coleridge, would be a pretty name for a Boy – If a Girl, let it be Gretha Coleridge – not *Greta* – but – Gretha – unless you prefer Rotha – or Laura. What do you think of Bridget?– Only it ought to end in a vowel. You may take your choice of Sara, Gretha, or rather Algretha, Rotha, Lara, Emily, or Lovenna. – The boy must be either Bracy, or Crescelly. – Algretha Coleridge will needs be a beautiful Girl.

No doubt the names were happily bandied about amongst the females gathered in the drawing room amongst whom he was in 'prodigious favour', according to Wedgwood. Yet one member of the circle regarded him with a very jaundiced eye indeed. Tom Wedgwood's sister, Kitty, was also amongst the party during December, and she imparted the following view of Coleridge's character in a letter to her brother:

> I don't know whether we shall ever agree in our sentiments respecting this gentleman, but I hope if we do not that we may agree to differ. I certainly felt no scruples of conscience in joining the attack at Cresselly. I have never seen enough of him to overcome the first disagreeable impression of his accent and exterior. I confess, too, that in what I have seen and heard of Mr Coleridge there is in my opinion too great a parade of superior feeling; and an excessive goodness and sensibility is put too forward, which gives an appearance, at least, of conceit, and excites suspicion that it is acting; . . . He appears to be an uncomfortable husband, and very negligent, of the worldly interest, of his children; leaving them in case of his death to be provided for by his

friends is a scheme more worthy of his desultory habits than of his talents.[6]

The 'attack' she mentions was probably made behind his back. Apparently Coleridge was rude to Fanny Allen when she laughed at a passage in Wordsworth's *Leech Gatherer*. There was further cause for raised eyebrows when he was irreverent about the Ten Commandments, and again, when speaking of his early days at Bristol, he had commented: 'There I had the misfortune to meet with my wife.'

By the 16 December he had left Crescelly and was travelling northwards. He was on his way home, and yet it was more of a coincidence than a decision to be at Greta for the birth of his child. Wedgwood wished to meet a Captain Charles Luff who lived at Glenridding in Patterdale, with a view to taking him on as a shooting companion. He would stay at Jackson's next door to the Coleridge's on his way up. Mrs Coleridge was duly forewarned and told not to be in the least disturbed by the coming of the great man: 'do not let him be any weight or bustle on your mind.' Meanwhile he advised that she should take in Sara Hutchinson as a companion during the rest of her confinement – not without the usual qualifications:

I hope, that Sara Hutchinson is well enough to have come in – it would be a great comfort, that one or the other of the three Women at Grasmere should be with you – & Sara rather than the other two because you will hardly have another opportunity of having her by yourself & to yourself, & of learning to know her, such as she really is. How much this lies at my Heart with respect to the Wordsworths, & Sara, and how much our common Love & Happiness depends on your loving those whom I love, – why should I repeat? – I am confident, my dear Love! that I have no occasion to repeat it.[7]

Sara Coleridge (the child was spared Algretha, not to mention Crescelly or Bracy) was born on 23 December, with no other remarkable occurrence than that she was 'somewhat disfigured with red gum'. Coleridge learnt of the birth when

13

he arrived at Grasmere on Christmas Eve and hurried on up to Keswick to be united with his wife. 'I had never thought of a Girl,' he told Southey, 'as a possible even – the words child & man child were perfect symonimes in my feelings – however I bore the sex with great fortitude.'

After a week at Keswick he went on with Wedgwood to Glenridding, and continued to journey back and forth to Grasmere for several days. He seems to have seen something of Sara Hutchinson at this time, and it is likely that he made a discovery that must have completely stunned him : that John Wordsworth, whose original hopes in marriage had been disappointed when William won Mary Hutchinson's hand, might seek the hand of Sara. Family tradition, endorsed by a letter of Coleridge's to Stuart in 1808[8] has it that there was indeed talk of John Wordsworth's marrying Sara Hutchinson, but whether she herself found the idea agreeable we do not know; she and Coleridge are both reticent on the subject. But E.K.Chambers's suggestion that Coleridge probably learnt of this proposal in the new Year of 1803, conjectural as it may be, remains unchallenged.[9] His supposition arises from a letter of Coleridge's dated 5 January, in which he says that he might come to Greta Hall on a double horse with Sara, 'whom I have *some few reasons* for wishing to be with you immediately'. Her health, he told his wife, had been affected by bad teeth, 'yet this Tooth ache I suspect to be in part nervous – & the cause, which, I more than suspect, has called this nervousness into action, I will tell you when I am alone with you'.

Yet whatever Coleridge was to tell his wife about Sara, there does not seem to have been any noticeable alteration in his activities or feelings during this time. As to the future, it was still a 'cloud'; Wedgwood, 'rapid in his movements, & sudden in his resolves', might be destined for Tarant Gunville in the West Country, or Trewern (other Wedgwood properties), after which, the Canary Islands, or Teneriffe, or Sicily and south Italy. Towards choosing the latter more warm and exotic locations he was encouraged by Coleridge: 'I have been in much dread respecting your long detention of the faeces – that alone seems to me to decide in favor of a hotter climate, somewhere or other.' Perhaps Wordsworth and his family would take a house in Sicily, and he, Coleridge, another, so that Wedgwood would always have pleasant society, if ever he chose to stay there.

At the same time he professed to be 'unfit', 'low and unwell', and was once more deeply preoccupied with dietary. Yet at this time he was not alone in such gloomy self-preoccupation; all his acquaintance seemed to be ill: Wordsworth with hypochondriasis, Tom Poole with the 'Dutch Ague', Sara Hutchinson with bad teeth, Southey with bad eyes, Wedgwood with the 'thickening gut'. 'God have mercy on us,' he told Southey, 'We are all sick all mad, all slaves!' But then, he was convinced that they were all poisoning themselves; and two weeks later he sent Southey a description of yet another régime:

I take the chalybeated Aquafortis, with benefit – & find considerable benefit from eating nothing at breakfast, & taking only a single cup of strong Coffee – then at eleven o'clock I take a couple of eggs, kept in boiling water one minute, folded up in a napkin for a minute & a half, & then put into the boiling water, which is now removed from the fire, & kept there with the sausepan covered from 4 to 6 minutes, according to the size of the eggs, & quantity of water in the saucepan. – the superiority of eggs thus boiled to those boiled in the common way proves to me the old proverb – there is reason in roasting of Eggs. – I empty the eggs out into a glass or tea cup, eat them with a little salt & cayenne pepper – but no bread.[10]

His lively interest in dietetics and regimens also prompted him to send directives to Mrs Coleridge: 'vigorous & persevering measures *must* be taken' with the children, he urged. It was entirely wrong to allow Hartley to stay up till eleven at night, then giving him coffee in the morning '&c &c &c – and this for a child whose nerves are as wakeful as the Strings of an Eolian Harp, & as easily put out of Tune!' The children were in a permanent malaise, he insisted, and it all came down to the one root cause :

Trash & general irregularity of Diet! – I know, you will say that you were dieted, & yet had worms. But this is no argument at all – for first it remains to be proved that you were *properly* dieted – secondly, it is as notorious as the Sun in heaven, that bad Diet will & does bring worms. – & lastly, Derwent has been manifestly tea-poisoned – as well as Hartley – & both of them are eat up by worms. Mary would not say, that Derwent had no Tea given him – she only said, that *he had but little*.[11]

Such was his confidence in the therapeutic powers of diet and regimens, and the lights he had thrown on these important matters, he had it in mind to write a 'pretty Book', entitled 'Le petite Soulagement, or little Comforts, by a Valetudinarian', 'comprizing cookery, sleeping, travelling, conversation, self-discipline – poetry, morals, metaphysics – all the alleviations, that reason & well-regulated self-indulgence, can give to a good sick man'.[12]

Ironically enough, at this very time Coleridge made himself extremely ill by a series of highly irregular and unwise activities. On New Year's day he had got his feet wet and dried his boots, still on his feet, in front of the fire. The result was the 'same deadly sweats – the same frightful Profluvium of Dysentery, burning Dregs, like melted Lead – with quantities of bloody mucus from the Coats of the Intestines'. But the next day, feeling better, he walked over to Mr Luff's, stayed there the night, then returned to Grasmere the day after, walking into a storm :

O it was a wild business! Such hurry-skurry of Clouds, such volleys of sound! In spite of the wet & the cold I should have had some pleasure in it, but for two vexations – first, an almost intolerable pain came into my right eye, a *smarting & burning* pain / & secondly, in consequence of riding with such cold water under my *fork* extremely uneasy & burthensome Feelings attacked my Groin & right Testicle – so that what with pain from the one, & the alarm from both, I had no enjoyment at all. Just on the brow of the Hill I met a man, dismounted who could not keep on horse-back – he seemed quite scared by the uproar – & said to me with much feeling – O Sir! it is a perilous Buffeting, but it is worse for you than for me – for I have it at my Back. – However I got safely over – and immediately on the Descent all was calm & breathless, as if it was some mighty Fountain just on the summit of Kirkstone, that shot forth it's volcano of Air, & precipitated a huge stream of invisible Lava down the Road to Patterdale.[13]

The adventure resulted in distressful dreams, a swollen eye, bowel attacks and the onset of rheumatism in the fingers. For relief he took, not opium, but 'two large Tea spoonfuls of Ether in a wine glass of Camphorated Gum water'. Tom Wedgwood, naturally bewildered by the discrepancy between Coleridge's vehement advice to others and his extraordinary negligence with regard to his own person, asked him why, 'in God's name', he went out in the storm in the first place. 'The true reason is simple, tho' it may be somewhat strange,' replied Coleridge, '– the thought never once entered my head.' He went on :

The *cause* of this I suppose to be, that (I do not remember it at least) I never once in my whole life turned back in fear of the weather. Prudence is a plant, of which I, no doubt, possess some valuable specimens – but they are always in my hot-house, never out of the glasses – & least of all things would endure the climate of the mountains. In simple earnest, I never find myself alone within the embracement of rocks & hills, a traveller up an alpine road, but my spirit courses, drives, and eddies, like a Leaf in Autumn : a wild activity, of thoughts, imaginations, feelings, and impulses of motion, rises up from within me – a sort of *bottom-wind*, that blows to no point of the compass, & comes from I know not whence, but agitates the whole of me; my whole Being is filled with waves, as it were, that roll & stumble, one this way, & one that way, like things that have no common master.[14]

No doubt Wedgwood could sympathize with his strange friend's answer, for he himself was a stern challenger to Coleridge's impulsiveness as the 'dreadful irritability' of his illness drove him relentlessly on an erratic career about the country. By the end of January the party was off again, returning to Cote House via Etruria and Bristol. 'I am a Comet tied to a Comet's Tail,' wrote Coleridge from Southey's place on 1 February, '& our combined Path must needs be damnably eccentric, & a defying Puzzle to all Astronomers.'

But back in Bristol Wedgwood at last decided that the state of Coleridge's health incapacitated him as a fit companion for continental travel. The change of plan, which hardly came as a surprise to Coleridge, urged him once more to complete arrangements for Southey's move to Greta Hall, although he had to warn Southey off any idea of bringing either Tom, his brother, or Mrs Lovell the widowed sister-in-law. The brother he disliked for his 'disrespectful & unbrotherly spirit of thwarting & contradicting', and Mrs Lovell, he feared, would only exacerbate domestic conflicts. 'I am so weak,' he informed Southey, 'that warmth of manner in a female House mate is as necessary to me, as warmth of internal attachment.' He also felt it necessary to advise Southey that he could not be relied on as a source of consolation or security : 'O dear Southey ! I am no Elm ! I am a crumbling wall, undermined at the foundation ! Why should the Vine with all its clusters be buried in my rubbish ?'[15]

Instead of returning to Keswick, however, Coleridge went on to Tarant Gunville, after a visit to Poole's at Stowey, where he remained up to his 'chin in comforts' until mid-March, when he moved on to London where his main business was to make arrangements for a life assurance which he contracted for £1000 at a premium of £27. The determination to make this arrangement had probably taken root as a result of Kitty Wedgwood's criticisms at Crescelly, no doubt reinforced by his intention to go abroad, with or without Wedgwood. There was also business to complete with Longman for a third edition of his poems, although an attempt to add a second volume was abandoned. He was seeing much of Charles and Mary Lamb during this period, and it fell to his lot to be involved in having the unfortunate Mary committed to an asylum as a new attack of insanity seemed imminent. Towards the end of March he wrote to Mrs Coleridge :

On Sunday she told her Brother that she was getting bad, with great agony – on Tuesday morning she layed hold of me with violent agitation, & talked wildly about George Dyer/I told Charles, there was not a moment to lose/and I did not lose a moment – but went for a Hackney Coach, & took her to the private Madhouse at Hogsden/ she was quite calm, & said – it was best to do so – but she wept bitterly two or three times, yet all in a calm way.

The period in London rounded off six months of hectic, enervating idleness. Coleridge's talents were hardly fed by country houses and fashionable dinner parties. And yet the more 'showy' side of his immense powers of conversation were clearly displayed to some advantage in such settings. Had he manifested his 'genius' in the Augustan tradition of wit, elegance, and satire, or even the mandarin style of Johnsonian observation, he might have derived some benefit from such an element. As it was, his talents and energies were being exploited and dissipated with no advantage to himself, not even financial. A comment made by John Rickman, Secretary to the Speaker in the House of Commons, and a friend of Lamb and Southey, emphasizes the sad predicament Coleridge had got into by the time he came to London :

I am a little annoyed by a habit of *assentation*, which I fancy I perceive in him ; and cannot but think he likes to talk well, rather than to give or receive much information. I understand he is terribly pestered with invitations to go to parties, as a singer does, to amuse the guests by his talent; a hateful task I should think : I would rather not talk finely, than talk to such a purpose.

Humphry Davy too found a change in his friend, although ironically enough Coleridge had himself commented that

Davy would be ruined by his habit of socializing too much in London. 'I saw him seldomer than usual,' says Davy; 'when I did see him it was generally in the midst of large companies, where he is the image of power and activity.'

His eloquence is unimpaired; perhaps it is softer and stronger. His will is probably less than ever commensurate with his ability. Brilliant images of greatness float upon his mind: like the images of the morning clouds upon the waters, their forms are changed by the motion of the waves, they are agitated by every breeze and modified by every sunbeam. He talked in the course of one hour of beginning three works, and he recited the poem of Christabel unfinished, and as I had before heard it. What talent does he waste in forming visions, sublime, but unconnected with the real world. I have looked to his efforts, as to the efforts of a creating being; but as yet, he has not even laid the foundations for the new world of intellectual form.[17]

14

Going Away

COLERIDGE finally arrived back in Keswick on Good Friday, 8 April, and immediately went down with 'flu. Having rid himself of this, or so he thought, with a dose of opium taken with camphor and rhubarb, he then caught a cold, and the influenza returned in the form of rheumatic fever. The rest of the household, indeed the whole of Keswick, seemed to have caught the same germ. Again it was the worst illness since his childhood,

... severe for it's continuance (3 fits in the 24 hours) than any attack since my first terrific one at Xt Hospital – it was sufficiently distinguished however from simple Rheumatic Fever by the immediate & total Prostration of Strength, confusion of senses & faculties, long tearing fits of coughing with great expectoration, & clammy treacle-sweats on awaking.

By mid-May he had recovered, and the assertions made by Davy in London had caught up with him. 'I am weary & ashamed of talking about my intended works,' he told Southey. 'I am still in the hopes that this summer will not pass away without something worthy of me.' He was determined to go abroad in the Autumn, to Valencia or Madeira 'which will be *our's* in some shape or other'. But first he must complete a philosophical work he had on hand. The task he was contemplating was connected with his investigations in the early months of 1801 : it was to be called '*Instrument* of practical Reasoning'[1] : 'I am now however ready to go to Press, with a work which I consider as introductory to A System, tho' to the public it will appear altogether a Thing by itself... I entitle it Organum verè Organum, or an *Instrument* of practical Reasoning in the business of real Life.' To this he would prefix an examination of systems from the earliest logic, Plato, Aristotle, Raymund Lully, Peter Ramus, Bacon, Descartes, Condillac and Hartley. Then would follow his own 'Organum verè Organum', a system of all '*possible* modes of true, probable, & false reasoning, arranged philosophically'.[2] But this immense task seemed already as nothing in his vaunting aspirations.

'When this book is fairly off my hands, I shall, if I live & have sufficient health, set seriously to work... in pushing forward my Studies, & my investigations relative to the omne scibile of human Nature – *what* we *are*, & *how* we *become* what we are; so as to solve the two grand Problems, how, being acted upon, we shall act; how, acting, we shall be acted upon.'

It was nothing less than the ambition to reconcile within a strict philosophical system the opposing tendencies in philosophy during his times – empiricism and idealism. But [he added], 'between me & this work there may be Death.'[3]

Coleridge never even completed the prefatory 'Organum', although he claims to have had it ready for the press in May of 1803. But there is, in fact, evidence that he had started the task at this time.[4]

As the summer wore on his reading, his investigations, and his plans veered in many different directions. He was involved again in undermining the 'doctrines of Materialism & mechanical necessity... Doctrines, that I have perhaps had a more various experience, or more intuitive knowledge, of such facts than most men!'[5] Again he was deep in Scotus Erigena – who was 'clearly the modern founder of the School of Pantheism'. He was absorbed with the idea of acquitting the 'notion of the *dark* Ages &c'. Were *they* in the early 19th century any better off? 'They had *Wells*; we are flooded, ancle-high – & what comes of it but grass rank

and rotten? Our age eats from that Poison-tree of Knowledge, yclept, Too much and too little.'[6]

In one sense at least he planned to counteract the dangers
of 'too little' by formulating another grand and daring
scheme – for nothing less than a *Bibliotheca Brittanica.*
Southey would write the first volume, which would 'exhaust'
the whole of 'Welch, Saxon & Erse Literature'.

> Good heavens! [he exploded] if you & I, Rickman & Lamb, were
> to put our shoulders to one volume/a compleat History of the Dark
> Ages – if Rickman would but take the physics, you the Romances &
> Legendary Theology, I the Metaphysics, and Lamb be left to say what
> he liked in his own way – what might not be done/as to the Canon &
> Roman Law, it is done admirably for all Countries by Hugo of
> Göttingen, & I would abridge his Book – / This alone would im-
> mortalize us – in Physics I comprehend Alchemy & Medicine/
> Enough of all this.[7]

And now strangely it all sounded as he discussed these
grandiose schemes in breathless letters to his friend in
Bristol, as if the fantastic substance was the least consideration. In many ways it resembled the old pantisocratic
squabbles, Coleridge insisting on a thematic treatment,
Southey staunchly proposing an encyclopaedic; Coleridge
countering with shrill vehemence, 'An encyclopaedia
appears to me a worthless monster. . . . You omit those
things only from your Encyclop. which are excrescences –
each volume will *set up* the reader, give him at once connected trains of thought & facts & a delightful miscellany
for lownge reading.'

But when it came down to it, it was all wistful talk, and he
had to admit to Southey the insuperable objection to the
plan – his health. And more than this a new and haunting
sense of weakness:

> – that I was an herbaceous Plant, as large as a large Tree, with a
> Trunk of the same Girth, & Branches as large & Shadowing – but
> with *pith within* the Trunk, not heart of Wood – that I had *power* not

strength – an involuntary Imposter – that I had no real Genius, no real Depth / – / This on my honor is as fair a statement of my habitual Haunting, as I could give before the tribunal of Heaven.[8]

Depressing as this sounds it was characteristic of his resilience to suggest that a study of this feeling would find a rightful place in that huge and ever growing circuit of curious knowledge that he longed to order and bring within his mastery. In the same way, the onset of illness this summer, 'a compleat & almost heartless Case of Atonic Gout', together with nightmares and hallucinatory experiences, induced him again to take soundings in the twilight depths of the subconscious :

There is a state of mind, wholly unnoticed, as far as I know, by any Physical or Metaphysical Writer, hitherto, & which yet is necessary to the explanation of some of the most important phenomena of Sleep & Disease / it is a transmutation of the *succession* of *Time* into the *juxtaposition* of *Space*, by which the smallest Impulses, if quickly & regularly recurrent, *aggregate* themselves – & attain a kind of visual magnitude with a correspondent Intensity of general Feeling. – The simplest Illustration would be the *circle* of Fire made by whirling round a live Coal – only here the mind is passive. Suppose the same effect produced ab intra – & you have a clue to the whole mystery of frightful Dreams, & Hypochondriacal Delusions. – I merely *hint* this ; but I could detail the whole process, complex as it is.[9]

Back in the world of daylight realities, however, his interest in painting was enlivened this summer by two visitors. The young Hazlitt had arrived to try his hand at painting portraits of Wordsworth, Coleridge and little Hartley, although only a sketch of Hartley has survived. And towards the end of July Sir George Beaumont, the art patron, came to stay next door at Jackson's. Beaumont had already met Coleridge as a guest of Sotheby the year before, and on that occasion had taken such a dislike to him that at first he wondered how he could shun him at Greta Hall. It was, he remarked to Joseph Farington, 'an instance why we should not give way to first prejudices'. The two men met in Jackson's house and on getting into conversation soon became attached to each other. Coleridge he now discovered was a man of great genius, with a prodigious command of words, and had read everthing.[10] All the same, he felt that Wordsworth was the greater in 'poetical power'. Coleridge, of course, would have agreed. In fact they discussed the effect of Hazlitt's portrait of Wordsworth, which seemed to Beaumont to give the impression of 'a profound strong-minded Philosopher, not as a Poet'. Upon which Coleridge remarked that this was just. Wordsworth was 'a great Poet by inspirations, & in the moments of revelation, but . . . a thinking feeling Philosopher habitually'. His poetry, he went on, was his philosophy 'under the action of strong winds of feeling – a sea rolling high'.[11]

Such was Beaumont's admiration he was prompted to give Wordsworth a piece of land at Applethwaite so that he could be closer to his friend. Wordsworth eventually accepted the land, but realizing that Coleridge was likely to leave the country made no plans for building a house. Hazlitt, on the other hand, came off rather badly in Sir George's estimation, by angrily contradicting Coleridge in discussion. He eventually repaired to Grasmere where, according to De Quincey, he proposed to Dorothy Wordsworth.

Coleridge's conviction throughout this summer that he was suffering from 'atonic gout' was mainly connected with his observation that the symptoms increased with the change of weather. 'The effects of weather are to the full as palpable upon me, as upon the little old Lady & Gentleman in the weather Box – Or on the Sea Weed in the Barber's Shop.' Yet when he came to talk of his symptoms he was accurately describing the most acute effects of opium addiction. We do not know to what extent he had increased his dosage over the past year; but it is certain that he had not only lost his fear of the drug while with Wedgwood, but that he had extended his repertoire to Ether, Bhang (or hashish), Hyosycamine Pills, Hensbane and Nepenthe.[12] It is hardly surprising, therefore, that by August he was suffering the full gamut of withdrawal symptoms as never before :

> ... indigestion/costiveness that makes my evacuations at times approach in all the symptoms to the pains of Labor viz – distortion of Body from agony, profuse & streaming Sweats, & fainting – at times, looseness with griping – frightful Dreams with screaming – *breezes* of Terror blowing from the Stomach up thro' the Brain/always when I am awaked, I find myself stifled with wind/& the wind the manifest cause of the Dream/frequent paralytic Feelings – sometimes approaches to Convulsion fit – three times I have wakened out of these frightful Dreams, & found my legs so *locked* into each other as to have *left* a bruise ... My mouth is endlessly full of water – itself no small Persecution.[13]

But the most agonizing of these symptoms were the frightful nightmares : 'with Sleep my Horrors commence ; & they are such, three nights out of four, as literally to *stun* the intervening Day, so that more often than otherwise I fall asleep, struggling to remain awake. ... Dreams are no Shadows with me ; but the real, substantial miseries of Life.'[14]

In a poem written during this summer, *The Pains of Sleep*, he tells of the terrifying sense of guilt which formed the content of these dreams :

> Rage, sensual Passion, mad'ning Brawl,
> And Shame, and Terror over all!
> Deeds to be hid that were not hid,
> Which, all confus'd I might not know,
> Whether I suffer'd or I did :
> For all was Horror, Guilt & Woe,
> My own or others, still the same,
> Life-stifling Fear, Soul-stifling Shame!

He tried to grapple with the significance of these fearful visitations ; such night horrors might be reconciled with the punishments of the damned, he thought, but what had they to do with him?

> Such punishments, I thought, were due
> To Nature's, deepliest stain'd with Sin,
> Still to be stirring up anew
> The self-created Hell within;
> The Horror of their Crimes to view,
> To know & loathe, yet wish & do!
> With such let Fiends make mockery –
> But I – O wherefore this on *me*?
> Frail is my Soul, yea, strengthless wholly,
> Unequal, restless, melancholy;
> But free from Hate, & sensual Folly!
> To live belov'd is all I need,
> And whom I love, I love indeed –

In 1814 Coleridge wrote that these lines were 'an exact and most faithful portraiture of the state of my mind under the influences of incipient bodily derangement from the use of Opium'. But in 1803 he remained, 'ignorant of the cause, & still *mighty proud* of my supposed grand discovery of Laudanum, as the Remedy or Palliative of Evils, which itself had mainly produced'. He was still convinced that the root cause of his sufferings lay elsewhere: and in the summer of this year he had been encouraged to believe that his basic illness was 'atonic gout'. Yet while his diagnosis remained inaccurate, he was nonetheless convinced that there would be a fatal outcome. 'If the Complaint does not settle – & very soon too – in my extremities, I do not see how it will be possible for me to avoid a paralytic or apoplectic Stroke', he wrote. ' . . . I have no heart to speak of the Children ! – God have mercy on them ; & raise them up friends when I am in the grave.'[15] And even if he were not to die of the illness, the depression occasioned by these nightly tortures made him feel that life was not worth living:

O God! when a man blesses the loud Scream of Agony that awakes him night after night; night after night! – & when a man's repeated

Night-screams have made him a nuisance in his own House, it is better to die than to live. I have a Joy in Life, that passeth all Understanding; but it is not in it's present Epiphany & Incarnation. Bodily Torture! all who have been with me can bear witness that I bear it, like an Indian/it is constitutional with me to sit still & look earnestly upon it, & ask it, what it is?[16]

In the second week of August he decided to make a fair trial of forcing the 'Disease into the extremities' by the exertions of a tour into Scotland with William and Dorothy Wordsworth. Yet even as they started out in their Irish jaunting car, he was far from optimistic : 'I never yet commenced a Journey with such inauspicious Heaviness of Heart.' They travelled by way of Carlisle and Gretna Green to Dumfries where they visited the grave of Robert Burns, then proceeded through Lanarkshire and Dunbartonshire, by the Falls of Clyde and Glasgow, to Loch Lomond. But Coleridge had not been happy. Forced to sit in the open carriage in bad weather he claimed that he had caught rheumatism in the head. In any case, relationships had been strained. Wordsworth's 'Hypochondraical Feelings keep him silent, & self-centered – ', he reported to Mrs Coleridge. But there was a growing discomfort between the two poets that ran much deeper than this. At Loch Lomond Coleridge listened to a recitation of Wordsworth's *Ruth*, probably read by Dorothy, and it occasioned the self-pitying reflection : 'tho' the World praise me, I have no dear Heart that loves my verses – I never hear them in snatches from a beloved Voice, fitted to some sweet occasion, of natural Prospect, in Winds at Night.'[17]

It is difficult not to read into this a degree of envy for his friend – so fortunate, so blessed, so cosseted by emotional comfort. At the same time it seems that Wordsworth had failed in the generosity of his regard for Coleridge, exactly from what cause we do not know ; but Dykes Campbell's suggestion that it had to do with Coleridge's consumption of opium sounds plausible. 'My words and actions imaged in his mind, distorted and snaky as the Boat man's Oar reflected in the Lake', wrote Coleridge in his notebook.[18] And later he commented: 'A = Coleridge; B = Wordsworth. A. thought himself unkindly used by B. – he had exerted himself for B. with warmth! honoring, praising B. beyond himself – etc. etc. – B. selfish – feeling all Fire respecting every Trifle of his own – quite backward to poor A. – The *up*, askance, pig look, in the Boat etc.'[19]

At Loch Lomond the poets agreed to separate, Coleridge deciding to continue his tour on foot and eventually to meet the Wordsworths in Edinburgh for the return journey. Dorothy Wordsworth comments in her journal entry for 29 August: 'So poor C. being very unwell, determined to send his clothes to Edinburgh and make the best way thither, being afraid to face much wet weather in an open carriage.' And when Coleridge reported his own version of the separation to his wife, he said much the same thing: 'I eagerly caught at the Proposal: for *sitting* in an open Carriage in the Rain is Death to me, and somehow or other I had not been quite comfortable.' But evidence of a mutual disenchantment during this tour has survived, indicating that there was something more than a disagreement over their mode of travel. In Wordsworth's *Memoirs* there is the remark, 'Coleridge was at that time in bad spirits, and somewhat too *much in love with his own dejection*.' But in Crabb Robinson's copy of this work, Sara Coleridge has underlined the words italicized above and added in the margin: 'My father gave a different account of this matter, & the cause of his departure, so far coincident indeed that his state of health made him sensitive to the cause as he might not have been otherwise.'[20] There can be little doubt that Coleridge's discomfort had been occasioned by what he saw as selfishness in his friend. Earlier on the tour he wrote, 'reflected how little there was in this World that could compensate for the loss or diminishment of the Love of such as truly love us/and what bad Calculators Vanity &

Selfishness prove to be in the long Run'.[21] Many years later he added to the entry in his notebook where he records their separation : 'utinam nonq. vidissem !' – which might be translated, 'Would that I had never set eyes upon them !' And in the following sentence he adds : 'O Esteesee ! that thou hadst from thy 22nd year indeed made *thy own* way and *alone* !'[22] But the most clear statement of his increasingly jaundiced attitude towards 'the God' in 1803 is plainly stated in a letter to Poole in the Autumn :

> I now see very little of Wordsworth : my own Health makes it inconvenient & unfit for me to go thither one third as often, as I used to do – and Wordsworth's Indolence, &c keeps him at home ... I saw him more & more benetted in hypochondriacal Fancies, living wholly among *Devotees* – having every the minutest Thing, almost his very Eating & Drinking, done for him by his Sister, or Wife – & trembled, lest a Film should rise, and thicken on his moral Eye.[23]

At last he was coming round to the view which Poole himself had so often expressed in the past, and that Southey would broadcast with his customary venom :

> Wordsworth and his sister who pride themselves upon having no selfishness, are of all human beings whom I have ever known the most intensely selfish. The one thing to which W. would sacrifice all others is his own reputation, concerning which his anxiety is perfectly childish – like a woman of her beauty : and so he can get Coleridge to talk his own writings over with him, and critise [*sic*] them, and (without commending them) teach him how to do it – to be in fact the very rain and air and sunshine of his intellect, he thinks C. is very well employed and this arrangement a very good one.[24]

In subsequent years this disenchantment with Wordsworth would take a bitter and unpleasant turn, as Coleridge began to see his friend as a rival in his love for Sara Hutchinson. How much this lay buried among his bitter thoughts towards Wordsworth in 1803 is difficult to say, but the first whisper of its suggestion was to occur in the following Spring when Coleridge wrote in his notebook : 'SICKLY

Thoughts about M. mort. & W. Sā – Hydrocarb. / died looking at the stars above the top mast.' Professor Coburn has interpreted this entry: '*unhealthy* thoughts of M(ary Wordsworth) dead and W(illiam) married to Sa(ra Hutchinson). Hydrocarb is himself? Hydro = water, i.e. dropsical, affected by various accumulations of serious fluid; also, an unstable element; and carbon is poetentially both charcoal (black and relatively valueless) and that to which the diamond of poetry and genius may be reduced.'[25]

So Coleridge departed from his friends in more ways than one at Arrochar in August of 1803, his bitterness exacerbated by the practical inconvenience that they gave him only £5 to continue his tour out of the £34 of their collected resources. But at once he felt released as he strode on by himself, covering forty-five miles of the road on his first day's walk. He had burnt his shoes drying them at a 'Boatman's Hovel', he had hurt his heel, and he was suffering from an inflamed leg, 'Rheumatism in the right of my head', and infected teeth. Nevertheless his spirits were high, 'such blessing is there in perfect liberty'. As he wrote to Mrs Coleridge, 'I am enjoying myself, having Nature with solitude & liberty; the liberty natural and solitary, the solitude natural & free!' Thus he marched on visiting Glencoe, Ballachulish and Fort William, and finally arriving at Fort Augustus where he was arrested on suspicion of being a spy.

From Fort Augustus he proceeded by way of Inverness and Cullen to Perth – arriving there on the eighth day of his lonely walk, having covered 263 miles on foot. Yet strangely, perversely, while his illness allowed him to perform such robust feats of energy, his sufferings were undiminished. At Fort William he suffered an 'hysterical Attack' and by the time he reached Perth he was again deeply depressed by nightmares. 'My spirits are dreadful, owing entirely to the Horrors of every night – I truly dread to sleep / it is no shadow with me, but substantial Misery foot-thick, that makes me sit by my bedside of a morning, & cry.' He adds the pathetic comment : 'I have abandoned all opiates except Ether be one ; & that only in *fits* – & that is a blessed medicine !'[26] At Perth, however, sad news awaited him. The Southeys had lost their daughter Margaret and had come to live at Greta Hall, finding Bristol unbearable. Coleridge decided to return home at once, so he hastened to Edinburgh where he was held up for several days waiting for a coach.

What a wonderful City Edinburgh is ! – What alternation of Height & Depth ! a city looked at in the polish'd back of a Brobdignag Spoon, held lengthways – so enormously *stretchd-up* are the Houses ! – When I first looked down on it, as the Coach drove in on the higher Street, I cannot express what I felt – such a section of a wasp's nest, striking you with a sort of bastard Sublimity from the enormity & infinity of it's littleness – the infinity swelling out the mind, the enormity striking it with wonder.[27]

It was in Edinburgh too that he composed his own epitaph while dreaming that he was dying :

> Here sleeps at length poor Col, & without Screaming,
> Who died, as he had always liv'd, a dreaming :
> Shot dead, while sleeping, by the Gout within,
> Alone, and all unknown, at E'nbro in an Inn.

By 15 September he had returned to Keswick, and the two Bristol friends were united once more. Again he could record his intense admiration for Southey: 'he is a good man / & his Industry is stupendous ! Take him all in all, his regularity & domestic virtues, Genius, Talents, Acquirements, & Knowlege – & he stands by himself.' But how long could it last? As it had happened so often in the past his exultancy was shortlived. Before very long the familiar criticisms would be confided in his notebook :

But now what is Australis? I can tell you, what he is NOT. He is not a man of warmth, or delicacy of Feeling, HE IS NOT self-oblivious or self-diffused, or acquainted with his own nature : & when warped by Resentment or Hatred, not incapable of doing base actions, at all events most *very*, or *damn'd*, indelicate actions, without hesitation at the moment, or any after-remorse. . . . He is a clear handsome piece of Water in a Park, moved from without – or at best, a smooth stream with one current, & tideless, & of which you can only avail yourself to one purpose.[28]

Yet it was probably the advent of the dependable Southey that at last made the prospect of escape feasible. And as winter approached, Coleridge became increasingly determined that he would now go abroad. The walk in Scotland had brought no improvement in his health : he had complaints that could be traced to infected teeth, rheumatism, gout, and an ulcer,[29] but the underlying problem of opium addiction was as strong as it ever was – and he continued to be tortured in his sleep : 'While I awake, & retain possession of my Will & Reason, I can contrive to keep the Fiend at Arms length ; but Sleep throws wide open all the Gates of the beleagured City – & an Host of Horrors rush in.' Neither had there been any improvement in his marriage. Of Mrs Coleridge he wrote, 'We go on, as usual – except that tho' I do not love her a bit better, I quarrel with her much less. We cannot be said to live at all as Husband & Wife/ but we are peaceable Housemates.'[30]

At the same time, while his love for Sara Hutchinson had increased, his illness and his late rift with the Wordsworths put her even more out of reach. He seemed to settle more and more into a state of self-pity and despair; to entertain a mood that would make his parting more bearable :

⌈O Σαρα Σαρα why am I⌉ not happy! why have I not an unencumbered Heart! these beloved Books still before me, this noble Room, the very centre to which a whole world of beauty converges, the deep reservoir into which all these streams & currents of lovely Forms flow – my own mind so populous, so active, so full of noble schemes, so capable of realising them/ this heart so loving, so filled with noble affections – ⌈Ασρα⌉ wherefore am I not happy! why for years have I not enjoyed one pure & sincere pleasure! – one full Joy! – one genuine

Delight, that rings sharp to the Beat of the Finger! – all cracked &
dull with base Alloy![31]

And in the loneliness and frustration of his love, Wordsworth, with his circle of 'Devotees' must have reproached him,
driven him even deeper into himself. 'Month after month,
year after year, the deepest Feeling of my Heart hid &
wrapped up in the depth & darkness – solitary chaos –
& solitariness', he wrote in his notebook.[32] Increasingly his
love was stifled by the grief of his frustrated longings :

> When I am sad & sick, I'd fain persuade my heart, I do not wish
> to see you but when my nature feels a vernal breeze, a gleam of
> sunshine, & begins to open, motions felt by me, & seen by none, for
> still I look sad; as the opening rose in its first opening seems shut, O
> then I *long* for you, till longing turns to Grief – & I close up again,
> despondent, sick at heart.[33]

Yet in this mood of hopelessness there was now nothing
to keep him in England, nothing to stop him realizing that
long heralded expatriate dream of rejuvenation in a southern
climate ; indeed, he was convinced that the fulfilment of that
dream stood between life and death : 'In bad weather,' he
told Southey in a moment of insight, 'I can not possess
Life without opiates . . . in fine weather I have not a Feeling
about me that ever reminds me that I have been Ill.'[34]

During the final weeks of 1803 he seemed to be getting
all in order for a long absence. He had settled his life
insurance, and by November his children had been publicly
baptized. Drawing up a list of works in progress and works
unfinished, he entered them into his notebook in order of
priority, 'with a deep groan from the Innermost of my
Heart, in the feeling of self-humiliation, & a lively sense of
my own weakness, & the distraction of my mind'. At the
head of the list was 'The Men and the Times : & then
absolutely to have done with all newspaper writing'. Then
came 'Christabel – or the Dramas'. Then 'Comforts and
Consolations'. This work had been at the forefront of his

mind throughout the latter half of 1803 – and he described it as 'Consolations and Comforts from the exercise and right application of the Reason, the Imagination, the Moral Feelings, addressed especially to those in Sickness, adversity, or distress of mind, from *speculative* gloom; etc.' It had clearly developed from his 'Le petite Soulagement' earlier in the year. But far down at the end of the list, beyond all the grandiose schemes of the past four years, he writes the brief and poignant note: 'As to Poems, I have said nothing – the wind bloweth as it listeth.'[35]

Already, too, he was developing that unhappily paranoid frame of mind that sees its unfruitful schemes and ideas filched away into the works of others – and even stolen by enemies to be turned against him. As he put it in a letter to Poole:

I lay too many Eggs in the hot Sands with Ostrich Carelessness & Ostrich oblivion – And tho' many are luckily trod on & smashed; as many crawl forth into Life, some to furnish Feathers for the Caps of others, and more alas! to plume the Shafts in the Quivers of my Enemies and of them 'that lie in wait against my Soul.'[36]

Little wonder that he could write to his brother George that his heart had been 'strangely shut up within itself'. But as the year drew to a close and the time for his fateful departure approached, he seemed to shrink even further into himself as if terrified of the enormous alteration in his life that lay ahead. On 23 November the house was turned upside down as the furniture was moved around to settle Southey's family permanently. Coleridge lay in his study, as if clinging to the last remnants of his security: 'Lo! on this day *we change Houses*! – All is in a bustle/and I do not greatly like *Bustle*; but it is not that that depresses me/it is the *Change*! – Change! – O Change doth trouble me with Pangs untold! – But change, and change! change about! – But they shall not get me out – from Thee, Dear Study!'[37]

Like a child nestling to his mother's bosom, he lay on

the couch or half-bed in his study, indulging fantasies of comfort and security :

When in a state of pleasurable & balmy Quietness I feel my Cheek and Temple on the nicely made up Pillow in Caelibe Toro meo, the fire-gleam on my dear Books, that fill up one whole side from ceiling to floor of my Tall Study – & winds, perhaps are driving the rain, or whistling in frost, at my blessed Window, whence I see Borrodale, the Lake, Newlands – wood, water, mountains, omniform Beauty – O then as I first sink on the pillow, as if Sleep had indeed a material *realm*, as if when I sank on my pillow, I was entering that region & realized Faery Land of Sleep – O then what visions have I had, what dreams – the Bark, the Sea, all the shapes & sounds & adventures made up of the Stuff of Sleep & Dreams, & yet my Reason at the Rudder/ O what visions, ⟨μαστου⟩ as if my Cheek & Temple were lying on me gale o' mast on – Seele meines Lebens! – & I sink down the waters, thro' Seas & Seas – yet warm, yet a Spirit – /

⟨οι⟩
Pillow = mast high[38]

As Professor Coburn has noted *me gale o' mast on*, signifies μεγαλόμαστον or, 'large breasted', and *mast high* (mast-οι), signifies 'breasts'.[39]

And at night he kept vigil, marking the progress of time in the stillness and silence – as if striving to withhold the destruction of change by the sheer effort of contemplation :

Wednesday Morning, 20 minutes past 2 o Clock. November 2nd. 1803. The Voice of the Greta, and the Cock-crowing: the Voice seems to grow, like a Flower on or about the water beyond the Bridge, while the Cock crowing is nowhere particular. . . . Now while I have been writing this & gazing between whiles (it is 40 m. past Two) the Break [in the clouds] over the road is swallowed up, & the Stars gone, the Break over the House is narrowed into a rude Circle, & on the edge of its circumference one very bright Star – see! already the white mass thinning at its edge *fights* with its Brilliance – see! it has bedimmed it – & now it is gone – & the Moon is gone. The Cock-crowing too has ceased. The Greta sounds on for ever. But I hear only the Ticking of my Watch, in the Pen-place of my Writing Desk, & the far lower note of the noise of the Fire – perpetual, yet seeming uncertain/it is the low voice of quiet change, of Destruction doing its work by little & little.[40]

Somehow the call to action, the opportunity to act, had found him paralysed. Yet as so often in the past self-knowledge led to insight. During his last days at Keswick he was buried in Kant's Ethics, where Kant teaches that reverence for the Law of Reason is to be identified with the rational concept itself. 'It is not enough that we act in conformity to the Law of moral Reason,' he comments in his notebook, ' – we must likewise FOR THE SAKE of that law/it must not only be our Guide, but likewise our Impulse – Like a strong current, it must make a visible Road on the Sea, & drive us along that road . . . '[41] It is the Will that produces impulse to action, like the wind in the sails of a ship, the mere presence of a rational concept leaves the ship becalmed. As he had noted lying in 'pleasurable & balmy Quietness' on his pillow, 'all the shapes & sounds & adventures' were but the 'Stuff of Sleep & Dreams, & yet my Reason at the Rudder'.

At last the impulse struck, and on 20 December he finally set out from Greta Hall, still uncertain whether he was bound for Madeira, Sicily or Malta. He got as far as Grasmere and collapsed once more with illness. Here for a whole month he was nursed by Dorothy and Mary Words-worth 'who tended me with Sister's and Mother's love'. The affection of the Wordsworth household must have weakened his resolve, it certainly found him regarding Wordsworth as he had in the past :

It does a man's heart good, I will not say, to know such a Family, but even – to know that there is such a Family. In spite of Words-worth's occasional Fits of Hypochondriacal Uncomfortableness – from which more or less . . . he has never been wholly free from his very Childhood . . . his is the happiest Family, I ever saw.[42]

There were moments when his better self seemed to have returned, especially in the sharp, dry cold after a fall of snow :

I observed the beautiful effects of *drifted Snow* upon the mountains/ the divine Tone of Color from the Top of the Mountain downward, from the powderiness Grass, a rich olive Green warmed with a little Brown/ & in this way harmonious & combined by insensible Gradation with the white — The Drifting took away all the monotony of Snow; & the whole Vale of Grasmere seen from the Terrace Wall in Easedale, called Lankrigg, was as varied, perhaps more so, than even in the pomp of Autumn.[43]

But the sense of wellbeing was shortlived, soon came 'Rain, soaking Rain : and my two last Nights have been poisoned by it'. Once again his sleep was persecuted with nightmares, the silence of the night rent with his screams.

At last on the 14 January he made a sudden recovery to 'a state of elastic health', and seizing the moment he walked the fateful nineteen miles through mud and rain to Kendal. It was the first stage of a journey that would end in two years' exile; a determined flight from sickness, misery and an early death. A few days before his departure he had written to Southey; 'if I can pass a year, a whole year, in a hot climate, I feel a deep confidence, that I shall (in some way or other) recover my Health/ & gladly should I purchase it at the price of an Eruption, that would kill all Love not purely spiritual.'

Postscript

AFTER many delays, Coleridge left England in April of 1804 to take up a post as secretary to the Governor of Malta, followed by a period spent in travelling in Sicily and Italy. When he arrived back in England in the summer of 1806 the 'death' he had anticipated seemed to have come to pass. Dorothy Wordsworth noted how 'the divine expression of his countenance' had fled. 'I never saw it, as it used to be,' she wrote, ' – a shadow, a gleam there was at times, but how faint and transitory.'

Yet when Coleridge left Grasmere in January of 1804 many of the dreams of his youth had already been long dead. The young radical who had warned Southey so sternly about taking office under government was now about to join the Civil Service, and gladly. The husband and father who had hoped for so much from marriage and family life was embarking on a journey that would eventually end in permanent separation; the man who depended for his happiness and security on the society of his intimate friends was taking himself off into voluntary exile. Above all, the poet who had seen himself as a possible successor to Milton had lapsed from achievements of high originality and great power to minor productions. He would continue to write verse, much of it unremarkable, but in a few memorable pieces achieving great poignancy out of the loss of the past. As he would write in *Youth and Age*:

> When I was young? – Ah, woful When!
> Ah! for the change 'twixt Now and Then!

This breathing house not built with hands,
This body that does me grievous wrong,
O'er aery cliffs and glittering sands,
How lightly then it flashed along: –
Like those trim skiffs, unknown of yore,
On winding lakes and rivers wide,
That ask no aid of sail or oar,
That fear no spite of wind or tide!
Nought cared this body for wind or weather
When Youth and I lived in't together.

The story of Coleridge's life can, and certainly has, been told in several different ways. A familiar version coincides with Hazlitt's view expressed in 1825 – 'All that he has done of moment, he had done twenty years ago : since then he may be said to have lived on the sound of his own voice.' But in our own day as the immense task of editing his private literary remains goes forward, some 2000 letters and 70 notebooks, the verdict of many of Coleridge's contemporaries, perpetuated by successive biographers and critics until at least the beginning of the last war, has undergone reappraisal. It is clear that after that sad journey from Grasmere in 1804 a new Coleridge emerged – a man of genius undoubtedly, but essentially a man who in spite of apparent external failure continued to lead an interior of life of extraordinary depth, insight and sensitivity; whose intellectual stature and influence is not to be judged on the achievement of works published in his lifetime alone. It has become common-place to talk of Coleridge's 'seminal' influence on the nineteenth century, but the full extent of our debt both in this century and the last to his wide ranging and penetrating thought is yet to be told.

Coleridge was born in 1772 in an age when the great literary epic, or the grand philosophical system still seemed possible. He died in 1834 when such schemes of total vision and reconciliation had for a long time been out of the question. Yet when Coleridge's contemporaries hailed him as the great genius of their times it was, almost without exception, in the expectation that he would write an epic of Miltonic majesty, or, later, when he turned to metaphysics and psychology, an all-embracing philosophical system. It is likely that his attempts to achieve such works helped to destroy the poet within him and conspired with the many other afflictions that led to a life of continued suffering. The great works never appeared, but the materials out of which he strove to realize a total vision of things still lie scattered and buried in a heap of faded manuscripts and notebooks; so too does the continuing story of a lifelong spiritual and psychological agony as he struggled with pain, disillusionment and self-doubt, and the burden of his extraordinary insights. As he once wrote in a notebook:

S.T.C. = who with long and large arm still collected precious Armfuls in whatever direction he pressed forward, yet still took up so much more than he could keep together that those who followed him gleaned more from his continual droppings than he himself brought home – Nay, made stately Corn-ricks therewith, while the Reaper himself was still seen only with a strutting armful of newly cut Sheaves. – But I should misinform you grossly, if I left you to infer that his collections were a heap of incoherent Miscellanea – No! – the very Contrary – Their variety conjoined with too great Coherency, the too great both desire & power of referring them in systematic, nay, genetic subordination was that which rendered his schemes gigantic & impracticable, as an Author – & his conversation less instructive, as a man / – Inopem sua *Copia* fecit – too much was given, all so weighty & brilliant as to preclude choice, & too many to be all received – so that it passed over the Hearers mind like a roar of Waters.[1]

The account of the hidden achievement of the latter period of his life along with the major prose works of that time deserves unique and separate treatment; it does not, perhaps, lend itself very well to chronological narrative, and it must in any case wait some few years before it can be told in detail. In this sense the narrative told in these pages is a prelude to those years in which Coleridge earned his ever growing intellectual reputation. And yet this earlier story nevertheless remains one of the most poignant pages in literary history, its interest lying not so much in the weakness and failings in his character as in the pressure of outward events, the conflicts and tensions of his unusual psychological make up, that combination of influences and circumstances which with ample justification might be termed 'The Enemies of Promise'.

Abbreviations

BM	British Museum
BNYPL	*Bulletin of the New York Public Library*
Campbell *Life*	J. D. Campbell, *Samuel Taylor Coleridge*, 1894
Carlyon	C. Carlyon, *Early Years and Late Reflections*, 1836–58
CH	*Coleridge: The Critical Heritage*, ed. J. R. de J. Jackson, 1970
Chambers *Life*	E. K. Chambers, *Coleridge*, 1938
CL	*Letters of Samuel Taylor Coleridge*, ed. E. L. Griggs, 6 vols, 1956–71
CRB	*Henry Crabb Robinson on Books and their Writers*, ed. E. J. Morley, 3 vols, 1938
Curry	*New Letters of Robert Southey*, ed. K. Curry, 2 vols, 1965
CWB	*S. T. Coleridge: Writers and their Background,* ed. R. L. Brett, 1971
E Rec.	J. Cottle, *Early Recollections; chiefly relating to S. T. C.*, 1837
Gillman	J. Gillman, *Life of Coleridge*, 1838
HLQ	*Huntington Library Quarterly*
Hucks	J. Hucks, *A Pedestrian Tour in North Wales*, 1795.
IJP	*International Journal of Psychoanalysis*
JEGP	*Journal of English and Germanic Philology*
JHI	*Journal of the History of Ideas*
Litchfield	R. B. Litchfield, *Tom Wedgwood*, 1903
LL	*Letters of Charles and Mary Lamb*, ed. E. V. Lucas, 1935
LPR	*Lectures 1795: On Politics and Religion*, ed. L. Patton and P. Mann, 1970, vol. ii, in *Collected Works of S. T. C.*, general ed. K. Coburn.

MLN	*Modern Language Notes*
Moorman	M. Moorman, *William Wordsworth: the Early Years*, 1957
N	*The Notebooks of Samuel Taylor Coleridge*, ed. K. Coburn, 2 double vols, 1957, 1961
Observer	*The Observer, Part 1st Being a transient glance at about Forty Youths of Bristol* (Bristol), 1795
Orsini	G. Orsini, *Coleridge and German Idealism*, New York, 1969
PMLA	*Proceedings of the Modern Language Association*
PW	*The Poems of Samuel Taylor Coleridge*, ed. E. H. Coleridge, 1912
REL	*Review of English Literature*
Rem.	J. Cottle, *Reminiscences of S.T.C. . . . and Robert Southey*, 1847
RES	*Review of English Studies*
SC Mem.	*Memoir and Letters of Sara Coleridge*, ed. by her Daughter, 1873
Seward	A. Seward, *Letters 1784*, Edinburgh, 1811
Shaver	*The Letters of William and Dorothy Wordsworth*, vol. 1, rec. by C. L. Shaver, 1967
SH Letters	*The Letters of Sara Hutchinson*, ed. K. Coburn, 1954
TPF	Mrs H. Sandford, *Thomas Poole and his Friends*, 1888
TLS	*The Times Literary Supplement*
TT	*Specimens of the Table Talk of S.T.C.*, ed. H. N. Coleridge, 1835
UTQ	*University of Toronto Quarterly*
VCL	Victoria College Library, Toronto
W	The *Watchman*, ed. Lewis Patton, 1970, vol. II in the *Collected Works of S. T. C.* general ed. K. Coburn
WPW	*Wordsworth's Poetical Works*, ed. E. de Selincourt and H. Darbishire, 1940–49

References

In order to keep references to a minimum I have omitted to give the sources of well-known passages. Also, when quoting the letters of Coleridge, Wordsworth and Lamb, where their correspondents and the date of writing are clear from the narrative, I have similarly omitted to give further citation.

ONE: CHILDHOOD AND YOUTH

1. *E Rec.* I, 243
2. E. Marcovitz, 'Bemoaning the Lost Dream', *I J P* 45, 1965, 411
3. Gillman, 20
4. Gillman, 28
5. See Orsini, 13
6. L. Werkmeister, 'Coleridge, Bowles and "Feelings of the Heart"', *Anglia* 78, 1960, 55
7. *CL* I, 545, 619
8. *TT* 15 Aug. 1833
9. *N* 1239
10. *N* 1176
11. *N* 2398
12. *N* 1250
13. *N* 1649
14. D. Beres, 'A Dream, A vision and a Poem', *I J P* 32, 1951, 97; Charles Baudouin, *Psychoanalysis and Aesthetics*, New York, 1924, 250; M. Schulz, 'Coleridge Agonistes', *J E G P* 61, 1962, 268
15. D. Fernbach, 'Sexuality and revolution', *New Left Review* 64, 1970, 87
16. *N* 848, 990, 1250, 1649, 1726, 1824; *CL* II, 1028
17. *N* 1403, 1726
18. *CL* II, 902
19. BM C. 126. k. 1. Marg.
20. Carlyon III, 1

21. J. Priestley, *Letters to Young Men*, 1787, 47
22. J. Priestley, *An Appeal*, 1792, 2
23. E.P.Thompson, *The Making of the Working Class*, Penguin edn 1968, 117
24. J.Priestley, *An Appeal*, 5, 7
25. J.Priestley, *Matter and Spirit*, 1782, 1, 37–8
26. *Ibid.*, 11, 42
27. Freda Knight, *University Rebel*, 1971, 69
28. P.Kaufman, 'New Light on Coleridge as an undergraduate', *REL* 7, 1966, 69
29. Freda Knight, *University Rebel*, 120
30. H.Gunning, *Reminiscences of the University, Town and County of Cambridge, from the year 1780*, 1854, 299–300
31. *CL* 1, 53
32. *CL* 1, 56
33. *CL* 1, 67

TWO : PANTISOCRACY

1. *CL* 1, 93
2. Hucks, 3
3. *CL* 1, 84
4. *E. Rec.* 1, 7
5. Curry, 1, 37
6. J. Simmonds, *Robert Southey*, 1945, 25
7. VCL MS BT Coleridge, Srah (Transcript) 9
8. Curry, 1, 38
9. *CL* 1, 86
10. Gillman, 69
11. *Ibid.*
12. Norman Cohn, *The Pursuit of the Millennium*, Paladin edn 1970, 179
13. J. Priestley, *Letters to Young Men*, 73
14. W.Godwin, *Political Justice*, 2nd edn, 1796, 1, 38
15. *Ibid.*, 1, 49
16. *Ibid.*, 11, 400
17. *Ibid.*, 11, 440
18. *CL* 1, 102
19. Hucks, 117
20. Hucks, 36
21. *CL* 1, 88
22. *CL* 1, 87–8
23. Trans. E.L.Griggs, *CL* 1, 88n
24. Curry, 1, 59

25. Curry, I, 54
26. Curry, I, 57
27. *Observer*, 16
28. Curry, I, 61
29. *SCMem.* 10
30. VCL MS
31. Curry, I, 71
32. VCL MS
33. VCL MS
34. Curry, I, 68–9
35. TPF I, 109
36. TPF I, 136
37. TPF I, 124
38. TPF I, 100–1
39. TPF I, 96–9
40. VCL MS
41. Seward, VI, 57
42. *PMLA* XLV, 1930, 1074
43. Brissot de Warville, *Travels in the United States*, 1794, I, 48, quoted *PMLA* XLV, 1930, 1089
44. Thomas Cooper, *Some Information Respecting America*, 1794, 64, quoted *REL* VII, 1966, 66
45. Carlyon, I, 27
46. *CL* I, 260
47. *CL* I, 119
48. *CL* I, 114
49. *The Fall of Robespierre*, Act III, ii, 189–91

THREE: THE EBULLIENCE OF 'SCHEMATISM'

1. *CL* II, 735
2. T.J.Hogg, *Life of Shelley*, 1933, I, 423
3. Curry, I, 57
4. *CL* I, 59
5. *N* 448
6. *CL* I, 102
7. *CL* I, 106
8. *CL* I, 109
9. *CL* I, 112–13
10. *CL* I, 129–30
11. *CL* I, 132
12. *CL* I, 170

13. *CL* I, 144
14. *CL* III, 86, 91
15. *CL* I, 145
16. *LL* I, 60
17. *LL* I, 8
18. H. Piper, 'Pantheistic sources of Coleridge', *JHI* xx, 1959, 47
19. BM C. 126. k. I, *Aurora*, 27
20. *CL* I, 126
21. *CL* I, 137
22. *CL* I, 137
23. *CL* I, 215
24. *CL* I, 138–9
25. *CL* I, 146
26. *CL* I, 148
27. *Rem.* 405
28. *LL* I, 4
29. Campbell, *Life*, 42

FOUR: BRISTOL

1. Curry, I, 37
2. Curry, I, 93
3. *CL* I, 260
4. G. Whalley, 'Coleridge and Southey in Bristol', *RES* I, 1950
5. *N* 566
6. *E Rec.* I, 3
7. *E Rec.* I, 7
8. *Observer*, 15
9. *Monthly Magazine*, XLVIII, 1819, 203
10. *Observer*, 15
11. *CL* II, 1000–1
12. *E Rec.* I, 178n
13. *CRB* I, 59
14. Seward, IV, 27
15. *LPR* 74
16. *CL* I, 152
17. *LPR* 12
18. *LPR* 43
19. *Observer*, 14
20. *E Rec.* I, 39
21. *E Rec.* I, 44–5
22. *CL* I, 172
23. *CL* I, 171–2

24. *RES* i, 1950
25. *CL* i, 165
26. *CL* i, 158

FIVE : MARRIAGE

1. This point has been discussed by the anonymous reviewer of Coleridge's *Lectures Political and Moral,* in *TLS,* 6 August 1971, 930
2. *LPR* lxxviii
3. *LPR* 229
4. *LPR* 227–8
5. *LPR* lvii
6. *N* 12n
7. Quoted Orsini, 14
8. Quoted Orsini, 25
9. *N* 203n
10. *CL* i, 160
11. *CL* i, 154
12. *PW* i, 97
13. Moorman, i, 271; see also Robert Woof's 'Wordsworth and Coleridge: some early matters', in *Bicentenary Wordsworth Studies,* ed. J. Wordsworth and B. Darlington, Cornell 1970, 76
14. TPF i, 128
15. *E Rec.* i, 58
16. Curry, i, 103
17. *CL* i, 173
18. *CL* i, 190
19. *CL* ii, 751

SIX : 'THE WATCHMAN'

1. *LPR* 361
2. *E Rec.* i, 150
3. *E Rec.* i, 150
4. *CL* i, 174
5. *W* xxxii
6. *W* xxxii–xxxiii
7. *CL* i, 175
8. *CL* i, 180
9. *CL* i, 179
10. *CL* i, 177
11. *CL* i, 179
12. *CL* i, 185–6
3. *W* xxxv

14. *CL* I, 207–8
15. *W* 13–14
16. *W* xxxviii
17. *W* 99
18. *W* xli–xlii
19. *CL* I, 208
20. *CL* I, 268–9
21. *W* 374–5

SEVEN: IN SEARCH OF A ROLE

1. *CH* 32
2. *CH* 35
3. *CH* 36
4. *CL* I, 207
5. *CL* I, 215–16. The first of the passages Coleridge refers to is as follows:

> When on some solemn jubilee of Saints
> The sapphire-blazing gates of Paradise
> Are thrown wide open; and thence voyage forth
> Detachments wide of seraph-warbled airs,
> And odors snatch'd from beds of amaranth,
> And they that from the crystal river of life
> Spring on freshn'd wing, ambrosial gales!
> The favor'd good man in his lonely walk
> Perceives them, and his silent spirit drinks
> Strange bliss that he shall recognise in heaven.

6. *CL* I, 214
7. *LL* I, 50
8. Quoted *CL* I, 220n
9. *CL* I, 222
10. *CL* I, 232
11. *CL* I, 228
12. *CL* I, 235
13. E.V. Lucas, *Charles Lamb and the Lloyds*, 1898, 20
14. *CL* I, 236
15. *LL* I, 72–3
16. *CL* I, 239
17. *LL* I, 72–3
18. *CL* I, 254
19. *CL* I, 240
20. *LL* I, 46–7
21. *CL* I, 249–50

22. *CL* i, 274
23. *CL* i, 271–2
24. *CL* i, 275
25. *CL* i, 288
26. *CL* i, 289
27. *PW* i, 160
28. *PW* i, 167n
29. *RES* i, 1950
30. *CL* i, 277
31. TPF i, 200–1

EIGHT : ALFOXDEN

1. *The Later Years*, ed. E. de Selincourt, 1939, 1584
2. *Memoirs of W. Wordsworth*, Christopher Wordsworth, 1851, i, 94
3. *CL* i, 320
4. *CL* vi, *Appendix B* 1009
5. *CL* i, 325
6. See MS D (dating 1799–1800), Jonathan Wordsworth's *The Music of Humanity*, 1968
7. Shaver, 189
8. J. Wordsworth, *The Music of Humanity*, 201
9. *CL* vi, 733
10. *LL* i, 112
11. *E Rec.* i, 275–7
12. *Illustrated London News*, 22 April 1893
13. TPF i, 233
14. Campbell, *Life* 73
15. *BNYPL* lxxvii, 1970, 82
16. *Ibid.*
17. *BL* 102
18. *WPW* i, 363
19. *TT*, 21 July, 1832
20. *CL* i, 339
21. *CL* i, 342
22. *CL* i, 344
23. For a discussion and full sources of 'the Spy' episode see H. Eaglestone, 'Wordsworth, Coleridge and the Spy', in *Coleridge. Studies by several hands*, 1934
24. For a full discussion of Wedgwood's 'Master-Stroke' see D. Erdman, 'Coleridge, Wordsworth and the Wedgwood Fund', *BNYPL* lx, 1956
25. *CL* i, 354

26. In opting for November of 1797 I am favouring M. L. Reed's argument in *Wordsworth: the chronology of the early years 1770–99* (Cambridge, Mass.) 1967; see also Chambers, *Life*, 100–3
27. Shaver, 194
28. *Works of William Hazlitt*, ed. P. P. Howe, 1930–34, XVII, 120
29. *PW* I, 296n
30. *PW* I, 296
31. *N* 383
32. *N* 1725
33. *CL* II, 853–4
34. *N* 2832
35. *CL* II, 814
36. *CL* II, 814; S. T. Coleridge, *Aids to Reflection*, 1825, 4n; *N* III, 4225, quoted CWB II, 43
37. *WPW* I, 361
38. Carlyon I, 143–4
39. *CL* VI, 1049
40. *N* 2372
41. *CL* VI, 1049
42. *N* 1772
43. *CL* II, 768
44. *CL* I, 367
45. *CL* I, 375
46. Chambers, *Life*, 90
47. E. Royston Pike, *Human Documents of the Industrial Revolution in Britain*, 1966, 104–5
48. *CL* II, 775
49. *CL* I, 396–7
50. *CL* I, 359
51. For the sources of the Lloyd affair, see E. K. Chambers, *A Sheaf of Studies*, 1942
52. *Ibid.*, 68–9

NINE: 'THE ANCIENT MARINER'

1. *CH* 53
2. *CH* 56
3. *CH* 57–8
4. *CL* I, 602n
5. Van Akin Burd, 'Background to Modern Painters', *PMLA* LXXIV, 1959
6. *N* III 4225, quoted *CWB* II

7. *CL* ii, 810
8. *CL* vi, 634
9. *Inquiring Spirit*, ed. K.Coburn, 1951, 143–4
10. S.T.Coleridge, *Aids to Reflection*, 1825, 4n
11. *N* 2357
12. J.Boehme, *Works* trans. W.Law, 1764–81, vol. i, *Aurora*, 118
13. *CL* ii, 814
14. BM C. 126. k. 1. Marg.
15. *UTQ* xvi, 381; also available in abridged form in *Coleridge: A Collection of Critical Essays*, ed. K.Coburn, 1967; and *The Rime of The Ancient Mariner*, ed. James D.Boulger, 1969
16. *N* 1561
17. P.Brown, *Augustine of Hippo*, 40
18. See *N* 161 (c)n
19. For a full discussion of Augustine and *The Ancient Mariner*, see J.A Stuart's study in *MLN* lxxvi, 1961, 116
20. *CL* ii, 949
21. *N* 1302
22. *N* 1247

TEN : GERMANY

1. *CL* i, 363
2. BM C. 126. k. 1. Marg.
3. *CL* i, 480
4. *CL* i, 416
5. *CL* i, 462
6. *CL* i, 508
7. *CL* i, 502
8. *CL* i, 524n
9. *CL* i, 543
10. *CL* i, 543
11. *CL* i, 544–5
12. *SH Letters*, ed. K.Coburn, xxxviii
13. *N* 1575
14. *N* 1575n
15. *N* 581
16. *N* 1592
17. T.J.Wise, *A Bibliography . . . of S.T.C.*, 1913, 257–64
18. *CL* i, 575
19. *CL* i, 582
20. *CL* i, 570

21. *CL* I, 579
22. *CL* I, 359
23. *CL* I, 582
24. *CL* I, 562

ELEVEN : GRETA HALL

1. *CL* I, 644
2. *CL* I 620
3. *N* 808
4. *N* 875
5. *N* 791
6. *CL* I, 643
7. *CL* I, 631n
8. *CL* I 623
9. Shaver, 305
10. *CL* I, 631n
11. *CL* I, 602n
12. *CL* I, 620
13. *CL* II, 714
14. *N* 834
15. *CL* I, 629
16. *CL* VI, 992
17. T.De Quincey, *Confessions of an Opium Eater*, Folio Society 1948, 150–1n
18. N.Retterstöl and A.Surd, 'Drug addiction and habituation', *Acta Psychiatrica Scandinavica*, XL, 1964, Suppl. 179
19. E.Slater and M.Roth, *Clinical Psychiatry*, 3rd ed., 1969, 424
20. *N* 848
21. *CL* I, 713–14
22. *CL* I, 656
23. *N* 932
24. *N* 918
25. *N* 924
26. *N* 925
27. *CL* I, 651
28. *CL* I, 625
29. *N* 886
30. *CL* I, 625
31. *N* 894
32. *N* 921
33. *Hazlitt Works*, ed. P.P.Howe, XX, 388, quoted R.Park, *Hazlitt and The Spirit of the Age*, 1971, 99

34. Quoted *ibid.*, 102
35. Quoted *ibid.*, 102
36. *N* 891
37. *CL* 11, 709
38. *CL* 11, 706
39. *CL* 11, 683
40. *CL* 11, 685–6
41. *CL* 11, 699–700
42. *CL* 11, 696
43. *CL* 11, 695
44. Quoted *CL* 11, 677n
45. TPF 11, 34
46. *CL* 11, 709
47. *N* 975
48. *N* 985
49. *CL* 11, 709
50. P.Colquhoun, *Wealth, Power and Resources of the British Empire,*
    1800, 111
51. *CL* 11, 709
52. *CL* 11, 726
53. *CL* 11, 747–8
54. *CL* 11, 757, 762, 765
55. *N* 926n
56. Shaver, 330–1
57. *N* 987
58. *N* 1030
59. *N* 979
60. *N* 985, 986
61. *CL* 11, 767
62. *Gent.Mag.* May 1838, 487
63. Southey to William Taylor, 6 Feb. 1802, quoted *CL* 11, 787n
64. *CL* 111, 782–3
65. *N* 1108
66. *N* 1032
67. *CL* 11, 785–6
68. *CL* 11, 789
69. *CL* 11, 788
70. *N* 1154
71. *CL* 11, 875
72. *CL* 11, 876
73. *CL* 11, 957n
74. *CL* 11, 832–3
75. *CL* 11, 875 6

76. *N* 2398
77. Quoted *N* 2398n
78. *CL* II, 831
79. *N* 1064
80. Moorman, I, 415, 539
81. *CL* I, 154
82. *N* 1421
83. *N* 1421n
84. See chapter 13, *Bicentenary Wordsworth Studies*, ed. J.Wordsworth and B.Darlington, 1970
85. *CL* II, 798

TWELVE: '. . . A LITTLE THEOLOGICAL'

1. Curry II, 294
2. *CL* II, 832–3
3. Shaver, 363
4. *N* 1156n
5. *N* 1153, 1156, 1157
6. *N* 1242n, 830n
7. *CL* II, 828
8. *CL* II, 871
9. Curry II, 294
10. *CL* II, 832
11. *CL* II, 819
12. *CL* II, 831
13. *CL* II, 805
14. *CL* II, 873
15. *CL* II, 830
16. *CL* II, 810
17. *CL* II, 864
18. *CL* II, 866
19. *CL* II, 814
20. *CL* II, 814
21. *N* 1718
22. *N* 1713
23. *N* 1715
24. BM C. 126. k. 1. Marg.
25. L.Wittgenstein, *Tractatus Logico-Philosophicus*, 1961, 147, 151
26. J.H.Newman, *Grammar of Assent*, 1947, 40
27. *CL* II, 841–2
28. *LL* IV, 314–15

29. *HLQ* xxiv, 1961, 67
30. *CL* ii, 853–4
31. *CL* ii, 875–8

THIRTEEN: 'A COMET TIED TO A COMET'S TAIL'

1. *CL* ii, 878–9
2. *CL* ii, 881–2
3. *CL* ii, 884
4. *CL* ii, 887–8
5. *CL* ii, 889–90
6. Litchfield, 139–40
7. *CL* ii, 894
8. *CL* ii, 909n
9. *SH Letters*, xxvi; Chambers, *Life*, 164–6
10. *CL* ii, 910
11. *CL* ii, 909
12. *CL* ii, 910–11
13. *CL* ii, 914
14. *CL* ii, 916
15. *CL* ii, 929
16. Litchfield, 139
17. Thorpe, *Davy*, 85

FOURTEEN: GOING AWAY

1. See Head note, Letter 504, *CL* ii, 946
2. *CL* ii, 947
3. *CL* ii, 949
4. *CL* ii, 946; and see Alice Snyder, *Coleridge on Logic and Learning*, 1929, 52–3
5. *CL* ii, 953
6. *CL* ii, 954
7. *CL* ii, 960
8. *CL* ii, 959
9. *CL* ii, 974
10. *The Farington Diary*, ed. J. Greig, 1923, ii, 172
11. *CL* ii, 957
12. *CL* ii, 934
13. *CL* ii, 976
14. *CL* ii, 986
15. *CL* ii, 981
16. *CL* ii, 990

17. *N* 1463
18. *N* 1473
19. *N* 1606
20. *N* 1471n
21. *N* 1436
22. *N* 1471
23. *CL* II, 1012
24. Curry, I, 449
25. *N* 2001n
26. *CL* II, 982
27. *CL* II, 988
28. *N* 1815
29. *CL* II, 992, 998–9
30. *CL* II, 1015
31. *N* 1577
32. *N* 1670
33. *N* 1669
34. *CL* II, 1027
35. *N* 1646
36. *CL* II, 1011
37. *N* 1682
38. *N* 1718
39. *N* 1718n
40. *N* 1635
41. *N* 1705; see also Basil Willey, *Samuel Taylor Coleridge*, 1972, 102–3
42. *CL* II, 1023
43. *N* 1812

POSTSCRIPT

1. *N* III, 4400; Quoted CWB 24

Index

Index

Abergavenny, 366
Abergeley, 48
Acton, 149
Adscombe, 146
Aeschylus, 26
Aiken, John, 135
Alfoxden, 168–9, 172, 280
Allen, Fanny, 371
Allen, John, 368
Ambleside, 268
America, 39, 49, 50–1, 53, 56–7, 64–5
An Address to the Inhabitants of Cambridge, 20
Analytic Review, 135
An Appeal to Candid Professors of Christianity, 20
Annals of Pleasure, 37
Aquinas, Thomas, 309, 322
Aristotle, 380
Arkwright, Richard, 22
Arrochar, 389
Asra, see Hutchinson, Sara
Augustine, 238–9
Aurora, 8, 234, 236, 245
Australis, see Southey, Robert
Azores, 313

Bacon, Francis, 266, 380

Bala, 415
Ballachulish, 389
Balliol College, 37
Bartram, 316
Bath, 103
Baudouin, Charles, 403
Beaumont, Sir George, 382–3
Beddoes, Thomas, 139, 178, 278
Bedford, Grosvenor, 49, 113
Bedford, Horace, 52
Beer, John, 183
Beres, D., 403
Berkeley, George, 7, 153–4, 304, 309
Biggs, Nathaniel, 288
Billington, Mrs, 325
Birmingham, 123
Blumenbach, J. F., 254
Boehme, Jacob, 8, 234, 236, 245
Bon Ton Magazine, 37
Bordeaux, 326
Borderers, 162, 181, 195
Borrodale, 284
Botanic Garden, 124
Botany Bay, 90
Bowles, William Lisle, 9–10, 193, 355
Boyer, James, 7–8
Brecon, 366

Bridge Street, 321
Brindley, James, 22
Bristol, 86
Bristol, Library, 153–4
British Critic, 134, 223
Brocken, 260
Brunton, Ann, 71–2, 132
Brunton, Elizabeth, 71
Bruton, 217
Buchan, Earl of, 117
Burd, Van Akin, 410
Burke, Edmund, 26
Burnett, George, 51, 85, 97, 99, 113, 126, 128
Burney, Charles, 223
Burns, Robert, 317, 350
Buttermere, 362
Byron, George Gordon, Lord, 183

Cambridge, 18–19, 26–32, 53, 58–9
Cambridge Intelligencer, 131, 150
Campbell, J. Dykes, 386
Canary Isles, 372
Carlisle, 372
Carlyle, Thomas, 197, 198
Carlyon, Clement, 19, 194, 254, 263
Castle of Indolence, 330
Chambers, E. K., 372
Chatterton, Thomas, 12, 31, 111, 149, 350
Cheapside, 284
Cheddar, 53
Chepstow, 95
Chester, John, 247, 253, 263
Chester, 283
Christ's Hospital, 6–14, 77, 127

Citizen, 86
Clarkson, Thomas, 86
Clyde, 386
Complaints of the Poor People of England, 57
Conclusion to Hartley's Observations, 79
Condillac, 380
Confessions, 242
Cooper, Thomas, 58
Cottle, Joseph, 4, 87, 94–5, 103, 112, 117, 121, 145, 167–8, 173, 217, 268
Covent Garden, 321
Clevedon, 129
Cobbett, William, 18
Coburn, Kathleen, 109, 270, 394
Cohn, Norman, 404
Coleridge, Ann (mother), 3–6, 16
Coleridge, Ann (sister), 1, 4–5, 28–9, 69
Coleridge, Berkeley, 219, 247, 254, 256
Coleridge, David Hartley, 142, 145, 267, 300, 351–2, 358
Coleridge, Derwent, 284, 300, 351–2, 358
Coleridge, Francis, 2–5, 29
Coleridge, George, 8, 30, 62–3, 140, 214, 266
Coleridge, James, 266
Coleridge, John (father), 1–2, 4–6, 12, 16
Coleridge, Luke, 8
Coleridge, Henry Nelson, 197, 224, 229, 264
Coleridge, Samuel Taylor: his early reading, 2; his relationships with mother and father,

Coleridge, Samuel Taylor – *cont.*
3–6; at Christ's Hospital, 6–10; and political awareness, and early poetry, 10–12; his dreams, 14–18; and Unitarianism, 18–27; loss of sister Ann, 28; and financial and emotional problems, 30–2; at Oxford, 35–42; and Pantisocracy, 39–42; in Wales, 45–50; his engagement to Sara Fricker, 50–3; and Pantisocratic quarrels, 60–65; and Southey, 66–8; his romantic misadventures, 69–76; in London, 77–8; and Hartley, 80–1; returns to Bristol and duty, 84; and Cottle, 87; and political lectures, 88–94; quarrels with Southey, 96–100; and religious lectures, 101–4; and lyrical poetry and *Eolian Harp*, 104–8; and transcendentalism, 108–9; and Nature, 109–110; marries, 111–13; breaks up with Southey, 114; and the *Watchman*, 121–3; and publication and reception of *Poems*, 134–6; and Thelwall, 136; and school plans, 136–7; and Charles Lamb, 143–4; his new seriousness, 145; and Poole, 146–50; his *Ode to the Departing Year*, 150–2; his determination to seek retirement, 152; and Berkeley, 153–4; at Nether Stowey, 154–6; and the Wordsworths,

157–62; and *This Lime Tree Bower*, 163–6; and Thelwall, 169–72; and the episode of the Spy, 172–6; and the Wedgwoods, 177–81; and *Kubla Khan*, 183–90; and inception of *The Ancient Mariner*, 190–192; and conversation, 196–200; and the Wedgwood annuity, 201–9; and *Frost at Midnight*, 210–14; and influence of Wordsworth, 214–217; and the Lloyd affair, 217–22; and *The Ancient Mariner*, 223–46; in Germany, 249–63; and death of Berkeley Coleridge, 254–5; and transcription and homesickness, 256–7; and failure to write descriptive prose, 257–260; and reconciliation with Southey, 264–6; and Sara Hutchinson, 269–71; and journalism in London, 272–280; moves to Keswick, 283; and *Christabel*, 287–91; and opium, 293–6; and illness, 296–8; his lapse from poetical inspiration, 298–9; his researches into language, perception and thought, 301–6; and Descartes and Locke, 307–9; and disgust with poverty, 310–13; and dreams of a warmer climate, 313–16; and the *Morning Post*, 321–2; and domestic affliction, 327–9; and *A Letter to [Asra]*, 330–8; his metaphysics and poetical

Coleridge, Samuel Taylor – *cont.*
loss, 338–9; and Mrs Coleridge and Sara Hutchinson, 340–1; and dejection, 342–4; and separation, 345–7; and the consolation of the Wordsworths, 347–51; and his children, 351–2; and Sotheby, 353–4; and criticism, 355–6; and imagination, 356–7; and religious experience, 358–9; as Thomas Wedgwood's companion, 364–6; and more domestic afflictions, 367–1; and dietry, 373–4; and London society, 377–8; and projected grand schemes, 380–1; and tyranny of opium and nightmares, 384–5; with the Wordsworths in Scotland, 386–90; and alienation from the Wordsworths, 389; and depression, 392; and emotional security, 394; decides to leave England, 395–6

Works (and projected works in inverted commas):
Aids to Reflection, 410
Ancient Mariner, The, 166, 191, 223–46, 290
[*Asra*], *A letter to*, 329–38, 344
Autumnal Evening, Lines on an, 29
Ave Atque Vale, 47
'*Biblioteca Brittanica*', 381
Biographia Literaria, 9–10, 123–4, 170, 173, 274–5, 277

Composed on a Journey Homewards, 153, 189
Conciones ad Populum, 93
Consolations and Comforts, 374
Christabel, 221, 285, 287–91
Day Dream, A, 326
Dejection: an Ode, 228, 344
Departing Year, Ode to the, 150–2
Destiny of Nations, 79
Discovery Made Too Late, On a, 73
Destruction of the Bastile, 10–12
Eolian Harp, The, 106–8, 111–12, 232, 303
Fall of Robespierre, The, 56, 63
Friend, The, 257
Frost at Midnight, 210–14, 216, 244
'*Hymns to the Sun, the Moon and the Elements*', 153
'*Imitations from the Modern Latin Poets*', 116, 121
'*Instrument of Practical Reasoning*', 379
King's Arms, Ross, Lines Written at the, 44
Kubla Khan, 181–90, 213, 221
Lime Tree Bower, This, 163–166, 189, 210
Lyrical Ballads, 158, 274, 287, 288, 290
Mad Monk, The, 331
'*Men and the Times, The*,' 392
Monody on the Death of Chatterton, 12–13

Works – cont.

Moral and Political Lecture, A, 88, 91
Nightingale, The, 106
Observing a Blossom on the First of February, On, 126
Oft of some unknown Past such Fancies roll, 142
One who Published In Print, To, 221
'Organum verè Organum', 380
Osorio, 162, 180, 189, 193, 194–51
O What a Life is the Eye! 255
Pains of Sleep, 384
Perspiration A Travelling Eclogue, 43
Poems, 121, 127, 134–5, 138, 145, 156
Plot Discovered, The, 119
Present War, On the, 91
Recantation: An Ode, 215
Receiving an Account that his only Sister's Death was inevitable, 28
Reflections on Entering Active Life, 24
Reflections on Having Left a Place of Retirement, 121
Religious Musings, 77–9, 91, 135, 153, 186
Shurton Bars, Lines Written at, 110
Statesman's Manual, 225
Seeing a Youth Affectionately Welcomed by a Sister, On, 29
Sight, The, 48, 135
Silver Thimble, The, 113
Two Bills, Against the, 119

Wanderings of Cain, 181, 190
'Wandering Jew', 153
Watchman, 120–22, 127–33, 138
Young Lady, With a Poem on the French Revolution, To a, 132
Youth and Age, 397
Coleridge, Mrs Sara (née Fricker), 36, 50–2, 58, 67–75, 82–4, 95–6, 104–5, 111–13, 126, 132, 138, 140, 142, 149, 163, 169, 223, 247, 265, 267, 270–1, 279, 282, 316–17, 320, 324–7, 329, 338, 341, 345–7, 365, 367–9
Coleridge, Sara (daughter), 371–2
Collins, William, 350
Collyer, Mrs, 191
Colquhoun, Patrick, 311–12
Coniston, 312
Connolly, Cyril, 14
Cote House, 180, 195
Copenhagen House, 118
Courier, 274
Crescelley, 368
Crewkerne, 157
Critical Review, 134–5, 155, 224
Crompton, Dr Peter, 140
Cudworth, Ralph, 109, 154, 304
Cuxhaven, 263
Cumberland, 157

Darwin, Erasmus, 124–5
Davy, Humphry, 278, 282, 377–8
Death of Abel, 182
Descartes, 300, 306–8, 380
Descriptive Sketches, 110

Denmark, 263
De Quincey, Thomas, 161, 162, 196, 293–4
Der Erste Schiffer, 353
Derby, 124, 139–40, 141, 145
Derwentwater, 269
Diderot, 79
Dovedale, 140
D'Oyley, Mr, 219
Dumfries, 368
Dunbartonshire, 386
Durham, 317
Dyer, George, 57, 109, 138

Early Recollections, 4, 87
East India Company, 77
Edinburgh, 387, 390
Edinburgh Review, 225, 237
Edmund Oliver, 219
Edwards, John, 123
Elbe, 249
Elton, Oliver, 219
Enemies of Promise, 14
Englishwoman's Domestic Magazine, 87
Erdman, David, 409
Essay on Human Understanding, 306
Essay on Man, 23
Estlin, John Prior, 18, 139, 208, 247
Etruria, 376
Euripedes, 31
Evans, Eliza, 46
Evans, Mary, 7, 29, 31, 37, 46–47, 51–2, 67, 71–6, 104
Evans, Mrs, 7
Evans, Mrs, of Derby, 139, 140, 141

Evening Walk, 110
Exeter, 266

Farington, Joseph, 197
Favell, Samuel, 70
Fawkes, Guy, 35
Fellowes, John, 125
Fernbach, D., 403
Fenwick, Dr, 318
Fisher, John, 312
Flagellant, 36
Flower, Benjamin, 131
Fort Augustus, 389
Fort William, 389
Fox, Charles James, 170, 273
France, 11, 34–5, 64, 92, 129–130, 214–15
Frend, William, 19–20, 25, 27, 34
Freud, Sigmund, 343
Fricker, Martha, 50–1, 329
Frost, John, 44

Gallow Hill, 318
Gazetteer, 131
Gentleman's Magazine, 2
George III, 11, 118
Germany, 136, 247–64
Gessner, Salomon, 182, 353
Gibbon, 11, 21, 284
Glasgow, 386
Glee and Pleasure, 37
Glencoe, 389
Glenridding, 371
Globe Inn, 175
Gloucester, 43
Godwin, William, 40–2, 103, 145, 274, 301

Gombrich, E. H., 304
Goneril, 377
Goslar, 250
Göttingen, 252–3
Grammar of Assent, 359
Grasmere, 268, 283
Greenough, George, 254, 263
Grenville, Lord, 119
Greta Hall, 283–4, 361–2
Gretna Green, 386
Grub Street, 273
Gutch Notebook, 104, 152

Hamburg, 249
Hamilton, Antony, 253
Hardy, Thomas, 42, 91
Hartley, David, 21, 63, 78, 80–1, 109–10, 304, 322, 380
Hawes Water, 268
Hawkeshead Grammar School, 157
Hazlitt, 24–5, 52, 159, 161, 182, 196, 205–7, 224, 383, 398
Heligoland, 249
Helvellyn, 285
Herder, 267
Higginbottom, Nehemiah, 218
Hill, Herbert, 98
History of Hindostan, 186
Hobbes, 300, 309
Holcroft, Thomas, 42, 82, 102, 178
Homer, 145
Hoppner, J., 224
Howell family, 321
Hubert de Sevrac, 156
Hucks, Joseph, 33–5, 43, 45–6, 48–9, 266

Hume, David, 22, 24, 282, 284, 300
Hutchinson, George, 268
Hutchinson, Johanna, 268
Hutchinson, Mary, 160, 168, 268, 335, 372
Hutchinson, Sara, 268–71, 316–317, 319, 324, 332, 337, 338, 343, 365, 371–2, 389, 391
Hutchinson, Thomas, 268

Ilam, 140
Immortality Ode, 142, 331
Ireland, 318
Iris, 126
Isaiah, 144
Islington, 118
Italian, The, 155
Italy, 188, 273

Jackson, William, 283
Jackson, J. R. de J., 401
Jamblichus, 8
Jardine, David, 103
Jesus College, 18, 28, 45
Jeffrey, Francis, 225
Joan of Arc, 50, 111
Johnson, Samuel, 10–11, 21, 23, 284
Jonas, 239

Kant, Immanuel, 137, 249, 300, 395
Keats, John, 197
Kempsford, 279
Keswick, 269
King, Mrs, 284
King Street, 321
Kirkstone, 375

Klopstock, F. G., 249
Knight, Freda, 404

Lamb, Charles, 8–9, 77, 82, 137, 143–5, 152, 156, 163–4, 166–7, 220–1, 223–5, 264, 279
Lamb, Mary, 77, 143–4
Lambert, 300
Lawson, Wilfred, 262
Lear, 327
Leech Gatherer, 349
Legrice, Charles, 26
Leibnitz, G. W., 300, 317
Lessing, G. E., 252, 263, 266, 279
Letters to Young Men at Oxford and Cambridge, 20
Lewis, M. G., 155
Lines Left Upon a Seat in a Yew Tree, 165–7
Lichfield, 126
Litchfield, R. B., 401
Liverpool, 283
Llangollin, 45–6
Llanvillin, 44
Lloyd, Charles (junior), 141–2, 148, 156, 167, 217, 220, 292
Lloyd, Charles (senior), 141, 144
Loch, Lomond, 386
Locke, John, 22, 63, 80, 300, 306–9
Lodore, 286, 362
London, 42, 76–7, 83, 126, 272, 321, 377
London Hospital, 8
Long Ashton, 97
Longman, Thomas, 276, 289, 309, 376

Louis XVI, King, 27
Lovell, Mary (née Fricker), 50, 128
Lovell, Robert, 49, 56, 128
Lucas, E. V., 401
Lucy Gray, 146, 333
Luff, Charles, 371
Lully, Raymond, 380
Lyme, 157
Lynmouth, 181
Lysons, Dr, 172

Mackintosh, James, 195–6, 200, 322
Madeira, 379
Malta, 293
Manchester, 26, 42, 126
Manchester College, 26
Mann, P., 407
Marcovitz, E., 5
Martin, James, 138
Matlock, 140
Matter and Spirit, 24, 233
Maurice, Charles, 219
Mediterranean, 273
Messiah, 249
Michaelis, 137
Middleham, 317
Mill, John Stuart, 398
Milner, Isaac, 19
Milton, John, 10, 105, 137, 145, 150, 159, 266, 276, 281, 305
Modern Painters, 303
Mogg, Charles, 172, 174
Monk, The, 155
Montagu, Basil (junior), 192
Montagu, Basil (senior), 192
Montgomery, James, 126
Monthly Magazine, 218

Monthly Review, 135, 223
Montpellier, 325
More, Hannah, 86
Morice, William, 266
Morley, E. J., 401
Morning Chronicle, 76, 126, 131, 139
Morning Post, 195, 200, 215, 257, 271, 321
Mosely, 141, 148

Naples, 366
Nelson, Horatio, 251
Nether Stowey, 53–4, 145, 154–155, 163, 167–8, 280, 322
Newlands, 286
Newman, J. H., 359
Newton, Isaac, 79, 300, 305
Nile, 251
Northmore, Thomas, 266
Norway, 263
Norwich, 200
Nottingham, 125

Oakover, 140
Observations on the Nature of Civil Liberty, 25
Observer, 88
Oracle, 131
Orestes, 354
Ottery Saint Mary, 1–7, 15, 30, 140, 266
Otway, 149
Owen, Robert, 26–7
Oxford, 18, 33–5, 49

Paine, Thomas, 35, 54
Park, Roy, 412–13

Patterdale, 371
Patton, L., 401
Peace and Union, 27
Pedlar, 289
Peel, Robert, 207
Pemberton, Sophia, 217
Penrith, 365
Perry, James, 139
Perth, 389
Phillips, Charles, 191, 311
Phalerius, Demetrius, 32
Pike, E. Royston, 410
Pinney family, 110, 314–15
Piper, H., 406
Plato, 380
Political Justice, 40–1
Poole, Charlotte, 54
Poole, John, 54
Poole, Thomas, 53–5, 63–4, 111, 131, 135–6, 138–40, 145, 147, 149, 150, 156, 171-2, 180, 202, 247, 254, 263, 280, 290, 314, 322, 376
Porlock, 181, 183
Portland, Duke of, 172
Portugal, 98, 113
Prelude, 180, 228, 251
Prothero, Rowland, 237
Public Advertiser, 36
Purchas his Pilgrimage, 182
Purkis, Samuel, 284

Quantocks, 163, 168
Quarterly Review, 227
Quiberon, 323

Racedown, 157, 160

Radcliffe, Ann, 155
Ramus, Peter, 380
Rasselas, 22
Ratzeburg, 250
Reed, M. L., 410
Rees, 289
Reflections on the Revolution, 26
Reynell, Richard, 168
Rich family, 267
Rights of Man, 21, 54
Rickman, John, 345, 352, 377
Robinson, Henry Crabb, 89, 197
Robinson, Mary, 155
Robespierre, 54
Ross on Wye, 44
Rowe, John, 200, 205
Ruined Cottage, 162, 216
Rummer Tabern, 121
Rush, William, 325
Ruskin, John, 303
Ruth, 386
Ruthin, 47
Rydal, 268

St Giles, 38
St John's College, 253
St Mary Redcliffe, 111
St Nevis, 314
St Paul, 145, 266
St Peter's Square, 188
Salisbury Plain, 181
'Salutation and Cat', 77, 83
Sandford, Mrs H., 112
Schiller, 136, 138
Schulz, M., 16
Scotland, 386–91
Scotus, Duns, 309, 322,
Scotus, Erigena, 380

Semler, 137
Seringapatam, 29
Severn, 44
Seward, Thomas, 57, 91
Shakespeare, 10, 91
Sheffield, 42, 126
Shelley, Percy Bishè, 67
Shelvock, 191
Sheridan, Richard Brinsley, 156, 193
Sheridan, William Linley, 193
Shrewsbury, 200
Sicily, 314
Skiddaw, 287
Smith, Adam, 22, 39
Some Information Respecting America, 58
Sotheby, William, 346, 354
Southey, Mrs Edith (née Fricker), 50, 95, 113, 265, 319
Southey, Mrs (mother), 50, 53
Southey, Robert, 17, 35–9, 49–50, 55–9, 60–1, 63, 65–70, 72, 74–5, 83–4, 86–7, 94–9, 113–16, 217–18, 225, 264–5, 276, 313–14, 319, 322, 345, 376, 390
Southey, Thomas, 50
Snyder, Alice, 415
Sockburn, 268–9
Spinoza, Benedict de, 176, 267
Stael, Mme de, 197
Star, 119, 126
State of Europe Compared with Ancient Prophecies, 79
Stockport, 42
Stuart, Daniel, 195, 200, 274, 321

Suarez, Francis, 309
Susquehanna, 152
Sweden, 263

Table Talk, 198
Tarant Gunville, 372
Taylor, Jeremy, 105, 199, 256
Taylor, William, 267
Telegraph, 86
Teneriffe, 366, 372
Thelwall, John, 102, 135, 169, 171–2, 176–7
Thompson, E. P., 404
Thoughts on Subscription to Religious Tests, 20
Threlkeld, 285
Thucidides, 26
Times, 131
Tintern, 95
Tintern Abbey, 165–6, 302
Tobin, James, 284, 289
Todd, Fryer, 76
Tooke, Horne, 91, 178
Trewern, 372
Trickie, Christopher, 174
True Intellectual System of the Universe, 109
Turner, J. M. W., 224, 227, 286, 303
Tyler, Elizabeth, 48, 61, 98

Vain, Frederick, 262
Valencia, 379
Vale of Usk, 366
Virgil, 6, 54, 145
Voltaire, 8

Wade, Josiah, 122, 141

Walla, 285
Wallenstein, 278, 287
Wales, 44–8
Walpole, Horace, 12
Walsh, 174
Wanthwaite, 285
Watchet, 191
Watt, James, 58
Wedgwood, John, 177, 195, 201
Wedgwood, Josiah, 177, 195, 207
Wedgwood, Kitty, 370–1
Wedgwood, Sally, 370
Wedgwood, Thomas, 177–8, 180–1, 193, 195, 200–1, 207, 272, 314, 322, 368
Weekes, Shadrack, 59
Wem, 205
Werkmeister, L., 403
West Indies, 314
Westminster, 321
Westminster School, 36
Whalley, George, 237
Willey, Basil, 416
Windermere, 268
Wittgenstein, L., 359
Wolfenbätel, 263
Woodforde, Parson, 118
Woof, Robert, 407
Worcester, 132
Wordsworth, Dorothy, 157, 160–3, 166, 168, 181, 191, 199, 209, 214, 220–1, 247–250, 269, 287, 303, 328, 330, 337, 347, 386–7
Wordsworth, John, 268, 372
Wordsworth, Jonathan, 166, 407, 409, 414
Wordsworth, Richard, 158

Wordsworth, William, 34, 97, 110–11, 136, 142, 157–63, 165–8, 171–80, 191–2, 208, 214, 217, 223–4, 228, 247–250, 256–7, 262–4, 268, 281, 289–92, 299, 302, 314, 330–331, 335, 337, 347, 350, 354–5, 386–9, 392

Wrangham, Francis, 299

Wrexham, 44, 46

Wynn, Charles, 98

Wythburn, 347